Existentialism

Second Edition

Robert C. Solomon

University of Texas at Austin

New York   Oxford
Oxford University Press
2005

Oxford University Press

Oxford New York
Auckland Bangkok Buenos Aires Cape Town Chennai
Dar es Salaam Delhi Hong Kong Istanbul Karachi Kolkata
Kuala Lumpur Madrid Melbourne Mexico City Mumbai Nairobi
São Paulo Shanghai Taipei Tokyo Toronto

Copyright © 2005 by Oxford University Press, Inc.

Published by Oxford University Press, Inc.
198 Madison Avenue, New York, New York 10016
www.oup.com

Oxford is a registered trademark of Oxford University Press

ISBN: 0-19-517463-1

Printing number: 9 8 7 6 5 4 3 2 1

Printed in the United States of America
on acid-free paper

The idea I have never ceased to develop is in the end that a man can always make something out of what is made of him.

—Jean-Paul Sartre, 1971 (interview in *New Left Review*)

Contents

Preface

This is the second edition of *Existentialism,* which was originally published in 1974 by Random House-Knopf in their classic Modern Library Series and then carried for years by McGraw-Hill Book Company. This is the first edition published under the auspices of Oxford University Press. I would like to thank my excellent editor, Robert Miller, and his very helpful assistant, Emily Voigt. I would also like to thank Jon-David Hague at McGraw-Hill for helping with the rights and Jane Cullen for helping me put together the first edition of the book. I would especially like to thank Clancy W. Martin for his help and advice in preparing this edition.

As in the first edition, *Existentialism* attempts to provide both ample material from the "big four" existentialists—Kierkegaard, Nietzsche, Heidegger, and Sartre—and give some sense of the breadth and variety of existentialist thought. In this edition, I have expanded the "big four" chapters and the introductions to those chapters so that those who prefer to concentrate their focus will find them adequate for an entire course. The "big four" contain extensive sections of major works and smaller bits that especially illuminate existentialism. I have not significantly lengthened the introductions, however, as I have done so at great length in some of my other publications (for example, *Continental Philosophy Since 1750,* Oxford University Press, 1988) and the purpose of this book is simply to provide substantial and now classic texts in the rich history of existentialism.

I have also tried to retain a sense of the rich variety of existentialist thought and writing by including many other figures. I have updated these, deleting several who once were cutting edge and important examples but no longer seem so. I have added other figures, notably Rainer Maria Rilke, Philip Roth, Gabriel Garcia Márquez, and Luis Borges, who seem more "hip" today. I have also included some "short takes" to round out the picture.

In teaching this course for many years, I have been embarrassed by the lack of representation of women—with the notable exception of Simone de Beauvoir—in existentialism as in philosophy. Consequently, and perhaps for other reasons too, existentialism has often been accused of being a "male" if not "macho" philosophy. (Norman Mailer's championing of existentialism in its early years in America did not blunt this charge, nor, I should add, did the infamous behavior of some of the leading French existentialists.) With this in mind, I have added the voice of at least one worthy feminist defender of existentialism (particularly Sartre's philosophy), Hazel Barnes. I cannot rewrite the history of the existentialist movement, but at least I can provide a more open forum.

I have expanded the global reach of the book to indicate that existentialism is no longer restricted to Europe and North America but now has a firm place in Asia and South America, for example. I have included both a Japanese author (Keiji Nishitani) and two Latin American authors (Luis Borges and Gabriel Garcia Márquez). In addition, I have added a much-missed piece to the Dostoyevsky chapter, "The Grand Inquisitor" from *The Brothers Karamazov,* as a response to something akin to popular demand.

I have not altered the form or format of the book, which remains an effort to present the works of the existentialists as works of philosophical art in an international gallery setting. That is what they are, works of philosophical art, despite their sometimes tangled and even artless prose. To say that existentialism is philosophy as art (and not, for example, science) is not meant to denigrate but to emphasize and enhance its value in questioning and appreciating the meaning of our lives.

Introduction

(1974)

I have left this introduction pretty much as I wrote it, in 1974, in a burst of still youthful enthusiasm. I have only made a few minor alterations to bring it up-to-date and contemporize some of the examples.

1. It is a commonly accepted half-truth that existentialism is a revolt against traditional Western rationalistic philosophy. It is also a demonstrable half-truth that existentialist philosophy is very much a continuation and logical expansion of themes and problems in Descartes, Kant, Hegel, Marx, and Husserl. But two half-truths provide us with less than the whole truth. Existentialism is not simply a philosophy or a philosophical revolt. Existentialist philosophy is the explicit conceptual manifestation of an existential attitude—a spirit of "the present age." It is a philosophical realization of a self-consciousness living in a "broken world" (Marcel), an "ambiguous world" (de Beauvoir), a "dislocated world" (Merleau-Ponty), a world into which we are "thrown" and "condemned" yet "abandoned" and "free" (Heidegger and Sartre), a world which appears to be indifferent or even "absurd" (Camus). It is an attitude that recognizes the unresolvable confusion of the human world, yet resists the all-too-human temptation to resolve the confusion by grasping toward whatever appears or can be made to appear firm or familiar—reason, God, nation, authority, history, work, tradition, or the "otherworldly," whether of Plato, Christianity, or utopian fantasy.

The existential attitude begins with a disoriented individual facing a confused world that she cannot accept. This disorientation and confusion is one of the by-products of the Renaissance, the Reformation, the growth of science, the decline of Church authority, the French Revolution, the growth of mass militarism and technocracy, two world wars, the "triumph" of capitalism, and the sudden onslaught of globalism and its

xi

consequences, for which the world was clearly not prepared. In philosophical terms, the modern stress on "the individual" provided the key
themes of the Enlightenment, the "Age of Reason," the philosophical rationalism of Descartes, Kant, and Hegel. In these authors, however, the
theme of individual autonomy was synthesized and absorbed into a transcendental movement of reason. But in a contemporary culture that
harps so persistently upon the themes of individual autonomy and freedom, there will always be individuals who carry these to their ultimate
conclusion. Existentialism begins with the expression of a few such isolated individuals of genius, who find themselves cut adrift in the dangerous abyss between the harmony of Hegelian reason and the romantic celebration of the individual, between the warmth and comfort of the
"collective idea" and the terror of finding oneself alone. Existentialism is
this self-discovery. Its presupposition is always the Cartesian "I am" (not
"I think"). Like its successor, "postmodernism" (which rejected even the
"I"), existentialism marks the ever-increasing failure of modern humanity to find itself "at home" in the world.

2. So long as we think of philosophy as a set of (one hopes) objective
propositions about nature, we will continue to be tempted by notions
that philosophy can be a "science," that there is a *correct* way of doing
philosophy, that a philosophical judgment or body of judgments can be
true. If instead we allow ourselves to think of philosophy as *expression*,
these rigid demands seem pointless or vulgar. Yet we surely do not want
to reduce philosophy to *mere* expression, to autobiography or poetry, to
"subjective truth" or psychic discharge. Although it is an expression of
personal attitude, a philosophical statement is better compared to a piece
of statuary than to a feeling or an attitude. The philosopher is a conceptual sculptor. He uses his language to give a shape to his prejudices and
values, to give his attitudes a life of their own, outside of him, for the
grasp of others. A philosophical statement, once made, is "in the world,"
free of its author, open to the public, a piece to be interpreted; it becomes universal. But "universal" does not mean universally *true*. Philosophical genius lies not in the discovery of universal truth, but in the se-
ductiveness with which one molds his personal attitudes as ideas for
others. The philosopher builds insight onto insight, illustration into argument, joins metaphysical slogan to concrete observation, perhaps
using himself as an example, the entire age as a foil. Nevertheless, the
philosophy is never merely a personal statement; if it is the individual
that has made existentialist philosophy possible, it is also the case that
existentialism has deepened our individualism. Nor is philosophy ever

merely an epiphenomenon of cultural attitudes; it gives them shape and direction, creates them as well as expresses them.

3. Existential philosophy, perhaps like all philosophies, typically finds itself going in circles, trying to prove axioms with theorems, converting premises into methodological rules, using repetition and restatement in place of argument and illustration in place of proof. Here "the individual" appears as a conclusion, there as the presupposition, and there again as the rule. The existential attitude finds itself in syndromes, interpreting a feeling as a mark of identity, converting an insight about oneself into an interpretation of the world, resolving self-doubt by exaggerating the self in everything. The existential attitude is first of all an attitude of self-consciousness. One feels herself separated from the world, from other people. In isolation, one feels threatened, insignificant, meaningless, and in response demands significance through a bloated view of self. One constitutes herself as a hero, as an offense, as a prophet or anti-Christ, as a revolutionary, as unique. As a result of this self-exaggeration, the world becomes—whether apparently or "really" is irrelevant—more threatening. So one attacks the world, discovering, with both despair and joy, that its threats are themselves without ultimate meaning, that there are no moral facts, no good and evil, that "the highest values devalue themselves," and that the human world is typically, even essentially, a hypocritical world. And so one self-righteously finds herself as the creator of meaning, which heightens one's role as absurd hero, prophet, revolutionary, as "underground," rebel, saint—or buffoon. Then there is at least slight paranoia, me or us against the others, the authorities, the public, the herd, the bourgeoisie, the pharisees, the oppressors. As the world becomes more threatening, one is thrown into her exaggerated concept of self all the more; and as she becomes more self-conscious, the world becomes increasingly "hers". Then one begins to feel impotent in the face of the responsibility for "her" world; it becomes more apparent how indifferent the world is, how contingent its events, how utterly absurd. One feels isolated from others, and in desperate loneliness one seeks camaraderie, through rebellion, through art, through writing existential philosophy. In the existential syndrome every tension increases self-consciousness, every increase in self-consciousness exaggerates the irresolvable tension with the world that is always there. As the existentialist becomes more sophisticated, as her feelings become formulated into ideas, as the existential attitude becomes philosophy, it becomes a mantra for similar attitudes in others. When those attitudes finally manifest themselves in the sardonic irony of Kierkegaard, the utter loneliness of Niet-

zsche's Zarathustra, the pathetic spitefulness of Dostoevsky's underground man, the struggle against nausea and "bad faith" in Sartre, the
struggle for the heights in Camus's Sisyphus, these attitudes are no longer
personal syndromes but widely accessible meanings that we can accept
as our own.

4. According to many existentialists, every act and every attitude must be
considered a choice. Yet the existential attitude itself is apparently not
chosen. One finds oneself in it. Dostoevsky tells us that selfconsciousness is a "disease"; Nietzsche adds, in his discussion of "bad conscience,"
that it is "a disease—but as pregnancy is a disease." Although many existentialists speak of the universality of "the human condition," this universality is itself a view from within an attitude which is less than universal. Most existentialists, no less than Descartes, Kant, and Hegel, take
self-consciousness to be the home of a universal first truth about everyone. But self-consciousness itself is not universal, although once one becomes self-conscious, he cannot go back, no matter how he denies himself, drugs himself, *leaps* or *falls* away from himself (the terms, from
Kierkegaard and Heidegger respectively, carry their evaluations with
them). In *Utilitarianism,* John Stuart Mill argues for "quality" of pleasures
by contrasting the dissatisfied Socrates with a satisfied pig. The first is
preferable, Mill argues, because Socrates has experienced both Socratic
pleasures and pig pleasures and he, like other men, has chosen to remain Socratic. Actually Socrates has no choice. He can *act like* a pig, but
he cannot enjoy himself as one. Socrates can no more imagine the self-
less indulgence of pig pleasure than the pig can appreciate the arguments of the *Apology.* Once expressed, the existential attitude appears as
a universal condition, but only to those who can understand it. It is a peculiarly Western attitude, and talk of "the human condition" is as pre-
sumptuous as it is overdramatic. Perhaps that is why, for many of us,
Hermann Hesse is convincing, even in the wild fantasies of his magic
theater, but lyrically unpersuasive as he attempts to capture the selflessness of his Eastern Siddhartha. If we begin by understanding Siddhartha's quest, it is because we, like Hesse, understand quests. However, we
may well have difficulty understanding the peace and satisfaction of Siddhartha's repetitive routine as a ferryman. Of course we, like Hesse, can
moon for that selflessness as a dream, a nostalgia for something lost. But
for us, even selflessness is something viewed self-consciously, something that would have to be striven for by each of us as an individual.
The existential attitude is not universal, and existential philosophy is not
a truth about the human condition. As Camus says, for many of us it is
simply necessary.

5. Most of us have experienced this existential attitude at several points in our lives. A threat of imminent death—or even a passing thought of our own mortality—is sufficient to wrench us out of our current involvements—even if but for a moment—and force us to look at our lives. Like Sartre's characters in hell in *No Exit,* it is perhaps everyone's private dream to see her own funeral, to see her life after its completion. In life, however, there can be no such viewpoint, as Kierkegaard complains against Hegel, since "at no particular moment can I find the necessary resting place from which to understand [my life] backwards." Inevitably the thought of death prompts existential questions, What have I done? Who have I been? What have I wanted to be? Is there still time? But anxiety about death is only one preface to existential anxiety. As Camus tells us, "at any streetcorner the absurd can strike a man in the face." Imagine yourself involved in any one of those petty mechanical tasks which fill so much of our waking hours—washing the car, boiling an egg, changing a printer cartridge—when a friend appears with a new movie camera. No warning: "Do something!" she commands, and the camera is already whirring. A frozen shock of self-consciousness, embarrassment, and confusion. "Do something!" Well of course one was already doing something, but that is now seen as insignificant. And one is doing something just standing there, or perhaps indignantly protesting like a man caught with his pants down. At such moments one appreciates the immobilization of people on the street accosted by aggressive TV hosts such as David Letterman, that paralyzing self-consciousness in which no action seems meaningful. In desperation one *falls* back into her everyday task, or she *leaps* into an absurd posture directed only toward the camera. In either case, one feels absurd. One remains as aware of the camera as of her actions, and then of her actions viewed by the camera. It is the Kantian transcendental deduction with a 16mm lens: there is the inseparable polarity between self and object; but in this instance the self is out there, in the camera, but it is also the object. An "I am" (not an "I think") accompanies my every presentation. "How do I look?" No one knows the existential attitude better than a ham actor.

6. Enlarge this moment, so that the pressure of self-consciousness is sustained. Those who audition for "Reality TV" programs may or may not realize the pressure of such heightened self-consciousness over a period of days or even weeks or months. To be sure, many people today *live* to be on television, but the question is always how to present oneself, how to live one's life, even if one is not always playing to the camera. This becomes a problem for all of us. In self-consciousness we play to an audience or we play to a mirror. We enjoy making love, but always with

the consciousness of how we appear to be enjoying ourselves. We think or suffer, but always with the consciousness of the "outer" significance of those thoughts or sufferings. A film of one's life: would it be a comedy? a tragedy? thrilling? boring? heartrending? Would it be, as Kierkegaard suggests, the film of "a life which put on the stage would have the audience weeping in ecstasy"? Would it be a film that you would be willing to see yourself? twice? infinitely? Or would eternal reruns force you to throw yourself down and gnash your teeth and curse this Nietzschean projectionist? And who would edit this extravagant film of every detail—of yet undetermined significances—of your life? How would the credits be distributed? Each of us finds himself in his own leading role—the hero, the protagonist, the buffoon. John Barth tells us that Hamlet could have been told from Polonius' point of view: "He didn't think he was a minor character in anything."

What does one do? "Be yourself!" An empty script; *myself* sounds like a mere word that points at "me" along with the camera. One wants to "let things happen," but in self-conscious reflection nothing ever "just happens." One seizes a plan (one chooses a self), and all at once one demands controls unimaginable in everyday life. Every demand becomes a need, yet every need is also seen as gratuitous. No one can predict all of the script-wrecking contingencies of real life. One cannot be an existential hero and also accept fate, yet no one is more aware of contingencies. Camus tells us that Sisyphus is happy, but perhaps he is so just because his routine is settled. He can afford to have scorn because his mythical reality is entirely structured within its predictable contingencies. Could Sisyphus remain the absurd hero if he had a normal life? How much does Camus' absurd hero and the existential attitude require the routine and leisure of the bourgeoisie? But then there would be no existentialists in foxholes.

7. The hero? The buffoon? Does any of us really think of herself that way? As Odysseus, Beowulf, James Bond, Woody Allen, perhaps not. But as the center, the one who endows all else with meaning, that is an attitude we recognize easily. Yet at the same instant we recognize ourselves as pelted by meanings, "sown on our path as thousands of little demands, like the signs which order us to keep off the grass" (Sartre). The existential attitude is the constant confusion of given meanings and our own. As this confusion becomes better formulated, one begins to suspect an impossible dilemma. Today, I am Dr. Pangloss, and the world is spectacular; yesterday I was a Schopenhauerian fecal monist, grumbling over a fine wine in a rotten world. Each day values are given to me, but each

day I find changes to explain how yesterday's differing values depended on differences in the world. (Yesterday I was there, now I'm here; yesterday she was friendly, today she insulted me.) My friends assure me, typically, that what has changed is only me, and that yesterday's depression was a symptom of a very real problem. It is today that is the illusion; my happiness is merely another symptom of my problem. But the values remain a problem. They are outside of me. Then, the exaggerated insight: It is *all* me (mine). No one can be in the existential attitude without feeling sometimes the hero, sometimes the megalomaniac (Nietzsche: "I am dynamite"). But again, one need not, should not, take this attitude for the truth. The realization that "I am the world" is a necessary step in the awakening of self-consciousness. In the existentialists' self-conscious sense, perhaps a person has never really "existed" if she has never once seen herself as everything.

8. What is self-consciousness? According to some recent existentialists and almost all postmodernists, there is no *self* as such. And what is consciousness? "It is nothing," Sartre tells us, and for Heidegger it is not even worth mentioning. One looks at paradigm cases. One is self-conscious because of the camera, "he is self-conscious about his baldness." To be self-conscious is to be embarrassed, to be ill-at-ease. Or is that a peculiarly American paradigm? Descartes sees selfconsciousness as a propositional attitude; consciousness of one's own existence seems in the light of reason to be not much different from a mathematical postulate. Hegel is centrally concerned with self-consciousness in his master-slave parable, but self-consciousness in Hegel carries with it a sense of dignity, pride, independence. We might well suspect that semantics is here becoming an ethology as well. What we begin to see, in our movie-making example as well as in Descartes and Hegel, is that self-consciousness is neither a subject aware nor an awareness of an object (the self) so much as it is a motivation, an attitude that illuminates the world as well as the individual in the world. Self-consciousness is not, strictly speaking, awareness of self, for there is no self. Rather, self-consciousness in the existential sense is this very recognition that there is no self. The self is an ideal, a chosen course of action and values, something one creates in the world. Self-consciousness does not add anything to consciousness; it is neither a Lockean "turning back on itself" nor a Cartesian reflective substance. Self-consciousness robs the world of its authority, its given values, and it robs consciousness of its innocence. Self-consciousness is not a premise or an object for study. It is rather the perspective within which existentialism attempts to focus itself.

9. Existentialism is forced to be centrally concerned with problems of justification. In self-consciousness one holds all given values suspect. How much of reason might be no more than *our* reason, the anonymous consensus of "the public"? How many of our values might be no more than relics of dead authority or products of our weaknesses, our fears of isolation, failure, or meaninglessness? How many of our values are prejudices, how much reason mere rationalization? Nevertheless, to simply pronounce the nihilist thesis that the highest values are without justification is not sufficient. The problem, we hear from every author, is *to live*. And so we continue to seek courses of action. We look to Kant and try to act in a way that would universalize our principles of action for everyone. But that supposes that we can identify those features of our own action which would be so universalizable. And then, already caught in the existential attitude, each of us realizes that she is always an exception. I can accept moral principles by the tabletful, but I am always without the rule which teaches me to apply such principles to my own case. One is tempted to turn away from principles to the concrete—to her feelings and attitudes. Yet to do so, as Kant had already argued, is to give up morality. And which feelings can I trust? How does one build a way of life on a foundation of tenuous, passing or even passionate feelings? How much does one value happiness? Pleasure? Self-interest? Feelings for others? Simple perversity and spite? Must my values change every time my feelings change? Can I trust my passions? And how can decisions for the future depend upon the undependability of passing whims, a bad night's sleep, too much coffee, or a hassle on the subway? To be consistent, in such a scheme, one must be impotent. Still, all of this supposes that there are feelings, that they are given—with directions and instructions—like concrete and intuited moral principles of the moment. But a feeling does not have an identity or a direction before it is already made self-conscious. For one who is not yet self-conscious, a feeling can be a cause of behavior. In one who is self-conscious, a feeling is but an obscure text which requires an interpretation, and that presupposes a set of values. In one and the same situation I might be ashamed or embarrassed, depending on my own sense of responsibility, angry or afraid, depending on my sense of self-worth, indignant or amused, depending on my sense of morality. One can always find values given, in her everyday tasks, by "the public," but the existential self-consciousness has already closed this escape behind itself. One can no longer turn to religion, for Kant had already destroyed its authority and reduced it to a mere "postulate" of morality. So, one *creates* a criterion, "leaps" to a set of values, resigns oneself to a life. Camus calls this "philosophical suicide," for every such attempt to adopt a value is at the same

time a pretense that the value is justified. However, no one can simply rest in the existential attitude of the absurd, any more than she can relax in Hegel's dialectic. Kierkegaard's "leap," like the lie in Kafka's *Trial,* becomes for existentialism a foundational principle.

10. The existential attitude, as we have been describing it, is not merely a piece of psychology, much less psychopathology. Existential statements are at once both personal and general. Personal, however, is not autobiographical. The same Kierkegaard who complains of the lack of passion in his age is thus described by a friend: "There is nothing spontaneous about him: I am surprised he can eat and sleep." The Nietzsche one might have met in Sils Maria in 1886 was surely not the Dionysian epic hero one pictures from his writings. This is not hypocrisy. It is the mark of these great philosophers that their personal discomfort could be so brilliantly transformed into matters of universal concern and inspiration. Kierkegaard describes himself as a "stormy petrel" (a bird that appears "when, in a generation, storms begin to gather") and as "an epigram to make people aware." Nietzsche often feared that he would be considered either a saint or a buffoon. (Hesse remarked that "a nature such as Nietzsche's had to suffer the ills of our society a generation in advance"; his personal suffering was at the same time "the sickness of the times themselves.") And Camus gives us, not just *his* feelings of alienation, but "an absurd sensitivity that is widespread in our age." If these feelings are not universal, neither are they exceptional. What is exceptional is their expression in these authors and their ability to provoke others who hold these still unformed and unexpressed existential attitudes as mere personal failures and not yet as philosophical insights. Kierkegaard and Nietzsche wrote only for "the few": Camus and Sartre write to generations. Nevertheless, in each case the philosopher is not simply striving after the truth but after converts as well. The philosopher becomes the seducer, the *provocateur.* The Socratic gadfly kept people annoyedly aware of reason. The existentialist Don Juan draws his power from other people's desires, from their loneliness, from feelings of inadequacy that we all share.

11. One might object that this sketch of the existential attitude and its philosophical expression has failed to give a definition of existentialism. But existentialism is not a dead doctrine to be bottled and labeled. It is a living attitude that is yet defining and creating itself. As Nietzsche warns us in his *Genealogy of Morals,* "Only that which has no history can be defined." And Sartre, rejecting an invitation to define existentialism, says, "It is in the nature of an intellectual quest to be undefined. To name it and

define it is to wrap it up and tie the knot. What is left? A finished, already outdated mode of culture, something like a brand of soap, in other words, an idea" (*Search for a Method*). Although one might develop a working definition of one aspect of one twentieth-century existentialist "movement," namely that series of attempts to develop an existential phenomenology in extension of and reaction to Edmund Husserl's "transcendental phenomenology," existentialism is but a growing series of expressions of a set of attitudes which can be recognized only in a series of portraits. Therefore, I have made no attempts to define existentialism as such, and the selection of authors and works in this book can be justified only by their tenuous appeal to my own sympathies and perspectives on the origins, directions, and extensions of the existential attitude. Existentialism is not a movement or a set of ideas or an established list of authors. It is an attitude which has found and is still finding philosophical expression in the most gifted writers of our times. But little more needs to be said *about* existentialism, for nothing could be further from the existential attitude than attempts to define existentialism, except perhaps a discussion *about* the attempts to define existentialism.

12. In conformity with my belief that philosophical statements are a form of conceptual sculpture, I have tried to arrange the following selections as in a gallery, with each author's works prefaced by a brief introduction to give the reader some orientation. Biographical material has been kept to bare essentials, namely, dates and native country (and, where different, country of residence).

Søren Kierkegaard

(1813–1855)
DANISH

It is generally acknowledged that if existentialism is a "movement" at all, Kierkegaard is its prime mover. Referring to himself as "that Individual," he directs his sarcastic wit and irony against the most powerful institutions of his day—the Lutheran Church, the press, and Hegel's philosophy. However, these indictments of the church and press and *ad hominem* attacks upon Hegel are but targets for Kierkegaard's fundamental objection to the hyperreflectiveness, lack of passion, and collective contempt for the individual that he takes to be endemic of "the present age." In place of the search for science and objectivity that had motivated Kant and Hegel, Kierkegaard substitutes "subjective truth," choice, personality, and passion, turning our attention back to the individual and away from the "collective idea" and philosophical systems. In *Either/Or* we are told that human existence (a very special notion for Kierkegaard and the later existentialists) is *choice*. *Either/Or* contains a dialogue between two life styles or "spheres of existence," the aesthetic life of pleasure, self-indulgence, and personal taste (represented by a young Don Juan) and the ethical life of moral principle and duty (represented by an elderly judge). The dialogue remains conscientiously without resolution, for it is a presupposition of Kierkegaard's existentialism that there is no "rational" resolution of such choices; the crucial thing is rather choice itself, because it is through choice that humans discover and create themselves. Yet Kierkegaard believes that by making choices, rather than living the fundamentally passive life of the aesthete, the individual is inevitably propelled into the ethical way of living and thinking. This seeming paradox—that there are no good reasons for choosing to live one way rather than another, and yet there seem to be better and worse ways to live—runs throughout the existentialists. It is central to their arguments that there is no "better" choice, yet each wants to defend and promote some particular position.

Throughout his work, Kierkegaard in fact distinguishes not two but three spheres of existence: the aesthetic, the ethical, and the religious. In the excerpt from *Fear and Trembling* that follows, Kierkegaard dramatizes a crisis of decision similar to that of *Either/Or* through a retelling and interpretation of the Old Testament story of Abraham and Isaac. Kierkegaard's own choice of existence is a "leap" to the religious; that is, the Christian way of life. Our awareness of the possibility of this leap and our need for it are exemplified for Kierkegaard in the psychological category of *Angst,* or anxiety (Heidegger will later develop in great detail Kierkegaard's concept of anxiety, which is sometimes also translated as dread). In the excerpts from the *Concept of Anxiety,* Kierkegaard argues that anxiety is essential to human selfhood because it is our awareness of our own radical freedom and our intimation of eternity. Kierkegaard once wrote that "a man loses his umbrella, and he searches desperately for it all day, but he loses himself—and does not even notice." If we ignore anxiety we lose ourselves, yet we can overcome anxiety only through faith.

After 1846, Kierkegaard defines his efforts as "a Socratic task—to revise the conception of what it is to be a Christian." His harsh attacks on Christendom—the secularized Christian public—are intended to dramatize just how opposed being a Christian in Christendom is to becoming a Christian in Kierkegaard's sense. For Kierkegaard, the popular idea that one becomes a Christian merely by being born into a Christian country, by being baptized, by going to church every Sunday and then one day being married by your local pastor, is dangerous and ridiculous. Christianity is a matter of the individual's relationship with God—with all of the great, fearful, life-transforming demands a genuine relationship with God must require.

Kierkegaard's most systematic work, written pseudony-mously, is his *Concluding Unscientific Postscript*. In selections from that work included here, he explains his central notion of subjective truth, a concept that supports the earlier arguments in *Either/Or* and *Fear and Trembling,* and is crucial to his under-standing of faith. The opening selection, from *The Present Age,* is a relatively late work (1846) that captures, as well as any other document of the existentialist movement, the temperament of personal revolt and sense of "untimeliness" that these thinkers share. This theme is expanded in Kierkegaard's justly famous polemic against "the crowd as untruth," from his *On the Point of View for My Work as an Author,* which is excerpted toward the end of the selections. And, because so much of Kierkegaard's best writing is to be found in scattered entries in his notebooks and journals—indeed, he always insisted on the "unsystematic" nature of good philosophy—I have placed a sampling of them among the longer selections.

❖ *from* The Present Age ❖

The present age is fundamentally one of prudence and reflection, without passion, momentarily bursting into enthusiasm, and shrewdly relapsing into repose.

If we had actuarial tables of the consumption of discretion from generation to generation as we have for liquor, we would be aston-ished at the tremendous amount of care and deliberation consumed by small, prosperous families living quietly, and at the quantity which the young and even children put away, for just as the Children's Cru-sade may be said to typify the Middle Ages, precocious children are typical of the present age. In fact one is tempted to ask whether there is even one left ready, for once, to act outrageously. These days not even a suicide kills himself in desperation; before taking the step he reflects so long and so thoroughly that he literally chokes with the idea, making one even wonder whether he should be called a suicide,

From The Present Age *by Søren Kierkegaard, translated by Clancy Martin and pub-lished with the permission of Clancy Martin.*

since it is thought itself which takes his life. He does not die *with* reflection but *from* reflection. It would therefore be very hard to prosecute the present generation on account of its legal difficulties: indeed, its ability, skill, and prudence consist in attempting to reach a judgment and a decision without ever going so far as action.

If it may be said of the revolutionary period that it runs amok, it should be said of the present that it runs poorly. The individual and his generation are always contradicting one another, and therefore a prosecuting attorney would find it all but impossible to admit any fact into evidence: because nothing really happens. To judge from the abundance of circumstantial evidence, one would conclude that something truly exceptional had either just occurred or was about to occur. Yet any such conclusions would indeed be mistaken. True, indications are the sole achievement of the age; and its virtuosity and creativity in constructing enthralling illusions, its spurts of enthusiasm, employing as a misleading escape some projected change of form, must be ranked as high in the scale of cleverness and of the negative use of strength as the passionate, creative energy of the revolution in the corresponding scale of energy. But the present generation, exhausted by its deceitful efforts, relapses into total indolence. Its condition is that of one who has only fallen asleep towards morning: first of all come great dreams, then a feeling of laziness, and finally a witty or clever excuse for staying in bed.

● ● ●

A revolutionary age is an age of action; ours is the age of advertisement and publicity. Nothing ever happens but there is instantaneous publicity everywhere. In the present age a rebellion is of all things the most unthinkable. Such a manifestation of strength would seem preposterous to the shrewd intelligence of our time. On the other hand, a political virtuoso might accomplish something nearly as extraordinary. He might write a manifesto proposing a general assembly at which people should resolve upon a rebellion, and it would be so prudently written that even the censor would let it pass. At the meeting itself he would be able to create the impression that his audience had rebelled, after which they would all go quietly home—having enjoyed a very pleasant evening.

● ● ●

This reflective tension ultimately forms itself into a principle, and just as in a passionate age enthusiasm is the unifying principle, so in an age which is very reflective and passionless *envy* is the negative unifying principle. However, this must not be understood as an ethical complaint; to put it one way, the idea of reflection is envy, and so it is twofold in its action: it is selfish in the individual, and it results in the selfishness of the society around him, which therefore works against him.

But the further it goes, the more obviously does reflection's envy become a moral *ressentiment*. Just as air in a closed space becomes poisonous, so the imprisonment of reflection develops a blamable *ressentiment* if it is not ventilated by action or event of some kind. In reflection the condition of strain (or tension as we called it) results in the annulment of all the higher powers, and all that is low and contemptible comes forward, its very impudence given the spurious effect of strength, while shielded by its very lowness it avoids attracting the attention of *ressentiment*.

It is a basic truth of human nature that mankind cannot stay always on the heights, nor constantly admire anything. Human nature demands variety. Even in the most enthusiastic ages people have always like to joke enviously about their superiors. That is fair enough and is perfectly reasonable so long as after having laughed at the great they can once more admire them; otherwise the game is not worth the candle. In this way *ressentiment* finds a release even in an enthusiastic age. And so long as an age, although less enthusiastic, has the strength to grant *ressentiment* its actual character and has recognized what its expression signifies, *ressentiment* has its own, though dangerous, importance. . . .

Contrarily, the more reflection gains the upper hand and so makes people listless, the more dangerous *ressentiment* becomes, because it no longer has enough character to make it conscious of its significance. Without that character reflection is cowardly and wandering, and depending on the circumstances understands the same thing in different ways. It attempts to treat it as a joke, and if that won't work, to regard it as an insult, and when that fails, to dismiss it as nothing at all; or else it will regard the thing as a little witticism, and if that fails then insist that it was intended as a moral satire deserving attention, and if that won't work, add that it is not worth worrying over.

• • •

The *ressentiment* which is *establishing itself* is the process of leveling, and while a passionate age storms ahead erecting new things and tearing down old, raising and demolishing as it goes, a reflective and passionless age does just the opposite: it interferes with and suppresses all action; it levels. Leveling is a quiet, mathematical, and abstract occupation which avoids upheavals.

• • •

In order that everything may be reduced to the same level it is first of all necessary to find a phantom, its spirit, a monstrous abstraction, an all-embracing something which is nothing, a mirage: and that phantom is *the public*. It is only in an age without passion, which is yet reflective, that such a phantom can develop itself with the aid of the press which itself becomes an abstraction. In times of passion and commotion and enthusiasm, even when a people want to achieve a pointless idea and bring down and destroy everything: even then there is no such thing as a public.

• • •

A public is everything and nothing, the most dangerous of all powers and the most trifling: one can speak to an entire nation in the name of the public and still the public is less than a single real person however modest. The stipulation *public* is produced by the deceptive juggling of an age of reflection which makes it seem flattering to the individual who in this way can claim for himself this monster which makes concrete realities seem meager. The public is the fairy tale of an age of understanding which in imagination transforms the individual into something even greater than a king above his people; but the public is also a gruesome abstraction by which the individual receives his religious characterization—or sinks.

❖ *from* The Journals ❖

People rarely make use of the freedom they have, for example, freedom of thought, instead they demand freedom of speech as compensation.

From The Journals *by Søren Kierkegaard, translated by Clancy Martin and published with the permission of Clancy Martin. (Ed. note: this acknowledgment also covers the excerpts from* The Journals *on pp. 26 and 29.)*

The method which begins by doubting in order to philosophize is as fit to its purpose as instructing a soldier to lie down in a heap so that he may learn to stand erect.

Certainly it is true, as philosophers say, that life must be understood backwards. But they forget the other proposition, that it must be loved forwards. And if one considers that proposition it grows more and more obvious that life can never truly be understood in time simply because at no one moment can I find the necessary resting place from which to understand it—backwards.

In relation to their systems most systematizers are like one who builds an immense castle and lives in a shack nearby: they do not live in their own gigantic systematic buildings. But spiritually that is a crucial objection. Spiritually thinking one's thought must be the building in which one lives—otherwise everything is upside down.

Like Leporello learned literary men make a list, but the problem is what they lack: while Don Juan seduces girls and enjoys himself—Leporello notes the time, the place, and a description of the girl.

I always say: all honor to the sciences, etc. But the point is that slowly but surely people have tried to popularize the scientific spirit, it has forced its way down into the people—true religiousness goes down the drain, and existential respect is lost.

I have just returned from a party of which I was the life and soul; wit poured from my lips, everyone laughed and admired me—but I went away—and the dash should be as long as the earth's orbit————————————and wanted to shoot myself.

What I really lack is to be clear in my mind *what I am to do, not* what I am to know, except insofar as a kind of understanding must precede every action. The thing is to understand myself, to see what God truly wishes *me* to do; the thing is to find a truth which is true *for me,* to find *the idea I can live and die for.* What would be the use of discovering so-called objective truth, of mastering all the systems of philosophy and of being able, if required, to discuss them all and reveal the inconsistencies within each; what good would it do me to be able to develop a theory of the state and synthesize all details into one whole, and so to create a world I did not live in, but only held up for others to see; what good would it do me to be able to explain the meaning of Christianity if it had *no* deeper significance *for me and for my life;* what good would it do me if truth herself stood before me, cold and naked, not caring whether I recognized her or not, and producing in me a shudder of terror rather than a trusting devotion? Indeed I do not deny that I yet acknowledge an *imperative of understanding* and that with it one can control men, *but it must be taken up into my life,* and *that* is what I now recognize as the most important thing. . . .

❖ The Rotation Method ❖

The Aesthete speaks:

Starting from a principle is affirmed by people of experience to be a very reasonable procedure; I am willing to humor them, and so begin with the principle that all men are bores. Surely no one will prove himself so great a bore as to contradict me in this. This principle possesses the quality of being in the highest degree repellent, an essential requirement in the case of negative principles, which are in the last analysis the principles of all motion. It is not merely repellent, but infinitely forbidding; and whoever has this principle back of him cannot but receive an infinite impetus forward, to help him make new discoveries. For if my principle is true, one need only consider how ruinous boredom is for humanity, and by properly adjusting the intensity of one's concentration upon this fundamental truth, attain any desired degree of momentum. Should one wish to attain the maximum momentum, even to the point of almost endangering the driving power, one need only say to oneself: Boredom is the root of all evil. Strange that boredom, in itself so staid and stolid, should have such power to set in motion. The influence it exerts is altogether magical, except that it is not the influence of attraction, but of repulsion.

• • •

From Either/Or *by Søren Kierkegaard, Vol. I, translated by David F. Swenson and Lillian Marvin Swenson; Vol. II, translated by Walter Lowrie; both Vols. I and II with Revisions and a Foreword by Howard A. Johnson. Copyright 1944 © 1959 by Princeton University Press; Princeton Paperback, 1971. Reprinted by permission of Princeton University Press. The "Response" (pp. 11–14) is translated by Clancy Martin and published with the permission of Clancy Martin.*

The history of this can be traced from the very beginning of the world. The gods were bored, and so they created man. Adam was bored because he was alone, and so Eve was created. Thus boredom entered the world, and increased in proportion to the increase of population. Adam was bored alone; then Adam and Eve were bored together; then Adam and Eve and Cain and Abel were bored *en famille;* then the population of the world increased, and the peoples were bored *en masse.* To divert themselves they conceived the idea of constructing a tower high enough to reach the heavens. This idea is itself as boring as the tower was high, and constitutes a terrible proof of how boredom gained the upper hand. The nations were scattered over the earth, just as people now travel abroad, but they continued to be bored. Consider the consequences of this boredom. Humanity fell from its lofty height, first because of Eve, and then from the Tower of Babel. What was it, on the other hand, that delayed the fall of Rome, was it not *panis and circenses?*[1] And is anything being done now? Is anyone concerned about planning some means of diversion? Quite the contrary, the impending ruin is being proclaimed. It is proposed to call a constitutional assembly. Can anything more tiresome be imagined, both for the participants themselves, and for those who have to hear and read about it? It is proposed to improve the financial condition of the state by practicing economy. What could be more tiresome? Instead of increasing the national debt, it is proposed to pay it off. As I understand the political situation, it would be an easy matter for Denmark to negotiate a loan of fifteen million dollars. Why not consider this plan? Every once in a while we hear of a man who is a genius, and therefore neglects to pay his debts—why should not a nation do the same, if we were all agreed? Let us then borrow fifteen millions, and let us use the proceeds, not to pay our debts, but for public entertainment. Let us celebrate the millennium in a riot of merriment. Let us place boxes everywhere, not, as at present, for the deposit of money, but for the free distribution of money. Everything would become gratis; theaters gratis, women of easy virtue gratis, one would drive to the park gratis, be buried gratis, one's eulogy would be gratis; I say gratis, for when one always has money at hand, everything is in a certain sense free. No one should be permitted to own any property. Only in my own case would there be an exception. I reserve to myself securities in the Bank of London to the value of one hundred

[1] Bread *and* circuses.

dollars a day, partly because I cannot do with less, partly because the idea is mine, and finally because I may not be able to hit upon a new idea when the fifteen millions are gone. . . .

All men are bores. The word itself suggests the possibility of a subdivision. It may just as well indicate a man who bores others as one who bores himself. Those who bore others are the mob, the crowd, the infinite multitude of men in general. Those who bore themselves are the elect, the aristocracy; and it is a curious fact that those who do not bore themselves usually bore others, while those who bore themselves entertain others. Those who do not bore themselves are generally people who, in one way or another, keep themselves extremely busy; these people are precisely on this account the most tiresome, the most utterly unendurable.

• • •

Now since boredom, as shown above, is the root of all evil, what can be more natural than the effort to overcome it? Here, as everywhere, however, it is necessary to give the problem calm consideration; otherwise one may find oneself driven by the demoniac spirit of boredom deeper and deeper into the mire, in the very effort to escape. Everyone who feels bored cries out for change. With this demand I am in complete sympathy, but it is necessary to act in accordance with some settled principle.

My own dissent from the ordinary view is sufficiently expressed in the use I make of the word "rotation." This word might seem to conceal an ambiguity, and if I wished to use it so as to find room in it for the ordinary method, I should have to define it as a change of field. But the farmer does not use the word in this sense. I shall, however, adopt this meaning for a moment, in order to speak of the rotation which depends on change in its boundless infinity, its extensive dimension, so to speak.

This is the vulgar and inartistic method, and needs to be supported by illusion. One tires of living in the country, and moves to the city; one tires of one's native land, and travels abroad; one is *europamüde,* and goes to America, and so on; finally one indulges in a sentimental hope of endless journeyings from star to star. Or the movement is different but still extensive. One tires of porcelain dishes and eats on silver; one tires of silver and turns to gold; one burns half of Rome to get an idea of the burning of Troy. This method defeats itself; it is plain endlessness. And what did Nero gain by it? Antonine was wiser; he says: "It is in your power to review your life, to look at things you saw before, but from another point of view."

My method does not consist in change of field, but resembles the true rotation method in changing the crop and the mode of cultivation. Here we have at once the principle of limitation, the only saving principle in the world. The more you limit yourself, the more fertile you become in invention. A prisoner in solitary confinement for life becomes very inventive, and a spider may furnish him with much entertainment. One need only hark back to one's schooldays, when aesthetic considerations were ignored in the choice of one's instructors, who were consequently very tiresome: how fertile in invention did not one prove to be! How entertaining to catch a fly and hold it imprisoned under a nut shell, watching it run around the shell; what pleasure, from cutting a hole in the desk, putting a fly in it, and then peeping down at it through a piece of paper! How entertaining sometimes to listen to the monotonous drip of water from the roof! How close an observer does not one become under such circumstances, when not the least noise nor movement escapes one's attention! Here we have the extreme application of the method which seeks to achieve results intensively, not extensively.

• • •

Judge Wilhelm responds:

My Friend,

What I have told you many times I repeat yet again, or to be precise, now I shout it: either/or, *aut/aut* . . . There are times and places in life where it would be ludicrous, or a kind of madness, to apply an either/or, but there are also people whose souls are too dissolute to apprehend what is implied in such a dilemma, whose personalities lack the vigor to be able to insist with pathos: either/or. These words have always made a profound impression on me, and still do, particularly when I say them this way plainly and on their own, for in this way they may activate the most dreadful contradictions. They influence me like the incantation of a magic spell, and my soul becomes exceedingly serious, almost frozen in shock. I think of my early youth, when without really understanding what it is to make a choice I listened with childish trust to the conversation of my elders, and the instant of choice became a very solemn and weighty thing, although in choosing I was only following another's direction. I think of moments in later life when I stood at the crossroads, when my soul was matured in the hour of decision. I think of the many less weighty but for me not trivial occasions in my life when it was a matter of choosing, for even if there is only a single situation in which these words have absolute significance, that is when truth, righteousness and sanctity are arrayed on one side and lust and instinct, dark passions and perdition are on the other; nonetheless, even in matters that in and of themselves are innocent, what one chooses is always important. It is important to choose correctly, to test oneself, so that some day one does not find oneself retreating to the place at which one began, and so might be grateful to God that there was no worse self-reproach than that time had been wasted thereby.

And now you, indeed you use these words [either/or] often enough—they have become almost a slogan for you. What meaning do they have for you? None at all. . . . You take great pleasure in "comforting" people when they turn to you in critical situations; you listen to their expositions and then reply: "Yes, I see it all perfectly: there are two possibilities—one can either do this or that. My sincere opinion and my friendly counsel is this: Do it or don't do it—you will regret both." But he who mocks others mocks himself, and it is not a frippery but a profound mockery of yourself, a sad proof of how slack your soul is, that your entire understanding of life is contained in one single sentence, "I say merely either/or". . . .

Now although every such remark from you has no effect of me or, if it does, it at most arouses righteous indignation, I will nonetheless respond for your own sake. Do you now know that there comes a midnight hour when everyone must unmask; do you believe that life will always let itself be mocked; do you believe you can sneak away before midnight in order to avoid it? Or are you not afraid of it? I have seen those in ordinary life who have deceived others for so long that at last they were unable to show their true nature; I have seen some who played hide and seek so long that at last in a kind of madness they thrust their secret thoughts on others as disgustingly as before they arrogantly had concealed them. Or can you think of anything more frightening than having it all end with the disintegration of your essence into a multiplicity, so that one really might become many, just as that miserable demoniac became a legion, and so you would have lost what is most inward and holy in a human being, the unifying power of personality? You really should not joke about that which is not merely serious but is also dreadful. In every person there is something that up to a point prevents him from becoming wholly transparent to himself, and this can be true to such a high degree, he can be so inextricably interwoven in the relationships of life that extend beyond him, that he cannot unveil himself. But he who cannot unveil himself cannot love, and he who cannot love is the unhappiest one of all.

• • •

. . . Your whole nature contradicts itself. But you can only get out of this contradiction by an either/or . . .

Now in case a man were able to maintain himself upon the pinnacle of the instant of choice, in case he could cease to be a man, in case he were in his inmost nature only an airy thought, in case personality meant nothing more than to be a kobold, which takes part indeed in the movements, but nevertheless remains unchanged; in case such were the situation, it would be foolish to say that it might ever be too late for a man to choose, for in a deeper sense there could be no question of a choice. The choice itself is decisive for the content of the personality, through the choice the personality immerses itself in the thing chosen, and when it does not choose it withers away in consumption. For an instant it is as if, for an instant it may seem as if the thing with regard to which a choice was made lay outside of the chooser, that he stands in no relationship to it, that he can preserve a state of indifference over against it. This is the instant of deliberation, but this, like the Platonic instant, has no existence, least of all in the abstract sense in which you would hold it fast, and the longer one stares at it the less it exists. That which has to be chosen stands in the deepest relationship to the chooser and, when it is a question of a choice involving a life problem, the individual must naturally be living in the meantime; hence it comes about that the longer he postpones the choice the easier it is for him to alter its character, notwithstanding that he is constantly deliberating and deliberating and believes that thereby he is holding the alternatives distinctly apart. When life's either/or is regarded in this way, one is not easily tempted to jest with it. One sees, then, that the inner drift of the personality leaves no time for thought-experiments, that it constantly hastens onward and in one way or another posits this alternative or that, making the choice the more difficult the next instant, because what has thus been posited must be revoked. Think of the captain on his ship at the instant when it has to come about. He will perhaps be able to say, "I can either do this or that"; but in case he is not a pretty poor navigator, he will be aware at the same time that the ship is all the while making its usual headway, and that therefore it is only an instant when it is indifferent whether he does this or that. So it is with a man. If he forgets to take account of the headway, there comes at last an instant when there no longer is any question of an either/or, not because he has chosen but because he has neglected to choose, which is equivalent to saying, because others have chosen for him, because he has lost his self.

• • •

What is it, then, that I distinguish in my either/or? Is it good and evil? No, I would only bring you up to the point where the choice between the evil and the good acquires significance for you. Everything hinges upon this. As soon as one can get a man to stand at the crossways in such a position that there is no recourse but to choose, he will choose the right. Hence if it should chance that, while you are in the course of reading this somewhat lengthy dissertation, you were to feel that the instant for choice had come, then throw the rest of this away, never concern yourself about it, you have lost nothing—but choose, and you shall see what validity there is in this act, yea, no young girl can be so happy in the choice of her heart as is a man who knows how to choose. So then, one either has to live aesthetically, or one has to live ethically. In this alternative, as I have said, there is not yet in the strictest sense any question of a choice; for he who lives aesthetically does not choose, and he who after the ethical has manifested itself to him chooses the aesthetical is not living aesthetically, for he is sinning and is subject to ethical determinants even though his life may be described as unethical. . . .

Is There Such a Thing as a Teleological Suspension of the Ethical?

The ethical as such is the universal, it applies to everyone and the same thing is expressed from another point of view by saying that it applies every instant. It reposes immanently in itself, it has nothing outside itself which is its *telos,* but is itself *telos* for everything outside it, and when this has been incorporated by the ethical it can go no further. Conceived immediately as physical and psychical, the particular individual is the particular which has its *telos* in the universal, and its task is to express itself constantly in it, to abolish its particularity in order to become the universal. As soon as the individual would assert himself in his particularity over against the universal he sins, and only by recognizing this can he again reconcile himself with the universal. . . .

Faith is precisely this paradox, that the individual as the particular is higher than the universal, is justified over against it, is not subordinate but superior—yet in such a way, be it observed, that it is the particular individual who, after he has been subordinated as the particular to the universal, now through the universal becomes the individual who as the particular is superior to the universal, *inasmuch as the individual as the particular stands in an absolute relation to the absolute.* This position cannot be mediated, for all mediation comes about precisely by virtue of the universal; it is and remains to all eternity a paradox, inaccessible to thought. And yet faith is this paradox. . . .

Now the story of Abraham contains such a teleological suspension of the ethical. . . . Abraham's relation to Isaac, ethically speaking, is quite simply expressed by saying that a father shall love his son more dearly than himself. Yet within its own compass the ethical has various gradations. Let us see whether in this story there is to be found any higher expression for the ethical such as would ethically explain his conduct, ethically justify him in suspending the ethical obligation toward his son, without in this search going beyond the teleology of the ethical.

From Fear and Trembling and The Sickness Unto Death *by Søren Kierkegaard, translated by Walter Lowrie. Copyright 1941, 1954 by Princeton University Press; Princeton Paperback, 1968. Reprinted by permission of Princeton University Press.*

• • •

The difference between the tragic hero and Abraham is clearly evident. The tragic hero still remains within the ethical. He lets one expression of the ethical find its *telos* in a higher expression of the ethical; the ethical relation between father and son, or daughter and father, he reduces to a sentiment which has its dialectic in the idea of morality. Here there can be no question of a teleological suspension of the ethical.

With Abraham the situation was different. By his act he overstepped the ethical entirely and possessed a higher *telos* outside of it, in relation to which he suspended the former. For I should very much like to know how one would bring Abraham's act into relation with the universal, and whether it is possible to discover any connection whatever between what Abraham did and the universal—except the fact that he transgressed it. It was not for the sake of saving a people, not to maintain the idea of the state, that Abraham did this, and not in order to reconcile angry deities. If there could be a question of the deity being angry, he was angry only with Abraham, and Abraham's whole action stands in no relation to the universal; it is a purely personal undertaking. Therefore, whereas the tragic hero is great by reason of his moral virtue, Abraham is great by reason of a personal virtue. In Abraham's life there is no higher expression for the ethical than this, that the father shall love his son. Of the ethical in the sense of morality there can be no question in this instance. Insofar as the universal was present, it was indeed cryptically present in Isaac, hidden as it were in Isaac's loins, and must therefore cry out with Isaac's mouth, "Do it not! Thou art bringing everything to naught."

Why then did Abraham do it? For God's sake, and (in complete identity with this) for his own sake. He did it for God's sake because God required this proof of his faith; for his own sake he did it in order that he might furnish the proof. The unity of these two points of view is perfectly expressed by the word which has always been used to characterize this situation: it is a trial, a temptation (*Fristelse*). A temptation—but what does that mean? What ordinarily tempts a man is that which would keep him from doing his duty, but in this case the temptation is itself the ethical—which would keep him from doing God's will.

Here is evident the necessity of a new category if one would understand Abraham. Such a relationship to the deity paganism did not know. The tragic hero does not enter into any private relationship with the deity, but for him the ethical is the divine, hence the paradox implied in his situation can be mediated in the universal.

• • •

The story of Abraham contains therefore a teleological suspension of the ethical. As the individual he became higher than the universal: this is the paradox which does not permit of mediation. It is just as inexplicable how he got into it as it is inexplicable how he remained in it. If such is not the position of Abraham, then he is not even a tragic hero but a murderer. To want to continue to call him the father of faith, to talk of this to people who do not concern themselves with anything but words, is thoughtless. A man can become a tragic hero by his own powers—but not a knight of faith. When a man enters upon the way, in a certain sense the hard way of the tragic hero, many will be able to give him counsel; to him who follows the narrow way of faith no one can give counsel, him no one can understand. Faith is a miracle, and yet no man is excluded from it; for that in which all human life is unified is passion, and faith is a passion.

❖ Truth Is Subjectivity ❖

In order to clarify the different ways of objective and subjective reflection, I shall now describe subjective reflection in its pursuit back and inward into inwardness. Inwardness in an existing subject is at its highest in passion; truth as a paradox corresponds to passion, and that truth becomes a paradox is grounded precisely in its relation to an existing subject. Thus the one corresponds to the other. By forgetting that one is an existing subject, passion is lost, and in turn truth does not become a paradox; but the knowing subject becomes something fantastic rather than an existing human being, and truth becomes a fantastic object for its knowing.

When the question of truth is posed objectively, reflection attends objectively to the truth, as an object to which the knower relates him-

From Concluding Unscientific Postscript *by Søren Kierkegaard, translated by Clancy Martin and published with the permission of Clancy Martin. (Ed. note: this acknowledgment also covers the excerpts from* Concluding Unscientific Postscript *on pp. 24, 26, 27, 28, and 29.)*

self. Reflection does not attend to the relation, however, but to the truthfulness of that to which he relates himself, the true. If only that to which he relates himself to is the truth, the true, then the subject is in truth. When the question of truth is posed subjectively, reflection attends subjectively to the individual's relation. If only the how of this relation is in truth, the individual is in truth, even if he in this way relates himself to untruth.

Let us take as an example the knowledge of God. Objectively, reflection attends to the question of whether this object is the true God; subjectively, the question is whether the individual relates himself to something *such that* his relation in truth is a God-relation. On which side is the truth now? Alas, may we not here resort to a mediation, and say: it is on neither side, it is in the mediation? Excellently spoken, provided there is someone who could say how an existing person manages to be in mediation; to be in mediation is to be finished, while to exist is to become. Nor can an existing person be in two places at the same time, be subject-object. When he is closest to being in two places at the same time, he is in passion, but passion is merely momentary, and passion is also subjectivity's highest expression. The existing one who chooses the objective way goes now into the whole process of approximation intended to bring forth God objectively, which in all eternity is not achieved, because God is a subject, and therefore exists only for subjectivity in inwardness. The existing one who chooses the subjective way comprehends in the same instant the entire dialectical difficulty because he must use some time, perhaps a long time, to find God objectively; he feels this dialectical difficulty in all its pain, because he must have recourse to God in the same instant, because every instant is wasted in which he does not have God. In the same instant he has God, not by virtue of some objective deliberation, but by virtue of the infinite passion of inwardness. The objective person is not embarrassed by such dialectical difficulties as these: what it means to put an entire research period into finding God—since it is indeed possible that the researcher will die tomorrow, and if he lived he could certainly not consider God as something to be taken along at his convenience, since God is something one takes along *a tout prix* [at any price], which in passion's understanding is the true relationship of inwardness with God.

It is at this dialectically so difficult point, that the way swings off for everyone who knows what it means to think dialectically, and to think dialectically as an existing person, which is something other than sitting as a fantastic being at a desk and writing about something one has never done oneself, which is something other to write *de omnibus dubitandum* [to doubt everything], and at the same time to be as credulous in one's existence as the most sensuous of men— here is where the way swings off, and the change is this, that where objective knowledge rambles comfortably along approximations lengthy road, itself not impelled by passion, for subjective knowledge every delay is life-threatening and the decision is so infinitely important that it is so instantly pressing that it is as if the opportunity had already passed.

Now when the problem is this: to calculate where there is more truth (and, as said, at the same time to be on both sides equally is not possible for an existing person, but is only the happy delusion of a deluded I-I), whether on the side of one who objectively seeks the true God and the approximation of the truth of the idea of God, or on the side of one who, driven by the infinite passion of the need of God, feels an infinite concern that he in truth is related to God: then there can be no doubt about the answer for anyone who has not been thoroughly muddled through the help of science. If one who lives in the midst of Christianity goes up to the House of God, to the House of the true God, with knowledge of the true conception of God, and now prays, but prays in untruth; and when one lives in a godless country, but prays with all of the passion of infinity, although his eyes rest upon the image of an idol: where is the most truth? The one prays in truth to God, although he worships an idol; the other prays falsely to the true God, and therefore truly worships an idol.

When one objectively investigates immortality, and another embraces an uncertainty with the passion of the infinite: where is there most truth, and who has the most certainty? The one has entered upon an endless approximation, because the certainty of immortality is rooted precisely in subjectivity; the other is immortal, and fights for immortality by struggling with uncertainty. Let us consider Socrates. Yes, these days everyone dabbles with some proofs, one with more, another with less. But Socrates! He poses the question objectively problematically: whether there is an immortality. Was he therefore a doubter in comparison with one of our modern thinkers with the three proofs? By no means. On this "if" he stakes his whole life, he is willing to die, and he has determined the course of his life in accordance with the passion of infinity, that it may be acceptable—*if* there is an immortality. Is there any better proof of the immortality of

the soul? But those who have the three proofs do not at all determine
their lives according to it; if there is an immortality it must be nause-
ated with their way of living: is there any better refutation of the three
proofs? Uncertainty's "fragment" helped Socrates, helped him because he himself contributed the passion of the infinite; the three
proofs are of no benefit to those others, because they are and remain
maggots, and failing to demonstrate anything else with their three
proofs have demonstrated precisely this. In the same way also, perhaps, a young girl may enjoy all the sweetness of love on the basis
of what is merely a weak hope of being loved by the beloved, because she rests everything on this weak hope: while many a wedded
matron, who more than once has submitted to the strongest expression of erotic love, has certainly had proofs, but strangely enough has
not enjoyed *quod erat demonstratum* [that which was to be demon-
strated]. The Socratic ignorance, firmly maintained with all the passion of inwardness, was thus an expression for the principle that eternal truth is related to an existing individual, and that this truth must
therefore be a paradox for him as long as he exists, and yet it is possible that there was more truth in the Socratic ignorance than in the
whole System's objective truth, which flirts with what the times demand and adapts itself to assistant professors.

Objectivity emphasizes: what is said; subjectivity: how it is said. Already in aesthetics this distinction applies, and is specifically expressed in the principle that what is in itself true may in the mouth
of such and such a person become untrue. This distinction is in these
times particularly noteworthy, for if we wish to express in a single
sentence the difference between ancient times and our own, we
should certainly have to say: In ancient times there were only a few
individuals who knew the truth, now all know it, but inwardness
stands in an inverse relation thereto. Aesthetically the contradiction
that emerges, when truth becomes falsehood in the mouth of such
and such a person, is best construed comically. Ethically-religiously,
the emphasis is again on: how; but this is not to be understood as
demeanor, modulation, expression etc., rather it refers to the relationship maintained by the existing individual, in his own existence,
to the content of his utterance. Objectively, the question is only about
categories of thought, subjectively, it is on inwardness. At its maximum this "how" is the passion of the infinite, and the passion of the
infinite is itself truth. But the passion of the infinite is just subjectivity, and so subjectivity is truth. Objectively viewed there is no infinite

decision, and so it is objectively correct that the difference between good and evil is cancelled together with the principle of contradiction, and thereby also the infinite distinction between truth and falsehood. Only in subjectivity is there decision, whereas wanting to become objective is untruth. The passion of the infinite is the deciding factor, not its content, for its content in just itself. Accordingly the subjective "how" and subjectivity are the truth.

But the "how" which subjectivity emphasizes is also, just because the subject is existing, dialectical with regard to time. In passion's decisive moment, where the road swings away from objective knowledge, it seems as if the infinite decision were thereby achieved. But in the same moment the existing person is in the temporal order, and the subjective "how" is transformed into a striving that is impelled and repeatedly refreshed by infinity's decisive passion, but is nevertheless a striving.

When subjectivity is truth, the definition of truth must also contain in itself an expression of the antithesis to objectivity, a memento of that fork in the road, and this expression will simultaneously indicate the resilience of the inwardness. Here is such a definition of truth: *the objective uncertainty, seized in the most passionately inward appropriation, is truth,* the highest truth there is for an *existing* person. At the point where the road swings off (and where that is cannot be objectively told, because it is precisely subjectivity), objective knowledge is suspended. Objectively he then has only uncertainty, but it is precisely this which increases the tension of that infinite passion of inwardness, and truth is precisely the daring venture of choosing the objective uncertainty with the passion of the infinite. I contemplate nature in order to find God, and I do indeed see power and wisdom, but I also see much more that excites anxiety and disturbs. The *summa summarum* [sum total] of this is an objective uncertainty, but it is therefore that the inwardness is so great, because inwardness grasps this objective uncertainty with infinity's entire passion. In the case of a mathematical proposition, for example, the objectivity is given, but therefore its truth is also an indifferent truth.

But the given definition of truth is a paraphrasing of faith. Without risk there is no faith. Faith is just the contradiction between inwardnesses infinite passion and the objective uncertainty. If I can grasp God objectively, I do not have faith, but just because I cannot do that, therefore I must have faith; and if I wish to keep myself in faith, I must constantly be wary, that I hold fast the objective uncertainty, that I in objective uncertainty am "over 70,000 fathoms of water," and I have faith.

• • •

It is impossible to exist without passion, unless existing means just any sort of so-called existence. For this reason every Greek thinker was essentially a passionate thinker. I have often wondered how one might bring a man to passion. So I have thought I might seat him on a horse and frighten the horse into a wild gallop, or still better, in order to bring out the passion properly, I might take a man who wants to go somewhere as quickly as possible (and so was already in a sort of passion) and seat him on a horse that can barely walk. But this is just how existence is, if one becomes conscious of it. Or if someone hitched a carriage with Pegasus and an old nag, and told the driver, who was not usually inclined to passion, "Now, drive": I think that would succeed. And this is just how existence is, if one becomes conscious of it. Eternity is the winged horse, infinitely quick, and time is the old nag, and the existing individual is the driver; that is to say, he is the driver when his existence is not merely a so-called existence, for then he is no driver, but a drunken peasant who sleeps in the wagon and lets the horses wander where they will. True, he also drives, he is a driver, and so there are perhaps many who—also exist.

• • •

The way of objective reflection makes the subject accidental, and thereby changes existence into something indifferent, something vanishing. The objective way of reflection leads away from the subject to the objective truth, and all the while the subject and his subjectivity become indifferent, and this indifference is precisely its objective validity; for all interest, like all decisiveness, is grounded in subjectivity. The way of objective reflection leads to abstract thought, to mathematics, to historical knowledge of different kinds; and it always leads away from the subject, whose existence or non-existence, and from the objective point of view entirely correctly, becomes infinitely indifferent. Entirely correctly, since as Hamlet says, existence and non-existence have only subjective significance. . . .

• • •

Despite all his effort, the subjective thinker obtains only a modest return. The more the collective idea comes to dominate even the ordinary perspective, the more forbidding seems the transition to becoming an individual existing human being instead of losing oneself in the race and saying "we," "our age," "the nineteenth century." That it is a very little thing [to be an existing human being] is not to be denied; thus it takes a great deal of resignation not to disparage it. For what is an individual existing human being? Our age knows all too well how little it is, but just here is the particular immorality of our age. Every age has its own particular immorality: the immorality of our age is perhaps not lust, pleasure and sensuality, but rather a degenerate and pantheistic contempt for the individual. In the midst of all our elation over our age and the nineteenth century there sounds a note of hidden contempt for the individual; in the midst of the self-importance of the generation there is a despair over being human. Everything must be joined to everything else; people strive to deceive themselves in the totality of things, in world history; no one wants to be an individual human being. Thus, perhaps, the numerous attempts to continue to hang on to Hegel, even by those who have seen through the questionable nature of his philosophy. They worry that if they became particular existing human beings, they would vanish without a trace, so that not even the newspapers could find them, still less academic journals, to say nothing of speculative philosophers immersed in world-history. As particular human beings they worry they will be condemned to a more lonely and forgotten existence than that of a man in the country: for if a man lets go of Hegel, he will not even be in a position to have a letter addressed to him.

❖ On Becoming A Christian ❖

My only analogy is Socrates. My task is a Socratic task—to rectify the concept of what it means to be a Christian.

*(Attack upon Christendom)**

---

*From Attack upon Christendom, *1854–1855, by Søren Kierkegaard, translated by Clancy Martin and published with the permission of Clancy Martin.*

What now is the absurd? The absurd is that the eternal truth has come into being in time, that God has come into being, has been born, has grown up, and so forth, has come into being just like any other individual human being, quite indistinguishable from other human beings. . . .

Precisely in its objective repulsion, the absurd is the measure of the intensity of faith in inwardness. There is a man who wants to have faith, well, let the comedy begin. He wants to have faith, but he also wants to ensure himself with the help of an objective inquiry and its approximation-process. What happens? With the help of the approximation-process, the absurd becomes something else; it becomes probable, it becomes more probable, it becomes extremely and exceedingly probable. Now he is prepared to believe it, and he boldly supposes that he does not believe as shoemakers and tailors and simple folk do, but only after long consideration. Now he is prepared to believe it, but lo and behold, now it has become impossible to believe it. The almost probable, the very probable, the extremely and exceedingly probable: that he can almost know, or as good as know, to a greater degree and exceedingly almost *know*— but *believe* it, that is impossible, for the absurd is precisely the object of faith, and only that can be believed.

(Concluding Unscientific Postscript)

But what is this unknown thing, with which reason in its paradoxical passion is affronted, and which even upsets for man his self-knowledge? It is the Unknown. But it is certainly something human, insofar as we know what it is to be human, nor is it some other thing humans know. Let us call this unknown something: *the God.* That is merely the name we give to it. To want to prove that this unknown something (the God) exists could hardly occur to reason. For of course if God does not exist, it would be impossible to prove it, but if God does exist, it would be folly to try to prove it; for, in the very moment I began my proof, I would have presupposed it, not as dubious but as certain (a presupposition is never dubious, just because it is a presupposition), since otherwise I would never begin, understanding that the whole would be impossible if he did not exist. But if when I speak of proving God's existence I mean that I propose to prove that the Unknown, which exists, is God, then I express myself less fortunately; for then I prove nothing, least of all existence, but merely develop the content of a concept. In general, to try to prove that something exists is a difficult matter, and what is still worse for the bold who would attempt it, the difficulty is of a kind that will not bring fame to those who occupy themselves with it. The whole proof always turns into something entirely different, turns into an additional development of the consequences that come from my having assumed that the object in question exists. Thus I continually deduce not toward existence, but I deduce from existence, whether I exert myself indeed in the world I can grasp with my hands or in thought. So I do not prove that a stone exists, but that something which exists is a stone; a court of justice does not prove that a criminal exists, but that the accused, who certainly exists, is a criminal. Whether one calls existence an *accessorium* [a predicate] or the eternal *prius* [first given], it can never be proven. Let us take our time; for us there is no reason to hurry, as there is for those, who from concern for themselves or for God or for some other thing, must hurry to show they exist. When it is so, there is indeed excellent reason to hurry, especially if the prover sincerely tries to appreciate the danger that he himself or the thing in question may not exist until the proof is complete, and does not secretly entertain the thought that it exists whether he succeeds in proving it or not.

So if from Napoleon's actions one tried to prove Napoleon's existence, would it not be of the greatest peculiarity, since his existence very well explains his actions, but actions cannot prove *his* existence, unless I have already understood the word "his" such that I assume that he exists. But Napoleon is only an individual, and insofar there is no absolute relationship between him and his actions; after all, another person may have performed the same actions. Perhaps this is why I cannot deduce from actions to existence. If I call these actions the actions of Napoleon, then the proof is superfluous, since I have already named him; if I ignore this, I can never prove from the actions that they are Napoleon's, but (purely ideally) prove that such actions are the actions of a great general, etc. But between God and his works there is an absolute relationship, God is not a name, but a concept, and perhaps it follows from that, that his *essentia involvit existentiam* [essence entails existence]. God's works can only be done by God; quite right, but where then are the works of God? The works from which I would deduce his existence are not immediately given. Or does the wisdom in nature, the goodness, the wisdom in the governance of the world, reside on the very face of things? Are we not here confronted with the most terrible temptations to doubt, and is it not impossible finally to dispose of those doubts? But from such an order of things I will certainly not prove God's existence, and even if I began I would never finish, and furthermore would live constantly *in suspenso* [in suspense], that something terrible should suddenly happen that would demolish my little proof. So, from what works will I prove it? From the works as apprehended through an ideal interpretation, i.e., such as they do not immediately reveal themselves. But in that case it is not from the works that I prove it, but I develop only the ideality I have presupposed; because of my confidence in *this* I boldly defy all objections, even those that have not yet been made. As soon as I begin I have presupposed the ideal interpretation, and presuppose that I will be successful in carrying it through; but this is just to presuppose that God exists, and that in confidence in him is how I am actually beginning.   *(Philosophical Fragments)**

The two ways. To suffer, or to become a professor of the fact that someone suffered.   *(Journals)*

Objective faith: what does that mean? It means a sum of dogmas. But suppose Christianity is nothing of the kind; suppose, on the contrary, it is inwardness, and therefore also the paradox, so as to push away objectively; and thus to acquire significance for the existing individual in the inwardness of his existence, in order to place him more decisively than any judge can place the accused, between time and eternity in time, between heaven and hell in the time of salvation. Objective faith: it is as if Christianity had also been heralded as a kind of little system, although not quite so good as the Hegelian system; it is as if Christ—yes, no offense intended—it is as if Christ were a professor, and as if the Apostles had formed a little professional society. Truly, if it was once no easy thing to become a Christian, I believe now it becomes more difficult every year, because by now it has become so easy to become one—one finds a little competition only in becoming a speculative philosopher. And yet the speculative philosopher is perhaps most removed from Christianity, and perhaps it is far preferable to be an offended individual who nonetheless continually relates himself to Christianity, than to be a speculative philosopher who supposes he has understood it.

(Concluding Unscientific Postscript)

*From Philosophical Fragments *by Søren Kierkegaard, translated by Clancy Martin and published with the permisssion of Clancy Martin.*

Suppose, however, that subjectivity is truth, and that subjectivity is the existing subjectivity, then, to put it this way, Christianity is an exact fit. Subjectivity culminates in passion, Christianity is paradox, paradox and passion fit one another exactly, and paradox exactly fits one whose situation is in the extremity of existence. Yes, in the wide world there could not be found two lovers so well fitted for one another as paradox and passion, and their argument is like a lovers' argument, when they argue whether he first aroused her passion, or she his. So it is here: by means of the paradox itself, the existing person has been situated in the extremity of existence. And what is more delightful for lovers than that they are allowed a long time together without any change in the relationship between them, except that it becomes more intensive in inwardness? And this is indeed given to the highly unspeculative understanding between passion and paradox, since the entirety of life in time is so entrusted, and the change comes first in eternity.   *(Ibid.)*

Subjectively, what it is to become a Christian is defined thus:

The decision resides in the subject. The appropriation is the paradoxical inwardness which is specifically dissimilar to all other inwardness. What it is to be a Christian is not determined by the *what* of Christianity but by the *how* of the Christian. This *how* corresponds with one thing only, the absolute paradox. Accordingly there is no confused chatter that being a Christian is to accept, and to accept, and to accept very differently, to appropriate, to believe, to appropriate by faith very differently (all of these merely rhetorical and fictitious characterizations); but to *believe* is specifically dissimilar from all other kinds of appropriation and inwardness. *Faith is the objective uncertainty along with the repulsion of the absurd seized in the passion of inwardness, which just is inwardness potentiated to the highest degree.* This formula applies only to the believer, no one else, not to a lover, not to an enthusiast, not to a thinker, but simply and solely to the believer who is related to the absolute paradox.   *(Ibid.)*

Can one prove from history that Christ was God? Let me first ask another question: Is it possible to imagine a sillier contradiction than that of wanting to PROVE—it does not matter for our purposes whether from history of from anything else in the wide world one wants to *prove* it—that a particular individual man is God? That an individual man is God, declares himself to be God, is indeed the offense *kat' eksochein*. But what is the offense, the offensive thing? What is at odds with (human) reason. And such a thing as that one would attempt to prove! To prove is to demonstrate something to be the rational actuality it is. Can one demonstrate that to be a rational actuality which is at odds with reason? Of course not, unless one would contradict oneself. One can prove only that it is at odds with reason. The proofs which Scripture advances for Christ's divinity—His miracles, His resurrection from the dead, His ascension into heaven—are accordingly only for faith, they are not proofs, they have no intention of proving that all this accord exactly with reason; quite the opposite, they would prove that it is at odds with reason and so is a matter of faith.   *(Training in Christianity)**

. . . So rather let us openly mock God, as has been done before in the world: this is always preferable to the demeaning air of self-importance with which one would prove God's existence. For to prove the existence of one who is present is the most shameless insult, since it is an attempt to make him ridiculous; but regrettably people haven't the faintest idea of this and out of sheer seriousness see it as a pious undertaking. But how could it occur to anyone to prove that he exists, unless one had allowed oneself to ignore him, and now makes it all the worse by proving his existence before his own nose? The existence of a king, his presence is generally acknowledged by the fitting attitude of subjection and submission: what if in his great presence one were to try to prove that he exists? Is that how one should proceed? No, that would be making a fool of him, for one proves his presence by the attitude of submission, which may have many different forms according to the customs of the country: and so it is also with God, that one proves his existence by worship—not by proofs. A miserable unknown author, who is brought from his obscurity by some later enquirer, may well be very pleased that the enquirer succeeds in proving his existence, but an omnipresent being can only be brought to a ridiculous embarrassment by some thinker's pious blundering.

                                      (Concluding Unscientific Postscript)

*From Training in Christianity *by Søren Kierkegaard, translated by Clancy Martin and published with the permission of Clancy Martin.*

To stand on one leg and prove God's existence is a very different thing from going down on one's knees and thanking Him.

(Journals)

Christianity is certainly not despair, it is, on the contrary, good news—for the despairing; but for the frivolous it is certainly not good news, for it wants first of all to make them serious.   *(Ibid.)*

. . . *It is easier to become a Christian when I am not a Christian than to become a Christian when I am one* . . .

(Concluding Unscientific Postscript)

The same thing happens with Christianity, or with becoming a Christian, as with all radical cures: one stalls as long as possible . . .

(Journals)

❖ *from* The Concept of Anxiety ❖

Anxiety as a Saving Experience Through Faith

In one of Grimm's fairy tales there is a story of a youth who goes in search of adventure to learn what it is to be anxious. We will let this adventurer go his way without troubling ourselves about whether he encountered the terrible on his way. However, I will say that to learn to be anxious is an adventure which every human being must endure, in order that he may not perish either by never having been anxious, or to sink in anxiety; and therefore he who has learned rightly to be anxious has learned the ultimate.

If a human being were a beast or an angel, then he could not be anxious. Since he is a synthesis he can be anxious, and indeed the deeper the anxiety, the greater the man; yet not in the sense usually understood, in which anxiety is about something external, about something outside the person, but in the sense that he himself produces the anxiety. Only in this sense can it be understood, when said of Christ, that he was anxious unto death, and just so when he said

From The Concept of Anxiety *by Søren Kierkegaard, translated by Clancy Martin and published with the permission of Clancy Martin.*

to Judas, "What you are going to do, do quickly." Not even the terrifying verse that Luther himself preached with anxiety, "My God, my God why have you forsaken me?", not even these words express suffering so strongly; for the latter signify a condition in which Christ actually is, while the former signify the relation to a condition that is not.

Anxiety (*Angest*) is freedom's possibility, and only this anxiety is through faith absolutely educative, laying bare as it does all finite ends and discovering all their deceptions. And no Grand Inquisitor has such terrifying torments in readiness as has anxiety, and no spy knows as cunningly as anxiety how to attack his suspect in his weakest moment, or how to lay the traps where he will be snared; and no sharp-witted judge knows how to examine indeed to interrogate the accused as anxiety does, which never releases him, neither in entertainment nor in noise, nor in work, neither in day nor in night.

He who is educated by anxiety is educated by possibility, and only he who is educated by possibility is educated according to his infinitude. Possibility is therefore the weightiest of all categories. True, one often hears the opposite, that possibility is so light, but reality so heavy. But from whom does one hear such talk? From miserable men who never have known what possibility is, and who, since reality showed them that they were good for nothing and would become nothing better, now mendaciously revived a possibility that was so beautiful, so enchanting, and the foundation of this possibility was at the most a little youthful giddiness, of which they ought rather to be ashamed. Therefore this possibility that is said to be so light is commonly regarded as the possibility of happiness, luck, etc. But this is certainly not possibility, it is a mendacious invention which human depravity falsely embellishes so as to have a reason to complain of life, of providence, and as a pretext for being self-important. No, in possibility everything is possible, and he who in truth was raised by possibility has comprehended the terrible as well as the cheerful. Therefore when one such goes out from possibility's school, and knows better than a child knows his ABC's that he can demand absolutely nothing from life, and that terror, perdition, annihilation dwell next door to every man, and when he has thoroughly learned that every anxiety about which he is anxious in the next instant came upon him, then he will give reality a different explanation; he will praise reality, and even when it weighs heavily upon him, he will remember that it is yet far, far lighter than possibility was. Only thus can possibility educate; for finiteness and the finite relationships in which every individual is assigned a place, whether it be small and everyday, or world-historical, educate one only finitely, and a person can always persuade them, always get a little more out of them, always bargain, always escape a little way from them, always keep a little distance, always prevent oneself from learning absolutely from them; and if he does this, the individual must in turn have the possibility in himself and himself develop that from which he is to learn, even though in the next instant it does not recognize that it was created by him but absolutely takes the power from him.

But in order that the individual may thus be educated absolutely and infinitely by possibility, he must be honest towards possibility and have faith. By faith I understand here what Hegel somewhere in his fashion calls quite rightly the inner certainty that anticipates infinity. When possibility's discoveries are honestly administered, then will possibility disclose all finitudes, but idealize them in the form of infinity and in anxiety overwhelm the individual until he again overcomes them in the anticipation of faith.

What I am saying here may to many seem to be a strange and foolish story, because they pride themselves on never having been anxious. To this I would reply that one certainly should not be anxious about mankind, about finite things, but that only he who has undergone possibility's anxiety is educated not to be anxious, not because he avoids the dreadful things of life, but because these always become weak by comparison with those of possibility.

If the individual cheats the possibility by which he is to be educated, he never reaches faith, his faith remains the cleverness of finitude, as his school was finitude's school. But one cheats possibility in every way; if it were otherwise any man, if he were only to stick his head out of the window, would have seen enough for possibility to use in beginning its exercises. . . .

When one or another extraordinary event occurs in life, when a world-historical hero gathers heroes about him and accomplishes great things, when a crisis occurs and everything gains significance, then men want to have a part in it, for all of this educates. Quite possibly. But there is a much simpler way of being educated more fundamentally. Take possibility's disciple, set him in the middle of the Jylland heath, where no event occurs, or the greatest event is that a grouse flies up noisily, and he will experience everything more perfectly, more precisely, more profoundly, than the one who received applause on the stage of world-history, if he was not educated by possibility.

Concerning the Dedication ❖
❖ to "The Individual"

There is a view of life which conceives that where the crowd is, there
also is the truth, and that in truth itself there is need of having the
crowd on its side. There is another view of life which conceives that
wherever there is a crowd there is untruth, so that (to consider for a
moment the extreme case), even if every individual, each for himself
in private, were to be in possession of the truth, yet in case they were
all to get together in a crowd—a crowd to which any sort of decisive
significance is attributed, a voting, noisy, audible crowd—untruth
would at once be in evidence.

• • •

A crowd—not this crowd or that, the crowd now living or the
crowd long deceased, a crowd of humble people or of superior people, of rich or of poor, &c.—a crowd in its very concept is the untruth, by reason of the fact that it renders the individual completely
impenitent and irresponsible, or at least weakens his sense of responsibility by reducing it to a fraction. Observe that there was not
one single soldier that dared lay hands upon Caius Marius—this was
an instance of truth. But given merely three or four women with the
consciousness or the impression that they were a crowd, and with
hope of a sort in the possibility that no one could say definitely who
was doing it or who began it—then they had courage for it. What a
falsehood! The falsehood first of all is the notion that the crowd does
what in fact only the individual in the crowd does, though it be every
individual. For 'crowd' is an abstraction and has no hands: but each
individual has ordinarily two hands, and so when an individual lays
his two hands upon Caius Marius they are the two hands of the individual, certainly not those of his neighbour, and still less those of
the . . . crowd which has no hands. In the next place, the falsehood
is that the crowd had the 'courage' for it, for no one of the individuals was ever so cowardly as the crowd always is. For every individual who flees for refuge into the crowd, and so flees in cowardice
from being an individual (who had not the courage to lay his hands

From The Point of View for My Work As an Author *by Søren Kierkegaard, translated*
by Walter Lowrie. Copyright 1962 by Harper and Row, Inc.

upon Caius Marius, nor even to admit that he had it not), such a man contributes his share of cowardliness to the cowardliness which we know as the 'crowd'.—Take the highest example, think of Christ—and the whole human race, all the men that ever were born or are to be born. But let the situation be one that challenges the individual, requiring each one for himself to be alone with Him in a solitary place and as an individual to step up to Him and spit upon Him—the man never was born and never will be born with courage or insolence enough to do such a thing. This is untruth.

❖ What Do I Want? ❖

March 31, 1855.

Quite simply: I want honesty. I am not, as well-meaning people have represented me—for I can pay no attention to the representations of me advanced by exasperation and anger and impotence and non-sense—I am not a Christian severity as opposed to a Christian leniency.

By no means, I am neither leniency nor severity—I am: a human honesty.

The leniency which is the ordinary Christianity here in the land, I want to hold up to the New Testament in order to see how these two relate to one another.

Then if it appears, if I or another can show, that it is equal to the New Testament's Christianity: then with the greatest happiness I will agree to it.

But one thing I will not do, not for any, any price: I will not by suppression or by performing tricks try to produce the impression that the ordinary Christianity in the land and the New Testament's Christianity are like one another.

From Kierkegaard's letters, translated by Clancy Martin and published with the permission of Clancy Martin.

Ivan Turgenev

(1818–1883)
RUSSIAN

Turgenev was a Russian novelist and contemporary of Dostoevsky. In his best-known work, *Fathers and Sons,* he popularized the concept of nihilism, a concept he may have picked up
from Nadezhdin and other current Russian authors. The term itself, however, goes at least as far back as Saint Augustine, who
used it to refer to unbelievers. Turgenev is very likely the source
for Nietzsche's adoption of the term, although the latter gives it
a much more profound place in his thought. In Turgenev, *nihilism* refers to lack of respect; in Nietzsche, it refers to a philosophical problem of justification as well as to the nihilistic attitudes exemplified by Turgenev's Bazarov. On its release in
Russia, Turgenev's book created considerable admiration for
him among the rebellious young, although he then took pains
to object that he had not at all attempted a sympathetic defense
of nihilism.

❖ *from* Fathers and Sons ❖

"What is Bazarov?" Arkady looked amused. "Shall I tell you what he
really is, Uncle?"

From Fathers and Sons *by Ivan Turgenev, translated by B. Isaacs for Washington Sq.
Press/Simon and Schuster, Inc. Reprinted by permission of Washington Sq. Press/Simon
and Schuster, Inc.*

"Please do, nephew."

"He is a nihilist."

"A what?" Nikolai Petrovich asked, while Pavel Petrovich stopped dead, his knife with a dab of butter on the tip arrested in mid-air.

"He is a nihilist," Arkady repeated.

"A nihilist," Nikolai Petrovich said. "That's from the Latin *nihil*—nothing, as far as I can judge. Does that mean a person who . . . who believes in nothing?"

"Say, 'Who respects nothing,'" put in Pavel Petrovich, applying himself to the butter again.

"Who regards everything critically," Arkady observed.

"Isn't that the same thing?" asked Pavel Petrovich.

"No, it isn't. A nihilist is a person who does not look up to any authorities, who does not accept a single principle on faith, no matter how highly that principle may be esteemed."

"Well, and is that a good thing?" Pavel Petrovich broke in.

"It all depends, Uncle. It may be good for some people and very bad for others."

"I see. Well, this, I see, is not in our line. We are men of the old school—we believe that without principles" (he pronounced the word softly, in the French manner, whereas Arkady clipped the word and accentuated the first syllable) "—principles taken on faith, as you put it, one cannot stir a step or draw a breath. *Vous avez changé tout cela,* God grant you good health and a generalship, but we'll be content to look on and admire, *Messieurs les* . . . what do you call them?"

"Nihilists," Arkady said distinctly.

"Yes. We used to have *Hegelists,* now we have nihilists. We shall see how you manage to live in a void, in a vacuum. And now please ring the bell, brother Nikolai Petrovich. It's time for my cocoa."

• • •

"Who wants that logic? We get along without it."

"What do you mean?"

"What I say. You, I trust, don't need logic to put a piece of bread into your mouth when you are hungry. Of what use are these abstract ideas?"

Pavel Petrovich threw up his hands.

"I don't understand you. You insult the Russian people. I don't understand how one can deny principles, maxims! What do you believe in?"

"I've already told you, Uncle, that we don't recognize authorities," interposed Arkady.

"We believe in whatever we consider useful," Bazarov said. "These days negation is more useful than anything else—so we negate."

"Everything?"

"Yes, everything."

"What? Not only art, poetry, but even . . . it's too shocking to utter. . . ."

"Everything," Bazarov repeated with indescribable coolness.

Pavel Petrovich stared at him. He had not expected this. Arkady, on the other hand, flushed with pleasure.

"But, look here," Nikolai Petrovich broke in. "You negate everything or, to be more exact, you destroy everything. But who is going to do the building?"

"That's not our affair. The ground has to be cleared first."

• • •

"I see," Pavel Petrovich interrupted. "So you have convinced yourself of all this and have made up your mind not to tackle anything seriously?"

"And have made up our mind not to tackle anything," Bazarov echoed grimly. He was suddenly annoyed with himself for having loosened his tongue before this aristocrat.

"And do nothing but damn?"

"Do nothing but damn."

"And that's called nihilism?"

"That's called nihilism," Bazarov repeated, this time with pointed insolence.

Pavel Petrovich narrowed his eyes slightly.

"I see!" he said in a singularly calm voice. "Nihilism is to cure all our ills—and you, *you* are our deliverers and heroes. So. But what makes you take the others to task, the denouncers, for instance? Don't you go about ranting like the rest of them?"

"Whatever our faults, that is not one of them," Bazarov muttered.

"What then? Do you act? Do you intend to act?"

Bazarov did not answer. Pavel Petrovich controlled himself with an effort.

Feodor Dostoevsky

(1821–1881)
RUSSIAN

Freedom, devotion, and rebellion are central themes in Dostoevsky's writings. In the first selection here, from *Notes from Underground,* the peculiar protagonist declares his freedom and
wages revolt against science and the Enlightenment, even against
nature itself. In direct opposition to the scientific emphasis on
self-interest and the utilitarianism of his time, the protagonist refuses to "obey" his own interests. He refuses medical attention
and he argues philosophically that nature has no bind on him.
For, as he becomes conscious of a law of nature, his very consciousness of it constitutes a new variable not accounted for by
the natural law. He can then formulate a second-level law that
takes the first-level law into account and countermands it. But the
becoming aware of the second-level law makes it possible to
countermand it as well. (It is like the logic of "reverse psychology" favored by parents and older siblings, telling someone not
to do something so that they will do it.) Even if the laws in question are laws of "human nature," laws that constitute one's own
self-interests, the demand for freedom—or just plain spite—can
always provide contrary motivation. For the "underground" man,
this hyperconsciousness becomes a disease that renders him incapable of even the simplest actions.

The second selection is from *The Brothers Karamazov.* It is a
parable called "The Grand Inquisitor," one of Dostoevsky's most
controversial pieces of religious speculation. In this parable, we

37

meet Ivan Karamazov and his younger brother Alyosha. Ivan is the troubled atheist and Alyosha the devout but naïve Christian. Dostoevsky himself was a devout if heterodox Christian, but neither Karamazov brother should be construed as an expression of Dostoevsky's own views. He certainly rejected Ivan's atheism, and he also rejected Alyosha's naïvete. In Dostoevsky's view, true Christian devotion requires doubt and despair. Dostoevsky is more convincing, however, in Ivan's desperate expressions of nihilism and despairing freedom than he is in presenting Alyosha's honeyed words of innocence and goodness. And the parable itself, "The Grand Inquisitor," can be interpreted in many different ways, all of them troublesome. On the face of it, it is the story of Christ's return to earth, though more as a visitor than the "second coming." But his return is not a time for rejoicing, and the grand inquisitor (the cardinal) makes the case that quite the contrary to improving people's lives, Jesus's first appearance and his promise of freedom based on faith has only added to their misery. So he is sent on his way and told never to return again! No wonder that Alyosha is horrified by the story, but his horror is an essential part of his growth from naïvete to mature devotion. Behind the story, however, is the whole Enlightenment scientific tradition, promising both freedom and happiness but culminating, in Dostoevsky's view, in the nihilism of the mid-nineteenth century and in Ivan's mad howl: "without God, everything is lawful." We can have either freedom *or* happiness, but not both. This idea of a purely "negative freedom" has plagued many philosophers and defines much of the history of existentialism.

❖ *from* Notes From Underground ❖

I am a sick man . . . I am a spiteful man. I am an unpleasant man. I think my liver is diseased. However, I don't know beans about my

From Notes from Underground *by Feodor Dostoevsky, translated by Ralph Matlaw (1960) for E. P. Dutton, Inc.*

disease, and I am not sure what is bothering me. I don't treat it and never have, though I respect medicine and doctors. Besides, I am extremely superstitious, let's say sufficiently so to respect medicine. (I am educated enough not to be superstitious, but I am.) No, I refuse to treat it out of spite. You probably will not understand that. Well, but *I* understand it. Of course, I can't explain to you just whom I am annoying in this case by my spite. I am perfectly well aware that I cannot "get even" with the doctors by not consulting them. I know better than anyone that I thereby injure only myself and no one else. But still, if I don't treat it, it is out of spite. My liver is bad, well then— let it get even worse!

• • •

. . . But these are all golden dreams. Oh, tell me, who first declared, who first proclaimed, that man only does nasty things because he does not know his own real interests; and that if he were enlightened, if his eyes were opened to his real normal interests, man would at once cease to do nasty things, would at once become good and noble because, being enlightened and understanding his real advantage, he would see his own advantage in the good and nothing else, and we all know that not a single man can knowingly act to his own disadvantage. Consequently, so to say, he would begin doing good through necessity. Oh, the babe! Oh, the pure, innocent child! Why, in the first place, when in all these thousands of years has there ever been a time when man has acted only for his own advantage? What is to be done with the millions of facts that bear witness that men, *knowingly,* that is, fully understanding their real advantages, have left them in the background and have rushed headlong on another path, to risk, to chance, compelled to this course by nobody and by nothing, but, as it were, precisely because they did not want the beaten track, and stubbornly, wilfully, went off on another difficult, absurd way seeking it almost in the darkness. After all, it means that this stubbornness and wilfulness were more pleasant to them than any advantage. Advantage! What is advantage? And will you take it upon yourself to define with perfect accuracy in exactly what the advantage of man consists of? And what if it so happens that a man's advantage *sometimes* not only may, but even must, consist exactly in his desiring under certain conditions what is harmful to himself and not what is advantageous. And if so, if there can be such a condition then the whole principle becomes worthless. What do you think—are there such cases? You laugh; laugh away, gentlemen, so long as you answer me: have man's advantages been calculated with perfect certainty? Are there not some which not only have been included but cannot possibly be included under any classification? After all, you, gentlemen, so far as I know, have taken your whole register of human advantages from the average of statistical figures and scientific-economic formulas. After all, your advantages are prosperity, wealth, freedom, peace—and so on, and so on. So that a man who, for instance, would openly and knowingly oppose that whole list would, to your thinking, and indeed to mine too, of course, be an obscurantist or an absolute madman, would he not? But, after all, here is something amazing: why does it happen that all these statisticians, sages and lovers of humanity, when they calculate human advantages invariably leave one out? They don't even take it into their calculation in the form in which it should be taken, and the whole reckoning depends upon that. There would be no great harm to take it, this advantage, and to add it to the list. But the trouble is, that this strange advantage does not fall under any classification and does not figure in any list. For instance, I have a friend. Bah, gentlemen! But after all he is your friend, too; and indeed there is no one, no one, to whom he is not a friend! When he prepares for any undertaking this gentleman immediately explains to you, pompously and clearly, exactly how he must act in accordance with the laws of reason and truth. What is more, he will talk to you with excitement and passion of the real normal interests of man; with irony he will reproach the short-sighted fools who do not understand their own advantage, for the true significance of virtue; and, within a quarter of an hour, without any sudden outside provocation, but precisely through that something internal which is stronger than all his advantages, he will go off on quite a different tack—that is, act directly opposite to what he has just been saying himself, in opposition to the laws of reason, in opposition to his own advantage—in fact, in opposition to everything. I warn you that my friend is a compound personality, and therefore it is somehow difficult to blame him as an individual. The fact is, gentlemen, it seems that something that is dearer to almost every man than his greatest advantages must really exist, or (not to be illogical) there is one most advantageous advantage (the very one omitted of which we spoke just now) which is more important and more advantageous than all other advantages, for which, if necessary, a man is ready to act in opposition to all laws, that is, in oppo-

sition to reason, honor, peace, prosperity—in short, in opposition to
all those wonderful and useful things if only he can attain that fundamental, most advantageous advantage which is dearer to him than
all.

"Well, but it is still advantage just the same," you will retort. But excuse me, I'll make the point clear, and it is not a case of a play on
words, but what really happens is that this advantage is remarkable
from the very fact that it breaks down all our classifications, and continually shatters all the systems evolved by lovers of mankind for the
happiness of mankind. In short, it interferes with everything. But before I mention this advantage to you, I want to compromise myself
personally, and therefore I boldly declare that all these fine systems—
all these theories for explaining to mankind its real normal interests,
so that inevitably striving to obtain these interests, it may at once become good and noble—are, in my opinion, so far, mere logical exercises! Yes, logical exercises. After all, to maintain even this theory of
the regeneration of mankind by means of its own advantage, is, after
all, to my mind almost the same thing as—as to claim, for instance,
with Buckle, that through civilization mankind becomes softer, and
consequently less bloodthirsty, and less fitted for warfare. Logically it
does not seem to follow from his arguments. But man is so fond of
systems and abstract deductions that he is ready to distort the truth intentionally, he is ready to deny what he can see and hear just to justify his logic. I take this example because it is the most glaring instance
of it. Only look about you: blood is being spilled in streams, and in
the merriest way, as though it were champagne. Take the whole of
the nineteenth century in which Buckle lived. Take Napoleon—both
the Great and the present one. Take North America—the eternal
union. Take farcical Schleswig-Holstein. And what is it that civilization softens in us? Civilization only produces a greater variety of sensations in man—and absolutely nothing more. And through the development of this variety, man may even come to find enjoyment in
bloodshed. After all, it has already happened to him. Have you noticed that the subtlest slaughterers have almost always been the most
civilized gentlemen, to whom the various Attilas and Stenka Razins
could never hold a candle, and if they are not so conspicuous as the
Attilas and Stenka Razins it is precisely because they are so often met
with, are so ordinary and have become so familiar to us. In any case
if civilization has not made man more bloodthirsty, it has at least made
him more abominably, more loathsomely bloodthirsty than before.

Formerly he saw justice in bloodshed and with his conscience at peace exterminated whomever he thought he should. And now while we consider bloodshed an abomination, we nevertheless engage in this abomination and even more than ever before. Which is worse? Decide that for yourselves. It is said that Cleopatra (pardon the example from Roman history) was fond of sticking gold pins into her slave-girls' breasts and derived enjoyment from their screams and writhing. You will say that that occurred in comparatively barbarous times; that these are barbarous times too, because (also comparatively speaking) pins are stuck in even now; that even though man has now learned to see more clearly occasionally than in barbarous times, he is still far from having *accustomed* himself to act as reason and science would dictate. But all the same you are fully convinced that he will inevitably accustom himself to it when he gets completely rid of certain old bad habits, and when common sense and science have completely reeducated human nature and turned it in a normal direction. You are confident that man will then refrain from erring *intentionally,* and will, so to say, willy-nilly, not want to set his will against his normal interests. More than that: then, you say, science itself will teach man (though to my mind that is a luxury) that he does not really have either caprice or will of his own and that he has never had it, and that he himself is something like a piano key or an organ stop, and that, moreover, laws of nature exist in this world, so that everything he does is not done by his will at all, but is done by itself, according to the laws of nature. Consequently we have only to discover these laws of nature, and man will no longer be responsible for his actions, and life will become exceedingly easy for him. All human actions will then, of course, be tabulated according to these laws, mathematically, like tables of logarithms up to 108,000, and entered in a table; or better still, there would be published certain edifying works like the present encyclopedic lexicons, in which everything will be so clearly calculated and designated that there will be no more incidents or adventures in the world.

Then—it is still you speaking—new economic relations will be established, all ready-made and computed with mathematical exactitude, so that every possible question will vanish in a twinkling, simply because every possible answer to it will be provided. Then the crystal palace will be built. Then—well, in short, those will be halcyon days. Of course there is no guaranteeing (this is my comment now) that it will not be, for instance, terribly boring then (for what will one have to do when everything is calculated according to the table?) but on the other hand everything will be extraordinarily rational. Of course boredom may lead you to anything. After all, boredom even sets one to sticking gold pins into people, but all that would not matter. What is bad (this is my comment again) is that for all I know people will be thankful for the gold pins then. After all, man is stupid, phenomenally stupid. Or rather he is not stupid at all, but he is so ungrateful that you could not find another like him in all creation. After all, it would not surprise me in the least, if, for instance, suddenly for no reason at all, general rationalism in the midst of the future, a gentleman with an ignoble, or rather with a reactionary and ironical, countenance were to arise and, putting his arms akimbo, say to us all: "What do you think, gentlemen, hadn't we better kick over all that rationalism at one blow, scatter it to the winds, just to send these logarithms to the devil, and to let us live once more according to our own foolish will!" That again would not matter; but what is annoying is that after all he would be sure to find followers— such is the nature of man. And all that for the most foolish reason, which, one would think, was hardly worth mentioning: that is, that man everywhere and always, whoever he may be, has preferred to act as he wished and not in the least as his reason and advantage dictated. Why, one may choose what is contrary to one's own interests, and sometimes one *positively ought* (that is my idea). One's own free unfettered choice, one's own fancy, however wild it may be, one's own fancy worked up at times to frenzy—why that is that very "most advantageous advantage" which we have overlooked, which comes under no classification and through which all systems and theories are continually being sent to the devil. And how do these sages know that man must necessarily need a rationally advantageous choice? What man needs is simply independent choice, whatever that independence may cost and wherever it may lead. Well, choice, after all, the devil only knows . . .

"Ha! ha! ha! But after all, if you like, in reality, there is no such thing as choice," you will interrupt with a laugh. "Science has even now succeeded in analyzing man to such an extent that we know already that choice and what is called freedom of will are nothing other than—"

Wait, gentlemen, I meant to begin with that myself. I admit that I was even frightened. I was just going to shout that after all the devil only knows what choice depends on, and that perhaps that was a very good thing, but I remembered the teaching of science—and pulled myself up. And here you have begun to speak. After all, really, well, if some day they truly discover a formula for all our desires and caprices—that is, an explanation of what they depend upon, by what laws they arise, just how they develop, what they are aiming at in one case or another and so on, and so on, that is, a real mathematical formula—then, after all, man would most likely at once stop to feel desire, indeed, he will be certain to. For who would want to choose by rule? Besides, he will at once be transformed from a human being into an organ stop or something of the sort; for what is a man without desire, without free will and without choice, if not a stop in an organ? What do you think? Let us consider the probability—can such a thing happen or not?

"H'm!" you decide. "Our choice is usually mistaken through a mistaken notion of our advantage. We sometimes choose absolute nonsense because in our stupidity we see in that nonsense the easiest means for attaining an advantage assumed beforehand. But when all that is explained and worked out on paper (which is perfectly possible, for it is contemptible and senseless to assume in advance that man will never understand some laws of nature), then, of course, so-called desires will not exist. After all, if desire should at any time come to terms completely with reason, we shall then, of course, reason and not desire, simply because, after all, it will be impossible to retain reason and *desire* something senseless, and in that way knowingly act against reason and desire to injure ourselves. And as all choice and reasoning can really be calculated, because some day they will discover the laws of our so-called free will—so joking aside, there may one day probably be something like a table of desires so that we really shall choose in accordance with it. After all, if, for instance, some day they calculate and prove to me that I stuck my tongue out at someone because I could not help sticking my tongue out at him and that I had to do it in that particular way, what sort of *freedom* is left me, especially if I am a learned man and have taken my degree somewhere? After all, then I would be able to calculate my whole life for thirty years in advance. In short, if that comes about, then, after all, we could do nothing about it. We would have to accept it just the same. And, in fact, we ought to repeat to ourselves incessantly that at such and such a time and under such and such circumstances, Nature does not ask our leave; that we must accept her as she is and not as we imagine her to be, and if we really aspire to tables and indices and well, even—well, let us say to the chemical retort, then it cannot be helped. We must accept the retort, too, or else it will be accepted without our consent."

Yes, but here I come to a stop! Gentlemen, you must excuse me for philosophizing; it's the result of forty years underground! Allow me to indulge my fancy for a minute. You see, gentlemen, reason, gentlemen, is an excellent thing, there is no disputing that, but reason is only reason and can only satisfy man's rational faculty, while will is a manifestation of all life, that is, of all human life including reason as well as all impulses. And although our life, in this manifestation of it, is often worthless, yet it is life nevertheless and not simply extracting square roots. After all, here I, for instance, quite naturally want to live, in order to satisfy all my faculties for life, and not simply my rational faculty, that is, not simply one-twentieth of all my faculties for life. What does reason know? Reason only knows what it has succeeded in learning (some things it will perhaps never learn; while this is nevertheless no comfort, why not say so frankly?) and human nature acts as a whole, with everything that is in it, consciously or unconsciously, and, even if it goes wrong, it lives. I suspect, gentlemen, that you are looking at me with compassion; you repeat to me that an enlightened and developed man, such, in short, as the future man will be, cannot knowingly desire anything disadvantageous to himself, that this can be proved mathematically. I thoroughly agree, it really can—by mathematics. But I repeat for the hundredth time, there is one case, one only, when man may purposely, consciously, desire what is injurious to himself, what is stupid, very stupid—simply in order *to have the right* to desire for himself even what is very stupid and not to be bound by an obligation to desire only what is rational. After all, this very stupid thing, after all, this caprice of ours, may really be more advantageous for us, gentlemen, than anything else on earth, especially in some cases. And in particular it may be more advantageous than any advantages even when it does us obvious harm, and contradicts the soundest conclusions of our reason about our advantage—because in any case it preserves for us what is most precious and most important—that is, our personality, our individuality. Some, you see, maintain that this really is the most precious thing for man; desire can, of course, if it desires, be in agreement with reason; particularly if it does not abuse this practice but does so in moderation, it is both useful and sometimes even praiseworthy. But very often, and even most often, desire completely and stubbornly opposes reason, and . . .

and . . . and do you know that that, too, is useful and sometimes
even praiseworthy? Gentlemen, let us suppose that man is not stupid.
(Indeed, after all, one cannot say that about him anyway, if only for
the one consideration that, if man is stupid, then, after all, who is
wise?) But if he is not stupid, he is just the same monstrously ungrateful! Phenomenally ungrateful. I even believe that the best definition of man is—a creature that walks on two legs and is ungrateful.
But that is not all, that is not his worst defect; his worst defect is his
perpetual immorality, perpetual—from the days of the Flood to the
Schleswig-Holstein period of human destiny. Immorality, and consequently lack of good sense; for it has long been accepted that lack of
good sense is due to no other cause than immorality. Try it, and cast
a look upon the history of mankind. Well, what will you see? Is it a
grand spectacle? All right, grand, if you like. The Colossus of Rhodes,
for instance, that is worth something. Mr. Anaevsky may well testify
that some say it is the work of human hands, while others maintain
that it was created by Nature herself. Is it variegated? Very well, it may
be variegated too. If one only took the dress uniforms, military and
civilian, of all peoples in all ages—that alone is worth something, and
if you take the undress uniforms you will never get to the end of it;
no historian could keep up with it. Is it monotonous? Very well. It may
be monotonous, too; they fight and fight; they are fighting now, they
fought first and they fought last—you will admit that it is almost too
monotonous. In short, one may say anything about the history of the
world—anything that might enter the most disordered imagination.
The only thing one cannot say is that it is rational. The very word sticks
in one's throat. And, indeed, this is even the kind of thing that continually happens. After all, there are continually turning up in life
moral and rational people, sages, and lovers of humanity, who make
it their goal for life to live as morally and rationally as possible, to be,
so to speak, a light to their neighbors, simply in order to show them
that it is really possible to live morally and rationally in this world. And
so what? We all know that those very people sooner or later toward
the end of their lives have been false to themselves, playing some
trick, often a most indecent one. Now I ask you: What can one expect
from man since he is a creature endowed with such strange qualities?
Shower upon him every earthly blessing, drown him in bliss so that
nothing but bubbles would dance on the surface of his bliss, as on a
sea; give him such economic prosperity that he would have nothing
else to do but sleep, eat cakes and busy himself with ensuring the con-

tinuation of world history and even then man, out of sheer ingratitude, sheer libel, would play you some loathsome trick. He would even risk his cakes and would deliberately desire the most fatal rubbish, the most uneconomical absurdity, simply to introduce into all this positive rationality his fatal fantastic element. It is just his fantastic dreams, his vulgar folly, that he will desire to retain, simply in order to prove to himself (as though that were so necessary) that men still are men and not piano keys, which even if played by the laws of nature themselves threaten to be controlled so completely that soon one will be able to desire nothing but by the calendar. And, after all, that is not all: even if man really were nothing but a piano key, even if this were proved to him by natural science and mathematics, even then he would not become reasonable, but would purposely do something perverse out of sheer ingratitude, simply to have his own way. And if he does not find any means he will devise destruction and chaos, will devise sufferings of all sorts, and will thereby have his own way. He will launch a curse upon the world, and, as only man can curse (it is his privilege, the primary distinction between him and other animals) then, after all, perhaps only by his curse will he attain his object, that is, really convince himself that he is a man and not a piano key! If you say that all this, too, can be calculated and tabulated, chaos and darkness and curses, so that the mere possibility of calculating it all beforehand would stop it all, and reason would reassert itself—then man would purposely go mad in order to be rid of reason and have his own way! I believe in that, I vouch for it, because, after all, the whole work of man seems really to consist in nothing but proving to himself continually that he is a man and not an organ stop. It may be at the cost of his skin! But he has proved it; he may become a caveman, but he will have proved it. And after that can one help sinning, rejoicing that it has not yet come, and that desire still depends on the devil knows what!

You will shout at me (that is, if you will still favor me with your shout) that, after all, no one is depriving me of my will, that all they are concerned with is that my will should somehow of itself, of its own free will, coincide with my own normal interests, with the laws of nature and arithmetic.

Bah, gentlemen, what sort of free will is left when we come to tables and arithmetic, when it will all be a case of two times two makes four? Two times two makes four even without my will. As if free will meant that!

❖ The Grand Inquisitor ❖

"My story is laid in Spain, in Seville, in the most terrible time of the Inquisition, when fires were lighted every day to the glory of God, and 'in the splendid *auto da fé* the wicked heretics were burnt.' Oh, of course, this was not the coming in which He will appear according to His promise at the end of time in all His heavenly glory, and which will be sudden "as lightning flashing from east to west." No, He visited His children only for a moment, and there where the flames were crackling round the heretics. In His infinite mercy, He came once more among men in that human shape in which He walked among men for three years fifteen centuries ago. He came down to the 'hot pavement' of the southern town in which on the day before almost a hundred heretics had, "For the greater glory of God" been burnt by the cardinal, the Grand Inquisitor, in a magnificent *auto da fé,* in the presence of the king, the court, the knights, the cardinals, the most charming ladies of the court, and the whole population of Seville.

"He came softly, unobserved, and yet, strange to say, everyone recognized Him. That might be one of the best passages in the poem. I mean, why they recognized Him. The people are irresistibly drawn to Him; they surround Him; they flock about Him, follow Him. He moves silently in their midst with a gentle smile of infinite compassion. The sun of love burns in His heart, light and power shine from His eyes, and their radiance, shed on the people, stirs their hearts with responsive love. He holds out His hands to them, blesses them, and a healing virtue comes from contact with Him, even with His garments. An old man in the crowd, blind from childhood, cries out, 'O Lord, heal me and I shall see Thee!' and, as it were, scales fall from his eyes and the blind man sees Him. The crowd weeps and kisses the earth under His feet. Children throw flowers before Him, sing, and cry hosannah. 'It is He—it is He!' all repeat. 'It must be He, it can be no one but Him!' He stops at the steps of the Seville cathedral at the moment when the weeping mourners are bringing in a little open white coffin. In it lies a child of seven, the only daughter of a prominent citizen. The dead child lies hidden in flowers. 'He will raise your child,' the crowd shouts

From The Brothers Karamazov *by Feodor Dostoevsky, translated by Constance Barnett (1912).*

to the weeping mother. The priest, coming to meet the coffin, looks perplexed and frowns, but the mother of the dead child throws herself at His feet with a wail. 'If it is Thou, raise my child!' she cries, holding out her hands to Him. The procession halts, the coffin is laid on the steps at His feet. He looks with compassion, and His lips once more softly pronounce, 'Maiden, arise!' and the maiden arises. The little girl sits up in the coffin and looks round, smiling with wide-open wondering eyes, holding a bunch of white roses they had put in her hand.

"There are cries, sobs, confusion among the people, and at that moment the cardinal himself, the Grand Inquisitor, passes by the cathedral. He is an old man, almost ninety, tall and erect, with a withered face and sunken eyes, in which there is still a gleam of light. He is not dressed in his gorgeous cardinal's robes, as he was the day before, when he was burning the enemies of the Roman Church—at that moment he is wearing his coarse, old monk's cassock. At a distance behind him come his gloomy assistant and slaves and the 'holy guard.' He stops at the sight of the crowd and watches it from a distance. He sees everything; he sees them set the coffin down at His feet, sees the child rise up, and his face darkens. He knits his thick grey brows and his eyes gleam with a sinister fire. He holds out his finger and bids the guards take Him. And such is his power, so completely are the people cowed into submission and trembling obedience to him, that the crowd immediately makes way for the guards, and in the midst of deathlike silence they lay hands on Him and lead Him away. The crowd instantly bows down to the earth, like one man, before the old inquisitor. He blesses the people in silence and passes on. The guards lead their prisoner to the close, gloomy, vaulted prison in the ancient palace of the Holy Inquisition and shut Him in it. The day passes and is followed by the dark, burning, 'breathless' night of Seville. The air is 'fragrant with laurel and lemon.' In the pitch darkness, the iron door of the prison is suddenly opened and the Grand Inquisitor himself comes in with a light in his hand. He is alone; the door is closed at once behind him. He stands in the doorway and for a minute or two gazes into His face. At last he goes up slowly, sets the light on the table, and speaks.

"'Is it Thou? Thou?' but receiving no answer, he adds at once, 'Don't answer; be silent. What canst Thou say, indeed? I know too well what Thou wouldst say. And Thou hast no right to add anything to what Thou hadst said of old. Why, then, art Thou come to hinder us? For Thou hast come to hinder us, and Thou knowest that. But dost Thou know what will be tomorrow? I know not who Thou art and care not to know whether it is Thou or only a semblance of Him, but tomorrow I shall condemn Thee and burn Thee at the stake as the worst of heretics. And the very people who have today kissed Thy feet, tomorrow at the faintest sign from me will rush to heap up the embers of Thy fire. Knowest Thou that? Yes, maybe Thou knowest it,' he added with thoughtful penetration, never for a moment taking his eyes off the Prisoner."

"I don't quite understand, Ivan. What does it mean?" Alyosha, who had been listening in silence, said with a smile. "Is it simply a wild fantasy, or a mistake on the part of the old man—some impossible case of mistaken identity?"

"Take it as the last," said Ivan, laughing, "if you are so corrupted by modern realism and can't stand anything fantastic. If you like it to be a case of mistaken identity, let it be so. It is true," he went on, laughing, "the old man was ninety, and he might well be crazy over his set idea. He might have been struck by the appearance of the Prisoner. It might, in fact, be simply his ravings, the delusion of an old man of ninety, overexcited by the *auto da fé* of a hundred heretics the day before. But does it matter to us after all whether it was a mistake of identity or a wild fantasy? All that matters is that the old man should speak out, should speak openly of what he has thought in silence for ninety years."

"And the Prisoner too is silent? Does He look at him and not say a word?"

"That's inevitable in any case," Ivan laughed again. "The old man has told Him He hasn't the right to add anything to what He has said of old. One may say it is the most fundamental feature of Roman Catholicism, in my opinion at least. 'All has been given by Thee to the Pope,' they say, 'and all, therefore, is still in the Pope's hands, and there is no need for Thee to come now at all. Thou must not meddle, for the time, at least.' That's how they speak and write too—the Jesuits, at any rate. I have read it myself in the works of their theologians. 'Hast Thou the right to reveal to us one of the mysteries of that world from which Thou hast come?' my old man asks Him, and answers the question for Him. 'No, Thou hast not; that Thou mayest not add to what has been said of old, and mayest not take from men the freedom which Thou didst exalt when Thou wast on earth. Whatsoever Thou revealest anew will encroach on men's freedom of faith, for it will be manifest as a miracle, and the freedom of their faith was dearer to Thee than anything in those days fifteen hundred years ago. Didst Thou not often say then, "I will make you free?" But now Thou hast seen these "free" men,' the old man adds suddenly, with a pensive smile. 'Yes, we've paid dearly for it,' he goes on, looking sternly at Him, 'but at last we have completed that work in Thy name. For fifteen centuries we have been wrestling with Thy freedom, but now it is ended and over for good. Dost Thou not believe that it's over for good? Thou lookest meekly at me and deignest not even to be wroth with me. But let me tell Thee that now, today, people are more persuaded than ever that they have perfect freedom, yet they have brought their freedom to us and laid it humbly at our feet. But that has been our doing. Was this what Thou didst? Was this Thy freedom?'"

"I don't understand again," Alyosha broke in. "Is he ironical? Is he jesting?"

"Not a bit of it! He claims it as a merit for himself and his Church that at last they have vanquished freedom and have done so to make men happy. 'For now' (he is speaking of the Inquisition, of course) 'for the first time it has become possible to think of the happiness of men. Man was created a rebel; and how can rebels be happy? Thou wast warned,' he says to Him. 'Thou hast had no lack of admonitions and warnings, but Thou didst not listen to those warnings; Thou didst reject the only way by which men might be made happy. But, fortunately, departing Thou didst hand on the work to us. Thou hast promised, Thou hast established by Thy word, Thou has given to us the right to bind and to unbind, and now, of course, Thou canst not think of taking it away. Why, then, hast Thou come to hinder us?'"

"And what's the meaning of 'no lack of admonitions and warnings'?" asked Alyosha.

"Why, that's the chief part of what the old man must say.

"'The wise and dread spirit, the spirit of self-destruction and nonexistence,' the old man goes on, 'the great spirit talked with Thee in the wilderness, and we are told in the books that he "tempted" Thee. Is that so? And could anything truer be said than what he revealed to Thee in three questions, and what Thou didst reject, and what in the books is called "the temptation"? And yet if there has ever been on earth a real, stupendous miracle, it took place on that day, on the day of the three temptations. The statement of those three questions was itself the miracle. If it were possible to imagine, simply for the sake of argument, that those three questions of the dread spirit had perished utterly from the books, and that we had to restore them and to invent them anew, and to do so had gathered together all the wise men of the earth—rulers, chief priests, learned men, philosophers, poets—and had set them the task to invent three questions, such as would not only fit the occasion, but express in three words, three human phrases, the whole future history of the world and of humanity—dost Thou believe that all the wisdom of the earth united could have invented anything in depth and force equal to the three questions which were actually put to Thee then by the wise and mighty spirit in the wilderness? From those questions alone, from the miracle of their statement, we can see that we have here to do not with the fleeting human intelligence, but with the absolute and eternal. For in those three questions the whole subsequent history of mankind is, as it were, brought together into one whole, and foretold, and in them are united all the unsolved historical contradictions of human nature. At the time, it could not be so clear, since the future was unknown; but now that fifteen hundred years have passed, we see that everything in those three questions was so justly divined and foretold, and has been so truly fulfilled, that nothing can be added to them or taken from them.

"'Judge Thyself who was right—Thou or he who questioned Thee then? Remember the first question; its meaning could be put this way: "Thou wouldst go into the world, and art going with empty hands, with some promise of freedom which men in their simplicity and their natural unruliness cannot even understand, which they fear and dread—for nothing has ever been more insupportable for a man and a human society than freedom. But seest Thou these stones in this parched and barren wilderness? Turn them into bread, and mankind will run after Thee like a flock of sheep, grateful and obedient, though forever trembling lest Thou withdraw. Thy hand and deny them Thy bread." But Thou wouldst not deprive man of freedom, and didst reject the offer, thinking what is that freedom worth if obedience is bought with bread? Thou didst reply that man lives not by bread alone. But dost Thou know that for the sake of that earthly bread the spirit of the earth will rise up against Thee and will strive with Thee and overcome Thee, and all will follow him, crying, "Who can compare with this beast? He has given us fire from heaven!" Dost Thou know that the ages will pass, and humanity will proclaim by the lips of their sages that there is no crime, and therefore no sin; there is only hunger? "Feed men, and then ask of them virtue!" that's what they'll write on the bannner, which they will raise against Thee, and with which they will destroy Thy temple. Where Thy temple stood will rise a new building; the terrible tower of Babel will be built again, and though, like the one of old, it will not be finished, yet Thou mightest have prevented that new tower and have cut short the sufferings of men for a thousand years; for they will come back to us after a thousand years of agony with their tower. They will seek us again, hidden underground in the catacombs, for we shall be again persecuted and tortured. They will find us and cry to us, "Feed us, for those who have promised us fire from heaven haven't given it!" And then we shall finish building their tower, for he finishes the building who feeds them. And we alone shall feed them in Thy name, declaring falsely that it is in Thy name. Oh, never, never can they feed themselves without us! No science will give them bread so long as they remain free. In the end, they will lay their freedom at our feet, and say to us, "Make us your slaves, but feed us." They will understand themselves, at last, that freedom and bread enough for all are inconceivable together, for never, never will they be able to share between them! They will be convinced, too, that they can never be free, for they are weak, vicious, worthless, and rebellious. Thou didst promise them the bread of Heaven, but, I repeat again, can it compare with earthly bread in the eyes of the weak, ever sinful, and ignoble race of man? And if for the sake of the bread of Heaven thousands and tens of thousands shall follow Thee, what is to become of the millions and tens of thousands of millions of creatures who will not have the strength to forego the earthly bread for the sake of the heavenly? Or dost Thou care only for the tens of thousands of the great and strong, while the millions, numerous as the sands of the sea, who are weak but love Thee, must exist only for the sake of the great and strong? No, we care for the weak too. They are sinful and rebellious, but in the end they too will become obedient. They will marvel at us and look on us as gods, because we are ready to endure the freedom which they have found so dreadful, and to rule over them—so awful it will seem to them to be free. But we shall tell them that we are Thy servants and rule them in Thy name. We shall deceive them again, for we will not let Thee come to us again. That deception will be our suffering, for we shall be forced to lie.

"'This is the significance of the first question in the wilderness, and this is what Thou hast rejected for the sake of that freedom which Thou hast exalted above everything. Yet in this question lies hidden the great secret of this world. Choosing "bread," Thou wouldst have satisfied the universal and everlasting craving of humanity—to find someone to worship. So long as man remains free, he strives for nothing so incessantly and so painfully as to find someone to worship. But man seeks to worship what is established beyond dispute, so that all men would agree at once to worship it. For these pitiful creatures are concerned not only to find what one or the other can worship, but to find something that all would believe in and worship; what is essential is that all may be *together* in it. This craving for *community* of worship is the chief misery of every man individually and of all humanity from the beginning of time. For the sake of common worship, they've slain each other with the sword. They have set up gods and challenged one another, "Put away your gods and come and worship ours, or we will kill you and your gods!" And so it will be to the end of the world, even when gods disappear from the earth; they will fall down before idols just the same. Thou didst know—Thou couldst not but have known—this fundamental secret of human nature, but Thou didst reject the one infallible banner that was offered Thee to make all men bow down to Thee alone—the banner of earthly bread; and Thou hast rejected it for the sake of freedom and the bread of Heaven. Behold what Thou didst further. And all again in the name of freedom! I tell Thee that man is tormented by no greater anxiety than to find someone quickly to whom he can hand over that gift of freedom with which the ill-fated creature is born. But only one who can appease their conscience can take over their freedom. In bread there was offered Thee an invincible banner; give bread, and man will worship Thee, for nothing is more certain than bread. But if someone else gains possession of his conscience—oh! then he will cast away Thy bread and follow after him who has ensnared his conscience. In that Thou wast right. For the secret of man's being is not only to live, but to have something to live for. Without a stable conception of the object of life, man would not consent to go on living, and would rather destroy himself than remain on earth, though he had bread in abundance. That is true. But what happened? Instead of taking men's freedom from them, Thou didst make it greater than ever! Didst Thou forget that man prefers peace, and even death, to freedom of choice in the knowledge of good and evil? Nothing is more seductive for man than his freedom of conscience, but nothing is a greater cause of suffering. And behold, instead of giving a firm foundation for setting the conscience of man at rest forever, Thou didst choose all that is exceptional, vague, and enigmatic; Thou didst choose what was utterly beyond the strength of men, acting as though Thou didst not love them at all—Thou, who didst come to give Thy life for them! Instead of taking possession of men's freedom, Thou didst increase it, and burdened the spiritual kingdom of mankind with its sufferings forever. Thou didst desire man's free love, that he should follow Thee freely, enticed and taken captive by Thee. In place of the rigid ancient law, man must hereafter, with free heart, decide for himself what is good and what is evil, having only Thy image before him as his guide. But didst Thou not know he would at last reject even Thy image and Thy truth, if he is weighed down with the fearful burden of free choice? They will cry aloud at last that the truth is not in Thee, for they could not have been left in greater confusion and suffering than Thou hast caused, laying upon them so many cares and unanswerable problems.

"'So that, in truth, Thou didst Thyself lay the foundation for the destruction of Thy kingdom, and no one is more to blame for it. Yet what was offered Thee? There are three powers, three powers alone, able to conquer and to hold captive forever the conscience of these impotent rebels for their happiness—those forces are miracle, mystery, and authority. Thou hast rejected all three, and hast set the example for doing so. When the wise and dread spirit set Thee on the pinnacle of the temple and said to Thee, "If Thou wouldst know whether Thou art the Son of God, then cast Thyself down, for it is written: the angels shall hold him up lest he fall and bruise himself, and Thou shalt know then whether Thou art the Son of God, and shalt prove then how great is Thy faith in Thy Father." But Thou didst refuse and wouldst not cast Thyself down. Oh, of course, Thou didst proudly and well, like God; but the weak, unruly race of men, are they gods? Oh, Thou didst know then that in taking one step, in making one movement to cast Thyself down, Thou wouldst be tempting God and have lost all Thy faith in Him, and wouldst have been dashed to pieces against that earth which Thou didst come to save. And the wise spirit that tempted Thee would have rejoiced. But I ask again, are there many like Thee? And couldst Thou believe for one moment that men, too, could face such a temptation? Is the nature of men such, that they can reject miracle and at the great moments of their lives, the moments of their deepest, most agonizing spiritual difficulties, cling only to the free verdict of the heart? Oh, Thou didst know that Thy deed would be recorded in books, would be handed down to remote times and the utmost ends of the earth, and Thou didst hope that man, following Thee, would cling to God and not ask for a miracle. But Thou didst not know that, when man rejects miracle, he rejects God too; for man seeks not so much God as the miraculous. And as man cannot bear to be without the miraculous, he will create new miracles of his own for himself, and will worship deeds of sorcery and witchcraft, though he might be a hundred times over a rebel, heretic, and infidel. Thou didst not come down from the Cross when they shouted to Thee, mocking and reviling Thee, "Come down from the cross and we will believe that Thou art He." Thou didst not come down, for again Thou wouldst not enslave man by a miracle, and didst crave faith given freely, not based on miracle. Thou didst crave free love and not the base raptures of the slave before the might that has overawed him forever. But Thou didst think too highly of men therein, for they are slaves, of course, though rebellious by nature. Look around and judge; fifteen centuries have passed; look upon them. Whom hast Thou raised up to Thyself? I swear, man is weaker and baser by nature than Thou hast believed him! Can he, can he do what Thou didst? By showing him so much respect, Thou didst, as it were, cease to feel for him, for Thou didst ask far too much from him—Thou who hast loved him more than Thyself! Respecting him less, Thou wouldst have asked less of him. That would have been more like love, for his burden would have been lighter. He is weak and vile. What matter that he is everywhere now rebelling against our power, and proud of his rebellion? It is the pride of a child and a schoolboy. They are little children rioting and barring the teacher from school. But their childish delight will end; it will cost them dearly. They will cast down temples and drench the earth with blood. But they will see at last, the foolish children, that, though they are rebels, they are impotent rebels, unable to keep up their own rebellion. Bathed in their foolish tears, they will recognize at last that He who created them rebels must have meant to mock at them. They will say this in despair, and their utterance will be a blasphemy, which will make them more unhappy still, for man's nature cannot bear blasphemy, and in the end always gets revenge for it. And so unrest, confusion, and unhappiness—that is the present lot of man after Thou didst bear so much for their freedom! Thy great prophet tells in vision and in image that he saw all those who took part in the first resurrection, and that there were of each tribe twelve thousand.

But even if there were so many of them, they must have been not men, but gods. They had borne Thy cross; they had endured scores of years in the barren, hungry wilderness, living upon locusts and roots—and Thou mayest indeed point with pride at those children of freedom, of free love, of free and splendid sacrifice for Thy name. But remember that they were only some thousands; and what of the rest? And how are the other weak ones to blame, because they could not endure what the strong have endured? How is the weak soul to blame that it is unable to receive such terrible gifts? Canst Thou have simply come to the elect and for the elect? But if so, it is a mystery, and we cannot understand it. And if it is a mystery, we too have a right to preach a mystery, and to teach them that it's not the free judgment of their hearts, not love that matters, but a mystery which they must follow blindly, even against their conscience. So we have done. We have corrected Thy work and have founded it upon *miracle, mystery,* and *authority.* And men rejoiced that they were again led like sheep, and that the terrible gift that had brought them such suffering was, at last, lifted from their hearts. Were we right teaching them this? Speak! Did we not love mankind, so meekly acknowledging their feebleness, lovingly lightening their burden, and permitting their weak nature, even sin, with our sanction? Why hast Thou come now to hinder us? And why dost Thou look silently and searchingly at me with Thy mild eyes? Be angry. I don't want Thy love, for I love Thee not. And what use is it for me to hide anything from Thee? Don't I know to Whom I am speaking? All that I can say is known to Thee already. And is it for me to conceal from Thee our mystery? Perhaps it is Thy will to hear it from my lips. Listen, then. We are not working with Thee, but with *him*— that is our mystery. It's long—eight centuries—since we have been on *his* side and not on Thine. Just eight centuries ago, we took from him what Thou didst reject with scorn, that last gift he offered Thee, showing Thee all the kingdoms of the earth. We took from him Rome and the sword of Cæsar, and proclaimed ourselves sole rulers of the earth, though hitherto we have not been able to complete our work. But whose fault is that? Oh, the work is only beginning, but it has begun. It has long to await completion, and the earth has yet much to suffer, but we shall triumph and shall be Cæsars, and then we shall plan the universal happiness of man. But Thou mightest have taken even then the sword of Cæsar. Why didst Thou reject that last gift? Hadst Thou accepted that last counsel of the mighty spirit, Thou wouldst have accomplished all that man seeks on earth—that is, someone to worship, someone to keep his conscience, and some means of uniting all in one unanimous and harmonious ant-heap, for the craving for universal unity is the third and last anguish of men. Mankind as a whole has always striven to organize a universal state. There have been many great nations with great histories, but the more highly they were developed the more unhappy they were, for they felt more acutely than other people the craving for worldwide union. The great conquerors, Tamerlanes and Ghenghis-Khans, whirled like hurricanes over the face of the earth striving to subdue its people, and they too were but the unconscious expression of the same craving for universal unity. Hadst Thou taken the world and Cæsar's purple, Thou wouldst have founded the universal state and have given universal peace. For who can rule men if not he who holds their conscience and their bread in his hands? We have taken the sword of Cæsar, and in taking it, of course, have rejected Thee and followed *him*. Oh, ages are yet to come of the confusion of free thought, of their science and cannibalism. For having begun to build their tower of Babel without us, they will end, of course, with cannibalism. But then the beast will crawl to us and lick our feet and spatter them with tears of blood. And we shall sit upon the beast and raise the cup, and on it will be written, "Mystery." But then, and only then, the reign of peace and happiness will come for men. Thou art proud of Thine elect, but Thou hast only the elect, while we give rest to all. And, besides, how many of those elect, those mighty ones who could become elect, have grown weary waiting for Thee, and have transferred and will transfer the powers of their spirit and the warmth of their heart to the other camp, and end by raising their *free* banner against Thee. Thou didst Thyself lift up that banner. But, with us, all will be happy and will no longer rebel or destroy one another as under Thy freedom. Oh, we shall persuade them that they will only become free when they renounce their freedom to us and submit to us. And shall we be right or shall we be lying? They will be convinced that we are right, for they will remember the horrors of slavery and confusion to which Thy freedom brought them. Freedom, free thought, and science, will lead them into such straits and will bring them face to face with such marvels and insoluble mysteries, that some of them, the fierce and rebellious, will destroy themselves, others, rebellious but weak, will destroy one another, while the rest, weak and unhappy, will crawl fawning to our feet and whine to us: "Yes, you were right, you alone possess His mystery, and we come back to you, save us from ourselves!"

"'Receiving bread from us, they will see clearly that we take the bread made by their hands from them, to give it to them, without any miracle. They will see that we do not change the stones to bread, but in truth they will be more thankful for taking it from our hands than for the bread itself! For they will remember only too well that in old days, without our help, even the bread they made turned to stones in their hands, while, since they have come back to us, the very stones have turned to bread in their hands. Too, too well they know the value of complete submission! And until men know that, they will be unhappy. Who is most to blame for their not knowing it, speak? Who scattered the flock and sent it astray on unknown paths? But the flock will come together again and will submit once more, and then it will be once and for all. Then we shall give them the quiet, humble happiness of weak creatures such as they are by nature. Oh, we shall persuade them at last not to be proud, for Thou didst lift them up and thereby taught them to be proud. We shall show them that they are weak, that they are only pitiful children, but that childlike happiness is the sweetest of all. They will become timid, and will look to us and huddle close to us in fear, as chicks to the hen. They will marvel at us, and will be awestricken before us, and will be proud at our being so powerful and clever that we have been able to subdue such a turbulent flock of thousands of millions. They will tremble impotently before our wrath; their minds will grow fearful; they will be quick to shed tears like women and children; but they will be just as ready at a sign from us to pass to laughter and rejoicing, to happy mirth and childish song. Yes, we shall set them to work, but in their leisure hours we shall make their life like a child's game, with children's songs and innocent dance. Oh, we shall allow them even sin, they are weak and helpless, and they will love us like children because we allow them to sin. We shall tell them that every sin will be expiated, if it is done with our permission, that we allow them to sin because we love them, and the punishment for these sins we take upon ourselves. And we shall take it upon ourselves, and they will adore us as their saviors who have taken on themselves their sins before God. And they will have no secrets from us. We shall allow or forbid them to live with their wives and mistresses, to have or not to have children—according to whether they have been obedient or disobedient—and they will submit to us gladly and cheerfully. The most painful secrets of their conscience, all, all they will bring to us, and we shall have an answer for all. And they will be glad to believe our answer, for it will save them from the great anxiety and terrible agony they endure at present in making a free decision for themselves. And all will be happy, all the millions of creatures except the hundred thousand who rule over them. For only we, we who guard the mystery, shall be unhappy. There will be thousands of millions of happy babes, and a hundred thousand sufferers who have taken upon themselves the curse of the knowledge of good and evil. Peacefully they will die, peacefully they will expire in Thy name, and beyond the grave they will find nothing but death. But we shall keep the secret, and for their happiness we shall allure them with the reward of heaven and eternity. Though, if there were anything in the other world, it certainly would not be for such as they. It is prophesied that Thou wilt come again in victory; Thou wilt come with Thy chosen, the proud and strong. But we will say that they have only saved themselves, but we have saved all. We are told that the harlot who sits upon the beast and holds in her hands the *mystery* shall be put to shame, that the weak will rise up again, and will rend her royal purple and will strip naked her loathsome body. But then I will stand up and point out to Thee the thousand millions of happy children who have known no sin. And we who have taken their sins upon ourselves for their happiness will stand up before Thee and say, "Judge us if Thou canst and darest." Know that I fear Thee not. Know that I too have been in the wilderness, I too have lived on roots and locusts, I too prized the freedom with which Thou hast blessed men, and I too was striving to stand among Thy elect, among the strong and powerful, thirsting "to make up the number." But I awakened and would not serve madness. I turned back and joined the ranks of those *who have corrected Thy work.* I left the proud and went back to the humble, for the happiness of the humble. What I say to Thee will come to pass, and our dominion will be built up. I repeat, tomorrow Thou shalt see that obedient flock who at a sign from me will hasten to heap up the hot cinders about the pile on which I shall burn Thee for coming to hinder us. For if any one has ever deserved our fires, it is Thou. Tomorrow I shall burn Thee.'"

Ivan stopped. He was carried away as he talked and spoke with excitement; when he had finished, he suddenly smiled.

Alyosha had listened in silence; towards the end he was greatly moved and seemed several times on the point of interrupting, but restrained himself. Now his words came with a rush.

"But . . . that's absurd!" he cried, flushing. "Your poem is in praise of Jesus, not in blame of Him—as you meant it to be. And who will believe you about freedom? Is that the way to understand it? That's not the idea of it in the Orthodox Church . . . That's Rome, and not even the whole of Rome; it's false—those are the worst of the Catholics, the Inquisitors, the Jesuits! . . . And there could not be such a fantastic creature as your Inquisitor. What are these sins of mankind they take on themselves? Who are these keepers of the mystery who have taken some curse upon themselves for the happiness of mankind? When have they been seen? We know the Jesuits; they are spoken ill of, but surely they are not what you describe. They are not that at all, not at all. . . . They are simply the Romish army for the earthly sovereignty of the world in the future, with the Pontiff of Rome for Emperor . . . that's their ideal, but there's no sort of mystery or lofty melancholy about it. . . . It's simple lust for power, for filthy earthly gain, for domination—something like a universal serfdom with them as masters—that's all they stand for. They don't even believe in God perhaps. Your suffering inquisitor is a mere fantasy."

"Stay, stay," laughed Ivan. "How hot you are! A fantasy you say; let it be so! Of course it's a fantasy. But allow me to say, do you really think that the Roman Catholic movement of the last centuries is actually nothing but the lust for power, for filthy earthly gain? Is that Father Paissy's teaching?"

"No, no, on the contrary; Father Paissy did once say something rather the same as you . . . but, of course, it's not the same, not a bit the same," Alyosha hastily corrected himself.

"A precious admission, in spite of your 'not a bit the same.' I ask you why your Jesuits and Inquisitors have united simply for vile material gain? Why can there not be among them one martyr oppressed by great sorrow and loving humanity? You see, only suppose that there was one such man among all those who desire nothing but filthy material gain—if there's only one like my old inquisitor, who had himself eaten roots in the desert and made frenzied efforts to subdue his flesh to make himself free and perfect. But yet all his life he loved humanity, and suddenly his eyes were opened, and he saw that it is no great moral blessedness to attain perfection and freedom, if at the same time one gains the conviction that millions of God's creatures have been created as a mockery, that they will never be capable of using their freedom, that these poor rebels can never turn into giants to complete the tower, that it was not for such geese that the great idealist dreamt his dream of harmony. Seeing all that, he turned back and joined—the clever people. Surely that could have happened?"

"Joined whom? What clever people?" cried Alyosha, completely carried away. "They have no such great cleverness and no mysteries and secrets. . . . Perhaps nothing but atheism, that's all their secret. Your inquisitor does not believe in God, that's his secret!"

"What if it is so! At last you have guessed it. It's perfectly true that that's the whole secret, but isn't that suffering, at least for a man like that, who has wasted his whole life in the desert and yet could not shake off his incurable love of humanity? In his old age, he reached the clear conviction that nothing but the advice of the great dread spirit could build up any tolerable sort of life for the feeble, unruly, 'incomplete, empirical creatures created in jest.' And so, convinced of this, he sees that he must follow the council of the wise spirit, the dread spirit of death and destruction, and therefore accept lying and deception, and lead men consciously to death and destruction, and yet deceive them all the way so that they may not notice where they are being led, that the poor blind creatures may at least on the way think themselves happy. And note, the deception is in the name of Him in Whose ideal the old man had so fervently believed all his life. Is not that tragic? And if only one such stood at the head of the whole army 'filled with the lust for power only for the sake of filthy gain'— would not one such be enough to make a tragedy? More than that, one such standing at the head is enough to create the actual leading idea of the Roman Church with all its armies and Jesuits, its highest idea. I tell you frankly that I firmly believe that there has always been such a man among those who stood at the head of the movement. Who knows, there may have been some such even among the Roman Popes. Who knows, perhaps the spirit of that accursed old man, who loves mankind so obstinately in his own way, is to be found even now in a whole multitude of such old men, existing not by chance but by agreement, as a secret league formed long ago for the guarding of the mystery, to guard it from the weak and the un- happy, so as to make them happy. No doubt it is so, and so it must be indeed. I fancy that even among the Masons there's something of the same mystery at the bottom, and that that's why the Catholics so detest the Masons as their rivals, breaking up the unity of the idea, while it is so essential that there should be one flock and one shep- herd. . . . But from the way I defend my idea, I might be an author impatient of your criticism. Enough of it."

"You are perhaps a Mason yourself!" broke suddenly from Alyosha. "You don't believe in God," he added, speaking this time very sorrowfully. He fancied besides that his brother was looking at him iron-ically. "How does your poem end?" he asked, suddenly looking down. "Or was it the end?"

"I meant to end it like this. When the Inquisitor ceased speaking, he waited some time for his Prisoner to answer him. His silence weighed down upon him. He saw that the Prisoner had listened in-tently all the time, looking gently in his face and evidently not wish-ing to reply. The old man longed for Him to say something, however bitter and terrible. But He suddenly approached the old man in si-lence and softly kissed him on his bloodless, aged lips. That was all his answer. The old man shuddered. His lips moved. He went to the door, opened it, and said to Him, 'Go, and come no more. . . . Come not at all; never, never!' And he let Him out into the dark al-leys of the town. The Prisoner went away."

"And the old man?"

"The kiss glows in his heart, but the old man adheres to his idea."

"And you with him, you too?" cried Alyosha, mournfully.

Ivan laughed.

"Why, it's all nonsense, Alyosha. It's only a senseless poem of a senseless student, who could never write two lines of verse. Why do you take it so seriously? Surely you don't suppose I am going straight off to the Jesuits, to join the men who are correcting His work? Good Lord, it's no business of mine. I told you, all I want is to live on to thirty, and then . . . dash the cup to the ground!"

"But the little sticky leaves, and the precious tombs, and the blue sky, and the woman you love! How will you live; how will you love them?" Alyosha cried sorrowfully. "With such a hell in your heart and your head, how can you? No, that's just what you are going away for, to join them . . . if not, you will kill yourself; you can't endure it!"

"There is a strength to endure everything," Ivan said with a cold smile.

"What strength?"

"The strength of the Karamazovs—the strength of the Karamazov baseness."

"To sink into debauchery, to stifle your soul with corruption, yes?"

"Possibly even that . . . only perhaps till I am thirty I shall escape it, and then."

"How will you escape it? By what will you escape it? That's im-possible with your ideas."

"In the Karamazov way, again."

"'Everything is lawful,' you mean? Everything is lawful, is that it?" Ivan scowled, and all at once turned strangely pale.

"Ah, you've picked up yesterday's phrase, which so offended Miusov—and which Dmitri pounced upon so naively and paraphrased!" he smiled queerly. "Yes, if you like, 'everything is lawful,' since the words have been said. I won't deny it."

Alyosha looked at him in silence.

"I thought that, going away from here, I have you at least," Ivan said suddenly, with unexpected feeling, "but now I see that there is no place for me even in your heart, my dear hermit. The formula, 'all is lawful,' I won't renounce—will you renounce me for that?"

Alyosha got up, went to him, and softly kissed him on the lips.

"That's plagiarism," cried Ivan, highly delighted. "You stole that from my poem. Thank you though. Get up, Alyosha, it's time we were going, both of us."

Friedrich Nietzsche

(1844-1900)
GERMAN ("EUROPEAN")

Nietzsche never read Kierkegaard, but there are remarkable parallels between them: their stress on the individual and disdain for the "herd" or "public"; their attacks on hypocritical Christendom and upon the bloated philosophical celebration of reason in Kant and Hegel; their hatred of personal weakness and anonymity. But Nietzsche will have no part of Kierkegaard's new Christian; indeed, he turns Kierkegaard on his head and defends the aesthetic life against both morality and Christianity. This defense, however, begins with the Dostoevskian premise that all of our claims—scientific, moral, and religious—are now without foundation. "God is dead," "the highest values devalue themselves," and the foundations of science are but errors ("necessary errors," perhaps, that is, necessary for the life of the species, yet not "true"). The negative, or "nihilistic," side of Nietzsche's philosophy consists of an attack on Christianity and Christian morality. One argument proceeds from the crumbling of the religious foundations and sanctions (the "death of God") to the invalidity of morality. More important, Nietzsche argues from a general thesis about values ("the value of value") to the rejection of both God and Christian morality. To do this, Nietzsche takes a naturalistic approach to moral reasoning. There are no a priori moral principles; there are only desires, all of them reducible to a single psychological drive, "the will to power." Values can be defended only insofar as they maximize one's power (in this regard, Nietzsche has in mind more the "spiritual" power of the artist or saint than political power). Christian morality, Nietzsche argues, is also a manifestation of the will to power, but the will of the weak, originating out of inferiority and *ressentiment,* a "slave morality" whose purpose is the preservation of the herd rather than the excellence of the strong. The positive side of Nietzsche's philosophy is much less focused, but it tends to celebrate the "this-worldly" and the creative potential of the greatest human beings. Frequently appearing in his mature works is the notion of the Will to Power, and Nietzsche was beginning to elaborate on this when he was struck down by a debilitating illness that ended his writing career. What remains of that effort are only unpublished notes, a few of which are included here. One of Nietzsche's most famous ideas is his fantasy of an "*Übermensch*"—a more than "human-all-too-human" being who is to serve as our new ideal. But this idea, too, is rather sketchy and limited to a single book, the prologue of Nietzsche's pseudo-biblical epic, *Thus Spoke Zarathustra.* Finally, Nietzsche seemed to take great pride in his idea of "eternal recurrence," the idea that what has happened and what will happen repeat themselves, over and over again. For Nietzsche, this would be the ultimate test of life-affirmation, whether one could accept his or her life with all of its joys and sufferings an infinite number of times.

Nietzsche developed his critique of morality and Christianity in a remarkable series of works over the last seven years of his productive life, 1882–1888. He begins with a famous slogan, "God is dead" (in the *Gay Science,* reprinted here), and in *Thus Spoke Zarathustra* he provides us with a complex portrait of the "this-worldly" attitude that is to take God's place. In quick succession, Nietzsche wrote *Beyond Good and Evil, On the Genealogy of Morals, Twilight of the Idols, The Antichrist,* and several other works. He considered himself a "good European" rather than German, and he spent virtually his entire career in Switzerland and Italy.

❖ *from* The Gay Science ❖

The madman.—Have you not heard of that madman who lit a lantern in the bright morning hours, ran to the market place, and cried incessantly: "I seek God! I seek God!"—As many of those who did not believe in God were standing around just then, he provoked much laughter. Has he got lost? asked one. Did he lose his way like a child? asked another. Or is he hiding? Is he afraid of us? Has he gone on a voyage? emigrated?—Thus they yelled and laughed.

The madman jumped into their midst and pierced them with his eyes. "Whither is God?" he cried; "I will tell you. *We have killed him—* you and I. All of us are his murderers. . . . God is dead. God remains dead. And we have killed him. . . .

Here the madman fell silent and looked again at his listeners; and they, too, were silent and stared at him in astonishment. At last he threw his lantern on the ground, and it broke into pieces and went out. "I have come too early," he said then; "my time is not yet. This tremendous event is still on its way, still wandering; it has not yet reached the ears of men. Lightning and thunder require time; the light of the stars requires time; deeds, though done, still require time to be seen and heard. This deed is still more distant from them than the most distant stars—*and yet they have done it themselves.*"

• • •

The meaning of our cheerfulness.—The greatest recent event—that "God is dead," that the belief in the Christian god has become unbelievable—is already beginning to cast its first shadows over Europe. For the few at least, whose eyes—the *suspicion* in whose eyes is strong and subtle enough for this spectacle, some sun seems to have set and some ancient and profound trust has been turned into doubt; to them our old world must appear daily more like evening, more mistrustful, stranger, "older." But in the main one may say: The event it-

From The Gay Science *by Friedrich Nietzsche, translated by Walter Kaufmann. Copyright 1946 by Random House, Inc. Reprinted by permission of the publisher. (Ed. note: this acknowledgment also covers the excerpts from* The Gay Science *on pp. 94–5 and 101.)*

self is far too great, too distant, too remote from the multitude's capacity for comprehension even for the tidings of it to be thought of as having *arrived* as yet. Much less may one suppose that many people know as yet *what* this event really means—and how much must collapse now that this faith has been undermined because it was built upon this faith, propped up by it, grown into it; for example, the whole of our European morality. This long plenitude and sequence of breakdown, destruction, ruin, and cataclysm that is now impending—who could guess enough of it today to be compelled to play the teacher and advance proclaimer of this monstrous logic of terror, the prophet of a gloom and an eclipse of the sun whose like has probably never yet occurred on earth?

Even we born guessers of riddles who are, as it were, waiting on the mountains, posted between today and tomorrow, stretched in the contradiction between today and tomorrow, we firstlings and premature births of the coming century, to whom the shadows that must soon envelop Europe really *should* have appeared by now—why is it that even we look forward to the approaching gloom without any real sense of involvement and above all without any worry and fear for *ourselves?* Are we perhaps still too much under the impression of the *initial consequences* of this event—and these initial consequences, the consequences for *ourselves,* are quite the opposite of what one might perhaps expect: They are not at all sad and gloomy but rather like a new and scarcely describable kind of light, happiness, relief, exhilaration, encouragement, dawn.

Indeed, we philosophers and "free spirits" feel, when we hear the news that "the old god is dead," as if a new dawn shone on us; our heart overflows with gratitude, amazement, premonitions, expectation. At long last the horizon appears free to us again, even if it should not be bright; at long last our ships may venture out again, venture out to face any danger; all the daring of the lover of knowledge is permitted again; the sea, *our* sea, lies open again; perhaps there has never yet been such an "open sea."—

Herd-Instinct.—Wherever we meet with a morality we find a valuation and order of rank of the human impulses and activities. These valuations and order of rank are always the expression of the needs of a community or herd: that which is in the first place to *its* advantage—and in the second place and third place—is also the authoritative standard for the worth of every individual. By morality the individual is taught to become a function of the herd, and to ascribe to himself value only as a function. As the conditions for the maintenance of one community have been very different from those of another community, there have been very different moralities; and in respect to the future essential transformations of herds and communities, states and societies, one can prophesy that there will still be very divergent moralities. Morality is the herd-instinct in the individual.

One Thing Is Needful.—To "give style" to one's character—that is a grand and a rare art! He who surveys all that his nature presents in its strength and in its weakness, and then fashions it into an ingenious plan, until everything appears artistic and rational, and even the weaknesses enchant the eye—exercises that admirable art. . . .

What does your conscience say? "You should become the person you are."

On the "genius of the species."—The problem of consciousness (more precisely, of becoming conscious of something) confronts us only when we begin to comprehend how we could dispense with it; and now physiology and the history of animals place us at the beginning of such comprehension (it took them two centuries to catch up with *Leibniz's* suspicion which soared ahead). For we could think, feel, will, and remember, and we could also "act" in every sense of that word, and yet none of all this would have to "enter our consciousness" (as one says metaphorically). The whole of life would be possible without, as it were, seeing itself in a mirror. Even now, for that matter, by far the greatest portion of our life actually takes place without this mirror effect; and this is true even of our thinking, feeling, and willing life, however offensive this may sound to older philosophers. For *what purpose,* then, any consciousness at all when it is in the main *superfluous?*

Now, if you are willing to listen to my answer and the perhaps extravagant surmise that it involves, it seems to me as if the subtlety and strength of consciousness always were proportionate to a man's (or animal's) *capacity for communication,* and as if this capacity in turn were proportionate to the *need for communication.* But this last point is not to be understood as if the individual human being who happens to be a master in communicating and making understandable his needs must also be most dependent on others in his needs.

But it does seem to me as if it were that way when we consider whole races and chains of generations: Where need and distress have forced men for a long time to communicate and to understand each other quickly and subtly, the ultimate result is an excess of this strength and art of communication—as it were, a capacity that has gradually been accumulated and now waits for an heir who might squander it. (Those who are called artists are these heirs; so are orators, preachers, writers—all of them people who always come at the end of a long chain, "late born" every one of them in the best sense of that word and, as I have said, by their nature squanderers.)

Supposing that this observation is correct, I may now proceed to the surmise that *consciousness has developed only under the pressure of the need for communication;* that from the start it was needed and useful only between human beings (particularly between those who commanded and those who obeyed); and that it also developed only in proportion to the degree of this utility. Consciousness is really only a net of communication between human beings; it is only as such that it had to develop; a solitary human being who lived like a beast of prey would not have needed it. That our actions, thoughts, feelings, and movements enter our own consciousness—at least a part of them—that is the result of a "must" that for a terribly long time lorded it over man. As the most endangered animal, he *needed* help and protection, he needed his peers, he had to learn to express his distress and to make himself understood; and for all of this he needed "consciousness" first of all, he needed to "know" himself what distressed him, he needed to "know" how he felt, he needed to "know" what he thought. For, to say it once more: Man, like every living being, thinks continually without knowing it; the thinking that rises to *consciousness* is only the smallest part of all this—the most superficial and worst part—for only this conscious thinking *takes the form of words, which is to say signs of communication,* and this fact uncovers the origin of consciousness.

In brief, the development of language and the development of consciousness (*not* of reason but merely of the way reason enters consciousness) go hand in hand. Add to this that not only language serves as a bridge between human beings but also a mien, a pressure, a gesture. The emergence of our sense impressions into our own consciousness, the ability to fix them and, as it were, exhibit them externally, increased proportionately with the need to communicate them to *others* by means of signs. The human being inventing signs is at the same time the human being who becomes ever more keenly conscious of himself. It was only as a social animal that man acquired self-consciousness—which he is still in the process of doing, more and more.

My idea is, as you see, that consciousness does not really belong to man's individual existence but rather to his social or herd nature; that, as follows from this, it has developed subtlety only insofar as this is required by social or herd utility. Consequently, given the best will in the world to understand ourselves as individually as possible, "to know ourselves," each of us will always succeed in becoming conscious only of what is not individual but "average." Our thoughts themselves are continually governed by the character of consciousness—by the "genius of the species" that commands it—and translated back into the perspective of the herd. Fundamentally, all our actions are altogether incomparably personal, unique, and infinitely individual; there is no doubt of that. But as soon as we translate them into consciousness *they no longer seem to be.*

This is the essence of phenomenalism and perspectivism as *I* understand them: Owing to the nature of *animal consciousness,* the world of which we can become conscious is only a surface- and sign-world, a world that is made common and meaner; whatever becomes conscious becomes by the same token shallow, thin, relatively stupid, general, sign, herd signal; all becoming conscious involves a great and thorough corruption, falsification, reduction to superficialities, and generalization. Ultimately, the growth of consciousness becomes a danger; and anyone who lives among the most conscious Europeans even knows that it is a disease.

You will guess that it is not the opposition of subject and object that concerns me here: This distinction I leave to the epistemologists who have become entangled in the snares of grammar (the metaphysics of the people). It is even less the opposition of "thing-in-itself" and appearance; for we do not "know" nearly enough to be entitled to any such distinction. We simply lack any organ for knowledge, for "truth": we "know" (or believe or imagine) just as much as may be *useful* in the interests of the human herd, the species; and even what is here called "utility" is ultimately also a mere belief, something imaginary, and perhaps precisely that most calamitous stupidity of which we shall perish some day.

❖ *from* Thus Spoke Zarathustra ❖

When Zarathustra came into the next town, which lies on the edge of the forest, he found many people gathered together in the market place; for it had been promised that there would be a tightrope walker. And Zarathustra spoke thus to the people:

"*I teach you the overman.* Man is something that shall be overcome. What have you done to overcome him?

"All beings so far have created something beyond themselves; and do you want to be the ebb of this great flood and even go back to the beasts rather than overcome man? What is the ape to man? A laughingstock or a painful embarrassment. And man shall be just that for the overman: a laughingstock or a painful embarrassment. You have made your way from worm to man, and much in you is still worm. Once you were apes, and even now, too, man is more ape than any ape.

• • •

"Behold, I teach you the overman. The overman is the meaning of the earth. Let your will say: the overman *shall be* the meaning of the earth! I beseech you, my brothers, *remain faithful to the earth,* and do not believe those who speak to you of otherworldly hopes! Poison-mixers are they, whether they know it or not. Despisers of life are they, decaying and poisoned themselves, of whom the earth is weary: so let them go.

"Once the sin against God was the greatest sin; but God died, and these sinners died with him. To sin against the earth is now the most dreadful thing, and to esteem the entrails of the unknowable higher than the meaning of the earth.

• • •

"What is the greatest experience you can have? It is the hour of the great contempt. The hour in which your happiness, too, arouses your disgust, and even your reason and your virtue.

From The Portable Nietzsche, *edited and translated by Walter Kaufmann. Copyright 1954 by The Viking Press, Inc. Reprinted by permission of The Viking Press, Inc. (Ed. note: this acknowledgment also covers the excerpt from* Thus Spoke Zarathustra *on p. 98.)*

"The hour when you say, 'What matters my happiness? It is poverty and filth and wretched contentment. But my happiness ought to justify existence itself.'"

• • •

Zarathustra, however, beheld the people and was amazed. Then he spoke thus:

"Man is a rope, tied between beast and overman—a rope over an abyss. A dangerous across, a dangerous on-the-way, a dangerous looking-back, a dangerous shuddering and stopping.

"What is great in man is that he is a bridge and not an end: what can be loved in man is that he is an *overture* and a *going under*."

• • •

When Zarathustra had spoken these words he beheld the people again and was silent. "There they stand," he said to his heart; "there they laugh. They do not understand me; I am not the mouth for these ears. Must one smash their ears before they learn to listen with their eyes? Must one clatter like kettledrums and preachers of repentance? Or do they believe only the stammerer?

"They have something of which they are proud. What do they call that which makes them proud? Education they call it; it distinguishes them from goatherds. That is why they do not like to hear the word 'contempt' applied to them. Let me then address their pride. Let me speak to them of what is most contemptible: but that is the *last man*."

And thus spoke Zarathustra to the people: "The time has come for man to set himself a goal. The time has come for man to plant the seed of his highest hope. His soil is still rich enough. But one day this soil will be poor and domesticated, and no tall tree will be able to grow in it. Alas, the time is coming when man will no longer shoot the arrow of his longing beyond man, and the string of his bow will have forgotten how to whir!

"I say unto you: one must still have chaos in oneself to be able to give birth to a dancing star. I say unto you: you still have chaos in yourselves.

"Alas, the time is coming when man will no longer give birth to a star. Alas, the time of the most despicable man is coming, he that is no longer able to despise himself. Behold, I show you the *last man*.

"'What is love? What is creation? What is longing? What is a star?' thus asks the last man, and he blinks.

"The earth has become small, and on it hops the last man, who makes everything small. His race is as ineradicable as the flea-beetle; the last man lives longest.

"'We have invented happiness,' say the last men, and they blink. They have left the regions where it was hard to live, for one needs warmth. One still loves one's neighbor and rubs against him, for one needs warmth.

"Becoming sick and harboring suspicion are sinful to them: one proceeds carefully. A fool, whoever still stumbles over stones or human beings! A little poison now and then: that makes for agreeable dreams. And much poison in the end, for an agreeable death.

"One still works, for work is a form of entertainment. But one is careful lest the entertainment be too harrowing. One no longer becomes poor or rich: both require too much exertion. Who still wants to rule? Who obey? Both require too much exertion.

"No shepherd and one herd! Everybody wants the same, everybody is the same: whoever feels different goes voluntarily into a madhouse.

"'Formerly, all the world was mad,' say the most refined, and they blink.

"One is clever and knows everything that has ever happened: so there is no end of derision. One still quarrels, but one is soon reconciled—else it might spoil the digestion.

"One has one's little pleasure for the day and one's little pleasure for the night: but one has a regard for health.

"'We have invented happiness,' say the last men, and they blink."

And here ended Zarathustra's first speech, which is also called "the Prologue"; for at this point he was interrupted by the clamor and delight of the crowd. "Give us this last man, O Zarathustra," they shouted. "Turn us into these last men! Then we shall make you a gift of the overman!" And all the people jubilated and clucked with their tongues.

But Zarathustra became sad and said to his heart: "They do not understand me: I am not the mouth for these ears. I seem to have lived too long in the mountains . . ."

❖ *from* Beyond Good and Evil ❖

Gradually it has become clear to me what every great philosophy so far has been: namely, the personal confession of its author and a kind of involuntary and unconscious memoir; also that the moral (or immoral) intentions in every philosophy constituted the real germ of life from which the whole plant had grown.

Indeed, if one would explain how the abstrusest metaphysical claims of a philosopher really came about, it is always well (and wise) to ask first: at what morality does all this (does *he*) aim? Accordingly, I do not believe that a "drive to knowledge" is the father of philosophy; but rather that another drive has, here as elsewhere, employed understanding (and misunderstanding) as a mere instrument. But anyone who considers the basic drives of man to see to what extent they may have been at play just here as *inspiring* spirits (or demons and kobolds) will find that all of them have done philosophy at some time—and that every single one of them would like only too well to represent just *itself* as the ultimate purpose of existence and the legitimate *master* of all the other drives. For every drive wants to be master—and it attempts to philosophize in *that spirit.*

To be sure: among scholars who are really scientific men, things may be different—"better," if you like—there you may really find something like a drive for knowledge, some small, independent clockwork that, once well wound, works on vigorously *without* any essential participation from all the other drives of the scholar. The real "interests" of the scholar therefore lie usually somewhere else— say, in his family, or in making money, or in politics. Indeed, it is almost a matter of total indifference whether his little machine is placed at this or that spot in science, and whether the "promising" young worker turns himself into a good philologist or an expert on fungi or a chemist: it does not *characterize* him that he becomes this or that. In the philosopher, conversely, there is nothing whatever that is impersonal; and above all, his morality bears decided and decisive witness to *who he is*—that is, in what order of rank the innermost drives of his nature stand in relation to each other.

From Beyond Good and Evil *by Friedrich Nietzsche, translated by Walter Kaufmann. Copyright 1966 by Random House. Reprinted by permission of the publisher. (Ed. note: this acknowledgment also covers the excerpt from Beyond Good and Evil on pp. 97–8.)*

Wandering through the many subtler and coarser moralities which have so far been prevalent on earth, or still are prevalent, I found that certain features recurred regularly together and were closely associated—until I finally discovered two basic types and one basic difference.

There are *master morality* and *slave morality*—I add immediately that in all the higher and more mixed cultures there also appear attempts at mediation between these two moralities, and yet more often the interpenetration and mutual misunderstanding of both, and at times they occur directly alongside each other—even in the same human being, within a *single* soul. The moral discrimination of values has originated either among a ruling group whose consciousness of its difference from the ruled group was accompanied by delight—or among the ruled, the slaves and dependents of every degree.

In the first case, when the ruling group determines what is "good," the exalted, proud states of the soul are experienced as conferring distinction and determining the order of rank. The noble human being separates from himself those in whom the opposite of such exalted, proud states finds expression: he despises them. It should be noted immediately that in this first type of morality the opposition of "good" and "*bad*" means approximately the same as "noble" and "contemptible." (The opposition of "good" and "*evil*" has a different origin.) One feels contempt for the cowardly, the anxious, the petty, those intent on narrow utility; also for the suspicious with their unfree glances, those who humble themselves, the doglike people who allow themselves to be maltreated, the begging flatterers, above all the liars: it is part of the fundamental faith of all aristocrats that the common people lie. "We truthful ones"—thus the nobility of ancient Greece referred to itself.

It is obvious that moral designations were everywhere first applied to *human beings* and only later, derivatively, to actions. Therefore it is a gross mistake when historians of morality start from such questions as: why was the compassionate act praised? The noble type of man experiences *itself* as determining values; it does not need approval; it judges, "what is harmful to me is harmful in itself"; it knows itself to be that which first accords honor to things; it is *value-creating*. Everything it knows as part of itself it honors: such a morality is self-glorification. In the foreground there is the feeling of fullness, of power that seeks to overflow, the happiness of high tension, the consciousness of wealth that would give and bestow: the noble human being, too, helps the unfortunate, but not, or almost not, from pity, but prompted more by an urge begotten by excess of power. The noble human being honors himself as one who is powerful, also as one who has power over himself, who knows how to speak and be silent, who delights in being severe and hard with himself and respects all severity and hardness. "A hard heart Wotan put into my breast," says an old Scandinavian saga: a fitting poetic expression, seeing that it comes from the soul of a proud Viking. Such a type of man is actually proud of the fact that he is *not* made for pity, and the hero of the saga therefore adds as a warning: "If the heart is not hard in youth it will never harden." Noble and courageous human beings who think that way are furthest removed from that morality which finds the distinction of morality precisely in pity, or in acting for others, or in *désintéressement;* faith in oneself, pride in oneself, a fundamental hostility and irony against "selflessness" belong just as definitely to noble morality as does a slight disdain and caution regarding compassionate feelings and a "warm heart."

It is the powerful who *understand* how to honor; this is their art, their realm of invention. The profound reverence for age and tradition—all law rests on this double reverence—the faith and prejudice in favor of ancestors and disfavor of those yet to come are typical of the morality of the powerful; and when the men of "modern ideas," conversely, believe almost instinctively in "progress" and "the future" and more and more lack respect for age, this in itself would sufficiently betray the ignoble origin of these "ideas."

A morality of the ruling group, however, is most alien and embarrassing to the present taste in the severity of its principle that one has duties only to one's peers; that against beings of a lower rank, against everything alien, one may behave as one pleases or "as the heart desires," and in any case "beyond good and evil"—here pity and like feelings may find their place. The capacity for, and the duty of, long gratitude and long revenge—both only among one's peers—refinement in repaying, the sophisticated concept of friendship, a certain necessity for having enemies (as it were, as drainage ditches for the affects of envy, quarrelsomeness, exuberance—at bottom, in order to be capable of being good *friends*): all these are typical characteristics of noble morality which, as suggested, is not the morality of "modern ideas" and therefore is hard to empathize with today, also hard to dig up and uncover.

• • •

It is different with the second type of morality, *slave morality*. Suppose the violated, oppressed, suffering, unfree, who are uncertain of themselves and weary, moralize: what will their moral valuations have in common? Probably, a pessimistic suspicion about the whole condition of man will find expression, perhaps a condemnation of man along with his condition. The slave's eye is not favorable to the virtues of the powerful: he is skeptical and suspicious, *subtly* suspicious, of all the "good" that is honored there—he would like to persuade himself that even their happiness is not genuine. Conversely, those qualities are brought out and flooded with light which serve to ease existence for those who suffer: here pity, the complaisant and obliging hand, the warm heart, patience, industry, humility, and friendliness are honored—for here these are the most useful qualities and almost the only means for enduring the pressure of existence. Slave morality is essentially a morality of utility.

Here is the place for the origin of that famous opposition of "good" and "evil": into evil one's feelings project power and dangerousness, a certain terribleness, subtlety, and strength that does not permit contempt to develop. According to slave morality, those who are "evil" thus inspire fear; according to master morality it is precisely those who are "good" that inspire, and wish to inspire, fear, while the "bad" are felt to be contemptible.

The opposition reaches its climax when, as a logical consequence of slave morality, a touch of disdain is associated also with the "good" of this morality—this may be slight and benevolent—because the good human being has to be *undangerous* in the slave's way of thinking: he is good-natured, easy to deceive, a little stupid perhaps, *un bonhomme.* Wherever slave morality becomes preponderant, language tends to bring the words "good" and "stupid" closer together.

One last fundamental difference: the longing for *freedom,* the instinct for happiness and the subtleties of the feeling of freedom belong just as necessarily to slave morality and morals as artful and enthusiastic reverence and devotion are the regular symptoms of an aristocratic way of thinking and evaluating.

❖ *from* On the Genealogy of Morality ❖

I. "Good and Evil," "Good and Bad"

• • •

2. . . . . Now in the first place it is obvious to me that the actual genesis of the concept "good" is sought and fixed in the wrong place by this theory: the judgment "good" does *not* stem from those to whom "goodness" is rendered! Rather it was "the good" themselves, that is the noble, powerful, higher-ranking, and high-minded who felt and ranked themselves and their doings as good, which is to say, as of the first rank, in contrast to everything base, low-minded, common, and vulgar. Out of this *pathos of distance* they first took for themselves the right to create values, to coin names for values: what did they care about usefulness! The viewpoint of utility is as foreign and inappropriate as possible, especially in relation to so hot an outpouring of highest rank-ordering, rank-distinguishing value judgments: for here feeling has arrived at an opposite of that low degree of warmth presupposed by every calculating prudence, every assessment of utility—and not just for once, for an hour of exception, but rather for the long run. As was stated, the pathos of nobility and distance, this lasting and dominant collective and basic feeling of a higher ruling nature in relation to a lower nature, to a "below"—*that* is the origin of the opposition "good" and "bad." (The right of lords to give names goes so far that we should allow ourselves to comprehend the origin of language itself as an expression of power on the part of those who rule: they say "this is such and such," they seal each thing and happening with a sound and thus, as it were, take possession of it.) It is because of this origin that from the outset the word "good" does *not* necessarily attach itself to "unegoistic" actions—as is the superstition of those genealogists of morality. On the contrary, only when aristocratic value judgments begin to *decline* does this entire opposition "egoistic" "unegoistic" impose itself more and more on the human conscience—to make use of my language,

From On the Genealogy of Morality *by Friedrich Nietzsche, translated by Maudemarie Clark and Alan J. Swenson. Copyright 1988 by Hackett Publ. Co. Reprinted by permission of the publisher. (Ed. note: this acknowledgment also covers the excerpt from* On the Genealogy of Morality *on pp. 95–6.)*

it is *the herd instinct* that finally finds a voice (also *words*) in this opposition. And even then it takes a long time until this instinct becomes dominant to such an extent that moral valuation in effect gets caught and stuck at that opposition (as is the case in present-day Europe: today the prejudice that takes "moral," "unegoistic," "*désintéressé*" to be concepts of equal value already rules with the force of an "*idée fixe*" and sickness in the head).

• • •

4.—The pointer to the *right* path was given to me by the question: what do the terms coined for "good" in the various languages actually mean from an etymological viewpoint? Here I found that they all lead back to the *same conceptual transformation*—that everywhere the basic concept is "noble," "aristocratic" in the sense related to the estates, out of which "good" in the sense of "noble of soul," "high-natured of soul," "privileged of soul" necessarily develops: a development that always runs parallel to that other one which makes "common," "vulgar," "base" pass over finally into the concept "bad." The most eloquent example of the latter is the German word "*schlecht*" [bad] itself: which is identical with "*schlicht*" [plain, simple]—compare "*schlechtweg*," "*schlechterdings*" [simply or downright]—and originally designated the plain, the common man, as yet without a suspecting sideward glance, simply in opposition to the noble one. Around the time of the Thirty-Years' War, in other words late enough, this sense shifts into the one now commonly used.

• • •

7.—One will already have guessed how easily the priestly manner of valuation can branch off from the knightly-aristocratic and then develop into its opposite; this process is especially given an impetus every time the priestly caste and the warrior caste confront each other jealously and are unable to agree on a price. The knightly-aristocratic value judgments have as their presupposition a powerful physicality, a blossoming, rich, even overflowing health, together with that which is required for its preservation: war, adventure, the hunt, dance, athletic contests, and in general everything which includes strong, free, cheerful-hearted activity. The priestly-noble manner of valuation—as we have seen—has other presuppositions: too bad for it when it comes to war! Priests are, as is well known, the *most evil enemies*—why is that? Because they are the most powerless. Out of their powerlessness their hate grows into something enormous and uncanny, into something most spiritual and most poisonous. The truly great haters in the history of the world have always been priests, also the most ingenious haters:—compared with the spirit of priestly revenge all the rest of spirit taken together hardly merits consideration. Human history would be much too stupid an affair without the spirit that has entered into it through the powerless:—let us turn right to the greatest example. Of all that has been done on earth against "the noble," "the mighty," "the lords," "the power-holders," nothing is worthy of mention in comparison with that which the *Jews* have done against them: the Jews, that priestly people who in the end were only able to obtain satisfaction from their enemies and conquerors through a radical revaluation of their values, that is, through an act of *spiritual revenge*. This was the only way that suited a priestly people, the people of the most suppressed priestly desire for revenge. It was the Jews who in opposition to the aristocratic value equation (good = noble = powerful = beautiful = happy = beloved of God) dared its inversion, with fear-inspiring consistency, and held it fast with teeth of the most unfathomable hate (the hate of powerlessness), namely: "the miserable alone are the good; the poor, powerless, lowly alone are the good; the suffering, deprived, sick, ugly are also the only pious, the only blessed in God, for them alone is there blessedness,—whereas you, you noble and powerful ones, you are in all eternity the evil, the cruel, the lustful, the insatiable, the godless, you will eternally be the wretched, accursed, and damned!" . . . We know *who* inherited this Jewish revaluation . . . In connection with the enormous and immeasurably doom-laden initiative provided by the Jews with this most fundamental of all declarations of war, I call attention to the proposition which I arrived at on another occasion ("Beyond Good and Evil" section 195)—namely, that with the Jews *the slave revolt in morality* begins: that revolt which has a two-thousand-year history behind it and which has only moved out of our sight today because it—has been victorious . . .

• • •

10. The slave revolt in morality begins when *ressentiment* itself becomes creative and gives birth to values: the *ressentiment* of beings denied the true reaction, that of the deed, who recover their losses

only through an imaginary revenge. Whereas all noble morality grows out of a triumphant yes-saying to oneself, from the outset slave morality says "no" to an "outside," to a "different," to a "not-self": and *this* "no" is its creative deed. This reversal of the value-establishing glance—this *necessary* direction toward the outside instead of back onto oneself—belongs to the very nature of *ressentiment:* in order to come into being, slave-morality always needs an opposite and external world; it needs, psychologically speaking, external stimuli in order to be able to act at all,—its action is, from the ground up, reaction. The reverse is the case with the noble manner of valuation: it acts and grows spontaneously, it seeks out its opposite only in order to say "yes" to itself still more gratefully and more jubilantly—its negative concept "low" "common" "bad" is only an after-birth, a pale contrast-image in relation to its positive basic concept, saturated through and through with life and passion: "we noble ones, we good ones, we beautiful ones, we happy ones!" When the noble manner of valuation lays a hand on reality and sins against it, this occurs relative to the sphere with which it is *not* sufficiently acquainted, indeed against a real knowledge of which it rigidly defends itself: in some cases it forms a wrong idea of the sphere it holds in contempt, that of the common man, of the lower people; on the other hand, consider that the affect of contempt, of looking down on, of the superior glance—assuming that it does *falsify* the image of the one held in contempt—will in any case fall far short of the falsification with which the suppressed hate, the revenge of the powerless, lays a hand on its opponent—in effigy, of course. Indeed there is too much carelessness in contempt, too much taking-lightly, too much looking-away and impatience mixed in, even too much of a feeling of cheer in oneself, for it to be capable of transforming its object into a real caricature and monster.

• • •

13.—But let us come back: the problem of the *other* origin of "good," of the good one as conceived by the man of *ressentiment,* demands its conclusion.—That the lambs feel anger toward the great birds of prey does not strike us as odd: but that is no reason for holding it against the great birds of prey that they snatch up little lambs for themselves. And when the lambs say among themselves "these birds of prey are evil; and whoever is as little as possible a bird of prey but rather its opposite, a lamb,—isn't he good?" there is nothing to criticize in this setting up of an ideal, even if the birds of prey should look on this a little mockingly and perhaps say to themselves: "*we* do not feel any anger towards them, these good lambs, as a matter of fact, we love them: nothing is more tasty than a tender lamb."— To demand of strength that it *not* express itself as strength, that it *not* be a desire to overwhelm, a desire to cast down, a desire to become lord, a thirst for enemies and resistances and triumphs, is just as nonsensical as to demand of weakness that it express itself as strength. A quantum of power is just such a quantum of drive, will, effect— more precisely, it is nothing other than this very driving, willing, effecting, and only through the seduction of language (and the basic errors of reason petrified therein), which understands and misunderstands all effecting as conditioned by an effecting something, by a "subject," can it appear otherwise. For just as common people separate the lightning from its flash and take the latter as a *doing,* as an effect of a subject called lightning, so popular morality also separates strength from the expressions of strength as if there were behind the strong an indifferent substratum that is free to express strength—or not to. But there is no such substratum; there is no "being" behind the doing, effecting, becoming; "the doer" is simply fabricated into the doing—the doing is everything. Common people basically double the doing when they have the lightning flash; this is a doing-doing: the same happening is posited first as cause and then once again as its effect. Natural scientists do no better when they say "force moves, force causes," and so on—our entire science, despite all its coolness, its freedom from affect, still stands under the seduction of language and has not gotten rid of the changelings slipped over on it, the "subjects" (the atom, for example, is such a changeling, likewise the Kantian "thing in itself"): small wonder if the suppressed, hiddenly glowing affects of revenge and hate exploit this belief and basically even uphold no other belief more ardently than this one, that *the strong one is free* to be weak, and the bird of prey to be a lamb:—they thereby gain for themselves the right to hold the bird of prey *accountable* for being a bird of prey.

• • •

16. Let us conclude. The two *opposed* values 'good and bad,' 'good and evil,' have fought a terrible millennia-long battle on earth; and as

certainly as the second value has had the upper hand for a long time, even so there is still no shortage of places where the battle goes on, undecided. One could even say that it has in the meantime been borne up ever higher and precisely thereby become ever deeper, ever more spiritual: so that today there is perhaps no more decisive mark of the "*higher nature,*" of the more spiritual nature, than to be conflicted in that sense and still a real battle-ground for those opposites. The symbol of this battle, written in a script that has so far remained legible across all of human history, is "Rome against Judea, Judea against Rome":—so far there has been no greater event than *this* battle, *this* formulation of the problem, *this* mortally hostile contradiction. Rome sensed in the Jew something like anti-nature itself, its antipodal monstrosity as it were; in Rome the Jew was held to have been "*convicted* of hatred against the entire human race": rightly so, insofar as one has a right to tie the salvation and the future of the human race to the unconditional rule of aristocratic values, of Roman values. What the Jews on the other hand felt towards Rome? One can guess it from a thousand indications; but it will suffice to recall again the Johannine Apocalypse, that most immoderate of all written outbursts that revenge has on its conscience. (Do not underestimate, by the way, the profound consistency of the Christian instinct when it gave precisely this book of hate the name of the disciple of love, the same one to whom it attributed that enamored-rapturous gospel—: therein lies a piece of truth, however much literary counterfeiting may have been needed for this purpose.) The Romans were after all the strong and noble ones, such that none stronger and nobler have ever existed, ever even been dreamt of; everything that remains of them, every inscription thrills, supposing that one can guess *what* is doing the writing there. The Jews, conversely, were that priestly people of *ressentiment* par excellence, in whom there dwelt a popular-moral genius without parallel: just compare the peoples with related talents—for instance the Chinese or the Germans—with the Jews in order to feel what is first and what fifth rank. Which of them has been victorious in the meantime, Rome or Judea? But there is no doubt at all: just consider before whom one bows today in Rome itself as before the quintessence of all the highest values—and not only in Rome, but over almost half the earth, everywhere that man has become tame or wants to become tame,—before *three Jews*, as everyone knows, and *one Jewess* (before Jesus of Nazareth, the fisher Peter, the carpet-weaver Paul, and the mother of the aforementioned Jesus, called Mary). This is very remarkable:

Rome has succumbed without any doubt. To be sure, in the Renaissance there was a brilliant-uncanny reawakening of the classical ideal, of the noble manner of valuing all things: Rome itself moved like one awakened from apparent death, under the pressure of the new Judaized Rome built above it, which presented the appearance of an ecumenical synagogue and was called "church": but immediately Judea triumphed again, thanks to that thoroughly mobbish (German and English) *ressentiment* movement called the Reformation, and that which had to follow from it, the restoration of the church—also the restoration of the old sepulchral sleep of classical Rome. In an even more decisive and more profound sense than before, Judea once again achieved a victory over the classical ideal with the French Revolution: the last political nobleness there was in Europe, that of the seventeenth and eighteenth *French* centuries, collapsed under the instincts of popular *ressentiment*—never on earth has a greater jubilation, a noisier enthusiasm been heard! It is true that in the midst of all this the most enormous, most unexpected thing occurred: the classical ideal itself stepped *bodily* and with unheard of splendor before the eyes and conscience of humanity—and once again, more strongly, more simply, more penetratingly than ever, the terrible and thrilling counter-slogan "the *privilege of the few*" resounded in the face of the old lie-slogan of *ressentiment,* "the privilege of the majority," in the face of the will to lowering, to debasement, to leveling, to the downward and evening-ward of man! Like a last sign pointing to the *other* path, Napoleon appeared, that most individual and late-born human being there ever was, and in him the incarnate problem of the *noble ideal in itself*—consider well, *what* kind of problem it is: Napoleon, this synthesis of an *inhuman* and a *superhuman* . . .

II.   "Guilt," "Bad Conscience," and Related Matters

1. To breed an animal that *is permitted to promise*—isn't this precisely the paradoxical task nature has set for itself with regard to man? isn't this the true problem *of* man? . . .

• • •

2. Precisely this is the long history of the origins of *responsibility.* As we have already grasped, the task of breeding an animal that is permitted to promise includes, as condition and preparation, the

more specific task of first *making* man to a certain degree necessary, uniform, like among like, regular, and accordingly predictable. The enormous work of what I have called "morality of custom" (cf. *Daybreak* 9, 14, 16)—the true work of man on himself for the longest part of the duration of the human race, his entire *prehistoric* work, has in this its meaning, its great justification—however much hardness, tyranny, mindlessness, and idiocy may be inherent in it: with the help of the morality of custom and the social straightjacket man was *made* truly calculable. If, on the other hand, we place ourselves at the end of the enormous process, where the tree finally produces its fruit, where society and its morality of custom finally brings to light that *to which* it was only the means: then we will find as the ripest fruit on its tree the *sovereign individual,* the individual resembling only himself, free again from the morality of custom, autonomous and supermoral (for "autonomous" and "moral" are mutually exclusive), in short, the human being with his own independent long will, the human being who *is permitted to promise*—and in him a proud consciousness, twitching in all his muscles, of *what* has finally been achieved and become flesh in him, a true consciousness of power and freedom, a feeling of the completion of man himself. This being who has become free, who is really *permitted* to promise, this lord of the *free* will, this sovereign—how could he not know what superiority he thus has over all else that is not permitted to promise and vouch for itself, how much trust, how much fear, how much reverence he awakens—he "*earns*" all three—and how this mastery over himself also necessarily brings with it mastery over circumstances, over nature and all lesser-willed and more unreliable creatures? The "free" human being, the possessor of a long, unbreakable will, has in this possession his *standard of value* as well: looking from himself toward the others, he honors or holds in contempt; and just as necessarily as he honors the ones like him, the strong and reliable (those who are *permitted* to promise),—that is, everyone who promises like a sovereign, weightily, seldom, slowly, who is stingy with his trust, who *conveys a mark of distinction* when he trusts, who gives his word as something on which one can rely because he knows himself to be strong enough to uphold it even against accidents, even "against fate"—: just as necessarily he will hold his kick in readiness for the frail dogs who promise although they are not permitted to do so, and his switch for the liar who breaks his word already the moment it leaves his mouth. The proud knowl-

edge of the extraordinary privilege of *responsibility,* the consciousness of this rare freedom, this power over oneself and fate, has sunk
into his lowest depth and has become instinct, the dominant instinct:—what will he call it, this dominant instinct, assuming that he
feels the need to have a word for it? But there is no doubt: this sovereign human being calls it his *conscience.* . . .

• • •

3. . . . We Germans certainly do not regard ourselves as a particularly cruel and hard-hearted people, still less as particularly frivolous or living-for-the-day; but one need only look at our old penal
codes to discover what amount of effort it takes to breed a "people
of thinkers" on earth (that is to say: *the* people of Europe, among
whom one still finds even today the maximum of confidence, seriousness, tastelessness, and matter-of-factness, qualities which give it
a right to breed every type of European mandarin). Using terrible
means these Germans have made a memory for themselves in order
to become master over their mobbish basic instincts and the brutal
heavy-handedness of the same: think of the old German punishments, for example of stoning (—even legend has the millstone fall
on the head of the guilty one), breaking on the wheel (the most characteristic invention and specialty of German genius in the realm of
punishment!), casting stakes, having torn or trampled by horses
("quartering"), boiling the criminal in oil or wine (as late as the four-
teenth and fifteenth centuries), the popular flaying ("*Riemenschnei-
den*"), cutting flesh from the breast; also, no doubt, that the evil-doer
was smeared with honey and abandoned to the flies under a burning sun. With the help of such images and processes one finally retains in memory five, six "I will nots," in connection with which one
has given one's *promise* in order to live within the advantages of society,—and truly! with the help of this kind of memory one finally
came "to reason"!—Ah, reason, seriousness, mastery over the affects,
this entire gloomy matter called reflection, all these prerogatives and
showpieces of man: how dearly they have been paid for! how much
blood and horror there is at the base of all "good things"! . . .

• • •

4. But how then did that other "gloomy thing," the consciousness
of guilt, the entire "bad conscience" come into the world?—And thus

we return to our genealogists of morality. To say it once more—or haven't I said it at all yet?—they aren't good for anything.

• • •

8. The feeling of guilt, of personal obligation—to take up the train of our investigation again—had its origin, as we have seen, in the oldest and most primitive relationship among persons there is, in the relationship between buyer and seller, creditor and debtor: here for the first time person stepped up against person, here for the first time a person *measured himself* by another person. No degree of civilization however low has yet been discovered in which something of this relationship was not already noticeable. Making prices, gauging values, thinking out equivalents, exchanging—this preoccupied man's very first thinking to such an extent that it is in a certain sense thinking *itself:* here that oldest kind of acumen was bred, here likewise we may suspect the first beginnings of human pride, man's feeling of preeminence with respect to other creatures. Perhaps our word "man" (*manas*) still expresses precisely something of this self-esteem: man designated himself as the being who measures values, who values and measures, as the "appraising animal in itself." Purchase and sale, together with their psychological accessories, are older than even the beginnings of any societal associations and organizational forms: it was out of the most rudimentary form of personal legal rights that the budding feeling of exchange, contract, guilt, right, obligation, compensation first *transferred* itself onto the coarsest and earliest communal complexes (in their relationship to similar complexes), together with the habit of comparing, measuring, and calculating power against power. The eye was simply set to this perspective: and with that clumsy consistency characteristic of earlier humanity's thinking—which has difficulty moving but then continues relentlessly in the same direction—one arrived straightaway at the grand generalization "every thing has its price; *everything* can be paid off"—at the oldest and most naive moral canon of *justice,* at the beginning of all "good-naturedness," all "fairness," all "good will," all "objectivity" on earth. Justice at this first stage is the good will among parties of approximately equal power to come to terms with one another, to reach an "understanding" again by means of a settlement—and in regard to less powerful parties, to *force* them to a settlement among themselves.—

• • •

16. At this point I can no longer avoid helping my own hypothesis on the origin of the "bad conscience" to a first, preliminary expression: it is not easy to present and needs to be considered, guarded, and slept over for a long time. I take bad conscience to be the deep sickness into which man had to fall under the pressure of that most fundamental of all changes he ever experienced—the change of finding himself enclosed once and for all within the sway of society and peace. Just as water animals must have fared when they were forced either to become land animals or to perish, so fared these half animals who were happily adapted to wilderness, war, roaming about, adventure—all at once all of their instincts were devalued and "disconnected." From now on they were to go on foot and "carry themselves" where they had previously been carried by the water: a horrible heaviness lay upon them. They felt awkward doing the simplest tasks; for this new, unfamiliar world they no longer had their old leaders, the regulating drives that unconsciously guided them safely—they were reduced to thinking, inferring, calculating, connecting cause and effect, these unhappy ones, reduced to their "consciousness," to their poorest and most erring organ! I do not believe there has ever been such a feeling of misery on earth, such a leaden discomfort—and yet those old instincts had not all at once ceased to make their demands! It's just that it was difficult and seldom possible to yield to them: for the most part they had to seek new and as it were subterranean gratifications. All instincts that do not discharge themselves outwardly *turn themselves inwards*—this is what I call the *internalizing* of man: thus first grows in man that which he later calls his "soul." The entire inner world, originally thin as if inserted between two skins, has spread and unfolded, has taken on depth, breadth, height to the same extent that man's outward discharging has been *obstructed*. Those terrible bulwarks with which the organization of the state protects itself against the old instincts of freedom—punishments belong above all else to these bulwarks— brought it about that all those instincts of the wild free roaming human turned themselves backwards *against man himself*. Hostility, cruelty, pleasure in persecution, in assault, in change, in destruction—all of that turning itself against the possessors of such instincts: *that* is the origin of "bad conscience." The man who, for lack of external enemies and resistance, and wedged into an oppressive narrowness and regularity of custom, impatiently tore apart, persecuted, gnawed at, stirred up, maltreated himself; this animal that one wants

to "tame" and that beats itself raw on the bars of its cage; this deprived one, consumed by homesickness for the desert, who had to
create out of himself an adventure, a place of torture, an uncertain
and dangerous wilderness—this fool, this longing and desperate prisoner became the inventor of "bad conscience." In him, however, the
greatest and most uncanny of sicknesses was introduced, one from
which man has not recovered to this day, the suffering of man *from
man,* from *himself*—as the consequence of a forceful separation
from his animal past, of a leap and plunge, as it were, into new situations and conditions of existence, of a declaration of war against
the old instincts on which his energy, desire, and terribleness had
thus far rested. Let us immediately add that, on the other hand, with
the appearance on earth of an animal soul turned against itself, taking sides against itself, something so new, deep, unheard of, enigmatic, contradictory, *and full of future* had come into being that the
appearance of the earth was thereby essentially changed. Indeed, divine spectators were necessary to appreciate the spectacle that thus
began and whose end is still by no means in sight—a spectacle too
refined, too wonderful, too paradoxical to be permitted to play itself
out senselessly-unnoticed on some ridiculous star! Since that time
man is *included* among the most unexpected and exciting lucky
throws in the game played by the "big child" of Heraclitus, whether
called Zeus or chance—he awakens for himself an interest, an anticipation, a hope, almost a certainty, as if with him something were an-
nouncing itself, something preparing itself, as if man were not a goal
but only a path, an incident, a bridge, a great promise . . .

• • •

19. It is a sickness, bad conscience—this admits of no doubt—but
a sickness as pregnancy is a sickness.

III.   What Do Ascetic Ideals Mean?

> *Carefree, mocking, violent—thus wisdom wants us: she is a*
> *woman, she always loves only a warrior.*
> —*Thus Spoke Zarathustra*

13. But let us return to our problem. In an accounting that is physiological and no longer psychological, a contradiction such as the as-

cetic seems to represent, "life *against* life," is—this much is immediately clear as day—simply nonsense. It can only be *apparent;* it must be a kind of provisional expression, an interpretation, formula, arrangement, a psychological misunderstanding of something whose actual nature could not be understood for a long time, could not be designated *in itself*—a mere word, jammed into an old *gap* in human knowledge. And to oppose this with a brief statement of the facts of the matter: *the ascetic ideal springs from the protective and healing instincts of a degenerating life* that seeks with every means to hold its ground and is fighting for its existence; it points to a partial physiological hindrance and tiredness against which the deepest instincts of life, which have remained intact, fight incessantly with new means and inventions. The ascetic ideal is such a means: it is exactly the opposite of what its venerators suppose—in it and through it life is wrestling with death and *against* death; the ascetic ideal is an artifice for the *preservation* of life. That this ideal has been able to rule and achieve power over humans to the extent that history teaches us it has, in particular wherever the civilization and taming of man has been successfully carried out, expresses a great fact: the *diseasedness* of the previous type of human, at least of the human made tame, the physiological struggle of man with death (more precisely: with satiety with life, with tiredness, with the wish for the "end"). The ascetic priest is the incarnate wish for a different existence, an existence somewhere else, and in fact the highest degree of this wish, its true fervor and passion: but the very *power* of his wishing is the shackle that binds him here; in this very process he becomes a tool that must work at creating more favorable conditions for being-here and being-human—with this very *power* he ties to existence the entire herd of the deformed, out of sorts, short-changed, failed, those of every kind who suffer from themselves, by instinctively going before them as shepherd. One understands me already: this ascetic priest, this seeming enemy of life, this *negating one*—precisely he belongs to the very great *conserving* and yes-*creating* forces of life . . . Whence it stems, this diseasedness? For man is sicker, more unsure, more changing, more undetermined than any other animal, of this there is no doubt—he is *the* sick animal: how does this come about? Certainly he has also dared more, innovated more, defied more, challenged fate more than all the other animals taken together: he, the great experimenter with himself, the unsatisfied, unsatiated one who wrestles with animal, nature, and gods for final dominion—he, the one

yet unconquered, the eternally future one who no longer finds any
rest from his own pressing energy, so that his future digs inexorably
like a spur into the flesh of every present:—how could such a courageous and rich animal not also be the most endangered, the most
prolongedly and most deeply sick among all sick animals? . . . Man
is fed up with it, often enough, there are entire epidemics of this
being-fed-up (—around 1348, at the time of the Dance of Death): but
even this loathing, this tiredness, this vexation with himself—everything emerges so powerfully in him that it immediately becomes a
new shackle. As if by magic, the "no" that he says to life brings to
light an abundance of tender "yes's"; even when he *wounds* himself,
this master of destruction, self-destruction—afterwards it is the
wound itself that compels him *to live.* . . .

• • •

28. . . . One simply cannot conceal from oneself *what* all the
willing that has received its direction from the ascetic ideal actually
expresses: this hatred of the human, still more of the animal, still
more of the material, this abhorrence of the senses, of reason itself,
this fear of happiness and of beauty, this longing away from all appearance, change, becoming, death, wish, longing itself—all of this
means—let us dare to grasp this—a *will to nothingness,* an aversion
to life, a rebellion against the most fundamental presuppositions of
life; but it is and remains a *will!* . . . And, to say again at the end
what I said at the beginning: man would much rather will *nothingness* than *not* will. . . .

❖ *from* Twilight of the Idols ❖

The Problem of Socrates

Concerning life, the wisest men of all ages have judged alike: *it is no
good.* Always and everywhere one has heard the same sound from
their mouths—a sound full of doubt, full of melancholy, full of weari-

From The Portable Nietzsche, *edited and translated by Walter Kaufmann. Copyright
1954 by The Viking Press, Inc. Reprinted by permission of The Viking Press, Inc. (Ed.
note: this acknowledgment also covers the excerpts from* Twilight of the Idols *on p. 97
and from* The Antichrist *on p. 99.)*

ness of life, full of resistance to life. Even Socrates said, as he died: "To live—that means to be sick a long time: I owe Asclepius the Savior a rooster." Even Socrates was tired of it. What does that evidence? What does it evince? Formerly one would have said (—oh, it has been said, and loud enough, and especially by our pessimists): "At least something of all this must be true! The consensus of the sages evidences the truth." Shall we still talk like that today? *May* we? "At least something must be *sick* here," *we* retort. These wisest men of all ages—they should first be scrutinized closely. Were they all perhaps shaky on their legs? late? tottery? decadents? Could it be that wisdom appears on earth as a raven, inspired by a little whiff of carrion?

• • •

When one finds it necessary to turn *reason* into a tyrant, as Socrates did, the danger cannot be slight that something else will play the tyrant. Rationality was then hit upon as the savior; neither Socrates nor his "patients" had any choice about being rational: it was *de rigeur,* it was their last resort. The fanaticism with which all Greek reflection throws itself upon rationality betrays a desperate situation; there was danger, there was but one choice: either to perish or—to be *absurdly rational.* The moralism of the Greek philosophers from Plato on is pathologically conditioned; so is their esteem of dialectics. Reason-virtue-happiness, that means merely that one must imitate Socrates and counter the dark appetites with a permanent daylight—the daylight of reason. One must be clever, clear, bright at any price: any concession to the instincts, to the unconscious, leads *downward.*

Morality as Anti-Nature

All passions have a phase when they are merely disastrous, when they drag down their victim with the weight of stupidity—and a later, very much later phase when they wed the spirit, when they "spiritualize" themselves. Formerly, in view of the element of stupidity in passion, war was declared on passion itself, its destruction was plotted; all the old moral monsters are agreed on this: *il faut tuer les passions.* The most famous formula for this is to be found in the New Testament, in that Sermon on the Mount, where, incidentally, things are by no means looked at from a height. There it is said, for example, with particular reference to sexuality: "If thy eye offend thee, pluck it out." Fortunately, no Christian acts in accordance with this precept. *Destroying* the passions and cravings, merely as a preventive measure against their stupidity and the unpleasant consequences of this stupidity—today this itself strikes us as merely another acute form of stupidity. We no longer admire dentists who "pluck out" teeth so that they will not hurt any more.

• • •

Let us finally consider how naïve it is altogether to say: "Man *ought* to be such and such!" Reality shows us an enchanting wealth of types, the abundance of a lavish play and change of forms—and some wretched loafer of a moralist comments: "No! Man ought to be different." He even knows what man should be like, this wretched bigot and prig: he paints himself on the wall and comments, "*Ecce homo!*" But even when the moralist addresses himself only to the single human being and says to him, "You ought to be such and such!" he does not cease to make himself ridiculous. The single human being is a piece of *fatum* from the front and from the rear, one law more, one necessity more for all that is yet to come and to be. To say to him, "Change yourself!" is to demand that everything be changed, even retroactively. And indeed there have been consistent moralists who wanted man to be different, that is, virtuous—they wanted him remade in their own image, as a prig: to that end, they *negated* the world! No small madness! No modest kind of immodesty!

. . . I am afraid we are not rid of God because we still have faith in grammar.

❖ On Truth ❖

Sense for Truth.—Commend me to all skepticism where I am permitted to answer: "Let us put it to the test!" But I don't wish to hear anything more of things and questions which do not admit of being tested. That is the limit of my "sense for truth": for bravery has there lost its right.

(Gay Science)

Life no Argument.—We have arranged for ourselves a world in which we can live—by the postulating of bodies, lines, surfaces, causes and effects, motion and rest, form and content: without these articles of faith no one could manage to live at present! But for all that they are still unproved. Life is no argument; error might be among the conditions of life.

(Ibid.)

Ultimate Scepticism.—But what after all are man's truths?—They are his irrefutable errors.

(Ibid.)

Truth is the kind of error without which a certain species of life could not live. The value for life is ultimately decisive.

(The Will to Power)*

The criterion of truth resides in the enhancement of the feeling of power.

(Ibid.)

What is truth?—Inertia; that hypothesis which gives rise to contentment; smallest expenditure of spiritual force, etc.

(Ibid.)

There are many kinds of eyes. Even the sphinx has eyes—and consequently there are many kinds of "truths," and consequently there is no truth.

(Ibid.)

Suppose such an incarnate will to contradiction and antinaturalness is induced to *philosophize:* upon what will it vent its innermost contrariness? Upon what is felt most certainly to be real and actual: it will look for error precisely where the instinct of life most unconditionally posits truth. It will, for example, like the ascetics of the Vedanta philosophy, downgrade physicality to an illusion; likewise pain, multiplicity, the entire conceptual antithesis "subject" and "object"—errors, nothing but errors! To renounce belief in one's ego, to deny one's own "reality"—what a triumph! not merely over the senses, over appearance, but a much higher kind of triumph, a violation and cruelty against *reason*—a voluptuous pleasure that reaches its height when the ascetic self-contempt and self-mockery of reason declares: "*there is* a realm of truth and being, but reason is *excluded* from it!" . . .

But precisely because we seek knowledge, let us not be ungrateful to such resolute reversals of accustomed perspectives and valuations with which the spirit has, with apparent mischievousness and

*From The Will to Power *by Friedrich Nietzsche, translated by Walter Kaufmann and R.J. Hollingdale, edited by Walter Kaufmann. Copyright © 1967 by Walter Kaufmann. Reprinted by permission of Random House, Inc. (Ed. note: this acknowledgment also covers the excerpts from* The Will to Power *on pp. 96, 99–100, and 101.)*

futility, raged against itself for so long: to see differently in this way for once, to want to see differently, is no small discipline and preparation of the intellect for its future "objectivity"—the latter understood not as "contemplation without interest" (which is a nonsensical absurdity), but as the ability *to control* one's Pro and Con and to dispose of them, so that one knows how to employ a *variety* of perspectives and affective interpretations in the service of knowledge.

Henceforth, my dear philosophers, let us be on guard against the dangerous old conceptual fiction that posited a "pure, will-less, painless, timeless knowing subject"; let us guard against the snares of such contradictory concepts as "pure reason," "absolute spirituality," "knowledge in itself": these always demand that we should think of an eye that is completely unthinkable, an eye turned in no particular direction, in which the active and interpreting forces, through which alone seeing becomes seeing *something,* are supposed to be lacking; these always demand of the eye an absurdity and a nonsense. There is *only* a perspective seeing, *only* a perspective "knowing"; and the *more* affects we allow to speak about one thing, the *more* eyes, different eyes, we can use to observe one thing, the more complete will our "concept" of this thing, our "objectivity," be. But to eliminate the will altogether, to suspend each and every affect, supposing we were capable of this—what would that mean but to *castrate* the intellect?—   *(Genealogy of Morality)*

My chief proposition: there are no moral phenomena, there is only a moral interpretation of these phenomena. This interpretation itself is of extra-moral origin.   *(Will to Power)*

Against positivism, which halts at phenomena—"There are only *facts*"—I would say: No, facts is precisely what there is not, only interpretations. We cannot establish any fact "in itself": perhaps it is folly to want to do such a thing.

"Everything is subjective," you say; but even this is interpretation. The "subject" is not something given, it is something added and invented and projected behind what there is.—Finally, is it necessary to posit an interpreter behind the interpretation? Even this is invention, hypothesis.

Insofar as the word "knowledge" has any meaning, the world is knowable; but it is *interpretable* otherwise, it has no meaning behind it, but countless meanings.—"Perspectivism."   *(Ibid.)*

How the "True World" Finally Became a Fable

The History of an Error

1. The true world—attainable for the sage, the pious, the virtuous man; he lives in it, *he is it.*

(The oldest form of the idea, relatively sensible, simple, and persuasive. A circumlocution for the sentence, "I, Plato, *am* the truth.")

2. The true world—unattainable for now, but promised for the sage, the pious, the virtuous man ("for the sinner who repents").

(Progress of the idea: it becomes more subtle, insidious, incomprehensible—*it becomes female,* it becomes Christian.)

3. The true world—unattainable, indemonstrable, unpromisable; but the very thought of it—a consolation, an obligation, an imperative.

(At bottom, the old sun, but seen through mist and skepticism. The idea has become elusive, pale, Nordic, Königsbergian [i.e., Kantian].)

4. The true world—unattainable? At any rate, unattained. And being unattained, also *unknown.* Consequently, not consoling, redeeming, or obligating: how could something unknown obligate us?

(Gray morning. The first yawn of reason. The cockcrow of positivism.)

5. The "true" world—an idea which is no longer good for anything, not even obligating—an idea which has become useless and superfluous—*consequently,* a refuted idea: let us abolish it!

(Bright day; breakfast; return of *bon sens* and cheerfulness; Plato's embarrassed blush; pandemonium of all free spirits.)

6. The true world—we have abolished. What world has remained? The apparent one perhaps? But no! *With the true world we have also abolished the apparent one.*

(Noon; moment of the briefest shadow; end of the longest error; high point of humanity; INCIPIT ZARATHUSTRA.)

(Twilight of the Idols)

❖ On The Will to Power ❖

Suppose nothing else were "given" as real except our world of desires and passions, and we could not get down, or up, to any other "reality" besides the reality of our drives—for thinking is merely a relation of these drives to each other: is it not permitted to make the experiment and to ask the question whether this "given" would not be *sufficient* for also understanding on the basis of this kind of thing the so-called mechanistic (or "material") world? I mean, not as a deception, as "mere appearance," an "idea" (in the sense of Berkeley and Schopenhauer) but as holding the same rank of reality as our affect—as a more primitive form of the world of affects in which everything still lies contained in a powerful unity before it undergoes ramifications and developments in the organic process (and, as is only fair, also becomes tenderer and weaker)—as a kind of instinctive life in which all organic functions are still synthetically intertwined along with self-regulation, assimilation, nourishment, excretion, and metabolism—as a *pre-form* of life.

In the end not only is it permitted to make this experiment; the conscience of *method* demands it. Not to assume several kinds of causality until the experiment of making do with a single one has been pushed to its utmost limit (to the point of nonsense, if I may say so)—that is a moral of method which one may not shirk today—it follows "from its definition," as a mathematician would say. The question is in the end whether we really recognize the will as *efficient,* whether we believe in the causality of the will: if we do—and at bottom our faith in this is nothing less than our faith in causality itself—then we have to make the experiment of positing the causality of the will hypothetically as the only one. "Will," of course, can affect only "will"— and not "matter" (not "nerves," for example). In short, one has to risk the hypothesis whether will does not affect will wherever "effects" are recognized—and whether all mechanical occurrences are not, insofar as a force is active in them, will force, effects of will.

Suppose, finally, we succeeded in explaining our entire instinctive life as the development and ramification of *one* basic form of the will—namely, of the will to power, as *my* proposition has it; suppose all organic functions could be traced back to this will to power and one could also find in it the solution of the problem of procreation and nourishment—it is *one* problem—then one would have gained the right to determine *all* efficient force univocally as—*will to power.* The world viewed from inside, the world defined and determined according to its "intelligible character"—it would be "will to power" and nothing else.—   (*Beyond Good and Evil*)

A tablet of the good hangs over every people. Behold, it is the tablet of their overcomings; behold, it is the voice of their will to power.   (*Zarathustra*)

I understand by "morality" a system of evaluations that partially coincides with the conditions of a creature's life. *(Will to Power)*

It is our needs that interpret the world; our drives and their For and Against. Every drive is a kind of lust to rule; each one has its perspective that it would like to compel all the other drives to accept as a norm. *(Ibid.)*

"Ends and means"
"Cause and effect"
"Subject and object"
"Acting and suffering"
"Thing-in-itself and appearance"
as interpretations (not as facts)
} and to what extent perhaps *necessary* interpretations? (as required for "preservation")— all in the sense of a will to power.

(Ibid.)

What are our evaluations and moral tables really worth? What is the outcome of their rule? For whom? In relation to what?—Answer: for life. But *what is life?* Here we need a new, more definite formulation of the concept "life." My formula for it is: Life is will to power. *(Ibid.)*

What is good? Everything that heightens the feeling of power in man, the will to power, power itself.

What is bad? Everything that is born of weakness.

What is happiness? The feeling that power is *growing,* that resistance is overcome.

Not contentedness but more power; not peace but war; not virtue but fitness (Renaissance virtue, *virtù,* virtue that is moraline-free).

The weak and the failures shall perish: first principle of *our* love of man. And they shall even be given every possible assistance.

What is more harmful than any vice? Active pity for all the failures and all the weak: Christianity. *(The Antichrist)**

And do you know what "the world" is to me? Shall I show it to you in my mirror? This world: a monster of energy, without beginning, without end; a firm, iron magnitude of force that does not grow

*From The Portable Nietzsche, *edited and translated by Walter Kaufmann. Copyright* 1954 by The Viking Press, Inc.*

bigger or smaller, that does not expend itself but only transforms itself; as a whole, of unalterable size, a household without expenses or losses, but likewise without increase or income; enclosed by "nothingness" as by a boundary; not something blurry or wasted, not something endlessly extended, but set in a definite space as a definite force, and not a space that might be "empty" here or there, but rather as force throughout, as a play of forces and waves of forces, at the same time one and many, increasing here and at the same time decreasing there; a sea of forces flowing and rushing together, eternally changing, eternally flooding back, with tremendous years of recurrence, with an ebb and a flood of its forms; out of the simplest forms striving toward the most complex, out of the stillest, most rigid, coldest forms toward the hottest, most turbulent, most self-contradictory, and then again returning home to the simple out of this abundance, out of the play of contradictions back to the joy of concord, still affirming itself in this uniformity of its courses and its years, blessing itself as that which must return eternally, as a becoming that knows no satiety, no disgust, no weariness: this, my *Dionysian* world of the eternally self-creating the eternally self-destroying, this mystery world of the twofold voluptuous delight my "beyond good and evil," without goal, unless the joy of the circle is itself a goal; without will, unless a ring feels good will toward itself—do you want a *name* for this world? A *solution* for all its riddles? A *light* for you too, you best-concealed, strongest, most intrepid, most midnightly men?—*This world is the will to power—and nothing besides!* And you yourselves are also this will to power—and nothing besides!   *(Will to Power)*

❖ On Eternal Recurrence ❖

The greatest stress. How, if some day or night a demon were to sneak after you into your loneliest loneliness and say to you, "This life as you now live it and have lived it, you will have to live once more and innumerable times more; and there will be nothing new in it, but every pain and every joy and every thought and sigh and everything immeasurably small or great in your life must return to you—all in the same succession and sequence—even this spider and this moonlight between the trees, and even this moment and I myself. The eternal hourglass of existence is turned over and over, and you with it, a dust grain of dust." Would you not throw yourself down and gnash your teeth and curse the demon who spoke thus? Or did you once experience a tremendous moment when you would have answered him, "You are a god, and never have I heard anything more godly." If this thought were to gain possession of you, it would change you, as you are, or perhaps crush you. The question in each and every thing, "Do you want this once more and innumerable times more?" would weigh upon your actions as the greatest stress. Or how well disposed would you have to become to yourself and to life to *crave nothing more fervently* than this ultimate eternal confirmation and seal?   *(Gay Science)*

The two most extreme modes of thought—the mechanistic and the Platonic—are reconciled in the *eternal recurrence:* both as ideals.
                                                          (Will to Power)

The law of the conservation of energy demands *eternal recurrence.*   *(Ibid.)*

If the world may be thought of as a certain definite quantity of force and as a certain definite number of centers of force—and every other representation remains indefinite and therefore useless—it follows that, in the great dice game of existence, it must pass through a calculable number of combinations. In infinite time, every possible combination would at some time or another be realized; more: it would be realized an infinite number of times. And since between every combination and its next recurrence all other possible combinations would have to take place, and each of these combinations conditions the entire sequence of combinations in the same series, a circular movement of absolutely identical series is thus demonstrated: the world as a circular movement that has already repeated itself infinitely often and plays its game *in infinitum.*   *(Ibid.)*

Hermann Hesse

(1877-1962)
GERMAN (SWISS)

Hesse is one of those rare writers who has mastered worlds of thought far removed from each other. He has captured the anguish of Kierkegaard and the frenzy of Nietzsche, the light rapture of the saint, the lust of the aesthete, the bliss of Eastern enlightenment. If it is ultimately the Nietzschean who emerges from his writings, it is not because the others have not been given a fair hearing. There are limits to freedom even in an imagination of genius, and Harry Haller and Emil Sinclair seem to emerge as far more convincing characters than Siddhartha. Haller, the *Steppenwolf,* in particular, seems to be born of Nietzschean heritage. He is the obviously "superior" cultured man, pursuing his virtue against and in the midst of the bourgeoisie ("this fat brood of mediocrity"), seeking Goethe and "the Immortals." If he is not yet Nietzsche's *Übermensch* (for one thing, he cannot dance), he is, with Nietzsche, the bridge between man and Übermensch. Yet he is torn between his two selves, wolf and man (the reference is primarily from Goethe's Faust: "Two souls, alas, are dwelling in my breast. And one is striving to foresake its brother"). Haller suffers nostalgia for the very bourgeoisie he despises, and he is overwhelmed by uncreative suffering. So he numbers himself among "the suicides." Haller seems to be giving up his pursuit of "the Immortals" when he is mysteriously handed a pamphlet, *Treatise on the Steppenwolf* (*Not for Everybody*). This pamphlet is his introduction to a Zarathustra more Eastern than Nietzsche's and a concept of self more radical than Nietzsche's ("man is an onion . . ."). Ultimately, it is the discovery of laughter and his plenitude of selves that allows Haller to see—to begin to see— what it is to be more than human-all-too-human.

❖ *from* Steppenwolf ❖

And now that we come to these records of Haller's, these partly diseased, partly beautiful and thoughtful fantasies, I must confess that if they had fallen into my hands by chance and if I had not known their author, I should most certainly have thrown them away in disgust. But owing to my acquaintance with Haller I have been able, to some extent, to understand them, and even to appreciate them. I should hesitate to share them with others if I saw in them nothing but the pathological fancies of a single and isolated case of a diseased temperament. But I see something more in them. I see them as a document of the times, for Haller's sickness of the soul, as I now know, is not the eccentricity of a single individual, but the sickness of the times themselves, the neurosis of that generation to which Haller belongs, a sickness, it seems, that by no means attacks the weak and worthless only but, rather, precisely those who are strongest in spirit and richest in gifts.

These records, however much or however little of real life may lie at the back of them, are not an attempt to disguise or to palliate this widespread sickness of our times. They are an attempt to present the sickness itself in its actual manifestation. They mean, literally, a journey through hell, a sometimes fearful, sometimes courageous journey through the chaos of a world whose souls dwell in darkness, a journey undertaken with the determination to go through hell from one end to the other, to give battle to chaos, and to suffer torture to the full.

It was some remembered conversation with Haller that gave me the key to this interpretation. He said to me once when we were talking of the so-called horrors of the Middle Ages: "These horrors were

From Steppenwolf *by Hermann Hesse, translated by Basil Creighton. Copyright 1929 by Holt, Rinehart, and Winston, Inc. Copyright renewed 1957 by Hermann Hesse. Reprinted by permission of the publisher, Holt, Rinehart, and Winston, Inc.*

really nonexistent. A man of the Middle Ages would detest the whole mode of our present-day life as something far more than horrible, far more than barbarous. Every age, every culture, every custom and tradition has its own character, its own weakness and its own strength, its beauties and ugliness; accepts certain sufferings as matters of course, puts up patiently with certain evils. Human life is reduced to real suffering, to hell, only when two ages, two cultures and religions overlap. A man of the Classical Age who had to live in medieval times would suffocate miserably just as a savage does in the midst of our civilization. Now there are times when a whole generation is caught in this way between two ages, two modes of life, with the consequence that it loses all power to understand itself and has no standard, no security, no simple acquiescence. Naturally, every one does not feel this equally strongly. A nature such as Nietzsche's had to suffer our present ills more than a generation in advance. What he had to go through alone and misunderstood, thousands suffer today."

I often had to think of these words while reading the records. Haller belongs to those who have been caught between two ages, who are outside of all security and simple acquiescence. He belongs to those whose fate it is to live the whole riddle of human destiny heightened to the pitch of a personal torture, a personal hell.

Treatise on the Steppenwolf

There was once a man, Harry, called the Steppenwolf. He went on two legs, wore clothes and was a human being, but nevertheless he was in reality a wolf of the Steppes. He had learned a good deal of all that people of a good intelligence can, and was a fairly clever fellow. What he had not learned, however, was this: to find contentment in himself and his own life. The cause of this apparently was that at the bottom of his heart he knew all the time (or thought he knew) that he was in reality not a man, but a wolf of the Steppes. Clever men might argue the point whether he truly was a wolf, whether, that is, he had been changed, before birth perhaps, from a wolf into a human being, or had been given the soul of a wolf, though born as a human being; or whether, on the other hand, this belief that he was a wolf was no more than a fancy or a disease of his. It might, for example, be possible that in his childhood he was a little wild and disobedient and disorderly and that those who brought him up had declared a war of extinction against the beast in him; and precisely this had given him the idea and the belief that he was in fact actually a beast with only a thin covering of the human. On this point one could speak at length and entertainingly, and indeed write a book about it. The Steppenwolf, however, would be none the better for it, since for him it was all one whether the wolf had been bewitched or beaten into him, or whether it was merely an idea of his own. What others chose to think about it or what he chose to think himself was no good to him at all. It left the wolf inside him just the same.

And so the Steppenwolf had two natures, a human and a wolfish one. This was his fate, and it may well be that it was not a very exceptional one. There must have been many men who have had a good deal of the dog or the fox, of the fish or the serpent in them without experiencing any extraordinary difficulties on that account. In such cases, the man and the fish lived on together and neither did the other any harm. The one even helped the other. Many a man indeed has carried this condition to such enviable lengths that he has owed his happiness more to the fox or the ape in him than to the man. So much for common knowledge. In the case of Harry, however, it was just the opposite. In him the man and the wolf did not go the same way together, but were in continual and deadly enmity. The one existed simply and solely to harm the other, and when there are two in one blood and in one soul who are at deadly enmity, then life fares ill. Well, to each his lot, and none is light.

Now with our Steppenwolf it was so that in his conscious life he lived now as a wolf, now as a man, as indeed the case is with all mixed beings. But, when he was a wolf, the man in him lay in ambush, ever on the watch to interfere and condemn, while at those times that he was man the wolf did just the same. For example, if Harry, as man, had a beautiful thought, felt a fine and noble emotion, or performed a so-called good act, then the wolf bared his teeth at him and laughed and showed him with bitter scorn how laughable this whole pantomime was in the eyes of a beast, of a wolf who knew well enough in his heart what suited him, namely, to trot alone over the Steppes and now and then to gorge himself with blood or to pursue a female wolf. Then, wolfishly seen, all human activities became horribly absurd and misplaced, stupid and vain. But it was exactly the same when Harry felt and behaved as a wolf and showed others his teeth and felt hatred and enmity against all human beings and their lying and degenerate manners and customs. For then the human part of him lay in ambush and watched the wolf, called him brute and beast, and spoiled and embittered for him all pleasure in his simple and healthy and wild wolf's being.

Thus it was then with the Steppenwolf, and one may well imagine that Harry did not have an exactly pleasant and happy life of it. This does not mean, however, that he was unhappy in any extraordinary degree (although it may have seemed so to himself all the same, inasmuch as every man takes the sufferings that fall to his share as the greatest). That cannot be said of any man. Even he who has no wolf in him, may be none the happier for that. And even the unhappiest life has its sunny moments and its little flowers of happiness between sand and stone. So it was, then, with the Steppenwolf too. It cannot be denied that he was generally very unhappy; and he could make others unhappy also, that is, when he loved them or they him. For all who got to love him saw always only the one side in him. Many loved him as a refined and clever and interesting man, and were horrified and disappointed when they had come upon the wolf in him. And they had to because Harry wished, as every sentient being does, to be loved as a whole and therefore it was just with those whose love he most valued that he could least of all conceal and belie the wolf. There were those, however, who loved precisely the wolf in him, the free, the savage, the untamable, the dangerous and strong, and these found it peculiarly disappointing and deplorable when suddenly the wild and wicked wolf was also a man, and had hankerings after goodness and refinement, and wanted to hear Mozart, to read poetry and to cherish human ideals. Usually these were the most disappointed and angry of all; and so it was that the Steppenwolf brought his own dual and divided nature into the destinies of others besides himself whenever he came into contact with them.

• • •

In this connection one thing more must be said. There are a good many people of the same kind as Harry. Many artists are of his kind. These persons all have two souls, two beings within them. There is God and the devil in them; the mother's blood and the father's; the capacity for happiness and the capacity for suffering; and in just such a state of enmity and entanglement toward and within each other as were the wolf and man in Harry. And these men, for whom life has no repose, live at times in their rare moments of happiness with such strength and indescribable beauty, the spray of their moment's happiness is flung so high and dazzlingly over the wide sea of suffering, that the light of it, spreading its radiance, touches others, too, with its enchantment. Thus, like a precious, fleeting foam over the sea of suffering arise all those works of art, in which a single individual lifts himself for an hour so high above his personal destiny that his happiness shines like a star and appears to all who see it as something eternal and as a happiness of their own. All these men, whatever their deeds and works may be, have really no life; that is to say, their lives are not their own and have no form. They are not heroes, artists or thinkers in the same way that other men are judges, doctors, shoemakers or schoolmasters. Their life consists of a perpetual tide, unhappy and torn with pain, terrible and meaningless, unless one is ready to see its meaning in just those rare experiences, acts, thoughts and works that shine out above the chaos of such a life. To such men the desperate and horrible thought has come that perhaps the whole of human life is but a bad joke, a violent and ill-fated abortion of the primal mother, a savage and dismal catastrophe of nature. To them, too, however, the other thought has come that man is perhaps not merely a half-rational animal but a child of the gods and destined to immortality.

Men of every kind have their characteristics, their features, their virtues and vices and their deadly sins. It was part of the sign manual of the Steppenwolf that he was a night prowler. The morning was a bad time of day for him. He feared it and it never brought him any good. On no morning of his life had he ever been in good spirits nor done any good before midday, nor ever had a happy idea, nor devised any pleasure for himself or others. By degrees during the afternoon he warmed and became alive, and only toward evening, on his good days, was he productive, active and, sometimes, aglow with joy. With this was bound up his need for loneliness and independence. There was never a man with a deeper and more passionate craving for independence than he. In his youth when he was poor and had difficulty in earning his bread, he preferred to go hungry and in torn clothes rather than endanger his narrow limit of independence. He never sold himself for money or an easy life or to women or to those in power, and had thrown away a hundred times what in the world's eyes was his advantage and happiness in order to safeguard his liberty. No prospect was more hateful and distasteful to him than that he

should have to go to an office and conform to daily and yearly routine and obey others. He hated all kinds of offices, governmental or
commercial, as he hated death, and his worst nightmare was confinement in barracks. He contrived, often at great sacrifice, to avoid
all such predicaments. It was here that his strength and his virtue
rested. On this point he could neither be bent nor bribed. Here his
character was firm and indeflectable. Only, through this virtue, he was
bound the closer to his destiny of suffering. It happened to him as it
does to all; what he strove for with the deepest and stubbornest instinct of his being fell to his lot, but more than is good for men. In the
beginning his dream and his happiness, in the end it was his bitter
fate. The man of power is ruined by power, the man of money by
money, the submissive man by subservience, the pleasure seeker
by pleasure. He achieved his aim. He was ever more independent. He
took orders from no man and ordered his ways to suit no man. Independently and alone, he decided what to do and to leave undone. For
every strong man attains to that which a genuine impulse bids him
seek. But in the midst of the freedom he had attained Harry suddenly
became aware that his freedom was a death and that he stood alone.
The world in an uncanny fashion left him in peace. Other men concerned him no longer. He was not even concerned about himself. He
began to suffocate slowly in the more and more rarefied atmosphere
of remoteness and solitude. For now it was his wish no longer, nor his
aim, to be alone and independent, but rather his lot and his sentence.
The magic wish had been fulfilled and could not be canceled, and it
was no good now to open his arms with longing and good will to wel-
come the bonds of society. People left him alone now. It was not,
however, that he was an object of hatred and repugnance. On the contrary, he had many friends. A great many people liked him. But it was
no more than sympathy and friendliness. He received invitations,
presents, pleasant letters; but no more. No one came near to him.
There was no link left, and no one could have had any part in his life
even had any one wished it. For the air of lonely men surrounded him
now, a still atmosphere in which the world around him slipped away,
leaving him incapable of relationship, an atmosphere against which
neither will nor longing availed. This was one of the significant ear-
marks of his life.

   Another was that he was numbered among the suicides. And here
it must be said that to call suicides only those who actually destroy
themselves is false. Among these, indeed, there are many who in a

sense are suicides only by accident and in whose being suicide has no necessary place. Among the common run of men there are many of little personality and stamped with no deep impress of fate, who find their end in suicide without belonging on that account to the type of the suicide by inclination; while on the other hand, of those who are to be counted as suicides by the very nature of their beings are many, perhaps a majority, who never in fact lay hands on themselves. The "suicide," and Harry was one, need not necessarily live in a peculiarly close relationship to death. One may do this without being a suicide. What is peculiar to the suicide is that his ego, rightly or wrongly, is felt to be an extremely dangerous, dubious and doomed germ of nature; that he is always in his own eyes exposed to an extraordinary risk, as though he stood with the slightest foothold on the peak of a crag whence a slight push from without or an instant's weakness from within suffices to precipitate him into the void. The line of fate in the case of these men is marked by the belief they have that suicide is their most probable manner of death. It might be presumed that such temperaments, which usually manifest themselves in early youth and persist through life, show a singular defect of vital force. On the contrary, among the "suicides" are to be found unusually tenacious and eager and also hardy natures. But just as there are those who at the least indisposition develop a fever, so do those whom we call suicides, and who are always very emotional and sensitive, develop at the least shock the notion of suicide. Had we a science with the courage and authority to concern itself with mankind, instead of with the mechanism merely of vital phenomena, had we something of the nature of an anthropology, or a psychology, these matters of fact would be familiar to every one.

• • •

As every strength may become a weakness (and under some circumstances must) so, on the contrary, may the typical suicide find a strength and a support in his apparent weakness. Indeed, he does so more often than not. The case of Harry, the Steppenwolf, is one of these. As thousands of his like do, he found consolation and support, and not merely the melancholy play of youthful fancy, in the idea that the way to death was open to him at any moment. It is true that with him, as with all men of his kind, every shock, every pain, every untoward predicament at once called forth the wish to find an escape in death. By degrees, however, he fashioned for himself out of this tendency a philosophy that was actually serviceable to life. He gained strength through familiarity with the thought that the emergency exit stood always open, and became curious, too, to taste his suffering to the dregs. If it went too badly with him he could feel sometimes with a grim malicious pleasure: "I am curious to see all the same just how much a man can endure. If the limit of what is bearable is reached, I have only to open the door to escape." There are a great many suicides to whom this thought imparts an uncommon strength.

• • •

. . . Humor alone, that magnificent discovery of those who are cut short in their calling to highest endeavor, those who falling short of tragedy are yet as rich in gifts as in affliction, humor alone (perhaps the most inborn and brilliant achievement of the spirit) attains to the impossible and brings every aspect of human existence within the rays of its prism. To live in the world as though it were not the world, to respect the law and yet to stand above it, to have possessions as though "one possessed nothing," to renounce as though it were no renunciation, all these favorite and often formulated propositions of an exalted worldly wisdom, it is in the power of humor alone to make efficacious.

And supposing the Steppenwolf were to succeed, and he has gifts and resources in plenty, in decocting this magic draft in the sultry mazes of his hell, his rescue would be assured. Yet there is much lacking. The possibility, the hope only are there. Whoever loves him and takes his part may wish him this rescue. It would, it is true, keep him forever tied to the bourgeois world, but his suffering would be bearable and productive. His relation to the bourgeois world would lose its sentimentality both in its love and its hatred, and his bondage to it would cease to cause him the continual torture of shame.

To attain to this, or, perhaps it may be, to be able at last to dare the leap into the unknown, a Steppenwolf must once have a good look at himself. He must look deeply into the chaos of his own soul and plumb its depths. The riddle of his existence would then be revealed to him at once in all its changelessness, and it would be impossible for him ever to escape first from the hell of the flesh to the comforts of a sentimental philosophy and then back to the blind orgy of his wolfishness. Man and wolf would then be compelled to recognize one another without the masks of false feeling and to look one another straight in the eye. Then they would either explode and separate forever, and there would be no more Steppenwolf, or else they would come to terms in the dawning light of humor.

It is possible that Harry will one day be led to this latter alternative. It is possible that he will learn one day to know himself. He may get hold of one of our little mirrors. He may encounter the Immortals. He may find in one of our magic theaters the very thing that is needed to free his neglected soul. A thousand such possibilities await him. His fate brings them on, leaving him no choice; for those outside of the bourgeoisie live in the atmosphere of these magic possibilities. A mere nothing suffices—and the lightning strikes.

And all this is very well known to the Steppenwolf, even though his eye may never fall on this fragment of his inner biography. He has a suspicion of his allotted place in the world, a suspicion of the Immortals, a suspicion that he may meet himself face to face; and he is aware of the existence of that mirror in which he has such bitter need to look and from which he shrinks in such deathly fear.

For the close of our study there is left one last fiction, a fundamental delusion to make clear. All interpretation, all psychology, all attempts to make things comprehensible, require the medium of theories, mythologies and lies; and a self-respecting author should not omit, at the close of an exposition, to dissipate these lies so far as may be in his power. If I say "above" or "below," that is already a statement that requires explanation, since an above and a below exist only in thought, only as abstractions. The world knows nothing of above or below.

So too, to come to the point, is the Steppenwolf a fiction. When Harry feels himself to be a werewolf, and chooses to consist of two hostile and opposed beings, he is merely availing himself of a mythological simplification. He is no werewolf at all, and if we appeared to accept without scrutiny this lie which he invented for himself and believes in, and tried to regard him literally as a twofold being and a Steppenwolf, and so designated him, it was merely in the hope of being more easily understood with the assistance of a delusion, which we must now endeavor to put in its true light.

The division into wolf and man, flesh and spirit, by means of which Harry tries to make his destiny more comprehensible to himself is a very great simplification. It is a forcing of the truth to suit a plausible, but erroneous, explanation of that contradiction which this man discovers in himself and which appears to himself to be the source of his by no means negligible sufferings. Harry finds in himself a "human being," that is to say, a world of thoughts and feelings, of culture and tamed or sublimated nature, and besides this he finds within himself also a "wolf," that is to say, a dark world of instinct, of savagery and cruelty, of unsublimated or raw nature. In spite of this apparently clear division of his being between two spheres, hostile to one another, he has known happy moments now and then when the man and the wolf for a short while were reconciled with one another. Suppose that Harry tried to ascertain in any single moment of his life, any single act, what part the man had in it and what part the wolf, he would find himself at once in a dilemma, and his whole beautiful wolf theory would go to pieces. For there is not a single human being, not even the primitive Negro, not even the idiot, who is so conveniently simple that his being can be explained as the sum of two or three principal elements; and to explain so complex a man as Harry by the artless division into wolf and man is a hopelessly childish attempt. Harry consists of a hundred or a thousand selves, not of two. His life oscillates, as everyone's does, not merely between two poles, such as the body and the spirit, the saint and the sinner, but between thousand and thousands.

We need not be surprised that even so intelligent and educated a man as Harry should take himself for a Steppenwolf and reduce the rich and complex organism of his life to a formula so simple, so rudimentary and primitive. Man is not capable of thought in any high degree, and even the most spiritual and highly cultivated of men habitually sees the world and himself through the lenses of delusive formulas and artless simplifications—and most of all himself. For it appears to be an inborn and imperative need of all men to regard the self as a unit. However often and however grievously this illusion is shattered, it always mends again. The judge who sits over the murderer and looks into his face, and at one moment recognizes all the emotions and potentialities and possibilities of the murderer in his own soul and hears the murderer's voice as his own, is at the next moment one and indivisible as the judge, and scuttles back into the shell of his cultivated self and does his duty and condemns the murderer to death. And if ever the suspicion of their manifold being dawns upon men of unusual powers and of unusually delicate perceptions, so that, as all genius must, they break through the illusion of the unity of the personality and perceive that the self is made up of a bundle of selves, they have only to say so and at once the majority puts them under lock and key, calls science to aid, establishes schizomania and protects humanity from the necessity of hearing the cry of truth from the lips of these unfortunate persons. Why then waste words, why utter a thing that every thinking man accepts as self-evident, when the mere utterance of it is a breach of taste? A man, therefore, who gets so far as making the supposed unity of the self twofold is already almost a genius, in any case a most exceptional and interesting person. In reality, however, every ego, so far from being a unity, is in the highest degree a manifold world, a constellated heaven, a chaos of forms, of states and stages, of inheritances and potentialities. It appears to be a necessity as imperative as eating and breathing for everyone to be forced to regard this chaos as a unity and to speak of his ego as though it were a onefold and clearly detached and fixed phenomenon. Even the best of us share the delusion.

The delusion rests simply upon a false analogy. As a body everyone is single, as a soul never. In literature, too, even in its ultimate achievement, we find this customary concern with apparently whole and single personalities. Of all literature up to our days the drama has been the most highly prized by writers and critics, and rightly, since it offers (or might offer) the greatest possibilities of representing the ego as a manifold entity, but for the optical illusion which makes us believe that the characters of the play are manifold entities by lodging each one in an undeniable body, singly, separately and once and for all. An artless aesthetic criticism, then, keeps its highest praise for this so-called character drama in which each character makes his appearance unmistakably as a separate and single entity. Only from afar and by degrees the suspicion dawns here and there that all this is perhaps a cheap and superficial aesthetic philosophy and that we make a mistake in attributing to our great dramatists those magnificent conceptions of beauty that come to us from antiquity. These conceptions are not native to us, but are merely picked up at second hand, and it is in them, with their common source in the visible body, that the origin of the fiction of an ego, an individual, is really to be found. There is no trace of such a notion in the poems of ancient India. The heroes of the epics of India are not individuals, but whole reels of individualities in a series of incarnations. And in modern times there are poems, in which, behind the veil of a concern with individuality and character that is scarcely, indeed, in the author's mind, the motive is to present a manifold activity of soul. Whoever wishes to recognize

this must resolve once and for all not to regard the characters of such
a poem as separate beings, but as the various facets and aspects of a
higher unity, in my opinion, of the poet's soul. If "Faust" is treated in
this way, Faust, Mephistopheles, Wagner and the rest form a unity and
a supreme individuality; and it is in this higher unity alone, not in the
several characters, that something of the true nature of the soul is revealed. When Faust, in a line immortalized among schoolmasters and
greeted with a shudder of astonishment by the Philistine, says, "Two
souls, alas, inhabit in my breast!" he has forgotten Mephisto and a
whole crowd of other souls that he has in his breast likewise. The Steppenwolf, too, believes that he bears two souls (wolf and man) in his
breast and even so finds his breast disagreeably cramped because of
them. The breast and the body are indeed one, but the souls that dwell
in it are not two, nor five, but countless in number. Man is an onion
made up of a hundred integuments, a texture made up of many
threads. The ancient Asiatics knew this well enough, and in the Bud-
dhist Yoga an exact technique was devised for unmasking the illusion
of the personality. The human merry-go-round sees many changes:
The illusion that cost India the efforts of thousands of years to unmask
is the same illusion that the West has labored just as hard to maintain
and strengthen.

If we consider the Steppenwolf from this standpoint it will be clear
to us why he suffered so much under his ludicrous dual personality.
He believes, like Faust, that two souls are far too many for a single
breast and must tear the breast asunder. They are on the contrary far
too few, and Harry does shocking violence to his poor soul when he
endeavors to apprehend it by means of so primitive an image. Although he is a most cultivated person, he proceeds like a savage that
cannot count further than two. He calls himself part wolf, part man,
and with that he thinks he has come to an end and exhausted the
matter. With the "man" he packs in everything spiritual and sublimated or even cultivated to be found in himself, and with the wolf
all that is instinctive, savage and chaotic. But things are not so simple in life as in our thoughts, nor so rough and ready as in our poor
idiotic language; and Harry lies about himself twice over when he
employs this niggardly wolf theory. He assigns, we fear, whole
provinces of his soul to the "man" which are a long way from being
human, and parts of his being to the wolf that long ago have left the
wolf behind.

• • •

That man is not yet a finished creation but rather a challenge of the spirit; a distant possibility dreaded as much as it is desired; that the way toward it has only been covered for a very short distance and with terrible agonies and ecstasies even by those few for whom it is the scaffold today and the monument tomorrow—all this the Steppenwolf, too, suspected. What, however, he calls the "man" in himself, as opposed to the wolf, is to a great extent nothing else than this very same average man of the bourgeois convention.

• • •

Man designs for himself a garden with a hundred kinds of trees, a thousand kinds of flowers, a hundred kinds of fruit and vegetables. Suppose, then, that the gardener of this garden knew no other distinction than between edible and inedible, nine-tenths of this garden would be useless to him. He would pull up the most enchanting flowers and hew down the noblest trees and even regard them with a loathing and envious eye. This is what the Steppenwolf does with the thousand flowers of his soul. What does not stand classified as either man or wolf he does not see at all. And consider all that he imputes to "man"! All that is cowardly and apish, stupid and mean— while to the wolf, only because he has not succeeded in making himself its master, is set down all that is strong and noble.

Now we bid Harry good-by and leave him to go on his way alone. Were he already among the immortals—were he already there at the goal to which his difficult path seems to be taking him, with what amazement he would look back to all this coming and going, all this indecision and wild zigzag trail. With what a mixture of encouragement and blame, pity and joy, he would smile at this Steppenwolf.

Martin Heidegger

(1889-1976)
GERMAN

The central problem of Heidegger's philosophy is the "problem of Being." In his early work the investigation of Being is inseparably tied to Edmund Husserl's phenomenology, though the differences between teacher and student were sufficient to cause uncomfortable friction between them. In his later work the problem of Being, although never openly theological, becomes increasingly tied to traditional religious themes. It is the earlier work, particularly *Being and Time,* that influenced Sartre, Merleau-Ponty, and other existentialists. There, the investigation of Being begins with the study of "human Being"—"Da-sein," or "Being-in-the-world." Unlike Sartre, Heidegger does not begin his investigation with human consciousness, and the hyphenated "Being-in-the-world" is intended to warn us against "detaching" Da-sein from the world in which it finds itself. Neither does Heidegger have sympathy for the Cartesian Ego and the Cartesian separation of subject and object. The Ego, he argues, is "a merely formal indicator," and the dualism of subject-object wrongly supposes that our "commerce" with the world is first of all to know it rather than to live in it. Accordingly, the identity of each Dasein ("the 'who' of Da-sein") is to be found in a collective "they" (*das Man*) engaged in joint endeavors in the world rather than in the solipsistic Cartesian *cogito.* Da-sein consists of both its facticity (its being "thrown" into the world at this place at this time) and *Existenz* (possibilities for personal choice). Da-sein can be

116

authentic insofar as it breaks away from the "they" to seek its own possibilities, of which the most necessary is *death*. In *in-authenticity,* Da-sein falls back to the "they," identifies itself with its facticity and ignores the possibility of its own death. In inauthenticity or fallenness, the search for authentic understanding becomes mere curiosity; philosophical discourse, mere idle talk; thinking, mere calculation. Heidegger often insists that authenticity and inauthenticity are not ethical notions. (They are "onto-logical" or "descriptive".) Yet Heidegger also insists that there is an intimate connection between how we describe ourselves (our ontology) and who we are (our *ontic* character). He says, for example, "Granted that we cannot do anything with philosophy, but might not philosophy . . . do something with us?" Heidegger has indeed avoided both ethical and political involvement, his apparent excursions into either as much a product of interpretation as intention.

❖ *from* Being and Time ❖

4. The Ontic Priority of the Question of Being

Science in general can be defined as the totality of fundamentally coherent true propositions. This definition is not complete, nor does it get at the meaning of science. As ways in which human beings behave, sciences have this being's (the human being's) kind of being. We are defining this being terminologically as Da-sein. Scientific research is neither the sole nor the most immediate kind of being of this being that is possible. Moreover, Da-sein itself is distinctly different from other beings. We must make this distinct difference visible in a preliminary way. Here the discussion must anticipate subsequent analyses which only later will become truly demonstrative.

Da-sein is a being that does not simply occur among other beings. Rather it is ontically distinguished by the fact that in its being this being is concerned *about* its very being. Thus it is constitutive of the being

From Being and Time *by Martin Heidegger, translated by Joan Stambaugh. Published by S.U.N.Y. Press, Inc. Sects. 4, 9, 25, 26, 27, 38, 40, 41, 47, 50, 51, and 53 reprinted with permission of S.U.N.Y. Press Inc.*

of Da-sein to have, in its very being, a relation of being to this being. And this in turn means that Da-sein understands itself in its being in some way and with some explicitness. It is proper to this being that it be disclosed to itself with and through its being. *Understanding of being is itself a determination of being of Da-sein.* The ontic distinction of Da-sein lies in the fact that it is ontological.

To be ontological does not yet mean to develop ontology. Thus if we reserve the term ontology for the explicit, theoretical question of the meaning of beings, the intended ontological character of Da-sein is to be designated as pre-ontological. That does not signify being simply ontical, but rather being in the manner of an understanding of being.

We shall call the very being to which Da-sein can relate in one way or another, and somehow always does relate, existence [*Existenz*]. And because the essential definition of this being cannot be accomplished by ascribing to it a "what" that specifies its material content, because its essence lies rather in the fact that it in each instance has to be its being as its own, the term Da-sein, as a pure expression of being, has been chosen to designate this being.

Da-sein always understands itself in terms of its existence, in terms of its possibility to be itself or not to be itself. Da-sein has either chosen these possibilities itself, stumbled upon them, or in each instance already grown up in them. Existence is decided only by each Da-sein itself in the manner of seizing upon or neglecting such possibilities. We come to terms with the question of existence always only through existence itself. We shall call *this* kind of understanding of itself *existentiell* understanding. The question of existence is an ontic "affair" of Da-sein. For this the theoretical transparency of the ontological structure of existence is not necessary. The question of structure aims at the analysis of what constitutes existence. We shall call the coherence of these structures *existentiality*. Its analysis does not have the character of an existentiell understanding but rather an *existential* one. The task of an existential analysis of Da-sein is prescribed with regard to its possibility and necessity in the ontic constitution of Da-sein.

• • •

Thus *fundamental ontology,* from which alone all other ontologies can originate, must be sought in the *existential analysis of Da-sein.*

Da-sein accordingly takes priority in several ways over all other beings. The first priority is an *ontic* one: this being is defined in its being by existence. The second priority is an *ontological* one: on the basis of its determination as existence Da-sein is in itself "ontological." But just as originally Da-sein possesses—in a manner constitutive of its understanding of existence—an understanding of the being of all beings unlike itself. Da-sein therefore has its third priority as the ontic-ontological condition of the possibility of all ontologies. Da-sein has proven to be what, before all other beings, is ontologically the primary being to be interrogated.

• • •

9. The Theme of the Analytic of Da-sein

The being whose analysis our task is, is always we ourselves. The being of this being is always *mine*. In the being of this being it is related to its being. As the being of this being, it is entrusted to its own being. It is being about which this being is concerned. From this characteristic of Da-sein two things follow:

1. The "essence" of this being lies in its to be. The whatness (*essentia*) of this being must be understood in terms of its being (*existentia*) insofar as one can speak of it at all. Here the ontological task is precisely to show that when we choose the word existence for the being of this being, this term does not and cannot have the ontological meaning of the traditional expression of *existentia*. Ontologically, *existentia* means *objective presence* [*Vorhandenheit*], a kind of being which is essentially inappropriate to characterize the being which has the character of Da-sein. We can avoid confusion by always using the interpretive expression *objective presence* [*Vorhandenheit*] for the term *existentia,* and by attributing existence as a determination of being only to Da-sein.

The "essence" of Da-sein lies in its existence. The characteristics to be found in this being are thus not objectively present "attributes" of an objectively present being which has such and such an "outward appearance," but rather possible ways for it to be, and only this. The thatness of this being is primarily being. Thus the term "Da-sein" which we use to designate this being does not express its what, as in the case of table, house, tree, but being.

2. The being which this being is concerned about in its being is always my own. Thus, Da-sein is never to be understood ontologi-

cally as a case and instance of a genus of beings as objectively present. To something objectively present its being is a matter of "indifference," more precisely, it "is" in such a way that its being can neither be indifferent nor non-indifferent to it. In accordance with the character of *always-being-my-own-being* [*Jemeinigkeit*], when we speak of Da-sein, we must always use the *personal* pronoun along with whatever we say: "I am," "You are."

Da-sein is my own, to be always in this or that way. It has somehow always already decided in which way Da-sein is always my own. The being which is concerned in its being about its being is related to its being as its truest possibility. Da-sein *is* always its possibility. It does not "have" that possibility only as a mere attribute of something objectively present. And because Da-sein is always essentially its possibility, it *can* "choose" itself in its being, it can win itself, it can lose itself, or it can never and only "apparently" win itself. It can only have lost itself and it can only have not yet gained itself because it is essentially possible as authentic, that is, it belongs to itself. The two kinds of being of *authenticity* and *inauthenticity*—these expressions are terminologically chosen in the strictest sense of the word—are based on the fact that Da-sein is in general determined by always being-mine. But the inauthenticity of Da-sein does not signify a "lesser" being or a "lower" degree of being. Rather, inauthenticity can determine Da-sein even in its fullest concretion, when it is busy, excited, interested, and capable of pleasure.

• • •

As a being, Da-sein always defines itself in terms of a possibility which it *is* and somehow understands in its being. That is the formal meaning of the constitution of the existence of Da-sein. But for the *ontological* interpretation of this being, this means that the problematic of its being is to be developed out of the existentiality of its existence. However, this cannot mean that Da-sein is to be construed in terms of a concrete possible idea of existence. At the beginning of the analysis, Da-sein is precisely not to be interpreted in the differentiation of a particular existence; rather, to be uncovered in the indifferent way in which it is initially and for the most part. This indifference of the everydayness of Da-sein is *not nothing;* but rather, a positive phenomenal characteristic. All existing is how it is out of this kind of being, and back into it. We call this everyday indifference of Da-sein *averageness.*

• • •

But the average everydayness of Da-sein must not be understood as a mere "aspect." In it, too, and even in the mode of inauthenticity, the structure of existentiality lies a priori. In it, too, Da-sein is concerned with a particular mode of its being to which it is related in the way of average everydayness, if only in the way of fleeing *from* it and of forgetting *it*.

• • •

25. The Approach to the Existential Question of the Who of Da-sein

The answer to the question of who this being actually is (Da-sein) seems to have already been given with the formal indication of the basic characteristics of Da-sein. Da-sein is a being which I myself am, its being is in each case mine. This determination *indicates* an *ontological* constitution, but no more than that. At the same time, it contains an *ontic* indication, albeit an undifferentiated one, that an I is always this being, and not others. The who is answered in terms of the I itself, the "subject," the "self." The who is what maintains itself in the changes throughout its modes of behavior and experiences as something identical and is, thus, related to this multiplicity. Ontologically, we understand it as what is always already and constantly objectively present in a closed region and for that region, as that which lies at its basis in an eminent sense, as the *subjectum*. As something self-same in manifold otherness, this subject has the character of the *self*. Even if one rejects a substantial soul, the thingliness of consciousness and the objectivity of the person, ontologically one still posits something whose being retains the meaning of objective presence, whether explicitly or not. Substantiality is the ontological clue for the determination of beings in terms of whom the question of the who is answered. Da-sein is tacitly conceived in advance as objective presence. In any case, the indeterminacy of its being always implies this meaning of being. However, objective presence is the mode of being of beings unlike Da-sein.

The ontic obviousness of the statement that it is I who is in each case Da-sein must not mislead us into supposing that the way for an ontological interpretation of what is thus "given" has been unmistakably prescribed. It is even questionable whether the ontic content of the above statement reaches the phenomenal content of everyday Da-sein. It could be the case that the who of everyday Da-sein is precisely *not* I myself.

• • •

In the present context of an existential analytic of factical Da-sein, the question arises whether the way of the giving of the I which we mentioned discloses Da-sein in its everydayness, if it discloses it at all. Is it then a priori self-evident that the access to Da-sein must be simple perceiving reflection of the I of acts? What if this kind of "self-giving" of Da-sein were to lead our existential analytic astray and do so in a way grounded in the being of Da-sein itself? Perhaps when Da-sein addresses itself in the way which is nearest to itself, it always says it is I, and finally says this most loudly when it is "not" this being. What if the fact that Da-sein is so constituted that it is in each case mine, were the reason for the fact that Da-sein *is,* initially and for the most part, *not itself?* What if, with the approach mentioned above, the existential analytic fell into the trap, so to speak, of starting with the givenness of the I for Da-sein itself and its obvious self-interpretation? What if it should turn out that the ontological horizon for the determination of what is accessible in simple giving should remain fundamentally undetermined? We can probably always correctly say ontically of this being that "I" am it. However, the ontological analytic which makes use of such statements must have fundamental reservations about them. The "I" must be understood only in the sense of a noncommittal *formal indication* of something which perhaps reveals itself in the actual phenomenal context of being as that being's "opposite." Then "not I" by no means signifies something like a being which is essentially lacking "I-hood," but means a definite mode of being of the "I" itself; for example, having lost itself.

But even the positive interpretation of Da-sein that has been given up to now already forbids a point of departure from the formal givenness of the I if the intention is to find a phenomenally adequate answer to the question of value. The clarification of being-in-the-world showed that a mere subject without a world "is" not initially and is also never given. And, thus, an isolated I without the others is in the end just as far from being given initially.

• • •

But if the self is conceived "only" as a way of the being of this being, then that seems tantamount to volatizing the true "core" of Da-
sein. But such fears are nourished by the incorrect preconception
that the being in question really has, after all, the kind of being of
something objectively present, even if one avoids attributing to it the
massive element of a corporeal thing. However, the *"substance"* of
human being is not the spirit as the synthesis of body and soul, but
existence.

26. The *Mitda-sein* of the Others and Everyday Being-with

• • •

But the characteristic of encountering the *others* is, after all, oriented
toward one's *own* Da-sein. Does not it, too, start with the distinction
and isolation of the "I," so that a transition from this isolated subject
to the others must then be sought? In order to avoid this misunderstanding, we must observe in what sense we are talking about "the
others." "The others" does not mean everybody else but me—those
from whom the I distinguishes itself. They are, rather, those from
whom one mostly does *not* distinguish oneself, those among whom
one is, too. This being-there-too with them does not have the ontological character of being objectively present "with" them within a
world. The "with" is of the character of Da-sein, the "also" means the
sameness of being as circumspect, heedful being-in-the-world.
"With" and "also" are to be understood existentially, not categorially.
On the basis of this *like-with* being-in-the-world, the world is always
already the one that I share with the others. The world of Da-sein is
a *with-world:* Being-in is *being-with* others. The innerworldly being-
in-itself of others is *Mitda-sein.*

• • •

One's own Da-sein, like the *Mitda-sein* of others, is encountered,
initially and for the most part, in terms of the world-together in the
surrounding world taken care of. In being absorbed in the world of
taking care of things, that is, at the same time in being-with toward

others, Da-sein is not itself. *Who* is it, then, who has taken over being as everyday being-with-one-another?

27. Everyday Being One's Self and the They

The *ontologically* relevant result of the foregoing analysis of being-with is the insight that the "subject character" of one's own Da-sein and of the others is to be defined existentially, that is, in terms of certain ways to be. In what is taken care of in the surrounding world, the others are encountered as what they are; they *are* what they do.

In taking care of the things which one has taken hold of, for, and against others, there is constant care as to the way one differs from them, whether this difference is to be equalized, whether one's own Da-sein has lagged behind others and wants to catch up in relation to them, whether Da-sein in its priority over others is intent on suppressing them. Being-with-one-another is, unknown to itself, disquieted by the care about this distance. Existentially expressed, being-with-one-another has the character of *distantiality*. The more inconspicuous this kind of being is to everyday Da-sein itself, all the more stubbornly and primordially does it work itself out.

But this distantiality which belongs to being-with is such that, as everyday being-with-one-another, Da-sein stands in *subservience* to the others. It itself *is* not; the others have taken its being away from it. The everyday possibilities of being of Da-sein are at the disposal of the whims of the others. These others are not *definite* others. On the contrary, any other can represent them. What is decisive is only the inconspicuous domination by others that Da-sein as being-with has already taken over unawares. One belongs to the others oneself, and entrenches their power. "The others," whom one designates as such in order to cover over one's own essential belonging to them, are those who *are there* initially and for the most part in everyday being-with-one-another. The who is not this one and not that one, not oneself and not some and not the sum of them all. The "who" is the neuter, *the they [das Man]*.

We have shown earlier how the public "surrounding world" is always already at hand and taken care of in the surrounding world nearest to us. In utilizing public transportation, in the use of information services such as the newspaper, every other is like the next. This being-with-one-another dissolves one's own Da-sein completely into the kind of being of "the others" in such a way that the others, as distinguishable and explicit, disappear more and more. In this inconspicuousness and unascertainability, the they unfolds its true dictatorship. We enjoy ourselves and have fun the way *they* enjoy themselves. We read, see, and judge literature and art the way *they* see and judge. But we also withdraw from the "great mass" the way *they* withdraw, we find "shocking" what *they* find shocking. The they, which is nothing definite and which all are, though not as a sum, prescribes the kind of being of everydayness.

The they has its own ways to be. The tendency of being-with which we called distantiality is based on the fact that being-with-one-another as such creates *averageness*. It is an existential character of the they. In its being, the they is essentially concerned with averageness. Thus, the they maintains itself factically in the averageness of what is proper, what is allowed, and what is not. Of what is granted success and what is not. This averageness, which prescribes what can and may be ventured, watches over every exception which thrusts itself to the fore. Every priority is noiselessly squashed. Overnight, everything primordial is flattened down as something long since known. Everything gained by a struggle becomes something to be manipulated. Every mystery loses its power. The care of averageness reveals, in turn, an essential tendency of Da-sein, which we call the *levelling down* of all possibilities of being.

Distantiality, averageness, and levelling down, as ways of being of the they, constitute what we know as "publicness." Publicness initially controls every way in which the world and Da-sein are interpreted, and it is always right, not because of an eminent and primary relation of being to "things," not because it has an explicitly appropriate transparency of Da-sein at its disposal, but because it does not get to "the heart of the matter," because it is insensitive to every difference of level and genuineness. Publicness obscures everything, and then claims that what has been thus covered over is what is familiar and accessible to everybody.

The they is everywhere, but in such a way that it has always already stolen away when Da-sein presses for a decision. However, because the they presents every judgment and decision as its own, it takes the responsibility of Da-sein away from it. The they can, as it were, manage to have "them" constantly invoking it. It can most easily be responsible for everything because no one has to vouch for anything. The they always "did it," and yet it can be said that "no one" did it. In the everydayness of Da-sein, most things happen in such a way that we must say "no one did it."

Thus, the they *disburdens* Da-sein in its everydayness. Not only that; by disburdening it of its being, the they accommodates Da-sein in its tendency to take things easily and make them easy. And since the they constantly accommodates Da-sein, it retains and entrenches its stubborn dominance.

Everyone is the other, and no one is himself. The *they,* which supplies the answer to the *who* of everyday Da-sein, is the *nobody* to whom every Da-sein has always already surrendered itself, in its being-among-one-another.

•   •   •

Nor is the they something like a "universal subject" which hovers over a plurality of subjects. One could understand it this way only if the being of "subjects" is understood as something unlike Da-sein, and if these are regarded as factually objectively present cases of an existing genus. With this approach, the only possibility ontologically is to understand everything which is not a case of this sort in the sense of genus and species. The they is not the genus of an individual Da-sein, nor can it be found in this being as an abiding characteristic. That traditional logic also fails in the face of these phenomena, cannot surprise us if we consider that it has its foundation in an ontology of objective presence—an ontology which is still rough at that. Thus, it fundamentally cannot be made more flexible no matter how many improvements and expansions might be made. These reforms of logic, oriented toward the "humanistic sciences," only increase the ontological confusion.

The they is an existential and belongs as a primordial phenomenon to the positive constitution of Da-sein. It itself has, in turn, various possibilities of concretion in accordance with Da-sein. The extent to which its dominance becomes penetrating and explicit may change historically.

The self of everyday Da-sein is the *they-self* which we distinguish from the *authentic self,* the self which has explicitly grasped itself. As the they-self, Da-sein is *dispersed* in the they and must first find itself. This dispersion characterizes the "subject" of the kind of being which we know as heedful absorption in the world nearest encountered. If *Da-sein* is familiar with itself as the they-self, this also means that the they prescribes the nearest interpretation of the world and of being-in-the-world. The they itself, for the sake of which Da-sein is every day, articulates the referential context of significance. The world of Da-sein frees the beings encountered for a totality of relevance which is familiar to the they in the limits which are established with the averageness of the they. *Initially,* factical Da-sein is in the with-world, discovered in an average way. *Initially,* "I" "am" not in the sense of my own self, but I am the others in the mode of the they. In terms of the they, and as the they, I am initially "given" to "myself." Initially, Da-sein is the they and for the most part it remains so. If Da-sein explicitly discovers the world and brings it near, if it discloses its authentic being to itself, this discovering of "world" and disclosing of Da-sein always comes about by clearing away coverings and obscurities, by breaking up the disguises with which Da-sein cuts itself off from itself.

$$\bullet \quad \bullet \quad \bullet$$

38. Falling Prey and Thrownness

$$\bullet \quad \bullet \quad \bullet$$

This term ["Falling"] which does not express any negative value judgment, means that Da-sein is initially and for the most part *together with* the "world" that it takes care of. This absorption in . . . mostly has the character of being lost in the publicness of the they. As an authentic potentiality for being a self, Da-sein has initially always already fallen away from itself and fallen prey to the "world." Falling prey to the "world" means being absorbed in being-with-one-another as it is guided by idle talk, curiosity, and ambiguity. What we called the inauthenticity of Da-sein may now be defined more precisely through the interpretation of falling prey. But inauthentic and unauthentic by no means signify "not really," as if Da-sein utterly lost its being in this kind of being. Inauthenticity does not mean anything like no-longer-being-in-the-world, but rather it constitutes precisely a distinctive kind of being-in-the-world which is completely taken in by the world and the *Mitda-sein* of the others in the they. Not-being-its-self functions as a *positive* possibility of beings which are absorbed in a world, essentially taking care of that world. This *nonbeing* must be conceived as the kind of being of Da-sein nearest to it and in which it mostly maintains itself.

Thus neither must the entanglement of Da-sein be interpreted as a "fall" from a purer and higher "primordial condition." Not only do we not have any experience of this ontically, but also no possibilities and guidelines of interpretation ontologically.

As factical being-in-the-world, Da-sein, falling prey, has already fallen *away from itself*; and it has not fallen prey to some being which it first runs into in the course of its being, or perhaps does not, but it has fallen prey to the *world* which itself belongs to its being. Falling prey is an existential determination of Da-sein itself, and says nothing about Da-sein as something objectively present, or about objectively present relations to beings from which it is "derived" or to beings with which it has subsequently gotten into a *commercium*.

The ontological-existential structure of falling prey would also be misunderstood if we wanted to attribute to it the meaning of a bad and deplorable ontic quality which could perhaps be removed in the advanced stages of human culture.

●　●　●

Idle talk discloses to Da-sein a being toward its world, to others and to itself—a being in which these are understood, but in a mode of groundless floating. Curiosity discloses each and every thing, but in such a way that being-in is everywhere and nowhere. Ambiguity conceals nothing from the understanding of Da-sein, but only in order to suppress being-in-the-world in this uprooted everywhere and nowhere.

With the ontological clarification of the kind of being of everyday being-in-the-world discernible in these phenomena, we first gain an existentially adequate determination of the fundamental constitution of Da-sein. What structure does the "movement" of falling prey show?

Idle talk and the public interpretedness contained in it are constituted in being-with-one-another. Idle talk is not objectively present for itself within the world, as a product detached from being-with-one-another. Nor can it be volatilized to mean something "universal" which, since it essentially belongs to no one, "really" is nothing and "actually" only occurs in individual Da-sein that speaks. Idle talk is the kind of being of being-with-one-another itself, and does not first originate through certain conditions which influence Da-sein "from the outside." But when Da-sein itself presents itself with the possibility in idle talk and public interpretedness of losing itself in the they, of falling prey to groundlessness, that means that Da-sein prepares for itself the constant temptation of falling prey. Being-in-the-world is in itself *tempting*.

Having already become a temptation for itself in this way, the way in which things have been publicly interpreted holds fast to Da-sein in its falling prey. Idle talk and ambiguity, having-seen-everything and having-understood-everything, develop the supposition that the disclosedness of Da-sein thus available and prevalent could guarantee to Da-sein the certainty, genuineness, and fullness of all the possibilities of its being. In the self-certainty and decisiveness of the they, it gets spread abroad increasingly that there is no need of authentic, attuned understanding. The supposition of the they that one is leading and sustaining a full and genuine "life" brings a *tranquillization* to Da-sein, for which everything is in "the best order" and for whom all doors are open. Entangled being-in-the-world, tempting itself, is at the same time *tranquillizing*.

This tranquillization in inauthentic being, however, does not seduce one into stagnation and inactivity, but drives one to uninhibited "busyness." Being entangled in the "world" does not somehow come to rest. Tempting tranquillization aggravates entanglement. With special regard to the interpretation of Da-sein, the opinion may now arise that understanding the most foreign cultures and "synthesizing" them with our own may lead to the thorough and first genuine enlightenment of Da-sein about itself. Versatile curiosity and restlessly knowing it all masquerade as a universal understanding of Da-sein. But fundamentally it remains undetermined and unasked *what* is then really to be understood; nor has it been understood that understanding itself is a potentiality for being which must become *free* solely in one's *ownmost* Da-sein. When Da-sein, tranquillized and "understanding" everything, thus compares itself with everything, it drifts toward an alienation in which its ownmost potentiality for being-in-the-world is concealed. Entangled being-in-the-world is not only tempting and tranquillizing, it is at the same time *alienating*.

However, alienation cannot mean that Da-sein is factically torn away from itself. On the contrary, this alienation drives Da-sein into a kind of being intent upon the most exaggerated "self-dissection" which tries out all kinds of possibilities of interpretation, with the result that the "characterologies" and "typologies" which it points out are themselves too numerous to grasp. Yet this alienation, which *closes off* to Da-sein its authenticity and possibility, even if only that of genuinely getting stranded, still does not surrender it to beings which it itself is not, but forces it into its inauthenticity, into a possible kind of being of *itself*. The tempting and tranquillizing alienation of falling prey has its own kind of movement with the consequence that Da-sein gets *entangled* in itself.

The phenomena pointed out of temptation, tranquillizing, alienation, and self-entangling (entanglement) characterize the specific kind of being of falling prey. We call this kind of "movement" of Da-sein in its own being the *plunge*. Da-sein plunges out of itself into itself, into the groundlessness and nothingness of inauthentic everydayness. But this plunge remains concealed from it by the way things have been publicly interpreted so that it is interpreted as "getting ahead" and "living concretely."

The kind of movement of plunging into and within the groundlessness of inauthentic being in the they constantly tears understanding away from projecting authentic possibilities, and into the tranquillized supposition of possessing or attaining everything. Since the understanding is thus constantly torn away from authenticity and into the they (although always with a sham of authenticity), the movement of falling prey is characterized by *eddying*.

Not only does falling prey determine being-in-the-world existentially; at the same time the eddy reveals the character of throwing and movement of thrownness which can force itself upon Da-sein in its attunement. Not only is thrownness not a "finished fact," it is also not a self-contained fact. The facticity of Da-sein is such that Da-sein, *as long as* it is what it is, remains in the throw and is sucked into the eddy of the they's inauthenticity. Thrownness, in which facticity can be seen phenomenally, belongs to Da-sein, which is concerned in its being about that being. Da-sein exists factically.

But now that falling prey has been exhibited, have we not set forth a phenomenon which directly speaks *against* the definition in which the formal idea of existence was indicated? Can Da-sein be conceived as a being whose being is concerned *with* potentiality for being if this being *has lost itself* precisely in its everydayness and "lives" *away from itself* in falling prey? Falling prey to the world is, however, phenomenal "evidence" *against* the existentiality of Da-sein only if Da-sein is posited as an isolated I-subject, as a self-point from which it moves away. Then the world is an object. Falling prey to the world is then reinterpreted onto-logically as objective presence in the manner of innerworldly beings. However, if we hold on to the being of Da-sein in the constitution indicated of *being-in-the-world,* it becomes evident that falling prey *as the kind of being of this being in* rather represents the most elemental proof *for* the existentiality of Da-sein. In falling prey, nothing other than our potentiality for being-in-the-world is the issue, even if in the mode of inauthenticity. Da-sein *can* fall prey *only* because it is concerned with understanding, attuned being-in-the-world. On the other hand, *authentic* existence is nothing which hovers over entangled everydayness, but is existentially only a modified grasp of everydayness.

Nor does the phenomenon of falling prey give something like a "night view" of Da-sein, a property occurring ontically which might serve to round out the harmless aspect of this being. Falling prey reveals an *essential,* ontological structure of Da-sein itself. Far from determining its nocturnal side, it constitutes all of its days in their everydayness.

Our existential, ontological interpretation thus does not make any ontic statement about the "corruption of human nature," not because the necessary evidence is lacking but because its problematic is *prior to* any statement about corruption or incorruption. Falling prey is an ontological concept of motion. Ontically, we have not decided whether human being is "drowned in sin," in the *status corruptionis,* or whether he walks in the *status integritatis* or finds himself in an interim stage, the *status gratiae.* But faith and "worldview," when they state such and such a thing and when they speak about Da-sein as being-in-the-world, must come back to the existential structures set forth, provided that their statements at the same time claim to be *conceptually* comprehensible.

The leading question of this chapter pursued the being of the there. Its theme was the ontological constitution of the disclosedness essentially belonging to Da-sein. The being of disclosedness is constituted in attunement, understanding, and discourse. Its everyday mode of being is characterized by idle talk, curiosity, and ambiguity. These show the kind of movement of falling prey with the essential characteristics of temptation, tranquillization, alienation, and entanglement.

But with this analysis the totality of the existential constitution of Da-sein has been laid bare in its main features and the phenomenal basis has been obtained for a "comprehensive" interpretation of the being of Da-sein as care.

• • •

40. The Fundamental Attunement of *Angst* as an Eminent Disclosedness of Da-sein

One possibility of being of Da-sein is to give ontic "information" about itself as a being. Such information is possible only in the disclosedness belonging to Da-sein which is based on attunement and understanding. To what extent is *Angst* a distinctive attunement? How is Da-sein brought before itself in it through its own being so that phenomenologically the being disclosed in *Angst* is defined as such in its being, or adequate preparations can be made for doing so?

With the intention of penetrating to the being of the totality of the structural whole, we shall take our point of departure from the concrete analysis of entanglement carried out in the last chapter. The absorption of Da-sein in the they and in the "world" taken care of reveals something like a *flight* of Da-sein from itself as an authentic potentiality for being itself. This phenomenon of the flight of Da-sein *from itself* and its authenticity seems, however, to be least appropriate to serve as a phenomenal foundation for the following inquiry. In this flight, Da-sein precisely does not bring itself before itself. In accordance with its own-most trait of entanglement, this turning away leads *away from* Da-sein. But in investigating such phenomena, our inquiry must guard against conflating ontic-existentiell characteristics with ontological-existential interpretation, and must not overlook the positive, phenomenal foundations provided for this interpretation by such a characterization.

It is true that existentielly the authenticity of being a self is closed off and repressed in entanglement, but this closing off is only the *privation* of a disclosedness which reveals itself phenomenally in the fact that the flight of Da-sein is a flight *from* itself. That from which Da-sein flees is precisely what Da-sein comes up "behind." Only because Da-sein is ontologically and essentially brought before itself by the disclosedness belonging to it, *can* it flee *from* that from which it flees. Of course, in this entangled turning away, that from which it flees is *not grasped,* nor is it experienced in a turning toward it. But in turning away *from* it, it is "there," disclosed. On account of its character of being disclosed, this existentielly-ontic turning away makes it phenomenally possible to grasp existentially and ontologically what the flight is from. Within the ontic "away from" which lies in turning away, that from which Da-sein flees can be understood and conceptualized by "turning toward" in a way which is phenomenologically interpretive.

• • •

We are not completely unprepared for the analysis of *Angst*. It is true that we are still in the dark as to how it is ontologically connected with fear. Obviously they are kindred phenomena. What tells us this is the fact that both phenomena remain mostly undifferentiated, and we designate as *Angst* what is really fear and call fear what has the character of *Angst*. We shall attempt to penetrate to the phenomenon of *Angst* step by step.

The falling prey of Da-sein to the they and the "world" taken care of, we called a "flight" from itself. But not every shrinking back from . . . , not every turning away from . . . is necessarily flight. Shrinking back from what fear discloses, from what is threatening, is founded upon fear and has the character of flight. Our interpretation of fear as attunement showed that what we fear is always a detrimental innerworldy being, approaching nearby from a definite region, which may remain absent. In falling prey, Da-sein turns away from itself. What it shrinks back from must have a threatening character; yet this being has the same kind of being as the one which shrinks back from it—it is Da-sein itself. What it shrinks back from cannot be grasped as something "fearsome"; because anything fearsome is always encountered as an innerworldly being. The only threat which can be "fearsome" and which is discovered in fear always comes from innerworldly beings.

The turning away of falling prey is thus not a flight which is based on a fear of innerworldly beings. Any flight based on that kind of fear belongs still less to turning away, as turning away precisely *turns toward* innerworldly beings while absorbing itself in them. *The turning away of falling prey is rather based on* Angst *which in turn first makes fear possible.*

In order to understand this talk about the entangled flight of Da-sein from itself, we must recall that being-in-the-world is the basic constitution of Da-sein. *That about which one has* Angst *is being-in-the-world as such.* How is what *Angst* is anxious about phenomenally differentiated from what fear is afraid of? What *Angst* is about is not an innerworldly being. Thus it essentially cannot be relevant. The threat does not have the character of a definite detrimentality which concerns what is threatened with a definite regard to a particular factical potentiality for being. What *Angst* is about is completely indefinite. This indefiniteness not only leaves factically undecided which innerworldly being is threatening us, but also means that innerworldly beings in general are not "relevant." Nothing of that which is at hand and objectively present within the world, functions as what *Angst* is anxious about. The totality of relevance discovered within the world of things at hand and objectively present is completely without importance. It collapses. The world has the character of complete insignificance. In *Angst* we do not encounter this or that thing which, as threatening, could be relevant

Thus neither does *Angst* "see" a definite "there" and "over here" from which what is threatening approaches. The fact that what is threatening is *nowhere* characterizes what *Angst* is about. *Angst* "does not know" what it is about which it is anxious. But "nowhere" does not mean nothing; rather, region in general lies therein, and disclosedness of the world in general for essentially spatial being-in. Therefore, what is threatening cannot approach from a definite direction within nearness, it is already "there"—and yet nowhere. It is so near that it is oppressive and stifles one's breath—and yet it is nowhere.

• • •

Angst is not only *Angst* about . . . , but is at the same time, as attunement, *Angst* for. . . . That for which *Angst* is anxious is not a *definite* kind of being and possibility of Da-sein. The threat itself is, after all, indefinite and thus cannot penetrate threateningly to this or that factically concrete potentiality of being. What *Angst* is anxious for is being-in-the-world itself. In *Angst,* the things at hand in the surrounding world sink away, and so do innerworldly beings in general. The "world" can offer nothing more, nor can the *Mitda-sein* of others. Thus *Angst* takes away from Da-sein the possibility of understanding itself, falling prey, in terms of the "world" and the public way of being interpreted. It throws Da-sein back upon that for which it is anxious, its authentic potentiality-for-being-in-the-world. . . .

Angst reveals in Da-sein its *being toward* its ownmost potentiality of being, that is, *being free for* the freedom of choosing and grasping itself. *Angst* brings Da-sein *before its being free for* . . . , the authenticity of its being as possibility which it always already is. But at the same time, it is this being to which Da-sein as being-in-the-world is entrusted.

That *about which Angst* is anxious reveals itself as that *for which* it is anxious: being-in-the-world. The identity of that about which and that for which one has *Angst* extends even to anxiousness itself. For as attunement, anxiousness is a fundamental mode of being-in-the-world. *The existential identity of disclosing and what is disclosed so that in what is disclosed the world is disclosed as world, as being-in, individualized, pure, thrown potentiality for being, makes it clear that with the phenomenon of* Angst *a distinctive kind of attunement has become the theme of our interpretation. Angst* individualizes and thus discloses Da-sein as "*solus ipse.*" This existential "solipsism," however, is so far from transposing an isolated subject-thing into the harmless vacuum of a worldless occurrence that it brings Da-sein in an extreme sense precisely before its world as world, and thus itself before itself as being-in-the-world.

• • •

41. The Being of Da-sein as Care

With the intention of grasping the totality of the structural whole ontologically, we must first ask whether the phenomenon of *Angst* and what is disclosed in it are able to give the whole of Da-sein in a way that is phenomenally equiprimordial, so that our search for totality can be fulfilled in this givenness. The total content of what lies in it can be enumerated: As attunement, being anxious is a way of being-in-the-world; that about which we have *Angst* is thrown being-in-the-world; that for which we have *Angst* is our potentiality-for-being-in-the-world. The complete phenomenon of *Angst* thus shows Da-sein as factical, existing being-in-the-world. The fundamental, ontological characteristics of this being are existentiality, facticity, and falling prey. These existential determinations are not pieces belonging to something composite, one of which might sometimes be missing, but a primordial content is woven in them which constitutes the totality of the structural whole that we are seeking. In the unity of the determinations of being of Da-sein that we have mentioned, this being becomes ontologically comprehensible as such. How is this unity it-self to be characterized?

Da-sein is a being which is concerned in its being about that be-ing. The "is concerned about . . ." has become clearer in the consti-tution of being of understanding as self-projective being toward its ownmost potentiality-for-being. This potentiality is that for the sake of which any Da-sein is as it is. Da-sein has always already compared itself, in its being, with a possibility of itself. Being free *for* its own-most potentiality-for-being, and thus for the possibility of authenticity and inauthenticity, shows itself in a primordial, elemental concretion in *Angst*. But ontologically, being toward one's ownmost potentiality-for-being means that Da-sein is always already *ahead* of itself in its being. Da-sein is always already "beyond itself," not as a way of be-having toward beings which it is *not,* but as being toward the poten-tiality-for-being which it itself is. This structure of being of the essen-tial "being concerned about" we formulate as the *being-ahead-of-itself* of Da-sein.

But this structure concerns the whole of the constitution of Da-sein. Being-ahead-of-itself does not mean anything like an isolated tendency in a worldless "subject," but characterizes being-in-the-world. But to being-in-the-world belongs the fact that it is entrusted to itself, that it is always already thrown *into a world*. The fact that Da-sein is entrusted to itself shows itself primordially and concretely in *Angst*. More completely formulated, being-ahead-of-itself means *being-ahead-of-itself-in-already-being-in-a-world*. As soon as this essentially unitary structure is seen phenomenally, what we worked out earlier in the analysis of worldliness also becomes clearer. There we found that the referential totality of significance (which is consti-tutive for worldliness) is "anchored" in a for-the-sake-of-which. The fact that this referential totality, of the manifold relations of the in-order-to, is bound up with that which Da-sein is concerned about, does not signify that an objectively present "world" of objects is welded together with a subject. Rather, it is the phenomenal expres-sion of the fact that the constitution of Da-sein, whose wholeness is now delineated explicitly as being-ahead-of-itself-in-already-being-in . . . is primordially a whole. Expressed differently: existing is al-ways factical. Existentiality is essentially determined by facticity.

Furthermore, the factical existing of Da-sein is not only in general and indifferently a thrown potentiality-for-being-in-the-world, but is always already also absorbed in the world taken care of. In this entangled being-together-with, fleeing from uncanniness (which mostly remains covered over by latent *Angst* because the publicness of the they suppresses everything unfamiliar) announces itself, whether it does so explicitly or not, and whether it is understood or not. In being-ahead-of-oneself-already-being-in-the-world, entangled *being-together* with innerworldly things at hand taken care of lies essentially included.

The formal existential totality of the ontological structural whole of Da-sein must thus be formulated in the following structure: The being of Da-sein means being-ahead-of-oneself-already-in (the world) as being-together-with (innerworldly beings encountered). This being fills in the significance of the term *care,* which is used in a purely ontological and existential way. Any ontically intended tendency of being, such as worry or carefreeness, is ruled out.

Since being-in-the-world is essentially care, being-together-with things at hand could be taken in our previous analyses as *taking care* of them, being with the *Mitda-sein* of others encountered within the world as *concern.* Being-together-with is taking care of things, because as a mode of being-in it is determined by its fundamental structure, care. Care not only characterizes existentiality, abstracted from facticity and falling prey, but encompasses the unity of these determinations of being. Nor does care mean primarily and exclusively an isolated attitude of the ego toward itself. The expression "care of oneself," following the analogy of taking care and concern, would be a tautology. Care cannot mean a special attitude toward the self, because the self is already characterized ontologically as being-ahead-of-itself; but in this determination the other two structural moments of care, already-being-in . . . and being-together-with, are *also posited.*

In being-ahead-of-oneself as the being toward one's ownmost potentiality-of-being lies the existential and ontological condition of the possibility of *being free for* authentic existential possibilities. It is the potentiality-for-being for the sake of which Da-sein always is as it factically is. But since this being toward the potentiality-for-being is itself determined by freedom, Da-sein *can* also be related to its possibilities *unwillingly,* it *can* be inauthentic, and it is so factically initially and for the most part. The authentic for-the-sake-of-which remains ungrasped, the project of one's potentiality-of-being is left to the disposal of the they. Thus in being-ahead-of-itself, the "self" actually means the self in the sense of the they-self. Even in inauthenticity, Da-sein remains essentially ahead-of-itself, just as the entangled fleeing of Da-sein from itself still shows *the* constitution of being of a being that *is concerned about its being*.

As a primordial structural totality, care lies "before" every factical "attitude" and "position" of Da-sein, that is, it is always already *in* them as an existential a priori. Thus this phenomenon by no means expresses a priority of "practical" over theoretical behavior. When we determine something objectively present by merely looking at it, this has the character of care just as much as a "political action," or resting and having a good time. "Theory" and "praxis" are possibilities of being for a being whose being must be defined as care.

• • •

Willing and wishing are necessarily rooted ontologically in Da-sein as care, and are not simply ontologically undifferentiated experiences which occur in a "stream" that is completely indeterminate as to the meaning of its being. This is no less true for predilection and urge. They, too, are based upon care insofar as they are purely demonstrable in Da-sein in general. This does not exclude the fact that urge and predilection are ontologically constitutive even for beings which are only "alive." The basic ontological constitution of "living," however, is a problem in its own right and can be developed only reductively and privatively in terms of the ontology of Da-sein.

Care is ontologically "prior" to the phenomena we mentioned, which can, of course, always be adequately "described" within certain limits without the complete ontological horizon needing to be visible or even known as such. For the present fundamental ontological study, which neither aspires to a thematically complete ontology of Da-sein nor even to a concrete anthropology, it must suffice to suggest how these phenomena are existentially based in care.

The potentiality-for-being for the sake of which Da-sein is, has itself the mode of being of being-in-the-world. Accordingly, the relation to innerworldly beings lies in it ontologically. Even if only privatively, care is always taking care of things and concern. In willing, a being that is understood, that is, projected upon its possibility, is grasped as something to be taken care of or to be brought to its being through concern. *For this reason,* something willed always belongs to willing, something which has already been determined in terms of a for the-sake-of-which. If willing is to be possible ontologically, the following factors are constitutive for it: the previous disclosedness of the for-the-sake-of-which in general (being-ahead-of-oneself), the disclosedness of what can be taken care of (world as the wherein of already-being), and the understanding self-projection of Da-sein upon a potentiality-for-being toward a possibility of the being "willed." The underlying totality of care shows through in the phenomenon of willing.

As something factical, the understanding self-projection of Da-sein is always already together with a discovered world. From this world it takes its possibilities, initially in accordance with the interpretedness of the they. This interpretation has from the outset restricted the possible options of choice to the scope of what is familiar, attainable, feasible, to what is correct and proper. The levelling down of the possibilities of Da-sein to what is initially available in an everyday way at the same time results in a phasing out of the possible as such. The average everydayness of taking care of things becomes blind to possibility and gets tranquillized with what is merely "real."

• • •

47. The Possibility of Experiencing the Death of Others and the Possibility of Grasping Da-sein as a Whole

When Da-sein reaches its wholeness in death, it simultaneously loses the being of the there. The transition to no-longer-being-there lifts Da-sein right out of the possibility of experiencing this transition and of understanding it as something experienced. This kind of thing is denied to actual Da-sein in relation to itself. The death of others, then, is all the more penetrating. In this way, an end of Da-sein becomes "objectively" accessible. Da-sein can gain an experience of death, all the more because it is essentially being-with with others. This "objective" givenness of death must then make possible an ontological analysis of the totality of Da-sein.

Thus from the kind of being that Da-sein possesses as being-with-one-another, we might glean the fairly obvious information that when the Da-sein of others has come to an end, it might be chosen as a substitute theme for our analysis of the totality of Da-sein. But does this lead us to our intended goal?

Even the Da-sein of others, when it has reached its wholeness in death, is a no-longer-being-there in the sense of no-longer-being-in-the-world. Does not dying mean going-out-of-the-world and losing being-in-the-world? Yet, the no-longer-being-in-the-world of the deceased (understood in an extreme sense) is still a being in the sense of the mere objective presence of a corporeal thing encountered. In the dying of others that remarkable phenomenon of being can be experienced that can be defined as the transition of a being from the kind of being of Da-sein (or of life) to no-longer-being-there. The *end* of the being qua Da-sein is the *beginning* of this being qua something objectively present.

This interpretation of the transition from Da-sein to something merely objectively present, however, misses the phenomenal content in that the being still remaining does not represent a mere corporeal thing. Even the objectively present corpse is, viewed theoretically, still a possible object for pathological anatomy whose understanding is oriented toward the idea of life. Merely-being-objectively-present is "more" than a *lifeless,* material thing. In it we encounter something *unliving* which has lost its life.

• • •

The more appropriately the no-longer-being-there of the deceased is grasped phenomenally, the more clearly it can be seen that in such being-with with the dead, the real having-come-to-an-end of the deceased is precisely *not* experienced. Death does reveal itself as a loss, but as a loss experienced by those remaining behind. However, in suffering the loss, the loss of being as such which the dying person "suffers" does not become accessible. We do not experience the dying of others in a genuine sense; we are at best always just "there" too.

• • •

However, this possibility of representation gets completely stranded when it is a matter of representing the possibility of being that constitutes the coming-to-an-end of Da-sein and gives it its totality as such. *No one can take the other's dying away from him.* Someone can go "to his death for an other." However, that always means to sacrifice oneself for the other "*in a definite matter.*" Such dying for . . . can never, however, mean that the other has thus had his death in the least taken away. Every Da-sein must itself actually take dying upon itself. Insofar as it "is," death is always essentially my own. And it indeed signifies a peculiar possibility of being in which it is absolutely a matter of the being of my own Da-sein. In dying, it becomes evident that death is ontologically constituted by mineness and existence. Dying is not an event, but a phenomenon to be understood existentially in an eminent sense still to be delineated more closely.

But if "ending," as dying, constitutes the totality of Da-sein, the being of the totality itself must be conceived as an existential phenomenon of my own Da-sein. In "ending," and in the totality thus constituted of Da-sein, there is essentially no representation. The way out suggested fails to recognize this existential fact when it proposes the dying of others as a substitute theme for the analysis of totality.

• • •

But if the analysis of the end and totality of Da-sein takes an orientation of such broad scope, this nevertheless cannot mean that the existential concepts of end and totality are to be gained by way of a deduction. On the contrary, it is a matter of taking the existential meaning of the coming-to-an-end of Da-sein from Da-sein itself and of showing how this "ending" can constitute a *being whole* of that being that *exists*.

What has been discussed up to now about death can be formulated in three theses:

1. As long as Da-sein is, a not-yet belongs to it, which it will be—what is constantly outstanding.

2. The coming-to-its-end of what is not-yet-at-an-end (in which what is outstanding is liquidated with regard to its being) has the character of no-longer-being-there.

3. Coming-to-an-end implies a mode of being in which the actual Da-sein absolutely cannot be represented by someone else.

• • •

50. A Preliminary Sketch of the Existential and Ontological Structure of Death

From our considerations of something outstanding, end, and totality there has resulted the necessity of interpreting the phenomenon of death as being-toward-the-end in terms of the fundamental constitution of Da-sein. Only in this way can it become clear how a wholeness constituted by being-toward-the-end is possible in Da-sein itself, in accordance with its structure of being. We have seen that care is the fundamental constitution of Da-sein. The ontological significance of this expression was expressed in the "definition": being-ahead-of-itself-already-being-in (the world) as being-together-with beings encountered (within the world). Thus the fundamental characteristics of the being of Da-sein are expressed: in being-ahead-of-itself, existence, in already-being-in . . . , facticity, in being-together-with . . . , falling prey. Provided that death belongs to the being of Da-sein in an eminent sense, it (or being-toward-the-end) must be able to be defined in terms of these characteristics.

• • •

But if being toward death belongs primordially and essentially to the being of Da-sein, it must also be demonstrated in everydayness, although initially in an inauthentic way. And if being-toward-the-end is even supposed to offer the existential possibility for an existentiell wholeness of Da-sein, this would give the phenomenal confirmation for the thesis that care is the ontological term for the wholeness of the structural totality of Da-sein. However, for the complete phenomenal justification of this statement, a preliminary sketch of the connection between being-toward-death and care is not sufficient. Above all, we must be able to see this connection in the concretion nearest to Da-sein, its everydayness.

51. Being-toward-Death and the Everydayness of Da-sein

The exposition of everyday, average being-toward-death was oriented toward the structures of everydayness developed earlier. In being-toward-death, Da-sein is related *to itself* as an eminent potentiality-of-being. But the self of everydayness is the they which is constituted in public interpretedness which expresses itself in idle talk. Thus, idle talk must make manifest in what way everyday Da-sein interprets its being-toward-death. Understanding, which is also always attuned, that is, mooded, always forms the basis of this interpretation. Thus we must ask how the attuned understanding lying in the idle talk of the they has disclosed being-toward-death. How is the they related in an understanding way to its ownmost nonrelational possibility not-to-be-bypassed of Da-sein? What attunement discloses to the they that it has been delivered over to death, and in what way?

The publicness of everyday being-with-one-another "knows" death as a constantly occurring event, as a "case of death." Someone or another "dies," be it a neighbor or a stranger. People unknown to us "die" daily and hourly. "Death" is encountered as a familiar event occurring within the world. As such, it remains in the inconspicuousness characteristic of everyday encounters. The they has also already secured an interpretation for this event. The "fleeting" talk about this which is either expressed or else mostly kept back says: One also dies at the end, but for now one is not involved.

The analysis of "one dies" reveals unambiguously the kind of being of everyday being toward death. In such talk, death is understood as an indeterminate something which first has to show up from somewhere, but which right now is *not yet objectively present* for oneself, and is thus no threat. "One dies" spreads the opinion that death, so to speak, strikes the they. The public interpretation of Da-sein says that "one dies" because in this way everybody can convince him/herself that in no case is it I myself, for this one is *no one.* "Dying" is levelled down to an event which does concern Da-sein, but which belongs to no one in particular. If idle talk is always ambiguous, so is this way of talking about death. Dying, which is essentially and irreplaceably mine, is distorted into a publicly occurring event which the they encounters. Characteristic talk speaks about death as a constantly occurring "case." It treats it as something always already "real," and veils its character of possibility and concomitantly the two factors belonging to it, that it is nonrelational and cannot-be-bypassed. With such ambiguity, Da-sein puts itself in the position of losing itself in the they with regard to an eminent potentiality-of-being that belongs to its own self. The they justifies and aggravates the *temptation* of covering over for itself its ownmost being-toward-death.

The evasion of death which covers over, dominates everydayness so stubbornly that, in being-with-one-another, the "neighbors" often try to convince the "dying person" that he will escape death and soon return again to the tranquillized everydayness of his world taken care of. This "concern" has the intention of thus "comforting" the "dying person." It wants to bring him back to Da-sein by helping him to veil completely his ownmost nonrelational possibility. Thus, the they makes sure of a *constant tranquillization about death*. But, basically, this tranquillization is not only for the "dying person," but just as much for "those who are comforting him." And even in the case of a demise, publicness is still not to be disturbed and made uneasy by the event in the carefreeness it has made sure of. Indeed, the dying of others is seen often as a social inconvenience, if not a downright tactlessness, from which publicness should be spared.

But along with this tranquillization, which keeps Da-sein away from its death, the they at the same time justifies itself and makes itself respectable by silently ordering the way in which *one* is supposed to behave toward death in general. Even "thinking about death" is regarded publicly as cowardly fear, a sigh of insecurity on the part of Da-sein and a dark flight from the world. *The they does not permit the courage to have* Angst *about death*. The dominance of the public interpretedness of the they has already decided what attunement is to determine our stance toward death. In *Angst* about death, Da-sein is brought before itself as delivered over to its possibility not-to-be-bypassed. The they is careful to distort this *Angst* into the fear of a future event. Angst, made ambiguous as fear, is, moreover, taken as a weakness which no self-assured Da-sein is permitted to know. What is "proper" according to the silent decree of the they is the indifferent calm as to the "fact" that one dies. The cultivation of such a "superior" indifference *estranges* Da-sein from its own-most nonrelational potentiality-of-being.

Temptation, tranquillization, and estrangement, however, characterize the kind of being of *falling prey*. Entangled, everyday being-toward-death is a constant *flight from death*. Being *toward* the end has the mode of *evading that end*—reinterpreting it, understanding it inauthentically, and veiling it. Factically one's own Da-sein is always already dying, that is, it is in a being-toward-its-end. And it conceals this fact from itself by reinterpreting death as a case of death occurring every day with others, a case which always assures us still more clearly that "one oneself" is still "alive." But in the entangled flight *from* death, the everydayness of Da-sein bears witness to the fact that the they itself is always already determined *as being toward death,* even when it is not explicitly engaged in "thinking about death." *Even in average everydayness, Da-sein is constantly concerned with its ownmost nonrelational potentiality-of-being not-to-be-bypassed, if only in the mode of taking care of things in a mode of untroubled indifference* toward *the most extreme possibility of its existence.*

• • •

53. Existential Project of an Authentic Being-toward-Death

• • •

Da-sein is constituted by disclosedness, that is, by attuned understanding. *Authentic* being-toward-death can*not evade* its ownmost non-relational possibility or *cover* it *over* in this flight and *reinterpret* it for the common sense of the they. The existential project of an authentic being-toward-death must thus set forth the factors of such a being which are constitutive for it as an understanding of death—in the sense of being toward this possibility without fleeing it or covering it over.

• • •

Death is the *ownmost* possibility of Da-sein. Being toward it discloses to Da-sein its *ownmost* potentiality-of-being in which it is concerned about the being of Da-sein absolutely. Here the fact can become evident to Da-sein that in the eminent possibility of itself it is torn away from the they, that is, anticipation can always already have torn itself away from the they. The understanding of this "ability," however, first reveals its factical lostness in the everydayness of the they-self.

• • •

In anticipating the indefinite certainty of death, Da-sein opens itself to a constant threat arising from its own there. Being-toward-the-end must hold itself in this very threat, and can so little phase it out that it rather has to cultivate the indefiniteness of the certainty. How is the genuine disclosing of this constant threat existentially possible? All understanding is attuned. Mood brings Da-sein before the thrownness of its "that-it-is-there." *But the attunement which is able to hold open the constant and absolute threat to itself arising from the ownmost individualized being of Da-sein* is Angst. In *Angst,* Da-sein finds itself *faced* with the nothingness of the possible impossibility of its existence. *Angst* is anxious *about* the potentiality-of-being of the being thus determined, and thus discloses the most extreme possibility. Because the anticipation of Da-sein absolutely individualizes and lets it, in this individualizing of itself, become certain of the wholeness of its potentiality-of-being, the fundamental attunement of Angst belongs to this self-understanding of Da-sein in terms of its ground. Being-toward-death is essentially Angst. This is attested unmistakably, although "only" indirectly, by being-toward-death as we characterized it, when it distorts *Angst* into cowardly fear and, in overcoming that fear, only makes known its own cowardliness in the face of *Angst.*

What is characteristic about authentic, existentially projected being-toward-death can be summarized as follows: *Anticipation reveals to Da-sein its lostness in the they-self, and brings it face to face with the possibility to be itself, primarily unsupported by concern taking care of things, but to be itself in passionate anxious **freedom toward death** which is free of the illusions of the they, factical, and certain of itself.*

❖ The Fundamental Question ❖
of Metaphysics

Why are there essents[1] rather than nothing? That is the question. Clearly it is no ordinary question. "Why are there essents, why is there anything at all, rather than nothing?"—obviously this is the first of all questions, though not in a chronological sense. Individuals and peoples ask a good many questions in the course of their historical passage through time. They examine, explore, and test a good many things before they run into the question "Why are there essents rather than nothing?" Many men never encounter this question, if by en-

From An Introduction to Metaphysics *by Martin Heidegger, translated by Ralph Manheim (1959) for Yale University Press, Inc. Reprinted by permission of Yale University Press, Inc.*

[1] Entities, things that exist. (Editor's note.)

counter we mean not merely to hear and read about it as an inter-
rogative formulation but to ask the question, that is, to bring it about,
to raise it, to feel its inevitability.

And yet each of us is grazed at least once, perhaps more than
once, by the hidden power of this question, even if he is not aware
of what is happening to him. The question looms in moments of
great despair, when things tend to lose all their weight and all meaning becomes obscured. Perhaps it will strike but once like a muffled
bell that rings into our life and gradually dies away. It is present in
moments of rejoicing, when all the things around us are transfigured
and seem to be there for the first time, as if it might be easier to think
they are not than to understand that they are and are as they are. The
question is upon us in boredom, when we are equally removed from
despair and joy, and everything about us seems so hopelessly commonplace that we no longer care whether anything is or is not—and
with this the question "Why are there essents rather than nothing?" is
evoked in a particular form.

But this question may be asked expressly, or, unrecognized as a
question, it may merely pass through our lives like a brief gust of
wind; it may press hard upon us, or, under one pretext or another,
we may thrust it away from us and silence it. In any case it is never
the question that we ask first in point of time.

But it is the first question in another sense—in regard to rank. This
may be clarified in three ways. The question "Why are there essents
rather than nothing?" is first in rank for us first because it is the most
far reaching, second because it is the deepest, and finally because it
is the most fundamental of all questions.

• • •

All essential philosophical questioning is necessarily untimely.
This is so because philosophy is always projected far in advance of
its time, or because it connects the present with its antecedent, with
what *initially* was. Philosophy always remains a knowledge which
not only cannot be adjusted to a given epoch but on the contrary imposes its measure upon its epoch.

Philosophy is essentially untimely because it is one of these few
things that can never find an immediate echo in the present. When
such an echo seems to occur, when a philosophy becomes fashionable, either it is no real philosophy or it has been misinterpreted and
misused for ephemeral and extraneous purposes.

Accordingly, philosophy cannot be directly learned like manual and technical skills; it cannot be directly applied, or judged by its usefulness in the manner of economic or other professional knowledge.

But what is useless can still be a force, perhaps the only real force. What has no immediate echo in everyday life can be intimately bound up with a nation's profound historical development, and can even anticipate it. What is untimely will have its own times. This is true of philosophy. Consequently there is no way of determining once and for all what the task of philosophy is, and accordingly what must be expected of it. Every stage and every beginning of its development bears within it its own law. All that can be said is what philosophy cannot be and cannot accomplish.

• • •

Every essential form of spiritual life is marked by ambiguity. The less commensurate it is with other forms, the more it is misinterpreted.

Philosophy is one of the few autonomous creative possibilities and at times necessities of man's historical being-there [Dasein]. The current misinterpretations of philosophy, all of which have some truth about them, are legion. Here we shall mention only two, which are important because of the light they throw on the present and future situation of philosophy. The first misinterpretation asks too much of philosophy. The second distorts its function.

Roughly speaking, philosophy always aims at the first and last grounds of the essent, with particular emphasis on man himself and on the meaning and goals of human being-there. This might suggest that philosophy can and must provide a foundation on which a nation will build its historical life and culture. But this is beyond the power of philosophy. As a rule such excessive demands take the form of a belittling of philosophy. It is said, for example: Because metaphysics did nothing to pave the way for the revolution it should be rejected. This is no cleverer than saying that because the carpenter's bench is useless for flying it should be abolished. Philosophy can never *directly* supply the energies and create the opportunities and methods that bring about a historical change; for one thing, because philosophy is always the concern of the few. Which few? The creators, those who initiate profound transformation. It spreads only indirectly, by devious paths that can never be laid out in advance, until at last, at some future date, it sinks to the level of a common-place; but by then it has long been forgotten as original philosophy.

What philosophy essentially can and must be is this: a thinking that breaks the paths and opens the perspectives of the knowledge that sets the norms and hierarchies, of the knowledge in which and by which a people fulfills itself historically and culturally, the knowledge that kindles and necessitates all inquiries and thereby threatens all values.

The second misinterpretation involves a distortion of the function of philosophy. Even if philosophy can provide no foundation for a culture, the argument goes, it is nevertheless a cultural force, whether because it gives us an overall, systematic view of what is, supplying a useful chart by which we may find our way amid the various possible things and realms of things, or because it relieves the sciences of their work by reflecting on their premises, basic concepts, and principles. Philosophy is expected to promote and even to accelerate—to make easier as it were—the practical and technical business of culture.

But—it is in the very nature of philosophy never to make things easier but only more difficult. And this not merely because its language strikes the everyday understanding as strange if not insane. Rather, it is the authentic function of philosophy to challenge historical being-there and hence, in the last analysis, being pure and simple. It restores to things, to the essents, their weight (being). How so? Because the challenge is one of the essential prerequisites for the birth of all greatness, and in speaking of greatness we are referring primarily to the works and destinies of nations. We can speak of historical destiny only where an authentic knowledge of things dominates man's being-there. And it is philosophy that opens up the paths and perspectives of such knowledge.

The misinterpretations with which philosophy is perpetually beset are promoted most of all by people of our kind, that is, by professors of philosophy. It is our customary business—which may be said to be justified and even useful—to transmit a certain knowledge of the philosophy of the past, as part of a general education. Many people suppose that this is philosophy itself, whereas at best it is the technique of philosophy.

In correcting these two misinterpretations I cannot hope to give you at one stroke a clear conception of philosophy. But I do hope that you will be on your guard when the most current judgments and even supposed observations assail you unawares. Such judgments are often disarming, precisely because they seem so natural. You hear remarks such as "Philosophy leads to nothing," "You can't do anything with philosophy," and readily imagine that they confirm an expression of your own. There is no denying the soundness of these two phrases, particularly common among scientists and teachers of science. Any attempt to refute them by proving that after all it does "lead to something" merely strengthens the prevailing misinterpretation to the effect that the everyday standards by which we judge bicycles or sulphur baths are applicable to philosophy.

It is absolutely correct and proper to say that "You can't do anything with philosophy." It is only wrong to suppose that this is the last word on philosophy. For the rejoinder imposes itself; granted that *we* cannot do anything with philosophy, might not philosophy, if we concern ourselves with it, do something *with us?* So much for what philosophy is not.

At the outset we stated a question: "Why are there essents rather than nothing?" We have maintained that to ask this question is to philosophize. When in our thinking we open our minds to this question, we first of all cease to dwell in any of the familiar realms. We set aside everything that is on the order of the day. Our question goes beyond the familiar and the things that have their place in everyday life. Nietzsche once said (*Werke*, 7, 269): "A philosopher is a man who never ceases to experience, see, hear, suspect, hope, and dream extraordinary things . . ."

To philosophize is to inquire into the *extra*-ordinary. But because, as we have just suggested, this questioning recoils upon itself, not only what is asked after is extra-ordinary but also the asking itself. In other words: this questioning does not lie along the way so that we bump into it one day unexpectedly. Nor is it part of everyday life: there is no requirement or regulation that forces us into it; it gratifies no urgent or prevailing need. The questioning itself is "out of order." It is entirely voluntary, based wholly and uniquely on the mystery of freedom, on what we have called the leap. The same Nietzsche said: "Philosophy . . . is a voluntary living amid ice and mountain heights (*Werke*, 15, 2). To philosophize, we may now say, is an extra-ordinary inquiry into the extra-ordinary.

❖ *from* Discourse on Thinking ❖

Let us not fool ourselves. All of us, including those who think professionally, as it were, are often enough thought-poor; we all are far too easily thought-less. Thoughtlessness is an uncanny visitor who comes and goes everywhere in today's world. For nowadays we take in everything in the quickest and cheapest way, only to forget it just as quickly, instantly. Thus one gathering follows on the heels of another. Commemorative celebrations grow poorer and poorer in thought. Commemoration and thoughtlessness are found side by side.

But even while we are thoughtless, we do not give up our capacity to think. We rather use this capacity implicitly, though strangely: that is, in thoughtlessness we let it lie fallow. Still only that can lie fallow which in itself is a ground for growth, such as a field. An expressway, where nothing grows, cannot be a fallow field. Just as we can grow deaf only because we hear, just as we can grow old only because we were young; so we can grow thought-poor or even thought-less only because man at the core of his being has the capacity to think; has "spirit and reason" and is destined to think. We can only lose or, as the phrase goes, get loose from that which we knowingly or unknowingly possess.

The growing thoughtlessness must, therefore, spring from some process that gnaws at the very marrow of man today: man today is in *flight from thinking.* This flight-from-thought is the ground of thoughtlessness. But part of this flight is that man will neither see nor admit it. Man today will even flatly deny this flight from thinking. He will assert the opposite. He will say—and quite rightly—that there were at no time such far-reaching plans, so many inquiries in so many areas, research carried on as passionately as today. Of course. And this display of ingenuity and deliberation has its own great usefulness. Such thought remains indispensable. But—it also remains true that it is thinking of a special kind.

Its peculiarity consists in the fact that whenever we plan, research, and organize, we always reckon with conditions that are given. We take them into account with the calculated intention of their serving specific purposes. Thus we can count on definite results. This calculation is the mark of all thinking that plans and investigates. Such thinking remains calculation even if it neither works with numbers nor uses an adding machine or computer. Calculative thinking computes. It computes ever new, ever more promising and at the same time more economical possibilities. Calculative thinking races from one prospect to the next. Calculative thinking never stops, never collects itself. Calculative thinking is not meditative thinking, not thinking which contemplates the meaning which reigns in everything that is.

There are, then, two kinds of thinking, each justified and needed in its own way: calculative thinking and meditative thinking.

This meditative thinking is what we have in mind when we say that contemporary man is in flight from thinking. Yet you may protest: mere meditative thinking finds itself floating unaware above reality. It loses touch. It is worthless for dealing with current business. It profits nothing in carrying out practical affairs.

And you may say, finally, that mere meditative thinking, persevering meditations, is "above" the reach of ordinary understanding. In this excuse only this much is true, meditative thinking does not just happen by itself any more than does calculative thinking. At times it requires a greater effort. It demands more practice. It is in need of even more delicate care than any other genuine craft. But it must also be able to bide its time, to await as does the farmer, whether the seed will come up and ripen.

Yet anyone can follow the path of meditative thinking in his own manner and within his own limits. Why? Because man is a *thinking,* that is, a *meditating* being. Thus meditative thinking need by no means be "high-flown." It is enough if we dwell on what lies close and meditate on what is closest; upon that which concerns us, each one of us, here and now; here, on this patch of home ground; now, in the present hour of history.

Rainer Maria Rilke

(1875-1926)
CZECH/(EUROPEAN)

Rilke was one of the great poets of the twentieth century. He was born in Prague, had an unhappy childhood, and, after beginning an inappropriate military career, he attended Charles University in Prague and decided to become a poet. By the time Rilke graduated in 1895, he had already published a volume of poetry. He then began a lifetime of travel, to Germany, Italy, Paris, Russia, and Switzerland, where he wrote his most famous work, *Duino Elegies*. He wrote, "poems are not . . . simply emotions . . . they are experiences. For the sake of a single poem, you must see many cities, many people and things . . . and know the gestures which small flowers make when they open in the morning . . ." Rilke's poetry is quite emotional and sensual and frequently raises "existential" questions about love, God, and the meaning of life. William Gass, who has written widely on Rilke, described him as "sensitive, insightful, gifted nearly beyond compare; a man with many devoted and distant friends, many extraordinary though frequently fatuous enthusiasms, but still a lonely unloving homeless boy as well, with fears words couldn't wave away, a self-pity there were rarely buckets enough to contain; yet a persistence in the pursuit of his goals, a courage, that overcame weakness and worry and made them into poems."

The following is excerpted from *The Notebooks of Malte Laurids Brigge*.

❖ *from* The Notebooks of ❖ Malte Laurids Brigge

How ridiculous. I sit here in my little room, I, Brigge, who am twenty-eight years old and completely unknown. I sit here and am nothing. And yet this nothing begins to think and thinks, five flights up, on a gray Paris afternoon, these thoughts:

Is it possible, it thinks, that we have not yet seen, known, or said anything real and important? Is it possible that we have had thousands of years to look, meditate, and record, and that we have let these thousands of years slip away like a recess at school, when there is just enough time to eat your sandwich and an apple?

Yes, it is possible.

Is it possible that despite our discoveries and advances, despite our culture, religion, and science, we have remained on the surface of life? Is it possible that even this surface, which might still have been something, has been covered with an incredibly tedious material, which makes it look like living-room furniture during the summer vacation?

Yes, it is possible.

. . . Is it possible that we say "women," "children," "boys," not suspecting (despite all our culture, not suspecting) that these words have long since had no plural, but only countless singulars?

Yes, it is possible.

Is it possible that there are people who say "God" and think that this is something they have in common?—Take a couple of schoolboys: one buys a pocket knife, and the same day his friend buys another exactly like it. And after a week they compare knives, and it turns out that there is now just a very distant resemblance between them—so differently have they developed in different hands. ("Oh," says the mother of one, "you can't own *any*thing without wearing it out in a day . . ."). In the same way: Is it possible to believe we could have a God without using him?

Yes, it is possible.

But if all this is possible, if it has even a semblance of possibility,—then surely, for the sake of everything in the world, something must

From The Notebooks of Malte Laurids Brigge *by Rainer Maria Rilke, translated by John Linton. Copyright 1997 by Oxford University Press.*

be done. The first comer, the one who has had these alarming thoughts, must begin to do some of the things that have been neg-lected; even though he is just anyone, certainly not the most suitable person: since there is no one else. This young, insignificant foreigner, Brigge, will have to sit down in his room, five flights up, and keep writing, day and night. Yes, he will have to write; that is how it will end.

Miguel de Unamuno

(1864-1936)
SPANISH

Unamuno took great pride in the fact that his philosophy was distinctively Spanish. Writing just after the devastation of World War I until the eve of the Spanish Civil War, he was obsessed with the problems of coping with a life so filled with anxiety, brutality, and disappointment. Unamuno was one of those very individual voices, crying out passionately on behalf of honesty and integrity. He supported the Allies against Germany in the first World War and he opposed Francisco Franco, the fascist dictator. He wrote elegantly about the "tragic sense of life," in poetry and novels as well as in philosophical essays and literary commentary. Kierkegaard was Unamuno's philosophical hero, and he, too, bemoaned the failure of objective science and reason to answer life's questions and defended a version of subjective truth. According to Unamuno, passion and commitment are more important in life than reason and rationality. Reason inevitably leads to skepticism, and skepticism to despair. Faith, by contrast, offers its own guarantees, even if they are "only" subjective. "All or nothing," Unamuno would say. What a human being wants is immortality, nothing less. Reason and science tell us that immortality is impossible. Faith satisfies that ultimate demand. For Unamuno, one "philosophizes in order to live," not the other way around.

❖ *from* The Tragic Sense of Life ❖

Several times in the wandering course of these observations I have been bold enough to define, in spite of my horror of definitions, my own position vis-à-vis the problem I have been examining. But I know there is bound to be some dissatisfied reader, indoctrinated in some dogmatism or other, who will say: "This man cannot make up his mind; he vacillates; first he seems to assert one proposition, then he maintains the opposite; he is full of contradictions; it is impossible to place him. What is he?" There you have me: a man who affirms opposites, a man of contradiction and quarrel, as Jeremiah said of himself; a man who says one thing with his heart and the opposite with his head, and for whom this strife is the stuff of life. It is a clear-cut case, as clear as the water which flows from the melted snow upon the mountain tops.

I shall be told that mine is an untenable position, that a foundation is needed upon which to build our actions and our works, that it is impossible to live by contradictions, that unity and clarity are essential conditions for life and thought, and that it is imperative to unify the latter. And so we are back where we started from. For it is precisely this inner contradiction which unifies my life and gives it a practical purpose.

Or, rather, it is the conflict itself, this selfsame passionate uncertainty which unifies my action and causes me to live and work.

We think in order that we may live I have said, but perhaps it would be more correct to say that we think because we live, and that the form of our thought corresponds to the form of our life. Once more I must point out that our ethical and philosophical doctrines in general are no more than a posteriori justifications of our conduct, of our actions. Our doctrines are usually the means by which we seek to explain and justify to others and to ourselves our own mode of action—to ourselves, be it noted, as well as to others. The man who does not really know why he acts as he does, and not otherwise, feels the need to explain to himself his reason for so acting, and so he manufactures a motive. What we believe to be the motives for our conduct are usually mere pretexts. The reason which impels one

From The Tragic Sense of Life *by Miguel de Unamuno, translated by Anthony Kerrigan. Published by Princeton University Press, Inc. (1972). Reprinted with permission of Princeton University Press, Inc.*

man carefully to preserve his life is the same reason given by another man for shooting himself in the head.

Nevertheless it cannot be denied that reasons, ideas, exert an influence on human actions, and sometimes even determine them by a process analogous to that of suggestion in the case of a hypnotized person, and this is due to the tendency of all ideas to resolve themselves in action—for an idea in itself is but an inchoate or aborted act. It was this tendency which suggested to Fouillée his theory of idea forces. But ordinarily ideas are forces which we reconcile with other deeper and much less conscious forces.

But leaving all this to one side for a moment, I should like to establish the fact that uncertainty, doubt, the perpetual wrestling with the mystery of our final destiny, the consequent mental despair, and the lack of any solid or stable dogmatic foundation, may all serve as basis for an ethic.

Whoever bases or thinks he bases his conduct—his inner or outward conduct, his feeling or his action—on a dogma or theoretical principle which he deems incontrovertible, runs the risk of becoming a fanatic; moreover, the moment this dogma shows any fissure or even any weakness, he finds the morality based on it giving way. If the ground he thought firm begins to rock, he himself trembles in the earthquake, for we are not all like the ideal Stoic who remains undaunted among the ruins of a world shattered to pieces. Luckily, the matter which underlies his ideas will tend to save him. For if a man should tell you that he does not defraud or cuckold his best friend because he fears hellfire, you may depend upon it that he would not do so even if he stopped believing in hell, but would instead invent some other excuse for not transgressing. And this truth is to the honor of the human race.

But whoever is convinced that he is sailing, perhaps without a set course, on an unstable or sinkable craft, will not be daunted if he finds the deck giving way beneath his feet and threatening to sink. For this type of man acts as he does, not because he believes his theory of action to be true, but because he believes that by acting thus he will make it true, prove it true, and that by thus acting he will create his spiritual world.

My conduct must be the best proof, the moral proof, of my supreme desire; and if I do not finally convince myself, within the limits of the ultimate and irremediable uncertainty, of the truth of what I hope for, it is because my conduct is not sufficiently pure. Virtue, therefore, is not based upon dogma, but dogma upon virtue, and it is not faith which creates martyrs but rather martyrs who create faith. There is no security or repose—so far as security and repose are attainable in this life which is essentially insecure and lacking in repose—save in passionately good conduct.

• • •

What is the anti-rational truth of our heart? It is the immortality of the human soul, the truth of the persistence of our consciousness without any termination whatever, the human finality of the Universe. And what is its moral proof? We may formulate it thus: Act so that in your own judgement and in the judgement of others you may deserve eternity, act so that you may be irreplaceable, act so that you do not deserve death. Or perhaps thus: Act as if you were to die tomorrow, but only in order to survive and become eternal. The end-purpose of morality is to give personal, human finality to the Universe; to discover the finality it possesses—if it does in fact possess any—and discover it by acting.

More than a century ago, in 1804, the deepest and most intense of the spiritual sons of the patriarch Rousseau, most tragic of French men of feeling (not excluding Pascal), Sénancour . . . wrote the words . . . "Man is perishable. . . . That may be; but let us perish resisting, and if annihilation must be our portion, let us not make it a just one." If you change this sentence from a negative to a positive form—"And if annihilation must be our portion, let us make it an unjust reward."—you get the firmest basis for action by the man who cannot or will not be a dogmatist.

All men deserve to be saved, but, as I have said in the previous chapter, whoever desires immortality with a passion and even against all reason deserves it most of all. The writer H. G. Wells, who has given himself over to prophecy (not an uncommon phenomenon in his country), tells us in his *Anticipations* that "Active and capable men of all forms of religious profession today tend in practice to disregard the question of immortality altogether." And this is so because the religious professions of these active and capable men of whom Wells speaks are usually no more than a lie, and their lives are a lie, too, if they pretend to base them upon religion. But perhaps what Wells tells us is not basically as true as he and others like him imagine. Those active and capable men live in the midst of a society imbued with Christian principles, surrounded by institutions and social reactions produced by Christianity, so that a belief in the immortality of the soul runs deep in their own souls like a subterranean river, neither seen nor heard, but watering the roots of their deeds and their motives.

In all truth it must be admitted that there exists no more solid foundation for morality than the foundation provided by the Catholic ethic. Man's end-purpose is eternal happiness, which consists in the vision and enjoyment of God *in saecula saeculorum*. Where that ethic errs, however, is in the choice of means conducive to this end; for to make the attainment of eternal happiness dependent upon believing or not believing that the Holy Ghost proceeds from the Father and the Son and not from the Father alone, or in the divinity of Jesus, or in the theory of the hypostatic union, or even in the existence of God is nothing less than monstrous, as a moment's reflection will show. A human God—and we can conceive of no other—would never reject whoever could not believe in Him with his head; it is not in his head but in his heart that the wicked man says there is no God, that is: he does not *want* God to exist. If any belief could be linked with the attainment of eternal happiness it would be the belief in this happiness itself and in the possibility of attaining it.

And what shall we say of that other notion of the emperor of pedants, to the effect that we have not come into the world to be happy but to fulfill our duty ("Wir sind nicht auf der Welt, um glücklich zu sein, sondern um unsere Schuldigkeit zu tun")? If we are in this world *for something* (*um etwas*), whence can this *for* be derived but from the very essence of our own will, which asks for happiness and not duty as ultimate end? And if we were to attempt to attribute some other value to this *for,* an "objective value," as some Sadducean pedant might say, then we would have to recognize that this objective reality—the reality which would remain though humanity should disappear—is as indifferent to our duty as to our happiness, as little concerned with our morality as with our felicity. I am not aware that Jupiter, Uranus, or Sirius would allow their courses to be affected because we do or do not fulfill our duty any more than because we are or are not happy.

Karl Jaspers

(1883–1969)
GERMAN

Jaspers entered philosophy from a medical career in psychiatry. Accordingly, his philosophy displays a fascinating combination of scientific knowledge and antiscientific humanism. Jaspers, perhaps the most systematic of the existentialists, is heavily influenced by Kant, Kierkegaard, and Nietzsche. Like Kant, he is interested in the limits of experience, the limitations of science. Like Kierkegaard and Nietzsche, he is interested in the individual, in "philosophizing as an exception." Philosophy for him is an activity, one developing out of the need to communicate to others one's own *Existenz*. *Existenz* is a notion Jaspers takes directly from Kierkegaard to refer to the authentic self. *Existenz* is, still following Kierkegaard, lived and not merely an object of knowledge. It is an experience of subjective freedom within certain boundary situations, exemplified by death and guilt. Authentic *Existenz* is the human attempt to push past these boundaries and reach the Encompassing ("transcendence"). This "will to infinity" is also called faith, the ideal attempt to go beyond the limits of experience. Again, one is very much reminded of Kant's philosophy—the separation of the world of our experience and world-in-itself, the world of knowledge and the world of faith. But this is Kant with a Kierkegaardian twist: for Jaspers there is no rationality to faith as there always is for Kant.

The selection here is taken from Jaspers's "Existenz" from *Philosophy,* vol. II, his most systematic exposition of these themes.

161

❖ Existenz ❖

Mundane Existence and Existenz

If by "world" I mean the sum of all that cognitive orientation can reveal to me as cogently knowable for everyone, the question arises whether the being of the world is all there is. Does cognitive thinking stop with world orientation? What we refer to in mythical terms as the soul and God, and in philosophical language as Existenz and transcendence, is not of this world. Neither one is knowable, in the sense of things in the world. Yet both might have another kind of being. They need not be nothing, even though they are not known. They could be objects of thought, if not of cognition.

What is there, as against all mundane being? In the answer to this question lies the basic decision of philosophy.

We answer: there is the being which in the phenomenality of existence *is not* but *can be, ought to be,* and therefore decides in time whether it is in eternity.

This being is myself as *Existenz.* I am Existenz if I do not become an object for myself. In Existenz I know, without being able to see it, that what I call my "self" is independent. The possibility of Existenz is what I live by; it is only in its realization that I am myself. Attempts to comprehend it make it vanish, for it is not a psychological subject. I feel more deeply rooted in its possibility than in my self-objectifying grasp of my nature and my character. Existenz appears to itself as existence, in the polarity of subjectivity and objectivity; but it is not the appearance of an object given anywhere, or uncoverable as underlying any reflection. It is phenomenal only for itself and for other Existenz.

It is thus not my existence that is Existenz; but, *being human,* I am possible Existenz *in existence.* I exist or I do not exist, but my Existenz, as a possibility, takes a step toward being or away from being, toward nothingness, in every choice or decision I make. My existence differs from other existence in scope; my world can be broad or narrow. But Existenz differs from other Existenz in essence, because of its freedom. As existence I live and die; my Existenz is un-

From Philosophy *(Vol. 2) by Karl Jaspers, translated by E. B. Ashton. Published by University of Chicago Press, Inc. Reprinted with permission of University of Chicago Press, Inc.*

aware of death but soars or declines in relation to its being. Existence exists empirically. Existenz as freedom only. Existence is wholly temporal, while Existenz, in time, is more than time. My existence is finite, since it is not all existence, and yet, for me, it is concluded within itself. Existenz is not everything and not for itself alone either, for its being depends on its relation to other Existenz and to transcendence—the wholly Other that makes it aware of being not by itself alone—but while existence may be termed infinite as relatively rounded endlessness, the infinity of Existenz is unrounded, an open possibility. Action on the ground of possible Existenz disconcerts me in existence; as existence, concerned with enduring in time, I cannot but turn against the doubtful path of unconditionality that may be costly, even ruinous, in existence. My concern with existence tends to make existential actions conditional upon the preservation of my existence; but to possible Existenz, the unqualified enjoyment of existence is already apostasy; to Existenz, the condition of its reality in existence is that it comprehends itself as unconditional. If I merely want to exist, without qualifications, I am bound to despair when I see that the reality of my existence lies in total foundering.

Existence is fulfilled in *mundane being;* to possible Existenz, the world is the field of its phenomenality.

The *known* world is the alien world. I am *detached* from it. What my intellect can know and what I can experience empirically repulses me as such, and I am irrelevant to it. Subject to overpowering causality in the realm of reality and to logical compulsion in the realm of validity, I am not sheltered in either. I hear no kindred language, and the more determined I am to comprehend the world, the more homeless will it make me feel; as the Other, as nothing but the world, it holds no comfort. Unfeeling, neither merciful nor unmerciful, subject to laws or foundering in coincidence, it is unaware of itself. I cannot grasp it, for it faces me impersonally, explicable in particulars but never intelligible as a whole.

And yet *there is another way in which I know the world.* It is akin to me then; I am at home in it and even sheltered in it. Its laws are the laws of my own reason. I find peace as I adjust to it, as I make my tools and expand my cognition of the world. It will speak to me now; it breathes a life that I share. I give myself up to it, and when I am in it I am with myself. It is familiar in small, present things, and thrilling in its grandeur; it will make me unwary in proximity or tend to sweep me along to its far reaches. Its ways are not the ways I expect, but though it may startle me with undreamed of fulfillments and incomprehensible failures, I shall trust it even as I perish.

This is no longer the world I know about in purely cognitive orientation. But my contentment in dealing with it is ambiguous. I may *crave* the world as the font of my joy of living, may be drawn to it and deceived about it by my blind will to live. I can indeed not exist without this craving, but as an absolute impulse it becomes self-destructive; it is against this impulse that my possible Existenz warns me to detach myself from the world lest I become its prey. Or, *in the world* that is so close to me, so much my kin, I may set out to *transcend* the world. Whether seeing it, thinking about it, acting and loving, producing and developing in it—in all that, then, I deal with something else at the same time, with a phenomenon of the transcendence that speaks to me. This is not a world I know but one that seems to have lost its continuity. It will change according to times and persons, and depending on my inner attitudes; it does not say the same things to all men, and not the same things at all times. I must be ready for it if I want to hear it. If I withhold myself, the very thing I might transcend to will withdraw. For it is only for freedom and by freedom, and there is nothing cogent about it at all.

Possible Existenz thus *sets itself off* from the world in order to find the right way into the world. It cuts loose from the world so that its grasp of the world will give it more than the world can be. The world attracts Existenz as the medium of its realization, and repels it as its possible decay to mere existence. There is a tension between the world and Existenz. They cannot become one, and they cannot separate either.

In philosophizing on the ground of possible Existenz we presuppose this tension. The world, as *what can be known,* and Existenz, as *what must be elucidated,* are dialectically distinguished and then reconsidered as one.

Mundane being, the being we know, is *general* because it is generally valid for everyone. It is the common property of all rational creatures who can agree on its being the same thing they mean. Its validity applies, in the endlessness of real things, to the definable particular.

Existenz is *never general,* and thus not a case that might be subsumed as particular under a universal. Objectified as a phenomenon, however, Existenz is also the individuality of the historic particular. We still comprehend this under general categories, limited only by the endlessness of individual factuality, which makes the individual inexhaustible and thus ineffable. But individuality as such is not Existenz. All that it is, to begin with, is the visible profusion of mundane existence—a profusion whose existential originality can be examined by the questioner's self-being, but not by any knowledge.

The union of Existenz and the world is the incalculable process of which no one who is a part of it can be sure.

Possible Existenz Unsatisfied in Existence

1. Doubts of the Being of Existenz

Once we divorce Existenz from existence, from the world, and from a general character, there seems to be nothing left. Unless Existenz becomes an object, it seems a vain hope to think of it; such thinking cannot last or produce results, so the attempted conception of Existenz seems bound to destroy itself. We can doubt the being of Existenz in every respect and let common sense tell us to stick to objectivity as both real and true. Was the attempt the outgrowth of a chimera?

There is no way to remove our doubts about Existenz. It is neither knowable as existence nor extant as validity. We can deny Existenz as we can deny the content of any philosophical thought—as opposed to particular objective cognition, whose object is demonstrable. I can never say of myself what I am, as if I were demonstrably extant. Whatever can be said of me by way of objectification applies to my empirical individuality, and as this can be the phenomenon of my Existenz, it is not subject to any definitive psychological analysis either—a limit of my self-knowledge which indirectly points to something else, without ever being able to compel that something to become apparent. Hence the elucidation of Existenz is a deliverance but not a fulfillment, as knowledge would be; it widens my scope, but it does not create substance by demonstrating any being that I might objectively comprehend.

Since Existenz is thus inaccessible to one who asks about it in terms of the purely objective intellect, it remains subject to lasting doubt. Yet though no proof can force me to admit its being, my thinking is still not an end: it gets beyond the bounds of objective knowability in a *leap* that exceeds the capacity of rational insight. Philosophizing begins and ends at a point to which that leap takes me. Existenz is the *origin* of existential philosophizing, not its goal. Nor is its origin the same as its beginning, beyond which I would go on asking for an earlier beginning; it is not my license either, which would drive me to despair, and it is not a will resulting from the endlessness of questionable motivations. The origin is free being. This is what I transcend to as *philosophizing, not knowing, brings me to myself.* The helplessness to which philosophizing reduces me when I doubt its origin is an expression of the helplessness of my self-being, and the reality of philosophizing is the incipient upsurge of that self-being. The premise of philosophizing, therefore, is to *take hold* of Existenz—which begins as no more than a dark striving for sense and support, turns into doubt and despair as reminders of its derivation from the realm of possibility, and then appears as the incomprehensible certainty that is elucidated in philosophizing.

2.   *Being Unsatisfied as an Expression of Possible Existenz*

If I reduce all things to mundane existence, either in theory or in practice, I feel unsatisfied. This feeling is a negative origin; in separating Existenz from mundane existence it makes me sense the truth of that separation. As there is no knowledge for which the world is conclusive, no "right" order of existence that could possibly be definitive, and no absolute final goal that all might see as one, I cannot help getting more unsatisfied the clearer I am in my mind about what I know, and the more honest I am about the sense of what I am doing.

No reasons will sufficiently explain this feeling. It expresses the being of possible Existenz, which understands itself, not something else, when it declares itself unsatisfied. What I feel then is not the impotence of knowledge. It is not the emptiness at the end of all my achievements in a world in which I face the brink of nothingness. Instead, I feel a discontent that eggs me on.

An inexplicable discontent is a step out of mere existence, the step into the *solitude of possibility* where all mundane existence disappears. This solitude is not the resignation of the scientist who buries his hopes for a cognition of intrinsic being. It is not the irritation of the man of action who has come to doubt the point of all action. Nor is it the grief of a man in flight from himself and loath to be alone. Instead, after all these disillusionments, it is my dissatisfaction with existence at large, *my need to have my own origin.* To be unsatisfied is a condition inadequate to existence, and when this condition has opposed me to the world, it is my freedom that conquers all disenchantment and returns me to the world, to my fellow man with whom I ascertain the origin. I do not, however, comprehend all this in thoughtful reflection—which is indeed what fails me—but in the reality of my actions and in total foundering.

This possible conquest alone lends substance and significance to the otherwise irremovable relativity of theoretical *knowledge* and practical *action.*

I may well derive a peculiar and profound satisfaction from a theoretical knowledge of things in general, from surveying world images, from contemplating forms and existence, and from expanding all of this farther and farther, under ideas. But it is my dissatisfaction that makes me feel that this whole world, for all its universality and validity, is not all of being. My attitude in it is not one of curiosity about every particular, shared with a fellow scientist who might be interchangeable according to his function; it is an attitude of original curiosity about being itself, shared with a friend. What grips me is a communion in asking and answering questions, and a communication which within objective validity goes indirectly beyond it.

When I face objective tasks in *practical* life, when I deal with them and ask about their meaning, no meaning that I can grasp in the world will satisfy me. My sense of possible Existenz will not rest even if my conscious comprehension feeds on the idea of a whole in which I have my place and do my job. The thought of fulfillment in an entirety will come to be merely relative, like a temptation to conceal the boundary situations which break up any entirety. Though each idea of the whole is also a step beyond the fission into sheer coincidence, I am never able to survey the whole; eventually it will be back at the mercy of the accidents of mundane existence. A place within the whole, a place that would lend importance to the individual as a member of the body of this kind of being, is always questionable. But what remains to me as an individual is what never fits into a whole: the choice of my tasks and my striving for accomplishment are simultaneous manifestations of *another* origin, unless the annihilating thought that all I do might be senseless makes me shut my eyes. While I devote my empirical individuality to my finite tasks, my possible Existenz is more than that empirical individuality, and more than the objective, realistic impersonality of my political, scientific, or economic achievements. Although its essence is realized solely by this participation in the historic process of mundane existence, Existenz is at war with the lower depths of the encompassing world in which it finds itself. It is against those depths that, failing in the world, it seeks to hold its own in the eternity of intrinsic being.

Not unless it is indeed unsatisfied—both theoretically, with the mere knowledge and contemplation of all things in the world, and practically, with the mere performance of a task in an ideal entirety— can possible Existenz *utter* and understand this dissatisfaction. It is never *motivated* by generally valid reasons; those rather tend to induce contentment and tranquillity in the totality of a mundane existence permeated by the idea and thus spiritualized. The discontent of possible self-being has broken through mundane existence and cast the individual back upon himself, back to the origin that lets him deal with his world and, with his fellow, realize his Existenz.

3.   *The Breakthrough Ascertained in Existential Elucidation*

If I am unsatisfied and want to clarify this not just by setting myself apart but by positive thoughts on what this is all about, I come to existential elucidation.

As Existenz results from the real act of breaking through mundane existence, existential elucidation is the *thinking ascertainment* of that act. The breakthrough goes from possible Existenz to its realization, without being able to leave the borderline of possibility. To have its reality—although it is not objectively demonstrable—in action itself is the peculiar quality of Existenz. In its philosophical elucidation we pursue each thought that leads to the breakthrough, no matter from what side.

a. The breakthrough occurs at the *limits* of mundane existence. Philosophical thinking leads up to such limits and puts us in mind of the experiences they involve and of the appeal they issue. From the situations in the world, it leads to "boundary situations"; from empirical consciousness, to "absolute consciousness"; from actions qualified by their purposes, to "unconditional actions."

b. But the breakthrough still does not lead us out of the world. It occurs in the world, and so philosophical thought follows the appearance of Existenz in the world, in "historic consciousness" and in the "tension of subjectivity and objectivity" in its existence.

c. The breakthrough is *original*. Events happen in the world, but in the breakthrough something is settled by me. Existenz is certain that no part of intrinsic being can stay unsettled for it as a phenomenon in temporal existence. For either I allow the course of things to

decide *about* me—vanishing as myself, since there is no real decision when everything just *happens*—or I deal with being originally,
as myself, with the feeling that there must be a decision. My thought,
aimed at the origin, seeks to elucidate "freedom."

d. Nothing I know in the world can give me any reasons for my
decision; but what I am to decide can be grasped in the medium of
that knowledge. Existential elucidation pervades my existence in the
world, not in the sense that what matters were now known, but so I
can sense possibilities that may give me a grasp on truth—on what
is true as I *become* true. "I myself" and "communication" as the premise of self-being are the things we try to cover in the fundamental
thoughts of all existential elucidation.

Franz Kafka

(1883-1924)
GERMAN-CZECH

It is now standard to link Kafka with Camus as a prophet of the absurd, but this view ignores the ultimate despair of Kafka that Camus rejects. In *The Trial,* for example, Kafka presents us with a terrifyingly concrete representation of Kierkegaardian sin and guilt, secularized in a bizarre indictment without a charge, by a court that is as comical as it is absurd. Joseph K is arrested without reason, and his protests of his "rights" never seem to make contact with the Power of the mysterious court itself. In Kafka's short story "Metamorphosis" Gregor Samsa, a young executive type, awakens to find himself turned into a giant cockroach. Samsa's attempts to hold onto his bourgeois self-identity become more horrifying than the metamorphosis itself. For Kafka, the absurdity of sin and guilt lies not in the indifferent world but rather in the very indistinguishability of the subjective and the objective: What first appears as an accusation from the senseless legal system becomes more and more K's own consciousness of guilt; and the absurdity of Samsa's metamorphosis lies, not in the change itself, but in Samsa's unchanged self-consciousness. One might say that the basic difference between Camus and Kafka is that Camus attempts to provide an answer for the problem Kafka sees as inescapable.

The first selection here is a brilliant Kafkaesque gem, reflecting in a short matter-of-fact parable all the horror and absurdity of the life of the middle-class so bitterly rejected by Kierkegaard,

Nietzsche, and Hesse. The second selection is an early parable, later expanded and incorporated into the heart of *The Trial*.

❖ Couriers ❖

They were offered the choice between becoming kings or the couriers of kings. The way children would, they all wanted to be couriers. Therefore there are only couriers who hurry about the world, shouting to each other—since there are no kings—messages that have become meaningless. They would like to put an end to this miserable life of theirs but they dare not because of their oaths of service.

❖ Before the Law ❖

Before the Law stands a doorkeeper. To this doorkeeper there comes a man from the country and prays for admittance to the Law. But the doorkeeper says that he cannot grant admittance at the moment. The man thinks it over and then asks if he will be allowed in later. "It is possible," says the doorkeeper, "but not at the moment." Since the gate stands open, as usual, and the doorkeeper steps to one side, the man stoops to peer through the gateway into the interior. Observing that, the doorkeeper laughs and says: "If you are so drawn to it, just try to go in despite my veto. But take note: I am powerful. And I am only the least of the doorkeepers. From hall to hall there is one doorkeeper after another, each more powerful than the last. The third doorkeeper is already so terrible that even I cannot bear to look at him." These are difficulties the man from the country has not expected; the Law, he thinks, should surely be accessible at all times and to everyone, but as he now takes a closer look at the doorkeeper in his fur coat, with his big sharp nose and long, thin, black Tartar beard, he decides that it is better to wait until he gets permission to enter. The doorkeeper gives him a stool and lets him sit down at one side of the door. There he sits for days and years. He makes many attempts to be admitted, and wearies the doorkeeper by his importunity. The doorkeeper frequently has little interviews with him, asking him questions about his home and many other things; but the questions are put indifferently, as great lords put them, and always finish with the statement that he cannot be let in yet. The man, who has furnished himself with many things for his journey, sacrifices all he has, however valuable, to bribe the doorkeeper. The doorkeeper accepts everything, but always with the remark: "I am only taking it to keep you from thinking you have omitted anything." During these many years the man fixes his attention almost continuously on the doorkeeper. He forgets the other doorkeepers, and this first one seems to him the sole obstacle preventing access to the Law. He curses his bad luck, in his early years boldly and loudly, later, as he grows old, he only grumbles to himself. He becomes childish, and since in his yearlong contemplation of the doorkeeper he has come to know even the fleas in his fur collar, he begs the fleas as well to help him and to change the doorkeeper's mind. At length his eyesight begins to fail, and he does not know whether the world is really darker or whether his eyes are only deceiving him. Yet in his darkness he is now aware of a radiance that streams inextinguishably from the gateway of the Law. Now he has not very long to live. Before he dies, all his experiences in these long years gather themselves in his head to one point, a question he has not yet asked the doorkeeper. He waves him nearer, since he can no longer raise his stiffening body. The doorkeeper has to bend low towards him, for the difference in height between them has altered much to the man's disadvantage. "What do you want to know now?" asks the doorkeeper; "you are insatiable." "Everyone strives to reach the Law," says the man, "so how does it happen that for all these many years no one but myself has ever begged for admittance?" The doorkeeper recognizes that the man has reached his end, and to let his failing senses catch the words roars in his ear: "No one else could ever be admitted here, since this gate was made only for you. I am now going to shut it."

Gabriel Marcel

(1889–1973)
FRENCH

Marcel is frequently referred to by Sartre as the contemporary
proponent of "theistic existentialism." Marcel, less than charmed
by his association with Sartre's atheistic existentialism, prefers to
call his work "Neo-Socratic." After a series of horrible experiences during World War I, Marcel found himself incapable of abstract philosophical thinking: he insisted upon a "philosophy of
the concrete." In his development of this philosophy he independently formulated many of the central insights of Husserl's
phenomenology, Heidegger's ontology, Sartre's notion of freedom, and Merleau-Ponty's theories of intersubjectivity and the
role of the body in perception. His philosophy shares many sim-
ilarities with Kierkegaard's, notably the conception of God as an
absolute presence. But unlike Kierkegaard, Marcel does not
argue that belief in God requires an irrational leap of faith, nor
does he share Kierkegaard's insistence that each of us face God
alone. His religious concept of Being is defended more in a Hei-
deggerian way—as the presupposition of *Existenz*—rather than
as one possibility of irrational choice. But Marcel's concerns remain centered upon the notions of freedom and the individual,
and his insistence upon the immediacy of our life with others is
not to be taken as a return to the anonymous warmth of Kierkegaard's despised "public," as the following selection from *Man
Against Mass Society* will show.

❖ What Is a Free Man? ❖

A problem such as the one we are dealing with in this chapter, "What is a free man?" cannot, or so it seems to me, be usefully discussed in the abstract. It cannot be discussed, that is, out of the context of historical situations, considered in their concrete fullness; it is, for that matter, of the very essence of the human lot that man always is in a situation of some sort or other, and that is what a too abstract kind of humanism always runs the risk of forgetting. We are not therefore here asking ourselves what a free man is *in se,* what the essential notion of a free man is; for that question very possibly has no meaning at all. But we are asking ourselves how in an historical situation which is *our* situation, which we have to face here and now, man's freedom can be conceived, and how we can bear witness to it.

About seventy-five years ago, Nietzsche asserted: "God is dead." To-day, we can hear, not so much boldly asserted as muttered in anguish, a statement that seems to echo that of Nietzsche: "Man is in his death-throes." Let us make ourselves clear; this statement, by those who make it sincerely, is not intended to have the force of prophecy; at the level of reflective awareness (and it is at this level that the statement is made) we cannot make any sort of pronouncement at all on coming events, we are in fact even forced to acknowledge our ignorance of the future. And there is a sense in which we ought even to rejoice in that ignorance, for it is that ignorance alone which makes possible that perpetual hopeful betting on the future without which human activity, as such, would find itself radically inhibited. To say that man is in his death-throes is only to say that man to-day finds himself facing, not some external event, such as the annihilation of our planet, for instance, which might be the consequence of some catastrophe in the heavens, but rather possibilities of complete self-destruction inherent in himself. These possibilities, always latent, become patent from the moment in which man makes a bad use, or rather an impious use, of the powers that constitute his nature. I am thinking here both of the atomic bomb and of techniques of human degradation, as these have been put into effect in all totalitarian states without exception. Between the physical destruction wrought by the

From "What Is a Free Man?" in Man Against Mass Society *by Gabriel Marcel. Copyright 1962 by the Henry Regnery Company, Inc.*

atomic bomb, and the spiritual destruction wrought by techniques of human degradation there exists, quite certainly, a secret bond; it is precisely the duty of reflective thinking to lay bare that secret.

The relationship which can exist between the two statements, "God is dead," "Man is in his death-throes," is not only a complex relationship, but an ambiguous one. We can ask ourselves, for instance, whether Nietzsche's cry of exultation or pain did not, just like the modern cry of mere pain, presuppose a concrete historical situation; linked itself, like our situation, to a preliminary misuse of human powers, of which men at that time had been guilty. No doubt we ought to recognize that the relationship between the two statements, "God is dead," and "Man is in his death-throes," is concrete and existential, not logical: it is quite impossible to extract from Nietzsche's statement about God by any method of analysis the other statement about man, though Nietzsche perhaps would have accepted the statement about man, at least during the ultimate or penultimate period of his working life. Even if he had accepted it, however, he would probably not have perceived all the overtones in the statement, "Man is in his death-throes," which we can perceive to-day. Also (this is a strange reflection, but a true one) it is perhaps by starting from the statement, "Man is in his death-throes," that we may be able to question once more the statement, "God is dead," and to discover that God is living after all. It is, as the reader will soon discover, towards the latter conclusion that the whole of my subsequent argument tends.

But what we have to ask ourselves first is the following question: what becomes of freedom in a world in which man, or at least man at a certain level of self-awareness, is forced to recognize that he has entered into his death-throes?

At this point, however, we may be faced with a preliminary objection. It is one which presents itself readily to the mind. Might it not be convenient to say that the question, "What is a free man?" can only receive a positive answer in a country which has itself remained a free country?

However, the very notion of a free country or a free people, on a little analysis, appears to be a much less distinct notion than we should be tempted to think it at first. I shall take two examples: Switzerland, as the sequel to a process of political blackmail, found itself under the necessity of putting its factories to work for the benefit of Nazi Germany—was Switzerland still a free country? Sweden, at the end of the war, was obliged to conclude with Soviet Russia a very burdensome trade treaty, which had the effect of throttling her economic life. Ought not Sweden to have admitted to herself that— at the level of facts, if not at the level of words—she was no longer a free country? If the freedom of a people or a country be defined as *absolute independence,* is it not obvious that in a world like ours freedom cannot exist, not only because of inevitable economic interdependence, but because of the part played by pressure, or, less politely, by blackmail, at all levels of international intercourse?

Following out this line of thought, we should be led to acknowledge that the individual himself, in any country whatsoever, not only finds himself dependent but finds himself, in a great many cases, obliged to carry out actions which his conscience disapproves. (We have only to think, for instance, of military conscription and its consequences to become aware of this fact.) All that we can say is that in countries where there is still a recognition of what we can call in a very general fashion the rights of the human person, a certain number of guarantees of freedom survive: but we ought immediately to add that such guarantees are becoming less and less numerous and that, failing a very improbable reversal of the present general tendency of things, there will be a continuing demand for their further reduction. It would be contrary to the facts of the case to assert that men, in what we broadly call "the free countries," enjoy absolute independence. That does not matter so much, for, except to a pedantic type of anarchist, such absolute independence is inconceivable. But it would also be contrary to the facts to assert that men in free countries to-day generally possess the power to square their conduct with their consciences.

This is the point at which we ought to pass to the extreme case and ask ourselves what becomes of the freedom of the individual, even of what we call his inner freedom, in a totalitarian country. Here, I believe, we shall find ourselves forced to recognize an exceptionally important fact: Stoicism (and I am thinking less of an abstract philosophical doctrine than of a spiritual attitude) has been to-day, I shall not say refuted by the facts, but uprooted by them from the soil which used to nourish it. This ancient and respectable attitude rested on the distinction made so forcibly and severely by such writers as Epictetus, Seneca, and Marcus Aurelius: the distinction between what depends on my will, and what does not depend on it. Stoic thought, in so far as it was not merely formulated in abstract terms but adopted with dauntless courage as a way of life, implied a belief in the inner tribunal of conscience: a tribunal unviolated, and indeed inviolable, by any intrusion of external power. There can be no Stoicism without a belief in an inalienable inner sovereignty, an absolute possession of the self by the self.

However, the very essence of those modern techniques of degradation, to which I made an earlier allusion, consists precisely in putting the individual into a situation in which he loses touch with himself, in which he is literally beside himself, even to the point of being able sincerely to disavow acts into which nevertheless he had put sincerely his whole heart, or on the other hand of being able to confess to acts which he had not committed. I shall not attempt at this point to define the *kind* of sincerity, obviously a factitious and artificial kind, that we are talking of. I shall note merely that, though in recent years such techniques of degradation have been brought to an almost unimaginable degree of refinement, they were already in use in periods much earlier than ours. I was told recently that during the trial of the Knights Templars under Philip the Fair confessions were obtained by processes which cannot have consisted merely of physical torture; since later on, during a second and last retraction of their original confessions, the accused, once more in possession of their faculties, declared that they had originally *sincerely* accused themselves of acts which they *had not committed*. Physical torture by itself seems incapable of producing such sincerity; it can be evoked only by those abominable methods of *psychological* manipulation to which so many countries, in such various latitudes, have in recent years had recourse.

Given these conditions, the situation that each one of us must face to-day is as follows: (I say *each one of us,* supposing that we do not want to lie to ourselves or to commit the sin of unwarranted presumption; given that supposition, we must admit that there are real and practical methods that can be applied to any of us to-morrow with the effect of depriving us of self-sovereignty or, less grandiosely, of self-control: even though in another age we should have had sound reasons for regarding that self-sovereignty as infrangible and inviolable). Our situation, then, is this: we ought not even to say, as the Stoics said, that even at the very worst there remains for us the possibility of suicide, as a happy way out. That is no longer a true statement of the case. A man to-day can be put into a situation in which he *will no longer want to kill himself;* in which suicide will appear to him as an *illicit* or *unfair* way out; in which he will think of himself as under an obligation not merely to suffer, but to wish for, the punishment appropriate to crimes which he will impute to himself *without having committed them.*

It may be objected here that the mere mention of such horrible possibilities is itself dangerous, almost criminal. Certainly, if I were addressing myself to a class of schoolboys or students, it might be proper to leave this aspect of my subject in the shadow. But I am addressing myself to mature minds, minds I assume already capable of higher reflection; and on such minds, just because of their maturity, a real responsibility rests.

What we have to recognize is this. Thanks to the techniques of degradation it is creating and perfecting, a materialistic mode of thought, in our time, is showing itself capable of bringing into being a world which more and more *tends to verify its own materialistic postulates.* I mean that a human being who has undergone a certain type of psychological manipulation tends progressively to be reduced to the status of a mere *thing;* a psychic thing, of course, but nevertheless a thing which falls quite tidily within the province of the theories elaborated by an essentially materialistic psychology. This assertion of mine is, of course, obviously ambiguous; it does not mean that this materialistic psychology, with however startling powers of reductive transformation it may become endowed, will ever be of a nature to grasp and reveal to us reality as it is in itself. Rather, my assertion emphasizes the fact that there is nothing surprising for a philosophy like my own, a philosophy of man as a being in a situation, in the fact that man depends, to a very great degree, on the idea he has of himself and that this idea cannot be degraded without at the same time degrading man. This is one more reason, and on the face of things the most serious and imperative reason for condemning materialistic thinking, root and branch. And it is relevant to note here that in our day the materialistic attitude has acquired a virulence and a cohesion which it was far from possessing in the last century. It was a common spectacle then to see thinkers who regarded themselves as thoroughly imbued with materialistic principles showing in their personal lives all the scrupulosity of Kantian rigorists.

It may seem that I am rather straying here from the question which I set out to answer at the beginning of this chapter, "What is a free man?" But this is not in fact by any means the case, for it is very important for us to recognize, whatever fancies certain thinkers incapable of the least coherence may have had about this question, that a materialistic conception of the universe is radically incompatible with the idea of a free man: more precisely, that, in a society ruled by materialistic principles, freedom is transmuted into its opposite, or becomes merely the most treacherous and deceptive of empty slogans.

Theoretically, of course, we can imagine the possibility of man's preserving a minimum of independence even in a society ruled on materialistic principles; but, as we ought to be immediately aware, this possibility is an evanescent one, implying contradictions: for freedom in such a society would consist, if I may put it so, in rendering oneself sufficiently insignificant to escape the attention of the men in power. But is it not fairly obvious that this wish for insignificance, supposing even that it is a wish that can be put into effect, is already in a sense a suicidal wish? In such a society, the mere keeping, for instance, of an intimate diary might be a capital crime, and one does not see why, by the use of tape recorders and tapped telephones, as well as by various quite conceivable extensions of the use of radio, it should not be quite possible to keep the police well informed about the thoughts and the feelings of any individual whatsoever.[1] From the point of view of the individual in such a society, there is no conceivable way out at all: private life, as such, does not exist any more.

But let us imagine, then, the situation of our country immediately after a *putsch* or a *coup d'état:* if rebellion is futile, and a retreat into insignificance impracticable, what, supposing that we are fully aware of our situation, does there remain for us to do? At the risk of discontenting and even of shocking those who still tend to think of solutions for political problems in terms of positive action, I shall say that in that region all the ways of escape seem to me to be barred. Our own recourse can be to the Transcendent: but what does that mean? "The transcendent," "transcendence," these are words which among philosophers and intellectuals, for a good many years past, have been strangely misused. When I myself speak here of a recourse to the transcendent, I mean, as concretely as possible, that our only chance in the sort of horrible situation I have imagined is to appeal, I should perhaps *not* say to a power, but rather to a level of being, an order of the spirit, which is also the level and order of grace, of mercy, of charity; and to proclaim, while there is still time,

---

[1] See George Orwell's *1984.*

that is to say before the state's psychological manipulations have produced in us the alienation from our true selves that we fear, that we repudiate *in advance* the deeds and the acts that may be obtained from us by any sort of constraint whatsoever. We solemnly affirm, by this appeal to the transcendent, that the reality of our selves lies *beyond* any such acts and any such words. It will be said, no doubt, that by this gesture we are giving ourselves a very ideal, a very unreal, sort of satisfaction; but to say so is to fail to recognize the real nature of the thought which I am groping to put into shape. What we have to do is to proclaim that we do *not* belong entirely to the world of objects to which men are seeking to assimilate us, in which they are straining to imprison us. To put it very concretely indeed, we have to proclaim that this life of ours, which it has now become technically possible to make into a hideous and grimacing parody of all our dreams, may in reality be only the most insignificant aspect of a grand process unfolding itself far beyond the boundaries of the visible world. In other words, this amounts to saying that *all philosophies of immanence have had their day,* that in our own day they have revealed their basic unreality or, what is infinitely more serious, their complicity with those modern idolatries which it is our duty to denounce without pity: the idolatry of race, the idolatry of class. I should add here that even the authentic religions may become similarly degraded in their very principle of being. They too can degenerate into idolatries; especially where the will to power is waiting to corrupt them; and this, alas, is almost invariably the case when the Church becomes endowed with temporal authority.

But we are now on the road towards a number of pretty positive conclusions. I should formulate them as follows: a man cannot be free or remain free, except in the degree to which he remains linked with that which transcends him, whatever the particular form of that link may be: for it is pretty obvious that the form of the link need not reduce itself to official and canonical prayers. I should say that in the case particularly of the true artist in paint, or stone, or music, or words, this relationship to the transcendent is something that is experienced in the most authentic and profound way. I am supposing, of course, that he does not yield to the innumerable temptations to which the artist is exposed to-day: the temptation to startle, to innovate at all costs, to shut oneself up in a private world leaving as few channels as possible open for communication with the world of eternal forms: and so on. But nothing could be falser and more dangerous than to base on these observations of mine some sort of neoaestheticism. We have to recognize that there are modes of creation which do not belong to the aesthetic order, and which are within the reach of everybody; and it is in so far as he is a creator, at however humble a level, that any man at all can recognize his own freedom. It would be necessary, moreover, to show that the idea of being creative, taken in this quite general sense, always implies the idea of being open towards others: that openness I have called in my Gifford Lectures, intersubjectivity, whether that is conceived as *agape* (charity) or *philia* (attachment): these two notions, in any case, I think, tend ultimately to converge. But what must be stated as forcibly as possible is that societies built on a materialistic basis, whatever place they tactfully leave for a collective and at bottom purely animal exaltation, sin radically against intersubjectivity; they exclude it in principle; and it is because they exclude it, that they grub up every possible freedom by its roots.

It is quite conceivable—and I put this idea forward not as an abstract hypothesis but as a familiar fact—that in a country enslaved by a totalitarian power, a man might find himself constrained, not merely in order to live but in order to draw his dependents from a state of absolute wretchedness, to accept, for instance, a job with the security police: a job which might compel him to carry out acts absolutely repugnant to his conscience. Is mere refusal to carry out such acts a solution to his problem? We may doubt this, for the very reason that such a refusal might entail direful consequences not only for the man himself but for his innocent dependents. But it could happen that the man who accepted such a job might make a religious vow to use the share of power which he has been given so much as possible to help the very people of whom he was officially the persecutor. Such a vow, with the creative power that it re-bestows on him who makes it, is a concrete example of that recourse to the transcendent of which I spoke earlier on. But it is obvious that there is nothing in such an extremely particular case out of which any general rule can be framed. A rigoristic moral formalism, an attempt to bring all human acts under very general rules, ceases almost entirely to be acceptable as soon as one becomes aware of that element of the unique and the incommensurable which is the portion of every concrete being, confronted with a concrete situation. No two beings, and no two situations, are really commensurable with each other. To become aware of this fact is to undergo a sort of crisis. But it is with the crisis in our moral awareness as a starting-point, that there becomes possible that cry from us towards the creative principle, and that demand by it on us, which each must answer in his own way, if he does not wish to become an accomplice of what Simone Weil called "the gross beast." In our world as it is to-day there can be hardly any set of circumstances in which we may not be forced to ask ourselves whether, through our free choice, through our particular decisions, we are not going to make ourselves guilty of just such a complicity.

Albert Camus

(1913–1960)
ALGERIAN-FRENCH

Camus is described by Sartre, in the obituary he wrote at the tragic end of a long and sometimes bitter feud between them, as the "Cartesian of the absurd," the "stubborn humanist." Whereas ambiguity, alienation, anxiety, *Existenz,* the polarity of for-itself/in-itself, are central in other authors, the key concept in Camus's philosophy is the "absurd," the confrontation between "rational man and the indifferent universe." Against the absurd there is rebellion, the scorn of Sisyphus, the "revolt of the flesh," the "I rebel, therefore we exist." For Camus there is no Kierkegaardian leap, which he degrades as "philosophical suicide"; there is no appeal to transcendence, which he dismisses as pointless hope; nor is there any role in Camus's philosophy for Sartre's notion of existential commitment. Rather, the point is to "keep the absurd alive." Politically, Camus's philosophical neglect of commitment manifests itself in his painful debates with Sartre and Merleau-Ponty. Always the moralist, the pacifist, Camus is hesitant about taking sides in the Algerian war, finding himself, like Meursault in *The Stranger* and like Clamence in *The Fall,* often feeling for both sides at once. He sympathizes with Sartre's and Merleau-Ponty's efforts to inaugurate a new Left, but he continuously moves away as they find themselves increasingly in alliance with the Communist Party. Camus objects to their Marxism, their lack of humanity, their violence, and their belief that ends justify means (a topic that ruptured

Camus's friendships with both Sartre and Merleau-Ponty). Central to Camus's works is a resolute moralistic concern with good and evil, the source of the absurd in *The Myth of Sisyphus,* the source of guilt in *The Fall.* In *The Stranger,* Camus creates an innocent young man whom he describes elsewhere as "totally honest," but honest in a peculiar way. He never reflects and thus never sees the significance of his actions. After committing a bizarre murder, neither intentional nor unintentional, Meursault (in the following selection) comes, while facing death, to the hesitant recognition of the absurd. In *The Fall* Clamence (a pseudonym) relates in restrospect his lucidity regarding the absurdity of his previous self-esteem as a successful defender of good causes and his "fall" into the role of Judge-Penitent. He is resentfully "happy" as Sisyphus is "happy," in scorn and in constant recognition of his avoidance of judgment ("Judge that ye not be judged").

❖ *from* The Stranger ❖

Then all day there was my appeal to think about. I made the most of this idea, studying my effects so as to squeeze out the maximum of consolation. Thus, I always began by assuming the worst; my appeal was dismissed. That meant, of course, I was to die. Sooner than others, obviously. "But," I reminded myself, "it's common knowledge that life isn't worth living, anyhow." And, on a wide view, I could see that it makes little difference whether one dies at the age of thirty or three-score and ten—since, in either case, other men and women will continue living, the world will go on as before. Also, whether I died now or forty years hence, this business of dying had to be got through, inevitably. Still, somehow this line of thought wasn't as consoling as it should have been; the idea of all those years of life in hand was a galling reminder! However, I could argue myself out of it, by picturing what would have been my feelings when my term was up, and death had cornered me. Once you're up against it, the precise manner of your death has obviously small importance. Therefore—but it was hard not to lose the thread of the argument leading up to that "therefore"—I should be prepared to face the dismissal of my appeal.

• • •

The chaplain gazed at me with a sort of sadness. I now had my back to the wall and light was flowing over my forehead. He muttered some words I didn't catch; then abruptly asked if he might kiss me. I said, "No." Then he turned, came up to the wall, and slowly drew his hand along it.

"Do you really love these earthly things so very much?" he asked in a low voice.

I made no reply.

For quite a while he kept his eyes averted. His presence was getting more and more irksome, and I was on the point of telling him to go, and leave me in peace, when all of a sudden he swung around on me, and burst out passionately:

"No! No! I refuse to believe it. I'm sure you've often wished there was an afterlife."

Of course I had, I told him. Everybody has that wish at times. But that had no more importance than wishing to be rich, or to swim very fast, or to have a better-shaped mouth. It was in the same order of things. I was going on in the same vein, when he cut in with a question. How did I picture the life after the grave?

I fairly bawled out at him: "A life in which I can remember this life on earth. That's all I want of it." And in the same breath I told him I'd had enough of his company.

But, apparently, he had more to say on the subject of God. I went close up to him and made a last attempt to explain that I'd very little time left, and I wasn't going to waste it on God.

Then he tried to change the subject by asking me why I hadn't once addressed him as "Father," seeing that he was a priest. That irritated me still more, and I told him he wasn't my father; quite the contrary, he was on the others' side.

"No, no, my son," he said, laying his hand on my shoulder. "I'm on *your* side, though you don't realize it—because your heart is hardened. But I shall pray for you."

Then, I don't know how it was, but something seemed to break inside me, and I started yelling at the top of my voice. I hurled insults at him, I told him not to waste his rotten prayers on me; it was better to burn than to disappear. I'd taken him by the neckband of his cassock, and, in a sort of ecstasy of joy and rage, I poured out on him all the thoughts that had been simmering in my brain. He seemed so cocksure, you see. And yet none of his certainties was worth one strand of a woman's hair. Living as he did, like a corpse, he couldn't even be sure of being alive. It might look as if my hands were empty. Actually, I was sure of myself, sure about everything, far surer than he; sure of my present life and of the death that was coming. That, no doubt, was all I had; but at least that certainty was something I could get my teeth into—just as it had got its teeth into me. I'd been right, I was still right, I was always right. I'd passed my life in a certain way, and I might have passed it in a different way, if I'd felt like it. I'd acted thus, and I hadn't acted otherwise; I hadn't done x, whereas I had done y or z. And what did that mean? That, all the time, I'd been waiting for this present moment, for that dawn, tomorrow's or another day's, which was to justify me. Nothing, nothing had the least importance, and I knew quite well why. He, too, knew why. From the dark horizon of my future a sort of slow, persistent breeze had been blowing toward me, all my life long, from the years that were to come. And on its way that breeze had leveled out all the ideas that people tried to foist on me in the equally unreal years I then was living through. What difference could they make to me, the deaths of others, or a mother's love, or his God; or the way a man decides to live, the fate he thinks he chooses, since one and the same fate was bound to "choose" not only me but thousands of millions of privileged people who, like him, called themselves my brothers. Surely, surely he must see that? Every man alive was privileged; there was only one class of men, the privileged class. All alike would be condemned to die one day; his turn, too, would come like the others'. And what difference could it make if, after being charged with murder, he were executed because he didn't weep at his mother's funeral, since it all came to the same thing in the end? The same thing for Salamano's wife and for Salamano's dog. That little robot woman was as "guilty" as the girl from Paris who had married Masson, or as Marie, who wanted me to marry her. What did it matter if Raymond was as much my pal as Céleste, who was a far worthier man? What did it matter if at this very moment Marie was kissing a new boy friend? As a condemned man himself, couldn't he grasp what I meant by that dark wind blowing from my future? . . .

I had been shouting so much that I'd lost my breath, and just then the jailers rushed in and started trying to release the chaplain from my grip. One of them made as if to strike me. The chaplain quietened them down, then gazed at me for a moment without speaking. I could see tears in his eyes. Then he turned and left the cell.

Once he'd gone, I felt calm again. But all this excitement had exhausted me and I dropped heavily on to my sleeping plank. I must have had a longish sleep, for, when I woke, the stars were shining down on my face. Sounds of the countryside came faintly in, and the cool night air, veined with smells of earth and salt, fanned my cheeks. The marvelous peace of the sleepbound summer night flooded through me like a tide. Then, just on the edge of daybreak, I heard a steamer's siren. People were starting on a voyage to a world which had ceased to concern me forever. Almost for the first time in many months I thought of my mother. And now, it seemed to me, I understood why at her life's end she had taken on a "fiancé"; why she'd played at making a fresh start. There, too, in that Home where lives were flickering out, the dusk came as a mournful solace. With death so near, Mother must have felt like someone on the brink of freedom, ready to start life all over again. No one, no one in the world had any right to weep for her. And I, too, felt ready to start life all over again. It was as if that great rush of anger had washed me clean, emptied me of hope, and, gazing up at the dark sky spangled with its signs and stars, for the first time, the first, I laid my heart open to the benign indifference of the universe. To feel it so like myself, indeed, so brotherly, made me realize that I'd been happy, and that I was happy still. For all to be accomplished, for me to feel less lonely, all that remained to hope was that on the day of my execution there should be a huge crowd of spectators and that they should greet me with howls of execration.

❖ *from* The Myth of Sisyphus ❖

An Absurd Reasoning

There is but one truly serious philosophical problem, and that is suicide. Judging whether life is or is not worth living amounts to an-

From The Myth of Sisyphus *by Albert Camus, translated by Justin O'Brien. Copyright* © *1955, by Alfred A. Knopf, 1983. Used by permission of Alfred A. Knopf, a division of Random House, Inc.*

swering the fundamental question of philosophy. All the rest—whether or not the world has three dimensions, whether the mind has nine or twelve categories—comes afterwards. These are games; one must first answer. And if it is true, as Nietzsche claims, that a philosopher, to deserve our respect, must preach by example, you can appreciate the importance of that reply, for it will precede the definitive act. These are facts the heart can feel; yet they call for careful study before they become clear to the intellect.

If I ask myself how to judge that this question is more urgent than that, I reply that one judges by the actions it entails. I have never seen anyone die for the ontological argument. Galileo, who held a scientific truth of great importance, abjured it with the greatest ease as soon as it endangered his life. In a certain sense, he did right.[1] That truth was not worth the stake. Whether the earth or the sun revolves around the other is a matter of profound indifference. To tell the truth, it is a futile question. On the other hand, I see many people die because they judge that life is not worth living. I see others paradoxically getting killed for the ideas or illusions that give them a reason for living (what is called a reason for living is also an excellent reason for dying). I therefore conclude that the meaning of life is the most urgent of questions. How to answer it? On all essential problems (I mean thereby those that run the risk of leading to death or those that intensify the passion of living) there are probably but two methods of thought: the method of La Palisse and the method of Don Quixote. Solely the balance between evidence and lyricism can allow us to achieve simultaneously emotion and lucidity. In a subject at once so humble and so heavy with emotion, the learned and classical dialectic must yield, one can see, to a more modest attitude of mind deriving at once and the same time from common sense and understanding.

Suicide has never been dealt with except as a social phenomenon. On the contrary, we are concerned here, at the outset, with the relationship between individual thought and suicide. An act like this is prepared within the silence of the heart, as is a great work of art. The man himself is ignorant of it. One evening he pulls the trigger or jumps. Of an apartment-building manager who had killed himself I was told that he had lost his daughter five years before, that he had

---

[1] From the point of view of the relative value of truth. On the other hand, from the point of view of virile behavior, this scholar's fragility may well make us smile.

changed greatly since, and that that experience had "undermined" him. A more exact word cannot be imagined. Beginning to think is beginning to be undermined. Society has but little connection with such beginnings. The worm is in man's heart. That is where it must be sought. One must follow and understand this fatal game that leads from lucidity in the face of existence to flight from light.

There are many causes for a suicide, and generally the most obvious ones were not the most powerful. Rarely is suicide committed (yet the hypothesis is not excluded) through reflection. What sets off the crisis is almost always unverifiable. Newspapers often speak of "personal sorrows" or of "incurable illness." These explanations are plausible. But one would have to know whether a friend of the desperate man had not that very day addressed him indifferently. He is the guilty one. For that is enough to precipitate all the rancors and all the boredom still in suspension.[2]

But if it is hard to fix the precise instant, the subtle step when the mind opted for death, it is easier to deduce from the act itself the consequences it implies. In a sense, and as in melodrama, killing yourself amounts to confessing. It is confessing that life is too much for you or that you do not understand it. Let's not go too far in such analogies, however, but rather return to everyday words. It is merely confessing that that "is not worth the trouble." Living, naturally, is never easy. You continue making the gestures commanded by existence for many reasons, the first of which is habit. Dying voluntarily implies that you have recognized, even instinctively, the ridiculous character of that habit, the absence of any profound reason for living, the insane character of that daily agitation, and the uselessness of suffering.

What, then, is that incalculable feeling that deprives the mind of the sleep necessary to life? A world that can be explained even with bad reasons is a familiar world. But, on the other hand, in a universe suddenly divested of illusions and lights, man feels an alien, a stranger. His exile is without remedy since he is deprived of the memory of a lost home or the hope of a promised land. This divorce between man and his life, the actor and his setting, is properly the feeling of absurdity. All healthy men having thought of their own sui-

---

[2] Let us not miss this opportunity to point out the relative character of this essay. Suicide may indeed be related to much more honorable considerations—for example, the political suicides of protest, as they were called, during the Chinese revolution.

cide, it can be seen, without further explanation, that there is a direct connection between this feeling and the longing for death.

• • •

Like great works, deep feelings always mean more than they are conscious of saying. The regularity of an impulse or a repulsion in a soul is encountered again in habits of doing or thinking, is reproduced in consequences of which the soul itself knows nothing. Great feelings take with them their own universe, splendid or abject. They light up with their passion an exclusive world in which they recognize their climate. There is a universe of jealousy, of ambition, of selfishness, or of generosity. A universe—in other words, a metaphysic and an attitude of mind. What is true of already specialized feelings will be even more so of emotions basically as indeterminate, simultaneously as vague and as "definite," as remote and as "present" as those furnished us by beauty or aroused by absurdity.

At any streetcorner the feeling of absurdity can strike any man in the face. As it is, in its distressing nudity, in its light without effulgence, it is elusive. But that very difficulty deserves reflection. It is probably true that a man remains forever unknown to us and that there is in him something irreducible that escapes us. But *practically* I know men and recognize them by their behavior, by the totality of their deeds, by the consequences caused in life by their presence. Likewise, all those irrational feelings which offer no purchase to analysis. I can define them *practically,* appreciate them *practically,* by gathering together the sum of their consequences in the domain of the intelligence, by seizing and noting all their aspects, by outlining their universe. It is certain that apparently, though I have seen the same actor a hundred times, I shall not for that reason know him any better personally. Yet if I add up the heroes he has personified and if I say that I know him a little better at the hundredth character counted off, this will be felt to contain an element of truth. For this apparent paradox is also an apologue. There is a moral to it. It teaches that a man defines himself by his make-believe as well as by his sincere impulses. There is thus a lower key of feelings, inaccessible in the heart but partially disclosed by the acts they imply and the attitudes of mind they assume. It is clear that in this way I am defining a method. But it is also evident that that method is one of analysis and not of knowledge. For methods imply metaphysics; unconsciously they disclose conclusions that they often claim not to know yet. Similarly, the last pages of a book are already contained in the first pages. Such a link is inevitable. The method defined here acknowledges the feeling that all true knowledge is impossible. Solely appearances can be enumerated and the climate make itself felt.

Perhaps we shall be able to overtake that elusive feeling of absurdity in the different but closely related worlds of intelligence, of the art of living, or of art itself. The climate of absurdity is in the beginning. The end is the absurd universe and that attitude of mind which lights the world with its true colors to bring out the privileged and implacable visage which that attitude has discerned in it.

All great deeds and all great thoughts have a ridiculous beginning. Great works are often born on a streetcorner or in a restaurant's revolving door. So it is with absurdity. The absurd world more than others derives its nobility from that abject birth. In certain situations, replying "nothing" when asked what one is thinking about may be pretense in a man. Those who are loved are well aware of this. But if that reply is sincere, if it symbolizes that odd state of soul in which the void becomes eloquent, in which the chain of daily gestures is broken, in which the heart vainly seeks the link that will connect it again, then it is as it were the first sign of absurdity.

It happens that the stage sets collapse. Rising, streetcar, four hours in the office or the factory, meal, streetcar, four hours of work, meal, sleep, and Monday Tuesday Wednesday Thursday Friday and Saturday according to the same rhythm—this path is easily followed most of the time. But one day the "why" arises and everything begins in that weariness tinged with amazement. "Begins"—this is important. Weariness comes at the end of the acts of a mechanical life, but at the same time it inaugurates the impulse of consciousness. It awakens consciousness and provokes what follows. What follows is the gradual return into the chain or it is the definitive awakening. At the end of the awakening comes, in time, the consequence: suicide or recovery. In itself weariness has something sickening about it. Here, I must conclude that it is good. For everything begins with consciousness and nothing is worth anything except through it. There is nothing original about these remarks. But they are obvious; that is enough for a while, during a sketchy reconnaissance in the origins of the absurd. Mere "anxiety," as Heidegger says, is at the source of everything.

Likewise and during every day of an unillustrious life, time carries us. But a moment always comes when we have to carry it. We live on the future: "tomorrow," "later on," "when you have made your way," "you will understand when you are old enough." Such irrelevancies are wonderful, for, after all, it's a matter of dying. Yet a day comes when a man notices or says that he is thirty. Thus he asserts his youth. But simultaneously he situates himself in relation to time. He takes his place in it. He admits that he stands at a certain point on a curve that he acknowledges having to travel to its end. He belongs to time, and by the horror that seizes him, he recognizes his worst enemy. Tomorrow, he was longing for tomorrow, whereas everything in him ought to reject it. That revolt of the flesh is the absurd.[3]

A step lower and strangeness creeps in: perceiving that the world is "dense," sensing to what a degree a stone is foreign and irreducible to us, with what intensity nature or a landscape can negate us. At the heart of all beauty lies something inhuman, and these hills, the softness of the sky, the outline of these trees at this very minutes lose the illusory meaning with which we had clothed them, henceforth more remote than a lost paradise. The primitive hostility of the world rises up to face us across millennia. For a second we cease to understand it because for centuries we have understood in it solely the images and designs that we had attributed to it beforehand, because henceforth we lack the power to make use of that artifice. The world evades us because it becomes itself again. That stage scenery masked by habit becomes again what it is. It withdraws at a distance from us. Just as there are days when under the familiar face of a woman, we see as a stranger her we had loved months or years ago, perhaps we shall come even to desire what suddenly leaves us so alone. But the time has not yet come. Just one thing: that denseness and that strangeness of the world is the absurd.

Men, too, secrete the inhuman. At certain moments of lucidity, the mechanical aspect of their gestures, their meaningless pantomime makes silly everything that surrounds them. A man is talking on the telephone behind a glass partition; you cannot hear him, but you see his incomprehensible dumb show: you wonder why he is alive. This discomfort in the face of man's own inhumanity, this incalculable tumble before the image of what we are, this "nausea," as a writer of today calls it, is also the absurd. Likewise the stranger who at certain

---

[3] But not in the proper sense. This is not a definition, but rather an enumeration of the feelings that may admit of the absurd. Still, the enumeration finished, the absurd has nevertheless not been exhausted.

seconds comes to meet us in a mirror, the familiar and yet alarming brother we encounter in our own photographs is also the absurd.

• • •

Now I can broach the notion of suicide. It has already been felt what solution might be given. At this point the problem is reversed. It was previously a question of finding out whether or not life had to have a meaning to be lived. It now becomes clear, on the contrary, that it will be lived all the better if it has no meaning. Living an experience, a particular fate, is accepting it fully. Now, no one will live this fate, knowing it to be absurd, unless he does everything to keep before him that absurd brought to light by consciousness. Negating one of the terms of the opposition on which he lives amounts to escaping it. To abolish conscious revolt is to elude the problem. The theme of permanent revolution is thus carried into individual experience. Living is keeping the absurd alive. Keeping it alive is, above all, contemplating it. Unlike Eurydice, the absurd dies only when we turn away from it. One of the only coherent philosophical positions is thus revolt. It is a constant confrontation between man and his own obscurity. It is an insistence upon an impossible transparency. It challenges the world anew every second. Just as danger provided man the unique opportunity of seizing awareness, so metaphysical revolt extends awareness to the whole of experience. It is that constant presence of man in his own eyes. It is not aspiration, for it is devoid of hope. That revolt is the certainty of a crushing fate, without the resignation that ought to accompany it.

This is where it is seen to what a degree absurd experience is remote from suicide. It may be thought that suicide follows revolt—but wrongly. For it does not represent the logical outcome of revolt. It is just the contrary by the consent it presupposes. Suicide, like the leap, is acceptance at its extreme. Everything is over and man returns to his essential history. His future, his unique and dreadful future—he sees and rushes toward it. In its way, suicide settles the absurd. It engulfs the absurd in the same death. But I know that in order to keep alive, the absurd cannot be settled. It escapes suicide to the extent that it is simultaneously awareness and rejection of death. It is, at the extreme limit of the condemned man's last thought, that shoelace that despite everything he sees a few yards away, on the very brink of his dizzying fall. The contrary of suicide, in fact, is the man condemned to death.

That revolt gives life its value. Spread out over the whole length of a life, it restores its majesty to that life. To a man devoid of blinders, there is no finer sight than that of the intelligence at grips with a reality that transcends it. The sight of human pride is unequaled. No disparagement is of any use. That discipline that the mind imposes on itself, that will conjured up out of nothing, that face-to-face struggle have something exceptional about them. To impoverish that reality whose inhumanity constitutes man's majesty is tantamount to impoverishing him himself. I understand then why the doctrines that explain everything to me also debilitate me at the same time. They relieve me of the weight of my own life, and yet I must carry it alone. At this juncture, I cannot conceive that a skeptical metaphysics can be joined to an ethics of renunciation.

Consciousness and revolt, these rejections are the contrary of renunciation. Everything that is indomitable and passionate in a human heart quickens them, on the contrary, with its own life. It is essential to die unreconciled and not of one's own free will. Suicide is a repudiation. The absurd man can only drain everything to the bitter end, and deplete himself. The absurd is his extreme tension, which he maintains constantly by solitary effort, for he knows that in that consciousness and in that day-to-day revolt he gives proof of his only truth, which is defiance. This is a first consequence.

• • •

But what does life mean in such a universe? Nothing else for the moment but indifference to the future and a desire to use up everything that is given. Belief in the meaning of life always implies a scale of values, a choice, our preferences. Belief in the absurd, according to our definitions, teaches the contrary. But this is worth examining.

Knowing whether or not one can live *without appeal* is all that interests me. I do not want to get out of my depth. This aspect of life being given me, can I adapt myself to it? Now, faced with this particular concern, belief in the absurd is tantamount to substituting the quantity of experiences for the quality. If I convince myself that this life has no other aspect than that of the absurd, if I feel that its whole equilibrium depends on that perpetual opposition between my conscious revolt and the darkness in which it struggles, if I admit that my freedom has no meaning except in relation to its limited fate, then I must say that what counts is not the best living but the most living.

It is not up to me to wonder if this is vulgar or revolting, elegant or deplorable. Once and for all, value judgments are discarded here in favor of factual judgments. I have merely to draw the conclusions from what I can see and to risk nothing that is hypothetical. Supposing that living in this way were not honorable, then true propriety would command me to be dishonorable.

The most living; in the broadest sense, that rule means nothing. It calls for definition. It seems to begin with the fact that the notion of quantity has not been sufficiently explored. For it can account for a large share of human experience. A man's rule of conduct and his scale of values have no meaning except through the quantity and variety of experiences he has been in a position to accumulate. Now, the conditions of modern life impose on the majority of men the same quantity of experiences and consequently the same profound experience. To be sure, there must also be taken into consideration the individual's spontaneous contribution, the "given" element in him. But I cannot judge of that, and let me repeat that my rule here is to get along with the immediate evidence. I see, then, that the individual character of a common code of ethics lies not so much in the ideal importance of its basic principles as in the norm of an experience that it is possible to measure. To stretch a point somewhat, the Greeks had the code of their leisure just as we have the code of our eight-hour day. But already many men among the most tragic cause us to foresee that a longer experience changes this table of values. They make us imagine that adventurer of the everyday who through mere quantity of experiences would break all records (I am purposely using this sports expression) and would thus win his own code of ethics. Yet let's avoid romanticism and just ask ourselves what such an attitude may mean to a man with his mind made up to take up his bet and to observe strictly what he takes to be the rules of the game.

Breaking all the records is first and foremost being faced with the world as often as possible. How can that be done without contradictions and without playing on words? For on the one hand the absurd teaches that all experiences are unimportant, and on the other it urges toward the greatest quantity of experiences. How, then, can one fail to do as so many of those men I was speaking of earlier—choose the form of life that brings us the most possible of that human matter, thereby introducing a scale of values that on the other hand one claims to reject?

But again it is the absurd and its contradictory life that teaches us. For the mistake is thinking that that quantity of experiences depends on the circumstances of our life when it depends solely on us. Here we have to be over-simple. To two men living the same number of years, the world always provides the same sum of experiences. It is up to us to be conscious of them. Being aware of one's life, one's revolt, one's freedom, and to the maximum, is living, and to the maximum. Where lucidity dominates, the scale of values becomes useless. Let's be even more simple. Let us say that the sole obstacle, the sole deficiency to be made good, is constituted by premature death. Thus it is that no depth, no emotion, no passion, and no sacrifice could render equal in the eyes of the absurd man (even if he wished it so) a conscious life of forty years and a lucidity spread over sixty years. Madness and death are his irreparables. Man does not choose. The absurd and the extra life it involves *therefore do not depend on man's will,* but on its contrary, which is death. Weighing words carefully, it is altogether a question of luck. One just has to be able to consent to this. There will never be any substitute for twenty years of life and experience.

By what is an odd inconsistency in such an alert race, the Greeks claimed that those who died young were beloved of the gods. And that is true only if you are willing to believe that entering the ridiculous world of the gods is forever losing the purest of joys, which is feeling, and feeling on this earth. The present and the succession of presents before a constantly conscious soul is the ideal of the absurd man. But the word "ideal" rings false in this connection. It is not even his vocation, but merely the third consequence of his reasoning. Having started from an anguished awareness of the inhuman, the meditation on the absurd returns at the end of its itinerary to the very heart of the passionate flames of human revolt.

Thus I draw from the absurd three consequences, which are my revolt, my freedom, and my passion. By the mere activity of consciousness I transform into a rule of life what was an invitation to death—and I refuse suicide. I know, to be sure, the dull resonance that vibrates throughout these days. Yet I have but a word to say: that it is necessary.

• • •

The preceding merely defines a way of thinking. But the point is to live.

The Myth of Sisyphus

The gods had condemned Sisyphus to ceaselessly rolling a rock to the top of a mountain, whence the stone would fall back of its own weight. They had thought with some reason that there is no more dreadful punishment than futile and hopeless labor.

• • •

You have already grasped that Sisyphus is the absurd hero. He *is,* as much through his passions as through his torture. His scorn of the gods, his hatred of death, and his passion for life won him that unspeakable penalty in which the whole being is exerted toward accomplishing nothing. This is the price that must be paid for the passions of this earth.

• • •

If this myth is tragic, that is because its hero is conscious. Where would his torture be, indeed, if at every step the hope of succeeding upheld him? The workman of today works every day in his life at the same tasks, and this fate is no less absurd. But it is tragic only at the rare moments when it becomes conscious. Sisyphus, proletarian of the gods, powerless and rebellious, knows the whole extent of his wretched condition: it is what he thinks of during his descent. The lucidity that was to constitute his torture at the same time crowns his victory. There is no fate that cannot be surmounted by scorn.

• • •

All Sisyphus' silent joy is contained therein. His fate belongs to him. His rock is his thing. Likewise, the absurd man, when he contemplates his torment, silences all the idols. In the universe suddenly restored to its silence, the myriad wondering little voices of the earth rise up. Unconscious, secret calls, invitations from all the faces, they are the necessary reverse and price of victory. There is no sun without shadow, and it is essential to know the night. The absurd man says yes and his effort will henceforth be unceasing. If there is a personal fate, there is no higher destiny, or at least there is but one which he concludes is inevitable and despicable. For the rest, he knows himself to be the master of his days. At that subtle moment when man glances backward over his life, Sisyphus returning toward his rock, in that slight pivoting he contemplates that series of unrelated actions which becomes his fate, created by him, combined under his memory's eye and soon sealed by his death. Thus, convinced of the wholly human origin of all that is human, a blind man eager to see who knows that the night has no end, he is still on the go. The rock is still rolling.

I leave Sisyphus at the foot of the mountain! One always finds one's burden again. But Sisyphus teaches the higher fidelity that negates the gods and raises rocks. He too concludes that all is well. This universe henceforth without a master seems to him neither sterile nor futile. Each atom of that stone, each mineral flake of that night-filled mountain, in itself forms a world. The struggle itself toward the heights is enough to fill a man's heart. One must imagine Sisyphus happy.

❖ *from* The Fall ❖

You don't understand what I mean? I'll admit my fatigue. I lose the thread of what I am saying; I've lost that lucidity to which my friends used to enjoy paying respects. I say "my friends," moreover, as a convention. I have no more friends; I have nothing but accomplices. To make up for this their number has increased; they are the whole human race. And within the human race, you first of all. Whoever is at hand is always the first. How do I know I have no friends? It's very easy: I discovered it the day I thought of killing myself to play a trick on them, to punish them, in a way. But punish whom? Some would be surprised, and no one would feel punished. I realized I had no friends. Besides, even if I had had, I shouldn't be any better off. If I had been able to commit suicide and then see their reaction, why then the game would have been worth the candle. But the earth is dark, *cher ami,* the coffin thick, and the shroud opaque. The eyes of the soul—to be sure—if there is a soul and it has eyes! But you see, we're not sure, we can't be sure. Otherwise, there would be a solution; at least one could get oneself taken seriously. Men are never convinced of your reasons, of your sincerity, of the seriousness of your sufferings, except by your death. So long as you are alive, your case is doubtful; you have a right only to their skepticism. So if there were the least certainty that one could enjoy the show, it would be worth proving to them what they are unwilling to believe and thus amazing them. But you kill yourself and what does it matter whether or not they believe you? You are not there to see their amazement and their contrition (fleeting at best), to witness, according to every man's dream, your own funeral. In order to cease being a doubtful case, one has to cease being, that's all.

Besides, isn't it better thus? We'd suffer too much from their indifference. "You'll pay for this!" a daughter said to her father who had prevented her from marrying a too well groomed suitor. And she killed herself. But the father paid for nothing. He loved fly-casting. Three Sundays later he went back to the river—to forget, as he said. He was right; he forgot. To tell the truth, the contrary would have been surprising. You think you are dying to punish your wife and actually you are freeing her. It's better not to see that. Besides the fact that you might hear the reasons they give for your action. As far as I am concerned, I can hear them now: "He killed himself because he couldn't bear . . ." Ah, *cher ami,* how poor in invention men are! They always think one commits suicide for a reason. But it's quite possible to commit suicide for two reasons. No, that never occurs to them. So what's the good of dying intentionally, of sacrificing yourself to the idea you want people to have of you? Once you are dead, they will take advantage of it to attribute idiotic or vulgar motives to your action. Martyrs, *cher ami,* must choose between being forgotten, mocked, or made use of. As for being understood—never!

Besides, let's not beat about the bush; I love life—that's my real weakness. I love it so much that I am incapable of imagining what is not life. Such avidity has something plebeian about it, don't you think? Aristocracy cannot imagine itself without a little distance surrounding itself and its life. One dies if necessary, one breaks rather than bending. But I bend, because I continue to love myself. For example, after all I have told you, what do you think I developed? An aversion for myself? Come, come, it was especially with others that I was fed up. To be sure, I knew my failings and regretted them. Yet I continued to forget them with a rather meritorious obstinacy. The prosecution of others, on the contrary, went on constantly in my heart. Of course—does that shock you? Maybe you think it's not logical? But the question is not to remain logical. The question is to slip through and, above all—yes, above all, the question is to elude judgment. I'm not saying to avoid punishment, for punishment without judgment is bearable. It has a name, besides, that guarantees our innocence: it is called misfortune. No, on the contrary, it's a matter of dodging judgment, of avoiding being forever judged without ever having a sentence pronounced.

• • •

Thus it is that in the end, to take but one example, women cost me dear. The time I used to devote to them I couldn't give to men, who didn't always forgive me this. Is there any way out? Your successes and happiness are forgiven you only if you generously consent to share them. But to be happy it is essential not to be too concerned with others. Consequently, there is no escape. Happy and judged, or absolved and wretched. As for me, the injustice was even greater: I was condemned for past successes. For a long time I had lived in the illusion of a general agreement, whereas, from all sides, judgments, arrows, mockeries rained upon me, inattentive and smiling. The day I was alerted I became lucid; I received all the wounds at the same time and lost my strength all at once. The whole universe then began to laugh at me.

That is what no man (except those who are not really alive—in other words, wise men) can endure. Spitefulness is the only possible ostentation. People hasten to judge in order not to be judged themselves. What do you expect? The idea that comes most naturally to man, as if from his very nature, is the idea of his innocence. From this point of view, we are all like that little Frenchman at Buchenwald who insisted on registering a complaint with the clerk, himself a prisoner, who was recording his arrival. A complaint? The clerk and his comrades laughed: "Useless, old man. You don't lodge a complaint here." "But you see, sir," said the little Frenchman, "My case is exceptional. I am innocent!"

We are all exceptional cases. We all want to appeal against something! Each of us insists on being innocent at all cost, even if he has to accuse the whole human race and heaven itself. You won't delight a man by complimenting him on the efforts by which he has become intelligent or generous. On the other hand, he will beam if you admire his natural generosity. Inversely, if you tell a criminal that his crime is not due to his nature or his character but to unfortunate circumstances, he will be extravagantly grateful to you. During the counsel's speech, this is the moment he will choose to weep.

❖ *from* "Albert Camus" ❖
by Jean-Paul Sartre

• • •

He represented in this century, and against History, the present heir of that long line of moralists whose works perhaps constitute what is most original in French letters. His stubborn humanism, narrow and pure, austere and sensual, waged a dubious battle against events of these times. But inversely, through the obstinacy of his refusals, he reaffirmed the existence of moral fact within the heart of our era and against the Machiavellians, against the golden calf of realism.

He *was,* so to speak, this unshakable affirmation. For, as little as people may read or reflect, they collide against the human values which he held in his closed fist. He put the political act in question. He had to be avoided or fought: indispensable, in a word, to this tension which makes the life of the mind. Even his silence, these last years, had a positive aspect: this Cartesian of the absurd refused to leave the sure ground of morality, and to engage upon the uncertain paths of the *practical.* We guessed this, and we also guessed the conflicts which he silenced: because morality, in order to take it up alone, demands revolt and condemns it at the same time.

• • •

I do not believe it [Camus' sudden death in an auto accident]. As soon as it manifests itself, the inhuman becomes part of the human. Every interrupted life—even that of so young a man—is, at the same time, *a record that is broken* and a complete life. For all those who loved him, there was an unbearable absurdity in this death. But we

From Situations *by Jean-Paul Sartre, translated from the French by Benita Eisler. English translation copyright 1965 by George Braziller, Inc. Originally published in* France-Observateur, *January 7, 1960, after Camus's untimely death.*

shall have to learn to see this mutilated life-work as a whole life-work. In the same measure that the humanism of Camus contained a humane attitude towards the death that was to take him by surprise, in the measure that his proud quest for human happiness implied and reclaimed the inhuman necessity of dying, we shall recognize in this work and in the life which is inseparable from it, the pure and victorious endeavor of a man to recover each instant of his existence from his future death.

Jean-Paul Sartre

(1905-1980)
FRENCH

During one series of arrests in the Algerian crisis, de Gaulle himself is said to have refused to have Sartre arrested on the grounds that "Sartre is France, and one cannot arrest France." Such is Sartre's importance, not only in French letters and politics, but in the spirit of the Western world in the twentieth century. It is Sartre who is mainly responsible for both the formulation and the popularization of existentialism. It is Sartre who defined the very identity of existentialism in his actions as well as his writings. He persisted in his demand that writing have a social conscience, and that the writer be a person of action as well as of words. The focus of his philosophy was freedom and responsibility, and the goal of his activities was always to maintain an honest stance in the struggle for freedom. It has been argued that there are two Sartres, Sartre the existentialist and Sartre the Marxist. Though there has always been tension between the intellectual and committed political action, there was just one Sartre, whose restless genius has led him to focus now on this problem, now on that one.

Sartre was trained as an academic philosopher, but his life in the provincial academy was tedious and boring in the extreme, and those characteristics emerged in his first novel, *Nausea* (1938). It was a phenomenological novel, utilizing Edmund Husserl's method of phenomenology but presenting a shockingly grim view of the world, a world of "contingency," which would be one of Sartre's central existentialist themes. (In a later novel, he would comment that all of us want to be "indispensable.") In *Nausea,* Sartre's character Roquentin describes for us his meaningless world, culminating in a now classic depiction of the sheer awfulness of existence as such, represented by the brute existence of the root of a chestnut tree (reprinted here). During these years, Sartre was steeped in phenomenology, both theory and practice. It is in Sartre's work, more than anywhere else, that we see the synthesis of phenomenology and existentialism, the logic of the "first-person standpoint" elaborated into a dramatic expression of the existential point of view.

In his early *Being and Nothingness* (1943) Sartre brings to a climax his several years' work in psychology and phenomenology. The theme of that work is individual freedom, and its central intention is to characterize human existence in such a way that it is "without excuse." The work begins with Descartes' cogito, Husserl's phenomenological method, and Heidegger's arguments against the primacy of knowledge. Sartre distinguishes between the being of things—"Being-in-itself"—and the being of consciousness—"Being-for-itself." Only consciousness, not things, has the property of "secreting nothingness," of imagining alternatives, of denying a situation. This ability to negate is also called freedom, and Sartre argues that it is the very condition of there being consciousness. Freedom, thus characterized as freedom of intention and not as freedom of successful action (I am always free to try to escape; I am not always free to succeed in escaping), is absolute. Yet this freedom is also always confronted with a specific situation, its facticity (the term is from Heidegger), which both directs the kinds of actions that are appropriate and limits the actions that can be successful. Between my freedom and my facticity there is the question who I am. On the one hand, one might say that I am whatever the facts about me (i.e., my facticity) say I am. But then, one might say that I am not those facts, that I am whatever I intend to be. Neither answer is correct, Sartre tells us, and any attempt to settle who one is on the basis of only the facts about him or his intentions is in *bad faith*. The central purpose of *Being and Nothingness* is to display for us the various pitfalls of bad faith and to warn us against them. The ideal (though Sartre, like Heidegger, insists that he is doing "ontology" and not ethics) is the recognition of both one's freedom and one's facticity, like, for example, the young Orestes toward the end of Sartre's play *The Flies*. In addition to bad faith, there is another serious threat to our attitude toward ourselves: other people. Sartre follows Hegel's master-slave parable in his description of relations between people which are essentially conflict. Even love, as well as sadism and hate, is a manifestation of conflict, of the attempt of each person to win his or her freedom from the other. In *No Exit* Sartre portrays three people in hell who discover that "hell is—other people." Similarly, the young child Jean Genet is reduced to a thing—a thief—by the accusations of others.

In his last twenty years Sartre focused his attention more on society than on the isolated individual. The culmination of his studies was *La Critique de la Raison Dialectique* with its introduction, *Search for a Method* (reprinted in part here). Concepts from *Being and Nothingness* have been made at home in this sociological context. For example, bad faith has its social analogue in seriality; the project (ultimate choice) of the individual remanifests itself as praxis. The two works are complementary, although one would expect that Sartre has had some changes of mind since 1943. For example, he no longer argues that the notion of freedom is absolute, largely due to objections raised by Merleau-Ponty (see the latter's "Freedom," reprinted in this volume). But Sartre's work—his two main studies plus his many essays, plays, novels, and discussions—form an integrated whole that had few parallels in the twentieth century.

The following montage of pieces includes quite a few selections from *Being and Nothingness* together with selections from contemporaneous novels and plays, such as *Nausea, The Flies, No Exit,* and *The Age of Reason*. The selection from *St. Genet: Actor and Martyr* is a brief illustration of Sartre's brilliant excursions into existential psychoanalysis, most recently applied to Flaubert in a voluminous study. The last selection reflects Sartre's "radical conversion" to Marxism and to political revolution. The opening selection is taken from a popular and somewhat popularized lecture Sartre delivered in 1946–1947.

❖ *from* Existentialism Is a Humanism ❖

. . . For in truth this is of all teachings the least scandalous and the most austere: it is intended strictly for technicians and philosophers. All the same, it can easily be defined.

The question is only complicated because there are two kinds of existentialists. There are, on the one hand, the Christians, amongst whom I shall name Jaspers and Gabriel Marcel, both professed Catholics; and on the other the existential atheists, amongst whom we must place Heidegger as well as the French existentialists and myself. What they have in common is simply the fact that they believe that *existence* comes before *essence*—or, if you will, that we must begin from the subjective. What exactly do we mean by that?

If one considers an article of manufacture—as, for example, a book or a paper-knife—one sees that it has been made by an artisan who had a conception of it; and he has paid attention, equally, to the conception of a paper-knife and to the pre-existent technique of production which is a part of that conception and is, at bottom, a formula. Thus the paper-knife is at the same time an article producible in a certain manner and one which, on the other hand, serves a definite purpose, for one cannot suppose that a man would produce a paper-knife without knowing what it was for. Let us say, then, of the paper-knife that its essence—that is to say the sum of the formulae and the qualities which made its production and its definition possible—precedes its existence. The presence of such-and-such a paper-knife or book is thus determined before my eyes. Here, then, we are viewing the world from a technical standpoint, and we can say that production precedes existence.

When we think of God as the creator, we are thinking of him, most of the time, as a supernal artisan. Whatever doctrine we may be considering, whether it be a doctrine like that of Descartes, or of Leibnitz himself, we always imply that the will follows, more or less, from the understanding or at least accompanies it, so that when God creates he knows precisely what he is creating. Thus, the conception of man in the mind of God is comparable to that of the paper-knife in the mind of the artisan: God makes man according to a procedure and a conception, exactly as the artisan manufactures a paper-knife, following a definition and a formula. Thus each individual man is the realisation of a certain conception which dwells in the divine understanding. In the philosophic atheism of the eighteenth century, the notion of God is suppressed, but not, for all that, the idea that essence is prior to existence; something of that idea we still find everywhere, in Diderot, in Voltaire and even in Kant. Man possesses a human nature; that "human nature," which is the conception of human being, is found in every man; which means that each man is a particular example of an universal conception, the conception of Man. In Kant, this universality goes so far that the wild man of the woods, man in the state of nature and the bourgeois are all contained in the same definition and have the same fundamental qualities. Here again, the essence of man precedes that historic existence which we confront in experience.

Atheistic existentialism, of which I am a representative, declares with greater consistency that if God does not exist there is at least one being whose existence comes before its essence, a being which exists before it can be defined by any conception of it. That being is man or, as Heidegger has it, the human reality. What do we mean by saying that existence precedes essence? We mean that man first of all exists, encounters himself, surges up in the world—and defines himself afterwards. If man as the existentialist sees him is not definable, it is because to begin with he is nothing. He will not be anything until later, and then he will be what he makes of himself. Thus, there is no human nature, because there is no God to have a conception of it. Man simply is. Not that he is simply what he conceives himself to be, but he is what he wills, and as he conceives himself after already existing—as he wills to be after that leap towards existence. Man is nothing else but that which he makes of himself. That is the first principle of existentialism. And this is what people call its "subjectivity," using the word as a reproach against us. But what do we mean to say by this, but that man is of a greater dignity than a stone or a table? For we mean to say that man primarily exists—that man is, before all else, something which propels itself towards a future and is aware that it is doing so. Man is, indeed, a project which possesses a sub-

jective life, instead of being a kind of moss, or a fungus or a cauli-
flower. Before that projection of the self nothing exists; not even in
the heaven of intelligence: man will only attain existence when he is
what he purposes to be. Not, however, what he may wish to be. For
what we usually understand by wishing or willing is a conscious decision taken—much more often than not—after we have made ourselves what we are. I may wish to join a party, to write a book or to
marry—but in such a case what is usually called my will is probably
a manifestation of a prior and more spontaneous decision. If, however, it is true that existence is prior to essence, man is responsible
for what he is. Thus, the first effect of existentialism is that it puts
every man in possession of himself as he is, and places the entire responsibility for his existence squarely upon his own shoulders. And,
when we say that man is responsible for himself, we do not mean
that he is responsible only for his own individuality, but that he is responsible for all men. The word "subjectivism" is to be understood
in two senses, and our adversaries play upon only one of them. Subjectivism means, on the one hand, the freedom of the individual subject and, on the other, that man cannot pass beyond human subjectivity. It is the latter which is the deeper meaning of existentialism.
When we say that man chooses himself, we do mean that every one
of us must choose himself; but by that we also mean that in choosing for himself he chooses for all men. For in effect, of all the actions
a man may take in order to create himself as he wills to be, there is
not one which is not creative, at the same time, of an image of man
such as he believes he ought to be. To choose between this or that
is at the same time to affirm the value of that which is chosen; for we
are unable ever to choose the worse. What we choose is always the
better; and nothing can be better for us unless it is better for all. If,
moreover, existence precedes essence and we will to exist at the
same time as we fashion our image, that image is valid for all and for
the entire epoch in which we find ourselves. Our responsibility is
thus much greater than we had supposed, for it concerns mankind
as a whole. If I am a worker, for instance, I may choose to join a
Christian rather than a Communist trade union. And if, by that membership, I choose to signify that resignation is, after all, the attitude
that best becomes a man, that man's kingdom is not upon this earth,
I do not commit myself alone to that view. Resignation is my will for
everyone, and my action is, in consequence, a commitment on behalf of all mankind. Or if, to take a more personal case, I decide to

marry and to have children, even though this decision proceeds simply from my situation, from my passion or my desire, I am thereby committing not only myself, but humanity as a whole, to the practice of monogamy. I am thus responsible for myself and for all men, and I am creating a certain image of man as I would have him to be. In fashioning myself I fashion man.

This may enable us to understand what is meant by such terms—perhaps a little grandiloquent—as anguish, abandonment and despair. As you will soon see, it is very simple. First, what do we mean by anguish? The existentialist frankly states that man is in anguish. His meaning is as follows—When a man commits himself to anything, fully realising that he is not only choosing what he will be, but is thereby at the same time a legislator deciding for the whole of mankind—in such a moment a man cannot escape from the sense of complete and profound responsibility. There are many, indeed, who show no such anxiety. But we affirm that they are merely disguising their anguish or are in flight from it. Certainly, many people think that in what they are doing they commit no one but themselves to anything: and if you ask them, "What would happen if everyone did so?" they shrug their shoulders and reply, "Everyone does not do so." But in truth, one ought always to ask oneself what would happen if everyone did as one is doing; nor can one escape from that disturbing thought except by a kind of self-deception. The man who lies in self-excuse, by saying "Everyone will not do it," must be ill at ease in his conscience, for the act of lying implies the universal value which it denies. By its very disguise his anguish reveals itself. This is the anguish that Kierkegaard called "the anguish of Abraham." You know the story: An angel commanded Abraham to sacrifice his son: and obedience was obligatory, if it really was an angel who had appeared and said, "Thou, Abraham, shalt sacrifice thy son." But anyone in such a case would wonder, first, whether it was indeed an angel and secondly, whether I am really Abraham. Where are the proofs? A certain mad woman who suffered from hallucinations said that people were telephoning to her, and giving her orders. The doctor asked, "But who is it that speaks to you?" She replied: "He says it is God." And what, indeed, could prove to her that it was God? If an angel appears to me, what is the proof that it is an angel; or, if I hear voices, who can prove that they proceed from heaven and not from hell, or from my own subconsciousness or some pathological condition? Who can prove that they are really addressed to me?

Who, then, can prove that I am the proper person to impose, by my own choice, my conception of man upon mankind? I shall never find any proof whatever; there will be no sign to convince me of it. If a voice speaks to me, it is still I myself who must decide whether the voice is or is not that of an angel. If I regard a certain course of action as good, it is only I who choose to say that it is good and not bad. There is nothing to show that I am Abraham: nevertheless I also am obliged at every instant to perform actions which are examples. Everything happens to every man as though the whole human race had its eyes fixed upon what he is doing and regulated its conduct accordingly. So every man ought to say, "Am I really a man who has the right to act in such a manner that humanity regulates itself by what I do?" If a man does not say that, he is dissembling his anguish. Clearly, the anguish with which we are concerned here is not one that could lead to quietism or inaction. It is anguish pure and simple, of the kind well known to all those who have borne responsibilities. When, for instance, a military leader takes upon himself the respon- sibility for an attack and sends a number of men to their death, he chooses to do it and at bottom he alone chooses. No doubt he acts under a higher command, but its orders, which are more general, re- quire interpretation by him and upon that interpretation depends the life of ten, fourteen or twenty men. In making the decision, he can- not but feel a certain anguish. All leaders know that anguish. It does not prevent their acting, on the contrary it is the very condition of their action, for the action presupposes that there is a plurality of pos- sibilities, and in choosing one of these, they realise that it has value only because it is chosen. Now it is anguish of that kind which exis- tentialism describes, and moreover, as we shall see, makes explicit through direct responsibility towards other men who are concerned. Far from being a screen which could separate us from action, it is a condition of action itself.

And when we speak of "abandonment"—a favourite word of Hei- degger—we only mean to say that God does not exist, and that it is necessary to draw the consequences of his absence right to the end. The existentialist is strongly opposed to a certain type of secular moralism which seeks to suppress God at the least possible expense. Towards 1880, when the French professors endeavoured to formu- late a secular morality, they said something like this:—God is a use- less and costly hypothesis, so we will do without it. However, if we are to have morality, a society and a law-abiding world, it is essential that certain values should be taken seriously; they must have an a priori existence ascribed to them. It must be considered obligatory a priori to be honest, not to lie, not to beat one's wife, to bring up children and so forth; so we are going to do a little work on this subject, which will enable us to show that these values exist all the same, inscribed in an intelligible heaven although, of course, there is no God. In other words—and this is, I believe, the purport of all that we in France call radicalism—nothing will be changed if God does not exist; we shall re-discover the same norms of honesty, progress and humanity, and we shall have disposed of God as an out-of-date hypothesis which will die away quietly of itself. The existentialist, on the contrary, finds it extremely embarrassing that God does not exist, for there disappears with Him all possibility of finding values in an intelligible heaven. There can no longer be any good a priori, since there is no infinite and perfect consciousness to think it. It is nowhere written that "the good" exists, that one must be honest or must not lie, since we are now upon the plane where there are only men. Dostoievsky once wrote "If God did not exist, everything would be permitted"; and that, for existentialism, is the starting point. Everything is indeed permitted if God does not exist, and man is in consequence forlorn, for he cannot find anything to depend upon either within or outside himself. He discovers forthwith, that he is without excuse. For if indeed existence precedes essence, one will never be able to explain one's action by reference to a given and specific human nature; in other words, there is no determinism—man is free, man *is* freedom. Nor, on the other hand, if God does not exist, are we provided with any values or commands that could legitimise our behaviour. Thus we have neither behind us, nor before us in a luminous realm of values, any means of justification or excuse. We are left alone, without excuse. That is what I mean when I say that man is condemned to be free. Condemned, because he did not create himself, yet is nevertheless at liberty, and from the moment that he is thrown into this world he is responsible for everything he does. The existentialist does not believe in the power of passion. He will never regard a grand passion as a destructive torrent upon which a man is swept into certain actions as by fate, and which, therefore, is an excuse for them. He thinks that man is responsible for his passion. Neither will an existentialist think that a man can find help through some sign being vouchsafed upon earth for his orientation: for he thinks that the man himself interprets the sign as he chooses. He thinks that every man, without any support or help whatever, is condemned at every instant to invent man. As Ponge has written in a very fine article, "Man is the future of man." That is exactly true. Only, if one took this to mean that the future is laid up in Heaven, that God knows what it is, it would be false, for then it would no longer even be a future. If, however, it means that whatever man may now appear to be, there is a future to be fashioned, a virgin future that awaits him— then it is a true saying. But in the present one is forsaken.

As an example by which you may the better understand this state of abandonment, I will refer to the case of a pupil of mine, who sought me out in the following circumstances. His father was quarrelling with his mother and was also inclined to be a "collaborator"; his elder brother had been killed in the German offensive of 1940 and this young man, with a sentiment somewhat primitive but generous, burned to avenge him. His mother was living alone with him, deeply afflicted by the semi-treason of his father and by the death of her eldest son, and her one consolation was in this young man. But he, at this moment, had the choice between going to England to join the Free French Forces or of staying near his mother and helping her to live. He fully realised that this woman lived only for him and that his disappearance—or perhaps his death—would plunge her into despair. He also realised that, concretely and in fact, every action he performed on his mother's behalf would be sure of effect in the sense of aiding her to live, whereas anything he did in order to go and fight would be an ambiguous action which might vanish like water into sand and serve no purpose. For instance, to set out for England he would have to wait indefinitely in a Spanish camp on the way through Spain; or, on arriving in England or in Algiers he might be put into an office to fill up forms. Consequently, he found himself confronted by two very different modes of action: the one concrete, immediate but directed towards only one individual; and the other an action addressed to an end infinitely greater, a national collectivity, but for that very reason ambiguous—and it might be frustrated on the way. At the same time, he was hesitating between two kinds of morality; on the one side the morality of sympathy, of personal devotion and, on the other side, a morality of wider scope but of more debatable validity. He had to choose between those two. What could help him to choose? Could the Christian doctrine? No. Christian doctrine says: Act with charity, love your neighbour, deny yourself for others, choose the way which is hardest, and so forth. But which is the harder road?

To whom does one owe the more brotherly love, the patriot or the mother? Which is the more useful aim, the general one of fighting in and for the whole community, or the precise aim of helping one particular person to live? Who can give an answer to that a priori? No one. Nor is it given in any ethical scripture. The Kantian ethic says, Never regard another as a means, but always as an end. Very well: if I remain with my mother, I shall be regarding her as the end and not as a means: but by the same token I am in danger of treating as means those who are fighting on my behalf; and the converse is also true, that if I go to the aid of the combatants I shall be treating them as the end at the risk of treating my mother as a means.

If values are uncertain, if they are still too abstract to determine the particular, concrete case under consideration, nothing remains but to trust in our instincts. That is what this young man tried to do; and when I saw him he said, "In the end, it is feeling that counts; the direction in which it is really pushing me is the one I ought to choose. If I feel that I love my mother enough to sacrifice everything else for her—my will to be avenged, all my longings for action and adventure—then I stay with her. If, on the contrary, I feel that my love for her is not enough, I go." But how does one estimate the strength of a feeling? The value of his feeling for his mother was determined precisely by the fact that he was standing by her. I may say that I love a certain friend enough to sacrifice such or such a sum of money for him, but I cannot prove that unless I have done it. I may say, "I love my mother enough to remain with her," if actually I have remained with her. I can only estimate the strength of this affection if I have performed an action by which it is defined and ratified. But if I then appeal to this affection to justify my action, I find myself drawn into a vicious circle.

• • •

What is at the very heart and centre of existentialism is the absolute character of the free commitment, by which every man realises himself in realising a type of humanity—a commitment always understandable, to no matter whom in no matter what epoch—and its bearing upon the relativity of the cultural pattern which may result from such absolute commitment. One must observe equally the relativity of Cartesianism and the absolute character of the Cartesian commitment. In this sense you may say, if you like, that every one of us makes the absolute by breathing, by eating, by sleeping or by behaving in any fashion whatsoever. There is no difference between free being—being as self-committal, as existence choosing its essence—and absolute being. And there is no difference whatever between being as an absolute, temporarily localised—that is, localised in history—and universally intelligible being.

• • •

. . . Existentialism is nothing else but an attempt to draw the full conclusions from a consistently atheistic position. . . . Not that we believe God does exist, but we think that the real problem is not that of His existence; what man needs is to find himself again and to understand that nothing can save him from himself, not even a valid proof of the existence of God. In this sense existentialism is optimistic, it is a doctrine of action, and it is only by self-deception, by confusing their own despair with ours that Christians can describe us as without hope.

❖ *from* Nausea ❖

• • •

I was in the park just now. The roots of the chestnut tree were sunk in the ground just under my bench. I couldn't remember it was a root any more. The words had vanished and with them the significance of things, their methods of use, and the feeble points of reference which men have traced on their surface. I was sitting, stooping forward, head bowed, alone in front of this black, knotty mass, entirely beastly, which frightened me. Then I had this vision.

It left me breathless. Never, until these last few days, had I understood the meaning of "existence." I was like the others, like the ones walking along the seashore, all dressed in their spring finery. I said, like them, "The ocean *is* green; that white speck up there *is* a seagull," but I didn't feel that it existed or that the seagull was an "existing seagull"; usually existence hides itself. It is there, around us, in us, it is *us,* you can't say two words without mentioning it, but you can never touch it. When I believed I was thinking about it, I must believe that I was thinking nothing, my head was empty, or there was just one word in my head, the word "to be." Or else I was thinking . . . how can I explain it? I was thinking of *belonging,* I was telling myself that the sea belonged to the class of green objects, or that the green was a part of the quality of the sea. Even when I looked at things, I was miles from dreaming that they existed: they looked like scenery to me. I picked them up in my hands, they served me as tools, I foresaw their resistance. But that all happened on the surface. If anyone had asked me what existence was, I would have answered, in good faith, that it was nothing, simply an empty form which was added to external things without changing anything in their nature. And then all of a sudden, there it was, clear as day: existence had suddenly unveiled itself. It had lost the harmless look of an abstract category: it was the very paste of things, this root was kneaded into existence. Or rather the root, the park gates, the bench, the sparse grass, all that had vanished: the diversity of things, their individuality, were only an appearance, a veneer. This veneer had melted, leaving soft, monstrous masses, all in disorder—naked, in a frightful, obscene nakedness.

I kept myself from making the slightest movement, but I didn't need to move in order to see, behind the trees, the blue columns and the lamp posts of the bandstand and the Velleda, in the midst of a mountain of laurel. All these objects . . . how can I explain? They inconvenienced me; I would have liked them to exist less strongly, more dryly, in a more abstract way, with more reserve. The chestnut tree pressed itself against my eyes. Green rust covered it half-way up; the bark, black and swollen, looked like boiled leather. The sound of the water in the Masqueret Fountain sounded in my ears, made a nest there, filled them with signs; my nostrils overflowed with a green, putrid odour. All things, gently, tenderly, were letting themselves drift into existence like those relaxed women who burst out laughing and say: "It's good to laugh," in a wet voice; they were parading, one in front of the other, exchanging abject secrets about their existence. I realized that there was no half-way house between non-existence and this flaunting abundance. If you existed, you had to *exist all the way,* as far as mouldiness, bloatedness, obscenity were concerned. In another world, circles, bars of music keep their pure and rigid lines. But existence is a deflection. Trees, night-blue pillars, the happy bubbling of a fountain, vital smells, little heat-mists floating in the cold air, a red-haired man digesting on a bench: all this somnolence, all these meals digested together, had its comic side. . . . Comic . . . no: it didn't go as far as that, nothing that exists can be comic; it was like a floating analogy, almost entirely elusive, with certain aspects of vaudeville. We were a heap of living creatures, irritated, embarrassed at ourselves, we hadn't the slightest reason to be there, none of us, each one, confused, vaguely alarmed, felt in the way in relation to the others. *In the way:* it was the only relationship I could establish between these trees, these gates, these stones. In vain I tried to *count* the chestnut trees, to *locate* them by their relationship to the Velleda, to compare their height with the height of the plane trees: each of them escaped the relationship in which I tried to enclose it, isolated itself, and overflowed. Of these relations (which I insisted on maintaining in order to delay the crumbling of the human world, measures, quantities, and directions)—I felt myself to be the arbitrator; they no longer had their teeth into things. *In the way,* the chestnut tree there, opposite me, a little to the left. *In the way,* the Velleda. . . .

And I—soft, weak, obscene, digesting, juggling with dismal thoughts—I, too, was *In the way.* Fortunately, I didn't feel it, although I realized it, but I was uncomfortable because I was afraid of feeling it (even now I am afraid—afraid that it might catch me behind my head and lift me up like a wave). I dreamed vaguely of killing myself to wipe out at least one of these superfluous lives. But even my death would have been *In the way. In the way,* my corpse, my blood on these stones, between these plants, at the back of this smiling garden. And the decomposed flesh would have been *In the way* in the earth which would receive my bones, at last, cleaned, stripped, peeled, proper and clean as teeth, it would have been *In the way:* I was *In the way* for eternity.

The word absurdity is coming to life under my pen; a little while ago, in the garden, I couldn't find it, but neither was I looking for it, I didn't need it: I thought without words, *on* things, *with* things. Absurdity was not an idea in my head, or the sound of a voice, only this long serpent dead at my feet, this wooden serpent. Serpent or claw or root or vulture's talon, what difference does it make. And without formulating anything clearly, I understood that I had found the key to Existence, the key to my Nauseas, to my own life. In fact, all that I could grasp beyond that returns to this fundamental absurdity. Absurdity: another word; I struggle against words; down there I touched the thing. But I wanted to fix the absolute character of this absurdity here. A movement, an event in the tiny coloured world of men is only relatively absurd: by relation to the accompanying circumstances. A madman's ravings, for example, are absurd in relation to the situation in which he finds himself, but not in relation to his delirium. But a little while ago I made an experiment with the absolute or the absurd. This root—there was nothing in relation to which it was absurd. Oh, how can I put it in words? Absurd: in relation to the stones, the tufts of yellow grass, the dry mud, the tree, the sky, the green benches. Absurd, irreducible; nothing—not even a profound, secret upheaval of nature—could explain it. Evidently I did not know everything, I had not seen the seeds sprout, or the tree grow. But faced with this great wrinkled paw, neither ignorance nor knowledge was important: the world of explanations and reasons is not the world of existence. A circle is not absurd, it is clearly explained by the rotation of a straight segment around one of its extremities. But neither does a circle exist. This root, on the other hand, existed in such a way that I could not explain it. Knotty, inert, nameless, it fascinated me, filled my eyes, brought me back unceasingly to its own existence. In vain to repeat: "This is a root"—it didn't work any more. I saw clearly that you could not pass from its function as a root, as a breathing pump, *to that,* to this hard and compact skin of a sea lion, to this oily, callous, headstrong look. The function explained nothing: it allowed you to understand generally that it was a root, but not *that one* at all. This root, with its colour, shape, its congealed movement, was . . . below all explanation. Each of its qualities escaped it a little, flowed out of it, half solidified, almost became a thing; each one was *In the way* in the root and the whole stump now gave me the impression of unwinding itself a little, denying its existence to lose itself in a frenzied excess. I scraped my heel against this black claw: I wanted to peel off some of the bark. For no reason at all, out of defiance, to make the bare pink appear absurd on the tanned leather: to *play* with the absurdity of the world. But, when I drew my heel back, I saw that the bark was still black.

• • •

This moment was extraordinary. I was there, motionless and icy, plunged in a horrible ecstasy. But something fresh had just appeared in the very heart of this ecstasy; I understood the Nausea, I possessed it. To tell the truth, I did not formulate my discoveries to myself. But

I think it would be easy for me to put them in words now. The essential thing is contingency. I mean that one cannot define existence as necessity. To exist is simply *to be there;* those who exist let themselves be encountered, but you can never deduce anything from them. I believe there are people who have understood this. Only they tried to overcome this contingency by inventing a necessary, causal being. But no necessary being can explain existence: contingency is not a delusion, a probability which can be dissipated; it is the absolute, consequently, the perfect free gift. All is free, this park, this city and myself. When you realize that, it turns your heart upside down and everything begins to float, as the other evening at the "Railwaymen's Rendezvous": here is Nausea; here there is what those bastards—the ones on the Coteau Vert and others—try to hide from themselves with their idea of their rights. But what a poor lie: no one has any rights; they are entirely free, like other men, they cannot succeed in not feeling superfluous. And in themselves, secretly, they are *superfluous,* that is to say, amorphous, vague, and sad.

❖ The Origin of Nothingness ❖

In order for negation to exist in the world and in order that we may consequently raise questions concerning Being, it is necessary that in some way Nothingness be given. We perceived then that Nothingness can be conceived neither *outside of* being, nor as a complementary, abstract notion, nor as an infinite milieu where being is suspended. Nothingness must be given at the heart of Being, in order for us to be able to apprehend that particular type of realities which we have called *négatités.* But this intra-mundane Nothingness can not be produced by Being-in-itself; the notion of Being as full positivity does not contain Nothingness as one of its structures. We can not even say that Being excludes it. Being lacks all relation with it. Hence the question which is put to us now with a particular urgency: if Nothingness can be conceived neither outside of Being, nor in terms of Being, and if on the other hand, since it is non-being, it can

From Being and Nothingness *by Jean-Paul Sartre, translated by Hazel E. Barnes et. Copyright 1956 by Philosophical Library, Inc. Reprinted by permission of Philosophical Library, Inc., of New York.*

not derive from itself the necessary force to "nihilate itself," *where does Nothingness come from?*

. . .

Nothingness is not, Nothingness "is made-to-be," Nothingness does not nihilate itself; Nothingness "is nihilated." It follows therefore that there must exist a Being (this cannot be the In-itself) of which the property is to nihilate Nothingness, to support it in its being, to sustain it perpetually in its very existence, *a being by which nothingness comes to things.* But how can this Being be related to Nothingness so that through it Nothingness comes to things? We must observe first that the being postulated can not be passive in relation to Nothingness, can not receive it; Nothingness could not *come* to this being except through another Being—which would be an infinite regress. But on the other hand, the Being by which Nothingness comes to the world can not *produce* Nothingness while remaining indifferent to that production—like the Stoic cause which produces its effect without being itself changed. It would be inconceivable that a Being which is full positivity should maintain and create outside itself a Nothingness or transcendent being, for there would be nothing in Being by which Being could surpass itself toward Non-Being. The Being by which Nothingness arrives in the world must nihilate Nothingness in its Being, and even so it still runs the risk of establishing Nothingness as a transcendent in the very heart of immanence unless it nihilates Nothingness in its being *in connection with its own being.* The Being by which Nothingness arrives in the world is a being such that in its Being, the Nothingness of its Being is in question. *The being by which Nothingness comes to the world must be its own Nothingness.* By this we must understand not a nihilating act, which would require in turn a foundation in Being, but an ontological characteristic of the Being required. It remains to learn in what delicate, exquisite region of Being we shall encounter that Being which is its own Nothingness.

. . .

Descartes following the Stoics has given a name to this possibility which human reality has to secrete a nothingness which isolates it— it is *freedom.* But freedom here is only a name. If we wish to penetrate further into the question, we must not be content with this reply

and we ought to ask now, What is human freedom if through it nothingness comes into the world?

• • •

If the nihilating consciousness exists only as consciousness of nihilation, we ought to be able to define and describe a constant mode
of consciousness, present *qua* consciousness, which would be consciousness of nihilation. Does this consciousness exist? Behold, a
new question has been raised here: if freedom is the being of consciousness, consciousness ought to exist as consciousness of freedom. What form does this consciousness of freedom assume? In freedom the human being *is* his own past (as also his own future) in the
form of nihilation. If our analysis has not led us astray, there ought
to exist for the human being, in so far as he is conscious of being, a
certain mode of standing opposite his past and his future, as being
both this past and this future and as not being them. We shall be able
to furnish an immediate reply to this question; it is in anguish that
man gets the consciousness of his freedom, or if you prefer, anguish
is the mode of being of freedom as consciousness of being; it is in
anguish that freedom is, in its being, in question for itself.

Kierkegaard describing anguish in the face of what one lacks
characterizes it as anguish in the face of freedom. But Heidegger,
whom we know to have been greatly influenced by Kierkegaard,
considers anguish instead as the apprehension of nothingness. These
two descriptions of anguish do not appear to us contradictory; on the
contrary the one implies the other.

First we must acknowledge that Kierkegaard is right; anguish is
distinguished from fear in that fear is fear of beings in the world
whereas anguish is anguish before myself. Vertigo is anguish to the
extent that I am afraid not of falling over the precipice, but of throwing myself over. A situation provokes fear if there is a possibility of
my life being changed from without; my being provokes anguish to
the extent that I distrust myself and my own reactions in that situation. The artillery preparation which precedes the attack can provoke
fear in the soldier who undergoes the bombardment, but anguish is
born in him when he tries to foresee the conduct with which he will
face the bombardment, when he asks himself if he is going to be able
to "hold up." Similarly the recruit who reports for active duty at the
beginning of the war can in some instances be afraid of death, but
more often he is "afraid of being afraid"; that is, he is filled with an-

guish before himself. Most of the time dangerous or threatening situations present themselves in facets; they will be apprehended through a feeling of fear or of anguish according to whether we envisage the situation as acting on the man or the man as acting on the situation. The man who has just received a hard blow—for example, losing a great part of his wealth in a crash—can have the fear of threatening poverty. He will experience anguish a moment later when nervously wringing his hands (a symbolic reaction to the action which is imposed but which remains still wholly undetermined), he exclaims to himself: "What am I going to do? But what am I going to do?" In this sense fear and anguish are exclusive of one another since fear is unreflective apprehension of the transcendent and anguish is reflective apprehension of the self; the one is born in the destruction of the other. The normal process in the case which I have just cited is a constant transition from the one to the other. But there exist also situations where anguish appears pure; that is, without ever being preceded or followed by fear. If, for example, I have been raised to a new dignity and charged with a delicate and flattering mission, I can feel anguish at the thought that I will not be capable perhaps of fulfilling it, and yet I will not have the least fear in the world of the consequences of my possible failure.

What is the meaning of anguish in the various examples which I have just given? Let us take up again the example of vertigo. Vertigo announces itself through fear; I am on a narrow path—without a guard rail—which goes along a precipice. The precipice presents itself to me as *to be avoided;* it represents a danger of death. At the same time I conceive of a certain number of causes, originating in universal determinism, which can transform that threat of death into reality: I can slip on a stone and fall into the abyss; the crumbling earth of the path can give way under my steps. Through these various anticipations, I am given to myself as a thing; I am passive in relation to these possibilities; they come to me from without; in so far as I am also an object in the world, subject to gravitation, they are *my* possibilities. At this moment *fear* appears, which in terms of the situation is the apprehension of myself as a destructible transcendent in the midst of transcendents, as an object which does not contain in itself the origin of its future disappearance. My reaction will be of the reflective order; I will pay attention to the stones in the road; I will keep myself as far as possible from the edge of the path. I realize myself as pushing away the threatening situation with all my strength,

and I project before myself a certain number of future conducts destined to keep the threats of the world at a distance from me. These
conducts are *my* possibilities. I escape fear by the very fact that I am
placing myself on a plane where *my own* possibilities are substituted
for the transcendent probabilities where human action had no place.

But these conducts, precisely because they are *my* possibilities, do
not appear to me as determined by foreign causes. Not only is it not
strictly certain that they will be effective; in particular it is not strictly
certain that they will be adopted, for they do not have existence sufficient in itself. We could say, varying the expression of Berkeley, that
their "being is a sustained-being" and that their "possibility of being
is only an ought-to-be-sustained." Due to this fact their possibility has
as a necessary condition the possibility of negative conduct (*not* to
pay attention to the stones in the road, to run, to think of something
else) and the possibility of the opposite conduct (to throw myself
over the precipice). The possibility which I make *my* concrete possibility can appear as my possibility only by raising itself on the basis
of the totality of the logical possibilities which the situation allows.
But these rejected possibilities in turn have no other being than their
"sustained-being"; it is I who sustain them in being, and inversely
their present non-being is an "ought-not-to-be-sustained." No external cause will remove them. I alone am the permanent source of their
non-being, I engage myself in them; in order to cause *my* possibility
to appear, I posit the other possibilities so as to nihilate them. This
would not produce anguish if I could apprehend myself in my relations with these possibles as a cause producing its effects. In this
case the effect defined as my possibility *would be strictly* determined.
But then it would cease to be *possible;* it would become simply
"about-to-happen." If then I wished to avoid anguish and vertigo, it
would be enough if I were to consider the motives (instinct of self-
preservation, prior fear, etc.), which make me reject the situation envisaged, as *determining* my prior activity in the same way that the
presence at a determined point of one given mass determines the
courses followed by other masses; it would be necessary, in other
words, that I apprehend in myself a strict psychological determinism.
But I am in anguish precisely because any conduct on my part is only
possible, and this means that while constituting a totality of motives
for pushing away that situation, I at the same moment apprehend
these motives as not sufficiently effective. At the very moment when
I apprehend my being as *horror* of the precipice, I am conscious of

that horror as *not determinant* in relation to my possible conduct. In one sense that horror calls for prudent conduct, and it is in itself a pre-outline of that conduct; in another sense, it posits the final developments of that conduct only as possible, precisely because I do not apprehend it as the *cause* of these final developments but as need, appeal, etc.

Now as we have seen, consciousness of being is the being of consciousness. There is no question here of a contemplation which I could make after the event, of a horror already constituted; it is the very being of horror to appear to itself as "not being the cause" of the conduct it calls for. In short, to avoid fear, which reveals to me a transcendent future strictly determined, I take refuge in reflection, but the latter has only an undetermined future to offer. This means that in establishing a certain conduct as a possibility and precisely because it is *my* possibility, I am aware that *nothing* can compel me to adopt that conduct. Yet I am indeed already there in the future; it is for the sake of that being which I will be there at the turning of the path that I now exert all my strength, and in this sense there is already a relation between my future being and my present being. But a nothingness has slipped into the heart of this relation; I *am* not the self which I will be. First I am not that self because time separates me from it. Secondly, I am not that self because what I am is not the foundation of what I will be. Finally I am not that self because no actual existent can determine strictly what I am going to be. Yet as I am already what I will be (otherwise I would not be interested in any one being more than another), *I am the self which I will be, in the mode of not being it.* It is through my horror that I am carried toward the future, and the horror nihilates itself in that it constitutes the future as possible. Anguish is precisely my consciousness of being my own future, in the mode of not-being. To be exact, the nihilation of horror as a *motive,* which has the effect of reinforcing horror as a *state,* has as its positive counterpart the appearance of other forms of conduct (in particular that which consists in throwing myself over the precipice) as *my* possible *possibilities.* If *nothing* compels me to save my life, *nothing* prevents me from precipitating myself into the abyss. The decisive conduct will emanate from a self which I am not yet. Thus the self which I am depends on the self which I am not yet to the exact extent that the self which I am not yet does not depend on the self which I am. Vertigo appears as the apprehension of this dependence. I approach the precipice, and my scrutiny is searching for myself in my very depths. In terms of this moment, I play with my possibilities. My eyes, running over the abyss from top to bottom, imitate the possible fall and realize it symbolically; at the same time suicide, from the fact that it becomes a *possibility* possible for *me,* now causes to appear possible motives for adopting it (suicide would cause anguish to cease). Fortunately these motives in their turn, from the sole fact that they are motives of a possibility, present themselves as ineffective, as non-determinant; they can no more *produce* the suicide than my horror of the fall can *determine me* to avoid it. It is this counter-anguish which generally puts an end to anguish by transmuting it into indecision. Indecision in its turn calls for decision. I abruptly put myself at a distance from the edge of the precipice and resume my way.

❖ Patterns of Bad Faith ❖

. . . "What must be the being of man if he is to be capable of bad faith?"

Take the example of a woman who has consented to go out with a particular man for the first time. She knows very well the intentions which the man who is speaking to her cherishes regarding her. She knows also that it will be necessary sooner or later for her to make a decision. But she does not want to realize the urgency; she concerns herself only with what is respectful and discreet in the attitude of her companion. She does not apprehend this conduct as an attempt to achieve what we call "the first approach"; that is, she does not want to see possibilities of temporal development which his conduct presents. She restricts this behavior to what is in the present; she does not wish to read in the phrases which he addresses to her anything other than their explicit meaning. If he says to her, "I find you so attractive!" she disarms this phrase of its sexual background; she attaches to the conversation and to the behavior of the speaker, the immediate meanings, which she imagines as objective qualities. The man who is speaking to her appears to be sincere and respectful as the table is round or square, as the wall coloring is blue or gray. The qualities thus attached to the person she is listening to are in this way fixed in a permanence like that of things, which is no other than the projection of the strict present of the qualities into the temporal flux. This is because she does not quite know what she wants. She is profoundly aware of the desire which she inspires, but the desire cruel and naked would humiliate and horrify her. Yet she would find no charm in a respect which would be only respect. In order to satisfy her, there must be a feeling which is addressed wholly to her *personality*—i.e., to her full freedom—and which would be a recognition of her freedom. But at the same time this feeling must be wholly desire; that is, it must address itself to her body as object. This time then she refuses to apprehend the desire for what it is; she does not even give it a name; she recognizes it only to the extent that it transcends itself toward admiration, esteem, respect and that it is wholly absorbed in the more refined forms which it produces, to the extent of no longer figuring anymore as a sort of warmth and density. But then suppose he takes her hand. This act of her companion risks changing the situation by calling for an immediate decision. To leave the hand there is to consent in herself to flirt, to engage herself. To withdraw it is to break the troubled and unstable harmony which gives the hour its charm. The aim is to postpone the moment of decision as long as possible. We know what happens next; the young woman leaves her hand there, but she *does not notice* that she is leaving it. She does not notice because it happens by chance that she is at this moment all intellect. She draws her companion up to the most lofty regions of sentimental speculation; she speaks of Life, of her life, she shows herself in her essential aspect—a personality, a consciousness. And during this time the divorce of the body from the soul is accomplished; the hand rests inert between the warm hands of her companion—neither consenting nor resisting—a thing.

We shall say that this woman is in bad faith. But we see immediately that she uses various procedures in order to maintain herself in this bad faith. She has disarmed the actions of her companion by reducing them to being only what they are; that is, to existing in the mode of the in-itself. But she permits herself to enjoy his desire, to the extent that she will apprehend it as not being what it is, will recognize its transcendence. Finally while sensing profoundly the presence of her own body—to the degree of being disturbed perhaps—she realizes herself as *not being* her own body, and she contemplates it as though from above as a passive object to which events can *happen* but which can neither provoke them nor avoid them because all its possibilities are outside of it. What unity do we find in these various aspects of bad faith? It is a certain art of forming contradictory concepts which unite in themselves both an idea and the negation of that idea. The basic concept which is thus engendered utilizes the double property of the human being, who is at once a *facticity* and a *transcendence*. These two aspects of human reality are and ought to be capable of a valid coordination. But bad faith does not wish either to coordinate them or to surmount them in a synthesis. Bad faith seeks to affirm their identity while preserving their differences. It must affirm facticity as *being* transcendence and transcendence as *being* facticity, in such a way that at the instant when a person apprehends the one, he can find himself abruptly faced with the other.

We can find the prototype of formulae of bad faith in certain famous expressions which have been rightly conceived to produce their whole effect in a spirit of bad faith. Take for example the title of a work by Jacques Chardonne, *Love Is Much More than Love.* We see here how unity is established between *present* love in its facticity—"the contact of two skins," sensuality, egoism, Proust's mechanism of jealousy, Adler's battle of the *sexes,* etc.—and love as transcendence—Mauriac's "river of fire," the longing for the infinite, Plato's *eros,* Lawrence's deep cosmic intuition, etc. Here we leave facticity to find ourselves suddenly beyond the present and the factual condition of man, beyond the psychological, in the heart of metaphysics. On the other hand, the title of a play by Sarment, *I Am Too Great for Myself,* which also presents characters in bad faith, throws us first into full transcendence in order suddenly to imprison us within the narrow limits of our factual essence. We will discover this structure again in the famous sentence: "He has become what he was" or in its no less famous opposite: "Eternity at last changes each man into himself." It is well understood that these various formulae have only the appearance of bad faith; they have been conceived in this paradoxical form explicitly to shock the mind and discountenance it by an enigma. But it is precisely this appearance which is of concern to us. What counts here is that the formulae do not constitute new, solidly structured ideas: on the contrary, they are formed so as to remain in perpetual disintegration and so that we may slide at any time from naturalistic present to transcendence and vice versa.

We can see the use which bad faith can make of these judgments which all aim at establishing that I am not what I am. If I were only what I *am,* I could, for example, seriously consider an adverse criticism which someone makes of me, question myself scrupulously, and perhaps be compelled to recognize the truth in it. But thanks to transcendence, I am not subject to all that I am. I do not even have to discuss the justice of the reproach. As Suzanne says to Figaro, "To prove that I am right would be to recognize that I can be wrong." I am on a plane where no reproach can touch me since what I really am is my transcendence. I flee from myself, I escape myself, I leave my tattered garment in the hands of the fault-finder. But the ambiguity necessary for bad faith comes from the fact that I affirm here that I *am* my transcendence in the mode of being of a thing. It is only thus, in fact, that I can feel that I escape all reproaches. It is in the sense that our young woman purifies the desire of anything humiliating by being willing to consider it only as pure transcendence, which she avoids even naming. But inversely "I Am Too Great for Myself," while showing our transcendence changed into facticity, is the source of an infinity of excuses for our failures or our weaknesses. Similarly the young coquette maintains transcendence to the extent that the respect, the esteem manifested by the actions of her admirer are already on the plane of the transcendent. But she arrests this transcendence, she glues it down with all the facticity of the present; respect is nothing other than respect, it is an arrested surpassing which no longer surpasses itself toward anything.

But although this *metastable* concept of "transcendence-facticity" is one of the most basic instruments of bad faith, it is not the only one of its kind. We can equally well use another kind of duplicity derived from human reality which we will express roughly by saying that its being-for-itself implies complementarily a being-for-others. Upon any one of my conducts it is always possible to converge two looks, mine and that of the Other. The conduct will not present exactly the same structure in each case. But as we shall see later, as each look perceives it, there is between these two aspects of my being, no difference between appearance and being—as if I were to my self the truth of myself and as if the Other possessed only a deformed image of me. The equal dignity of being, possessed by my being-for-others and by my being-for-myself, permits a perpetually disintegrating synthesis and a perpetual game of escape from the for-itself to the for-others and from the for-others to the for-itself. We have seen also the use

which our young lady made of our being-in-the-midst-of-the-world—
i.e., of our inert presence as a passive object among other objects—
in order to relieve herself suddenly from the functions of her being-
in-the-world—that is, from the being which causes there to be a world
by projecting itself beyond the world toward its own possibilities. Let
us note finally the confusing syntheses which play on the nihilating
ambiguity of these temporal ekstases, affirming at once that I am what
I have been (the man who deliberately *arrests himself* at one period
in his life and refuses to take into consideration the later changes) and
that I am not what I have been (the man who in the face of reproaches
or rancor dissociates himself from his past by insisting on his freedom
and on his perpetual re-creation). In all these concepts, which have
only a transitive role in the reasoning and which are eliminated from
the conclusion (like hypochondriacs in the calculations of physicians),
we find again the same structure. We have to deal with human reality
as a being which is what it is not, and which is what it is.

But what exactly is necessary in order for these concepts of disintegration to be able to receive even a pretence of existence, in order
for them to be able to appear for an instant to consciousness, even
in a process of evanescence? A quick examination of the idea of sincerity, the antithesis of bad faith, will be very instructive in this connection. Actually sincerity presents itself as a demand and consequently is not a *state*. Now what is the ideal to be attained in this
case? It is necessary that a man be *for himself* only what he *is*. But is
this not precisely the definition of the in-itself—or if you prefer—the
principle of identity? To posit as an ideal the being of things, is this
not to assert by the same stroke that this being does not belong to
human reality and that the principle of identity, far from being a universal axiom universally applied, is only a synthetic principle enjoying a merely regional universality? Thus in order that the concepts of
bad faith can put us under illusion at least for an instant, in order that
the candor of "pure hearts" (*cf.* Gide, Kessel) can have validity for
human reality as an ideal, the principle of identity must not represent
a constitutive principle of human reality and human reality must not
be necessarily what it is but must be able to be what it is not. What
does this mean?

If man is what he is, bad faith is forever impossible and candor
ceases to be his ideal and becomes instead his being. But is man
what he is? And more generally, how can he *be* what he is when he
exists as consciousness of being? If candor or sincerity is a universal

value, it is evident that the maxim "one must be what one is" does not serve solely as a regulating principle for judgments and concepts by which I express what I am. It posits not merely an ideal of knowing but an ideal of *being;* it proposes for us an absolute equivalence of being with itself as a prototype of being. In this sense it is necessary that we *make ourselves* what we are. But what *are we* then if we have the constant obligation to make ourselves what we are, if our mode of being is having the obligation to be what we are?

Let us consider this waiter in the café. His movement is quick and forward, a little too precise, a little too rapid. He comes toward the patrons with a step a little too quick. He bends forward a little too eagerly; his voice, his eyes express an interest a little too solicitous for the order of the customer. Finally there he returns, trying to imitate in his walk the inflexible stiffness of some kind of automaton while carrying his tray with the recklessness of a tight-rope-walker by putting it in a perpetually unstable, perpetually broken equilibrium which he perpetually re-establishes by a light movement of the arm and hand. All his behavior seems to us a game. He applies himself to chaining his movements as if they were mechanisms, the one regulating the other; his gestures and even his voice seem to be mechanisms; he gives himself the quickness and pitiless rapidity of things. He is playing, he is amusing himself. But what is he playing? We need not watch long before we can explain it: he is playing at *being* a waiter in a café. There is nothing there to surprise us. The game is a kind of marking out and investigation. The child plays with his body in order to explore it, to take inventory of it; the waiter in the café plays with his condition in order to *realize* it. This obligation is not different from that which is imposed on all tradesmen. Their condition is wholly one of ceremony. The public demands of them that they realize it as a ceremony; there is the dance of the grocer, of the tailor, of the auctioneer, by which they endeavor to persuade their clientele that they are nothing but a grocer, an auctioneer, a tailor. A grocer who dreams is offensive to the buyer, because such a grocer is not wholly a grocer. Society demands that he limit himself to his function as a grocer, just as the soldier at attention makes himself into a soldier-thing with a direct regard which does not see at all, which is no longer meant to see, since it is the rule and not the interest of the moment which determines the point he must fix his eyes on (the sight "fixed at ten paces"). There are indeed many precautions to imprison a man in what he is, as if we lived in perpetual fear that he might escape from it, that he might break away and suddenly elude his condition.

In a parallel situation, from within, the waiter in the café can not be immediately a café waiter in the sense that this inkwell *is* an inkwell, or the glass is a glass. It is by no means that he can not form reflective judgments or concepts concerning his condition. He knows well what it "means"; the obligation of getting up at five o'clock, of sweeping the floor of the shop before the restaurant opens, of starting the coffee pot going, etc. He knows the rights which it allows: the right to the tips, the right to belong to a union, etc. But all these concepts, all these judgments refer to the transcendent. It is a matter of abstract possibilities, of rights and duties conferred on a "person possessing rights." And it is precisely this person *who I have to be* (if I am the waiter in question) and who I am not. It is not that I do not wish to be this person or that I want this person to be different. But rather there is no common measure between his being and mine. It is a "representation" for others and for myself, which means that I can be he only in *representation*. But if I represent myself as him, I am not he; I am separated from him as the object from the subject, separated *by nothing,* but this nothing isolates me from him. I cannot be he, I can only play *at being* him; that is, imagine to myself that I am he. And thereby I affect him with nothingness. In vain do I fulfill the functions of a café waiter. I can be he only in the neutralized mode, as the actor is Hamlet, by mechanically making the *typical gestures* of my state and by aiming at myself as an imaginary café waiter through those gestures taken as an "analogue." What I attempt to realize is a being-in-itself of the café waiter, as if it were not just in my power to confer their value and their urgency upon my duties and the rights of my position, as if it were not my free choice to get up each morning at five o'clock or to remain in bed, even though it meant getting fired. As if from the very fact that I sustain this role in existence I did not transcend it on every side, as if I did not constitute myself as one *beyond* my condition. Yet there is no doubt that I *am* in a sense a café waiter—otherwise could I not just as well call myself a diplomat or a reporter? But if I am one, this cannot be in the mode of being in-itself. I am a waiter in the mode of *being what I am not*.

Furthermore we are dealing with more than mere social positions; I am never any one of my attitudes, any one of my actions. The good speaker is the one who *plays at* speaking, because he cannot *be*

speaking. The attentive pupil who wishes to *be* attentive, his eyes riveted on the teacher, his ears open wide, so exhausts himself in playing the attentive role that he ends up by no longer hearing anything.
Perpetually absent to my body, to my acts, I am despite myself that
"divine absence" of which Valéry speaks. I cannot say either that I
am here or that I *am* not here, in the sense that we say "that box of
matches *is* on the table"; this would be to confuse my "being-in-the-
world" with a "being-in-the-midst-of-the-world." Nor that I *am* standing, nor that I *am* seated; this would be to confuse my body with the
idiosyncratic totality of which it is only one of the structures. On all
sides I escape being and yet—I am.

But take a mode of being which concerns only myself: I am sad.
One might think that surely I am the sadness in the mode of being
what I am. What is the sadness, however, if not the intentional unity
which comes to reassemble and animate the totality of my conduct? It
is the meaning of this dull look with which I view the world, of my
bowed shoulders, of my lowered head, of the listlessness in my whole
body. But at the very moment when I adopt each of these attitudes,
do I not know that I shall not be able to hold on to it? Let a stranger
suddenly appear and I will lift up my head, I will assume a lively
cheerfulness. What will remain of my sadness except that I obligingly
promise it an appointment for later after the departure of the visitor?
Moreover is not this sadness itself a *conduct?* Is it not consciousness
which affects itself with sadness as a magical recourse against a situation too urgent? And in this case even, should we not say that being
sad means first to make oneself sad? That may be, someone will say,
but after all doesn't giving oneself the being of sadness mean to *receive* this being? It makes no difference from where I receive it. The
fact is that a consciousness which affects itself with sadness is sad precisely for this reason. But it is difficult to comprehend the nature of
consciousness; the being-sad is not a ready-made being which I give
to myself as I can give this book to my friend. I do not possess the
property of *affecting myself with being.* If I make myself sad, I must
continue to make myself sad from beginning to end. I cannot treat my
sadness as an impulse finally achieved and put it on file without re-
creating it, nor can I carry it in the manner of an inert body which continues its movement after the initial shock. There is no inertia in consciousness. If I make myself sad, it is because I *am* not sad—the being
of the sadness escapes me by and in the very act by which I affect myself with it. The being-in-itself of sadness perpetually haunts my con-

sciousness (of) being sad, but it is as a value which I cannot realize; it stands as a regulative meaning of my sadness, not as its constitutive modality.

Someone may say that my consciousness at least *is,* whatever may be the object or the state of which it makes itself consciousness. But how do we distinguish my consciousness (of) being sad from sadness? Is it not all one? It is true in a way that my consciousness *is,* if one means by this that for another it is a part of the totality of being on which judgments can be brought to bear. But it should be noted, as Husserl clearly understood, that my consciousness appears originally to the Other as an absence. It is the object always present as the *meaning* of all my attitudes and all my conduct—and always absent, for it gives itself to the intuition of another as a perpetual question—still better, as a perpetual freedom. When Pierre locks at me, I know of course that he is looking at me. His eyes, things in the world, are fixed on my body, a thing in the world—that is the objective fact of which I can say: it *is*. But it is also a fact *in the world*. The meaning of this look is not a fact in the world, and this is what makes me uncomfortable. Although I make smiles, promises, threats, nothing can get hold of the approbation, the free judgment which I seek; I know that it is always beyond. I sense it in my very attitude, which is no longer like that of the worker toward the things he uses as instruments. My reactions, to the extent that I project myself toward the Other, are no longer for myself but are rather mere *presentations;* they await being constituted as graceful or uncouth, sincere or insincere, etc., by an apprehension which is always beyond my efforts to provoke, an apprehension which will be provoked by my efforts only if of itself it lends them force (that is, only in so far as it causes itself to be provoked from the outside), *which is its own mediator with the transcendent.* Thus the objective fact of the being-in-itself of the consciousness of the Other is posited in order to disappear in negativity and in freedom: consciousness of the Other is as not-being; its being-in-itself "here and now" is not-to-be.

Consciousness of the Other is what it is not.

Furthermore the being of my own consciousness does not appear to me as the consciousness of the Other. It *is* because it makes itself, since its being is consciousness of being. But this means that making sustains being; consciousness has to be its own being, it is never sustained by being; it sustains being in the heart of subjectivity, which means once again that it is inhabited by being but that it is not being: *consciousness is not what it is.*

Under these conditions what can be the significance of the ideal of sincerity except as a task impossible to achieve, of which the very meaning is in contradiction with the structure of my consciousness. To be sincere, we said, is to be what one is. That supposes that I am not originally what I am. But here naturally Kant's "You ought, therefore you can" is implicitly understood. I can *become* sincere; this is what my duty and my effort to achieve sincerity imply. But we definitely establish that the original structure of "not being what one is" renders impossible in advance all movement toward being in itself or "being what one is." And this impossibility is not hidden from consciousness; on the contrary, it is the very stuff of consciousness; it is the embarrassing constraint which we constantly experience; it is our very incapacity to recognize ourselves, to constitute ourselves as being what we are. It is this necessity which means that, as soon as we posit ourselves as a certain being, by a legitimate judgment, based on inner experience or correctly deduced from a priori or empirical premises, then by that very positing we surpass this being—and that not toward another being but toward emptiness, toward *nothing.*

How then can we blame another for not being sincere or rejoice in our own sincerity since this sincerity appears to us at the same time to be impossible? How can we in conversation, in confession, in introspection, even attempt sincerity since at the very time when we announce it we have a prejudicative comprehension of its futility? In introspection I try to determine exactly what I am, to make up my mind to be my true self without delay—even though it means consequently to set about searching for ways to change myself. But what does this mean if not that I am constituting myself as a thing? Shall I determine the ensemble of purposes and motivations which have pushed me to do this or that action? But this is already to postulate a causal determinism which constitutes the flow of my states of consciousness as a succession of physical states. Shall I uncover in myself "drives," even though it be to affirm them in shame? But is this not deliberately to forget that these drives are realized with my consent, that they are not forces of nature but that I lend them their efficacy by a perpetually renewed decision concerning their value? Shall I pass judgment on my character, on my nature? Is this not to veil from myself at that moment what I know only too well, that I thus judge a past to which by definition my present is not subject? The proof of this is that the same man who in sincerity posits that he is what in actuality he was, is indignant at the reproach of another and tries to disarm it by asserting that he can no longer be what he was. We are readily astonished and upset when the penalties of the court affect a man who in his new freedom *is no longer* the guilty person he was. But at the same time we require of this man that he recognize himself as *being* this guilty one. What then is sincerity except precisely a phenomenon of bad faith? Have we not shown indeed that in bad faith human reality is constituted as a being which is what it is not and which is not what it is?

Let us take an example: A homosexual frequently has an intolerable feeling of guilt, and his whole existence is determined in relation to this feeling. One will readily foresee that he is in bad faith. In fact it frequently happens that this man, while recognizing his homosexual inclination, while avowing each and every particular misdeed which he has committed, refuses with all his strength to consider himself "*a paederast.*" His case is always "different," peculiar; there enters into it something of a game, of chance, of bad luck; the mistakes are all in the past; they are explained by a certain conception of the beautiful which women cannot satisfy; we should see in them the results of a restless search, rather than the manifestations of a deeply rooted tendency, etc., etc. Here is assuredly a man in bad faith who borders on the comic since, acknowledging all the facts which are imputed to him, he refuses to draw from them the conclusion which they impose. His friend, who is his most severe critic, becomes irritated with this duplicity. The critic asks only one thing—and perhaps then he will show himself indulgent: that the guilty one recognize himself as guilty, that the homosexual declare frankly—whether humbly or boastfully matters little—"I am a paederast." We ask here: Who is in bad faith? The homosexual or the champion of sincerity?

The homosexual recognizes his faults, but he struggles with all his strength against the crushing view that his mistakes constitute for him a *destiny.* He does not wish to let himself be considered as a thing. He has an obscure but strong feeling that a homosexual is not a homosexual as this table is a table or as this red-haired man is red-haired. It seems to him that he has escaped from each mistake as soon as he has posited it and recognized it; he even feels that the psychic duration by itself cleanses him from each misdeed, constitutes for him an undetermined future, causes him to be born anew.

Is he wrong? Does he not recognize in himself the peculiar, irreducible character of human reality? His attitude includes then an undeniable comprehension of truth. But at the same time he needs this perpetual rebirth, this constant escape in order to live; he must constantly put himself beyond reach in order to avoid the terrible judgment of collectivity. Thus he plays on the word *being*. He would be right actually if he understood the phrase "I am not a paederast" in the sense of "I am not what I am." That is, if he declared to himself, "To the extent that a pattern of conduct is defined as the conduct of a paederast and to the extent that I have adopted this conduct, I am a paederast. But to the extent that human reality cannot be finally defined by patterns of conduct, I am not one." But instead he slides surreptitiously toward a different connotation of the word "being." He understands "not being" in the sense of "not-being-in-itself." He lays claim to "not being a paederast" in the sense in which this table *is not* an inkwell. He is in bad faith.

But the champion of sincerity is not ignorant of the transcendence of human reality, and he knows how at need to appeal to it for his own advantage. He makes use of it even and brings it up in the present argument. Does he not wish, first in the name of sincerity, then of freedom, that the homosexual reflect on himself and acknowledge himself as a homosexual? Does he not let the other understand that such a confession will win indulgence for him? What does this mean if not that the man who will acknowledge himself as a homosexual will no longer be *the same* as the homosexual whom he acknowledges being and that he will escape into the region of freedom and of good will? The critic asks the man then to be what he is in order no longer to be what he is. It is the profound meaning of the saying, "A sin confessed is half pardoned." The critic demands of the guilty one that he constitute himself as a thing, precisely in order no longer to treat him as a thing. And this contradiction is constitutive of the demand of sincerity. Who cannot see how offensive to the Other and how reassuring for me is a statement such as, "He's just a paederast," which removes a disturbing freedom from a trait and which aims at henceforth constituting all the acts of the Other as consequences following strictly from his essence. That is actually what the critic is demanding of his victim—that he constitute himself as a thing, that he should entrust his freedom to his friend as a fief, in order that the friend should return it to him subsequently—like a suzerain to his vassal. The champion of sincerity is in bad faith to the degree that in order to reassure himself, he pretends to judge, to the extent that he demands that freedom as freedom constitute itself as a thing. We have here only one episode in that battle to the death of consciousnesses which Hegel calls "the relation of the master and the slave." A person appeals to another and demands that in the name of his nature as consciousness he should radically destroy himself as consciousness, but while making this appeal he leads the other to hope for a rebirth beyond this destruction.

Very well, someone will say, but our man is abusing sincerity, playing one side against the other. We should not look for sincerity in the relation of the *mit-sein* but rather where it is pure—in the relations of a person with himself. But who cannot see that objective sincerity is constituted in the same way? Who cannot see that the sincere man constitutes himself as a thing in order to escape the condition of a thing by the same act of sincerity? The man who confesses that he is evil has exchanged his disturbing "freedom-for-evil" for an inanimate character of evil; he *is* evil, he clings to himself, he is what he is. But by the same stroke, he escapes from that thing, since it is he who contemplates it, since it depends on him to maintain it under his glance or to let it collapse in an infinity of particular acts. He derives a *merit* from his sincerity, and the deserving man is not the evil man as he is evil but as he is beyond his evilness. At the same time the evil is disarmed since it is nothing, save on the plane of determinism, and since in confessing it, I posit my freedom in respect to it; my future is virgin; everything is allowed to me.

Thus the essential structure of sincerity does not differ from that of bad faith since the sincere man constitutes himself as what he is *in order not to be it*. This explains the truth recognized by all that one can fall into bad faith through being sincere. As Valéry pointed out, this is the case with Stendhal. Total, constant sincerity as a constant effort to adhere to oneself is by nature a constant effort to dissociate oneself from oneself. A person frees himself from himself by the very act by which he makes himself an object for himself. To draw up a perpetual inventory of what one is means constantly to redeny oneself and to take refuge in a sphere where one is no longer anything but a pure, free regard. The goal of bad faith, as we said, is to put oneself out of reach; it is an escape. Now we see that we must use the same terms to define sincerity. What does this mean?

In the final analysis the goal of sincerity and the goal of bad faith are not so different. To be sure, there is a sincerity which bears on the past and which does not concern us here; I am sincere if I confess *having had* this pleasure or that intention. We shall see that if this sincerity is possible, it is because in his fall into the past, the being of man is constituted as a being-in-itself. But here our concern is only with the sincerity which aims at itself in present immanence. What is its goal? To bring me to confess to myself what I am in order that I may finally coincide with my being; in a word, to cause myself to be, in the mode of the in-itself, what I am in the mode of "not being what I am." Its assumption is that fundamentally I am already, in the mode of the in-itself, what I have to be. Thus we find at the base of sincerity a continual game of mirror and reflection, a perpetual passage from the being which is what it is to the being which is not what it is and inversely from the being which is not what it is to the being which is what it is. And what is the goal of bad faith? To cause me to be what I am, in the mode of "not being what one is," or not to be what I am in the mode of "being what one is." We find here the same game of mirrors. In fact in order for me to have an intention of sincerity, I must at the outset simultaneously be and not be what I am. Sincerity does not assign to me a mode of being or a particular quality, but in relation to that quality it aims at making me pass from one mode of being to another mode of being. This second mode of being, the ideal of sincerity, I am prevented by nature from attaining; and at the very moment when I struggle to attain it, I have a vague prejudicative comprehension that I shall not attain it. But all the same, in order for me to be able to conceive an intention in bad faith, I must have such a nature that within my being I escape from my being. If I were sad or cowardly in the way in which this inkwell is an inkwell, the possibility of bad faith could not even be conceived. Not only should I be unable to escape from my being; I could not even imagine that I could escape from it. But if bad faith is possible by virtue of a simple project, it is because so far as my being is concerned, there is no difference between being and non-being if I am cut off from my project.

Bad faith is possible only because sincerity is conscious of missing its goal inevitably, due to its very nature. I can try to apprehend myself as "*not being cowardly*," when I *am* so, only on condition that the "being cowardly" is itself "in question" at the very moment when it exists, on condition that it is itself *one* question, that at the very moment when I wish to apprehend it, it escapes me on all sides and annihilates itself. The condition under which I can attempt an effort in bad faith is that in one sense, I *am not* this coward which I do not wish to be. But if I *were not* cowardly in the simple mode of not-being-what-one-is-not, I would be "in good faith" by declaring that I am not cowardly. Thus this inapprehensible coward is evanescent; in order for me not to be cowardly, I must in some way also be cowardly. That does not mean that I must be "a little" cowardly, in the sense that "a little" signifies "to a certain degree cowardly—and not cowardly to a certain degree." No. I must at once both be and not be totally and in all respects a coward. Thus in this case bad faith requires that I should not be what I am; that is, that there be an imponderable difference separating being from non-being in the mode of being of human reality.

But bad faith is not restricted to denying the qualities which I possess, to not seeing the being which I am. It attempts also to constitute myself as being what I am not. It apprehends me positively as courageous when I am not so. And that is possible, once again, only if I am what I am not; that is, if non-being in me does not have being even as non-being. Of course necessarily I *am not* courageous; otherwise bad faith would not be *bad* faith. But in addition my effort in bad faith must include the ontological comprehension that even in my usual being what I *am,* I am not it really and that there is no such difference between the being of "being-sad," for example—which I *am* in the mode of not being what I am—and the "non-being" of not-being-courageous which I wish to hide from myself. Moreover it is particularly requisite that the very negation of being should be itself the object of a perpetual nihilation, that the very meaning of "non-being" be perpetually in question in human reality. If I *were not* courageous in the way in which this inkwell is not a table; that is, if I were isolated in my cowardice, propped firmly against it, incapable of putting it in relation to its opposite, if I were not capable of *determining* myself as cowardly—that is, to deny courage to myself and thereby to escape my cowardice in the very moment that I posit it—if it were not on principle *impossible* for me to coincide with my *not-being-courageous* as well as with my being-courageous—then any project of bad faith would be prohibited me. Thus in order for bad faith to be possible, sincerity itself must be in bad faith. The condition of the possibility for bad faith is that human reality, in its most immediate being, in the intra-structure of the pre-reflective *cogito,* must be what it is not and not be what it is.

❖ Freedom and Facticity: The Situation ❖

The decisive argument which is employed by common sense against freedom consists in reminding us of our impotence. Far from being able to modify our situation at our whim, we seem to be unable to change ourselves. I am not "free" either to escape the lot of my class, of my nation, of my family, or even to build up my own power or my fortune or to conquer my most significant appetites or habits. I am born a worker, a Frenchman, an hereditary syphilitic, or a tubercular. The history of a life, whatever it may be, is the history of a failure. The coefficient of adversity of things is such that years of patience are necessary to obtain the feeblest result. Again it is necessary "to obey nature in order to command it"; that is, to insert my action into the network of determinism. Much more than he appears "to make himself," man seems "to be made" by climate and the earth, race and class, language, the history of the collectivity of which he is a part, heredity, the individual circumstances of his childhood, acquired habits, the great and small events of his life.

This argument has never greatly troubled the partisans of human freedom. Descartes, first of all, recognized both that the will is infinite and that it is necessary "to try to conquer ourselves rather than fortune." Here certain distinctions ought to be made. Many of the facts set forth by the determinists do not actually deserve to enter into our considerations. In particular the coefficient of adversity in things can not be an argument against our freedom, for it is *by* us—i.e., by the preliminary positing of an end—that this coefficient of adversity arises. A particular crag, which manifests a profound resistance if I wish to displace it, will be on the contrary a valuable aid if I want to climb upon it in order to look over the countryside. In itself—if one can even imagine what the crag can be in itself—it is neutral; that is, it waits to be illuminated by an end in order to manifest itself as adverse or helpful. Again it can manifest itself in one or the other way only within an instrumental-complex which is already established. Without picks and piolets, paths already worn, and a technique of climbing, the crag would be neither easy nor difficult to climb; the question would not be posited, it would not support any relation of any kind with the technique of mountain climbing. Thus although brute things (what Heidegger calls "brute existents") can from the start limit our freedom of action, it is our freedom itself which must first constitute the framework, the technique, and the ends in relation to which they will manifest themselves as limits. Even if the crag is revealed as "too difficult to climb," and if we must give up the ascent, let us note that the crag is revealed as such only because it was originally grasped as "climbable"; it is therefore our freedom which constitutes the limits which it will subsequently encounter. . . .

In addition it is necessary to point out to "common sense" that the formula "to be free" does not mean "to obtain what one has wished" but rather "by oneself to determine oneself to wish" (in the broad sense of choosing). In other words success is not important to freedom. The discussion which opposes common sense to philosophers stems here from a misunderstanding: the empirical and popular concept of "freedom" which has been produced by historical, political, and moral circumstances is equivalent to "the ability to obtain the ends chosen." The technical and philosophical concept of freedom, the only one which we are considering here, means only the autonomy of choice. It is necessary, however, to note that the choice, being identical with acting, supposes a commencement of realization in order that the choice may be distinguished from the dream and the wish. Thus we shall not say that a prisoner is always free to go out of prison, which would be absurd, nor that he is always free to long for release, which would be an irrelevant truism, but that he is always free to try to escape (or get himself liberated); that is, that whatever his condition may be, he can project his escape and learn the value of his project by undertaking some action. Our description of freedom, since it does not distinguish between choosing and doing, compels us to abandon at once the distinction between the intention and the act. The intention can no more be separated from the act than thought can be separated from the language which expresses it; and as it happens that our speech informs us of our thought, so our acts will inform us of our intentions—that is, it will enable us to disengage our intentions, to schematize them, and to make objects of them instead of limiting us to living them—i.e., to assume a non-thetic consciousness of them. This essential distinction between the freedom of choice and the freedom of obtaining was certainly perceived by Descartes, following Stoicism. It puts an end to all arguments based on the distinction between "willing" and "being able," which are still put forth today by the partisans and the opponents of freedom.

It is nonetheless true that freedom encounters or seems to encounter limitations on account of the *given* which it surpasses or nihilates. To show that the coefficient of adversity of the thing and its character as an obstacle (joined to its character as an instrument) is indispensable to the existence of a freedom is to use an argument that cuts two ways; for while it enables us to establish that freedom is not invalidated by the given, it indicates, on the other hand, something like an ontological conditioning of freedom. Would it not be reasonable to say, along with certain contemporary philosophers: if no obstacle, then no freedom? And as we can not admit that freedom by itself creates its own obstacle—which would be absurd for anyone who has understood the meaning of spontaneity—there seems to be here a kind of ontological priority of the in-itself over the for-itself. Therefore we must consider the previous remarks as simple attempts to clear the ground, and we must take up again from the beginning the question of facticity. . . . The *situation,* the common product of the contingency of the in-itself and of freedom, is an ambiguous phenomenon in which it is impossible for the for-itself to distinguish the contribution of freedom from that of the brute existent. In fact, just as freedom is the escape from a contingency which it has to be in order to escape it, so the situation is the free coordination and the free qualification of a brute given which does not allow itself to be qualified in any way at all. Here I am at the foot of this crag which appears to me as "not scalable." This means that the rock appears to me in the light of a projected scaling—a secondary project which finds its meaning in terms of an initial project which is my being-in-the-world. Thus the rock is carved out on the ground of the world by the effect of the initial choice of my freedom. But on the other hand, what my freedom can not determine is whether the rock "to be scaled" will or will not lend itself to scaling. This is part of the brute being of the rock. Nevertheless the rock can show its resistance to the scaling only if the rock is integrated by freedom in a "situation" of which the general theme is scaling. For the simple traveler who passes over this road and whose free project is a pure aesthetic ordering of the landscape, the crag is not revealed either as scalable or as not-scalable; it is maintained only as beautiful or ugly.

Thus it is impossible to determine in each particular case what comes from freedom and what comes from the brute being of the for-itself. The given in-itself as *resistance* or as *aid* is revealed only in the light of the projecting freedom. But the projecting freedom organizes an illumination such that the in-itself is revealed by it *as it is* (i.e., resisting or favorable); but we must clearly understand that the resistance of the given is not directly admissible as an in-itself quality of the given but only as an indication—across a free illumination and a free refraction—of an inapprehensible *quid*. Therefore it is only in and through the free upsurge of a freedom that the world develops and reveals the resistance which can render the projected end unrealizable. Man encounters an obstacle only within the field of his freedom. Better yet, it is impossible to decree a priori what comes from the brute existent and what from freedom in the character of this or that particular existent functioning as an obstacle. What is an obstacle for me may not be so for another. There is no obstacle in an absolute sense, but the obstacle reveals its coefficient of adversity across freely invented and freely acquired techniques. The obstacle reveals this coefficient also in terms of the value of the end posited by freedom. The rock will not be an obstacle if I wish at any cost to arrive at the top of the mountain. On the other hand, it will discourage me if I have freely fixed limits to my desire of making the projected climb. Thus the world by coefficients of adversity reveals to me the way in which I stand in relation to the ends which I assign myself, so that I can never know if it is giving me information about myself or about it. Furthermore the coefficient of adversity of the given is never a simple relation to my freedom as a pure nihilating thrust. It is a relation, illuminated by freedom, between the *datum* which is the cliff and the *datum* which my freedom has to be; that is, between the contingent which it is not and its pure facticity. If the desire to scale it is equal, the rock will be easy for one athletic climber but difficult for another, a novice, who is not well trained and who has a weak body. But the body in turn is revealed as well or poorly trained only in relation to a free choice. It is because I am there and because I have made of myself what I am that the rock develops in relation to my body a coefficient of adversity. For the lawyer who has remained in the city and who is pleading a case, whose body is hidden under his lawyer's robe, the rock is neither hard nor easy to climb; it is dissolved in the totality "world" without in any way emerging from it. And in one sense it is I who choose my body as weak by making it face the difficulties which I cause to be born (mountain climbing, cycling, sport). If I have not chosen to take part in sports, if I live in the city, and if I concern myself exclusively with business or intellectual work, then from this point of view my body will have no quality whatsoever.

Thus we begin to catch a glimpse of the paradox of freedom: there is freedom only in a *situation,* and there is a situation only through freedom. Human-reality everywhere encounters resistance and obstacles which it has not created, but these resistances and obstacles have meaning only in and through the free choice which human-reality *is. . . .* Human freedom precedes essence in man and makes it possible; the essence of the human being is suspended in his freedom. What we call freedom is impossible to distinguish from the *being* of "human reality." Man does not exist *first* in order to be free *subsequently;* there is no difference between the being of man and his *being-free. . . .* Freedom is total and infinite, which does not mean that it has no limits but that it *never encounters them.* The only limits which freedom bumps up against at each moment are those which it imposes on itself.

❖ Being-for-Others ❖

. . . the upsurge of the Other touches the for-itself in its very heart. By the Other and for the Other the pursuing flight is fixed in in-itself. Already the in-itself was progressively recapturing it; already it was at once a radical negation of fact, an absolute positing of value and yet wholly paralyzed with facticity. But at least it was escaping by temporalization; at least its character as a totality detotalized conferred on it a perpetual "elsewhere." Now it is this very totality which the Other makes appear before him and which he transcends toward his own "elsewhere." It is this totality which is totalized. For the Other I am irremediably what I am, and my very freedom is a given characteristic of my being. Thus the in-self recaptures me at the threshold of the future and fixes me wholly in my very flight, which becomes a flight foreseen and contemplated, a *given* flight. But this fixed flight is never the flight which I am for myself; it is fixed *outside.* The objectivity of my flight I experience as an alienation which

From Being and Nothingness *by Jean-Paul Sartre, translated by Hazel E. Barnes. Copyright 1956 by Philosophical Library, Inc. Reprinted by permission of Philosophical Library, Inc., of New York.*

I can neither transcend nor know. Yet by the sole fact that I experience it and that it confers on my flight that in-itself which it flees, I must turn back toward it and assume *attitudes* with respect to it.

Such is the origin of my concrete relations with the Other; they are wholly governed by my attitudes with respect to the object which I am for the Other. And as the Other's existence reveals to me the being which I am without my being able either to appropriate that being or even to conceive it, this existence will motivate two opposed attitudes: First—The Other *looks* at me and as such he holds the secret of my being, he knows what I *am*. Thus the profound meaning of my being is outside of me, imprisoned in an absence. The Other has the advantage over me. Therefore in so far as I am fleeing the in-itself which I am without founding it, I can attempt to deny that being which is conferred on me from outside; that is, I can turn back upon the Other so as to make an object out of him in turn since the Other's objectness destroys my object-ness for him. But on the other hand, in so far as the Other as freedom is the foundation of my being-in-itself. I can seek to recover that freedom and to possess it without removing from it its character as freedom. In fact if I could identify myself with that freedom which is the foundation of my being-in-itself, I should be to myself my own foundation. To transcend the Other's transcendence, or, on the contrary, to incorporate that transcendence within me without removing from it its character as transcendence—such are the two primitive attitudes which I assume confronting the Other. Here again we must understand the words exactly. It is not true that I first am and then later "seek" to make an object of the Other or to assimilate him; but to the extent that the upsurge of my being is an upsurge in the presence of the Other, to the extent that I am a pursuing flight and a pursued-pursuing, I am—at the very root of my being—the project of assimilating and making an object of the Other. I am the proof of the Other. That is the original fact. But this proof of the Other is in itself an attitude toward the Other; that is, I can not *be in the presence of the Other* without being that "in-the-presence" in the form of having to be it. Thus again we are describing the for-itself's structures of being although the Other's presence in the world is an absolute and self-evident fact, but a contingent fact—that is, a fact impossible to deduce from the ontological structures of the for-itself.

These two attempts which I am are opposed to one another. Each attempt is the death of the other; that is, the failure of the one moti-

vates the adoption of the other. Thus there is no dialectic for my relations toward the Other but rather a circle—although each attempt
is enriched by the failure of the other. Thus we shall study each one
in turn. But it should be noted that at the very core of the one the
other remains always present, precisely because neither of the two
can be held without contradiction. Better yet, each of them is in the
other and endangers the death of the other. Thus we can never get
outside the circle. We must not forget these facts as we approach the
study of these fundamental attitudes toward the Other. Since these
attitudes are produced and destroyed in a circle, it is as arbitrary to
begin with the one as with the other. Nevertheless since it is necessary to choose, we shall consider first the conduct in which the for-
itself tries to assimilate the Other's freedom.

First Attitude Toward Others: Love, Language, Masochism

Everything which may be said of me in my relations with the Other
applies to him as well. While I attempt to free myself from the hold
of the Other, the Other is trying to free himself from mine; while I
seek to enslave the Other, the Other seeks to enslave me. We are by
no means dealing with unilateral relations with an object-in-itself, but
with reciprocal and moving relations. The following descriptions of
concrete behavior must therefore be envisaged within the perspective of *conflict*. Conflict is the original meaning of being-for-others.

  If we start with the first revelation of the Other as a *look,* we must
recognize that we experience our inapprehensible being-for-others
in the form of a *possession*. I am possessed by the Other; the Other's
look fashions my body in its nakedness, causes it to be born, sculp-
tures it, produces it as it *is,* sees it as I shall never see it. The Other
holds a secret—the secret of what I am. He makes me be and thereby
he possesses me, and this possession is nothing other than the consciousness of possessing me. I in the recognition of my object-state
have proof that he has this consciousness. By virtue of consciousness
the Other is for me simultaneously the one who has stolen my being
from me and the one who causes "there to be" a being which is my
being. Thus I have a comprehension of this ontological structure: I
am responsible for my being-for-others, but I am not the foundation
of it. It appears to me therefore in the form of a contingent given for
which I am nevertheless responsible; the Other founds my being in

so far as this being is in the form of the "there is." But he is not responsible for my being although he founds it in complete freedom—
in and by means of his free transcendence. Thus to the extent that I
am revealed to myself as responsible for my being, I *lay claim* to this
being which I am; that is, I wish to recover it, or, more exactly, I am
the project of the recovery of my being. I want to stretch out my hand
and grab hold of this being which is presented to me as *my being* but
at a distance—like the dinner of Tantalus; I want to found it by my
very freedom. For if in one sense my being-as-object is an unbearable contingency and the pure "possession" of myself by another, still
in another sense this being stands as the indication of what I should
be obliged to recover and found in order to be the foundation of myself. But this is conceivable only if I assimilate the Other's freedom.
Thus my project of recovering myself is fundamentally a project of
absorbing the Other.

* * *

❖ *from* No Exit ❖

    INEZ: It's obvious what they're after—an econ-
omy of man-power—or devil-power, if you prefer. The same idea as in the cafeteria, where
customers serve themselves.

    ESTELLE: What ever do you mean?

    INEZ: I mean that each of us will act as torturer
of the two others.

    *There is a short silence while they digest this in-
formation.*

    GARCIN (*gently*): No, I shall never be your tor-
turer. I wish neither of you any harm, and I've
no concern with you. None at all. So the solution's easy enough; each of us stays put in his

or her corner and takes no notice of the others.
You here, you here, and I there. . . .

ESTELLE: Have *I* got to keep silent, too?

GARCIN: Yes. And that way we—we'll work out
our salvation. Looking into ourselves, never
raising our heads. Agreed?

INEZ: Agreed.

ESTELLE (*after some hesitation*): I agree.

GARCIN: Then—good-by.

*He goes to his sofa and buries his head in his
hands. There is a long silence; then INEZ begins
singing to herself. Meanwhile ESTELLE has been
plying her powder-puff and lipstick. She looks
round for a mirror, fumbles in her bag, then turns
towards GARCIN.*

ESTELLE: Excuse me, have you a glass?
(GARCIN *does not answer.*) Any sort of glass, a
pocket-mirror will do. (GARCIN *remains silent.*)
Even if you won't speak to me, you might lend
me a glass.

*His head still buried in his hands, GARCIN ig-
nores her.*

INEZ (*eagerly*): Don't worry. I've a glass in my
bag. (*She opens her bag. Angrily.*) It's gone!
They must have taken it from me at the en-
trance.

ESTELLE: How tiresome!

*A short silence. ESTELLE shuts her eyes and
sways, as if about to faint. Inez runs forward and
holds her up.*

INEZ: What's the matter?

ESTELLE (*opens her eyes and smiles*): I feel so
queer. (*She pats herself.*) Don't you ever get
taken that way? When I can't see myself I begin
to wonder if I really and truly exist. I pat myself
just to make sure, but it doesn't help much.

INEZ: You're lucky. I'm always conscious of myself—in my mind. Painfully conscious.

ESTELLE: Ah yes, in your mind. But everything that goes on in one's head is so vague, isn't it? It makes one want to sleep. (*She is silent for a while.*) I've six big mirrors in my bedroom. There they are. I can see them. But they don't see me. They're reflecting the carpet, the settee, the window—but how empty it is, a glass in which I'm absent! When I talked to people I always made sure there was one near by in which I could see myself. I watched myself talking. And somehow it kept me alert, seeing myself as the others saw me. . . . Oh dear! My lipstick! I'm sure I've put it on all crooked. No, I can't do without a looking-glass for ever and ever. I simply can't.

INEZ: Suppose I try to be your glass? Come and pay me a visit, dear. Here's a place for you on my sofa.

ESTELLE: But—(*Points to* GARCIN).

INEZ: Oh, he doesn't count.

ESTELLE: But we're going to—to hurt each other. You said it yourself.

INEZ: Do I look as if I wanted to hurt you?

ESTELLE: One never can tell.

INEZ: Much more likely *you'll* hurt *me.* Still, what does it matter? If I've got to suffer, it may as well be at your hands, your pretty hands. Sit down. Come closer. Closer. Look into my eyes. What do you see?

ESTELLE: Oh, I'm there! But so tiny I can't see myself properly.

INEZ: But *I* can. Every inch of you. Now ask me questions. I'll be as candid as any looking-glass.

ESTELLE seems rather embarrassed and turns to GARCIN, as if appealing to him for help.

ESTELLE: Please, Mr. Garcin. Sure our chatter isn't boring you?

GARCIN makes no reply.

INEZ: Don't worry about him. As I said, he doesn't count. We're by ourselves. . . . Ask away.

ESTELLE: Are my lips all right?

INEZ: Show! No, they're a bit smudgy.

ESTELLE: I thought as much. Luckily (*throws a quick glance at* GARCIN) no one's seen me. I'll try again.

INEZ: That's better. No. Follow the line of your lips. Wait! I'll guide your hand. There. That's quite good.

ESTELLE: As good as when I came in?

INEZ: Far better. Crueler. Your mouth looks quite diabolical that way.

ESTELLE: Good gracious! And you say you like it! How maddening, not being able to see for myself! You're quite sure, Miss Serrano, that it's all right now?

INEZ: Won't you call me Inez?

ESTELLE: Are you sure it looks all right?

INEZ: You're lovely. Estelle.

ESTELLE: But how can I rely upon your taste? Is it the same as *my* taste? Oh, how sickening it all is, enough to drive one crazy!

INEZ: I *have* your taste, my dear, because I like you so much. Look at me. No, straight. Now smile. I'm not so ugly, either. Am I not nicer than your glass?

ESTELLE: Oh, I don't know. You scare me rather. My reflection in the glass never did that; of course, I knew it so well. Like something I had tamed. . . . I'm going to smile, and my smile will sink down into your pupils, and heaven knows what it will become.

INEZ: And why shouldn't you "tame" *me? (The women gaze at each other,* ESTELLE *with a sort of fearful fascination*.) Listen! I want you to call me Inez. We must be great friends.

ESTELLE: I don't make friends with women very easily.

INEZ: Not with postal clerks, you mean? Hullo, what's that—that nasty red spot at the bottom of your cheek? A pimple?

ESTELLE: A pimple? Oh, how simply foul! Where?

INEZ: There. . . . You know the way they catch larks—with a mirror? I'm your lark-mirror, my dear, and you can't escape me. . . . There isn't any pimple, not a trace of one. So what about it? Suppose the mirror started telling lies? Or suppose I covered my eyes—as he is doing—and refused to look at you, all that love-liness of yours would be wasted on the desert air. No, don't be afraid, I can't help looking at you, I shan't turn my eyes away. And I'll be nice to you, ever so nice. Only you must be nice to me, too.

A short silence.

ESTELLE: Are you really—attracted by me?

INEZ: Very much indeed.

Another short silence.

ESTELLE (*indicating* GARCIN *by a slight move-ment of her head*): But I wish he'd notice me, too.

INEZ: Of course! Because he's a Man! (*To* GARCIN) You've won. (GARCIN *says nothing.*) But look at her, damn it! (*Still no reply from* GARCIN.) Don't pretend. You haven't missed a word of what we've said.

GARCIN: Quite so; not a word. I stuck my fin-gers in my ears, but your voices thudded in my brain. Silly chatter. Now will you leave me in peace, you two? I'm not interested in you.

INEZ: Not in me, perhaps—but how about this child? Aren't you interested in her? Oh, I saw through your game; you got on your high horse just to impress her.

GARCIN: I asked you to leave me in peace. There's someone talking about me in the newspaper office and I want to listen. And, if it'll make you any happier, let me tell you that I've no use for the "child," as you call her.

ESTELLE: Thanks.

GARCIN: Oh, I didn't mean it rudely.

ESTELLE: You cad!

They confront each other in silence.

• • •

GARCIN: . . . (*He swings round abruptly.*) What? Only two of you? I thought there were more; many more. (*Laughs.*) So this is hell. I'd never have believed it. You remember all we were told about the torture-chambers, the fire and brimstone, the "burning marl." Old wives' tales! There's no need for red-hot pokers. Hell is—other people. . . .

❖ Freedom and Responsibility ❖

Although the considerations which are about to follow are of interest primarily to the ethicist, it may nevertheless be worth-while after these descriptions and arguments to return to the freedom of the for-itself and try to understand what the fact of this freedom represents for human destiny.

The essential consequence of our earlier remarks is that man being condemned to be free carries the weight of the whole world on his shoulders; he is responsible for the world and for himself as a way of being. We are taking the word "responsibility" in its ordinary sense as "consciousness (of) being the incontestable author of an event or of an object." In this sense the responsibility of the for-itself is overwhelming since he is the one by whom it happens that *there is* a world; since he is also the one who makes himself be, then whatever may be the situation in which he finds himself, the for-itself must wholly assume this situation with its peculiar coefficient of adversity, even though it be insupportable. He must assume the situation with the proud consciousness of being the author of it, for the very worst disadvantages or the worst threats which can endanger my person have meaning only in and through my project; and it is on the ground of the engagement which I am that they appear. It is therefore senseless to think of complaining since nothing foreign has decided what we feel, what we live, or what we are.

Furthermore this absolute responsibility is not resignation; it is simply the logical requirement of the consequences of our freedom. What happens to me happens through me, and I can neither affect myself with it nor revolt against it nor resign myself to it. Moreover everything which happens to me is *mine*. By this we must understand first of all that I am always equal to what happens to me *qua* man, for what happens to a man through other men and through himself can be only human. The most terrible situations of war, the worst tortures do not create a non-human state of things; there is no non-human situation. It is only through fear, flight, and recourse to magical types of conduct that I shall decide on the non-human, but this decision is human, and I shall carry the entire responsibility for it. But in addition the situation is *mine* because it is the image of my free choice of myself, and everything which it presents to me is *mine* in that this represents me and symbolizes me. Is it not I who decide the coefficient of adversity in things and even their unpredictability by deciding myself?

Thus there are no *accidents* in a life; a community event which suddenly bursts forth and involves me in it does not come from the outside. If I am mobilized in a war, this war is my war; it is in my image and I deserve it. I deserve it first because I could always get out of it by suicide or by desertion; these ultimate possibles are those which must always be present for us when there is a question of envisaging a situation. For lack of getting out of it, I have *chosen* it. This can be due to inertia, to cowardice in the face of public opinion, or because I prefer certain other values to the value of the refusal to join in the war (the good opinion of my relatives, the honor of my family, etc.). Any way you look at it, it is a matter of a choice. This choice will be repeated later on again and again without a break until the end of the war. Therefore we must agree with the statement by J. Romains, "In war there are no innocent victims." If therefore I have preferred war to death or to dishonor, everything takes place as if I bore the entire responsibility for this war. Of course others have declared it, and one might be tempted perhaps to consider me as a simple accomplice. But this notion of complicity has only a juridical sense, and it does not hold here. For it depended on me that for me and by me this war should not exist, and I have decided that it does exist. There was no compulsion here, for the compulsion could have got no hold on a freedom. I did not have any excuse; . . . the peculiar character of human-reality is that it is without excuse. Therefore it remains for me only to lay claim to this war.

But in addition the war is *mine* because by the sole fact that it arises in a situation which I cause to be and that I can discover it there only by engaging myself for or against it, I can no longer distinguish at present the choice which I make of myself from the choice which I make of the war. To live this war is to choose myself through it and to choose it through my choice of myself. There can be no question of considering it as "four years of vacation" or as a "reprieve," as a "recess," the essential part of my responsibilities being elsewhere in my married, family, or professional life. In this war which I have chosen I choose myself from day to day, and I make it mine by making myself. If it is going to be four empty years, then it is I who bear the responsibility for this.

Finally, . . . each person is an absolute choice of self from the standpoint of a world of knowledges and of techniques which this choice both assumes and illumines; each person is an absolute upsurge at an absolute date and is perfectly unthinkable at another date. It is therefore a waste of time to ask what I should have been if this war had not broken out, for I have chosen myself as one of the possible meanings of the epoch which imperceptibly led to war. I am not distinct from this same epoch; I could not be transported to another epoch without contradiction. Thus *I am* this war which restricts and limits and makes comprehensible the period which preceded it. In this sense we may define more precisely the responsibility of the for-itself if to the earlier quoted statement, "There are no innocent victims," we add the words, "We have the war we deserve." Thus, totally free, undistinguishable from the period for which I have chosen to be the

meaning, as profoundly responsible for the war as if I had myself declared it, unable to live without integrating it in *my* situation, engaging myself in it wholly and stamping it with my seal, I must be without remorse or regrets as I am without excuse; for from the instant of
my upsurge into being, I carry the weight of the world by myself alone
without anything or any person being able to lighten it.

Yet this responsibility is of a very particular type. Someone will say,
"I did not ask to be born." This is a naïve way of throwing greater emphasis on our facticity. I am responsible for everything in fact, except
for my very responsibility, for I am not the foundation of my being.
Therefore everything takes place as if I were compelled to be responsible. I am *abandoned* in the world, not in the sense that I might
remain abandoned and passive in a hostile universe like a board floating on the water, but rather in the sense that I find myself suddenly
alone and without help, engaged in a world for which I bear the whole
responsibility without being able, whatever I do, to tear myself away
from this responsibility for an instant. For I am responsible for my very
desire of fleeing responsibilities. To make myself passive in the world,
to refuse to act upon things and upon Others is still to choose myself,
and suicide is one mode among others of being-in-the-world. Yet I
find an absolute responsibility for the fact that my facticity (here the
fact of my birth) is directly inapprehensible and even inconceivable,
for this fact of my birth never appears as a brute fact but always across
a projective reconstruction of my for-itself. I am ashamed of being
born or I am astonished at it or I rejoice over it, or in attempting to get
rid of my life I affirm that I live and I assume this life as bad. Thus in
a certain sense I *choose* being born. This choice itself is integrally affected with facticity since I am not able not to choose, but this facticity in turn will appear only in so far as I surpass it toward my ends.
Thus facticity is everywhere but inapprehensible; I never encounter
anything except my responsibility. That is why I can not ask, "*Why*
was I born?" or curse the day of my birth or declare that I did not ask
to be born, for these various attitudes toward my birth—i.e., toward
the *fact* that I realize a presence in the world—are absolutely nothing
else but ways of assuming this birth in full responsibility and of making it *mine*. Here again I encounter only myself and my projects so
that finally my abandonment—i.e., my facticity—consists simply in
the fact that I am condemned to be wholly responsible for myself. I
am the being which *is* in such a way that in its being its being is in
question. And this "is" of my being is as present and inapprehensible.

Under these conditions since every event in the world can be revealed to me only as an *opportunity* (an opportunity made use of, lacked, neglected, etc.), or better yet since everything which happens to us can be considered as a *chance* (i.e., can appear to us only as a way of realizing this being which is in question in our being) and since others as transcendences-transcended are themselves only *opportunities* and *chances,* the responsibility of the for-itself extends to the entire world as a peopled-world. It is precisely thus that the for-itself apprehends itself in anguish; that is, as a being which is neither the foundation of its own being nor of the Other's being nor of the in-itselfs which form the world, but a being which is compelled to decide the meaning of being—within it and everywhere outside of it. The one who realizes in anguish his condition as *being* thrown into a responsibility which extends to his very abandonment has no longer either remorse or regret or excuse; he is no longer anything but a freedom which perfectly reveals itself and whose being resides in this very revelation. But as we pointed out . . . , most of the time we flee anguish in bad faith.

❖ *from* The Flies ❖

> ZEUS: A pity you can't see yourself as you are
> now, you fool, for all your boasting! What a
> heroic figure you cut there, cowering between
> the legs of a protecting god, with a pack of
> hungry vixen keeping guard on you! If you *can*
> brag of freedom, why not praise the freedom of
> a prisoner languishing in fetters, or a slave
> nailed to the cross?
> ORESTES: Certainly. Why not?

• • •

> *The walls draw together. ZEUS comes into view,*
> *tired and dejected, and he now speaks in his nor-*
> *mal voice.*

ZEUS: Impudent spawn! So I am not your king?
Who, then, made you?

ORESTES: You. But you blundered; you should
not have made me free.

ZEUS: I gave you freedom so that you might
serve me.

ORESTES: Perhaps. But now it has turned
against its giver. And neither you nor I can
undo what has been done.

ZEUS: Oh, at last! So this is your excuse?

ORESTES: I am not excusing myself.

ZEUS: No? Let me tell you it sounds much like
an excuse, this freedom whose slave you claim
to be.

ORESTES: Neither slave nor master. I *am* my
freedom. No sooner had you created me than I
ceased to be yours.

❖ *from* The Age of Reason ❖

Mathieu, who was about to get up, subsided into his chair, and the
old fraternal resentment took possession of him once more. That firm
but gentle pressure on his shoulder was more than he could stand;
he threw his head back and saw Jacques's face foreshortened.

"Tell myself a lie! Look here, Jacques, say you don't want to be
mixed up in a case of abortion, that you disapprove of it, or that you
haven't the ready money and you're perfectly within your rights, nor
shall I resent it. But this talk of lying is nonsense, there's no lying in
it at all. I don't want a child: a child is coming, and I propose to suppress it; that's all."

Jacques withdrew his hand and took a few steps with a meditative
air. "He's going to make me a speech," thought Mathieu. "I oughtn't
to have let myself in for an argument."

From The Age of Reason *by Jean-Paul Sartre, translated by Eric Sutton. Copyright
1947 by Eric Sutton. Reprinted by permission of Alfred A. Knopf, a division of Random
House, Inc.*

"Mathieu," said Jacques in a calm tone, "I know you better than you think, and you distress me. I've long been afraid that something like this would happen: this coming child is the logical result of a situation into which you entered of your own free will, and you want to suppress it because you won't accept all the consequences of your acts. Come, shall I tell you the truth? I dare say you aren't lying to yourself at this precise moment: the trouble is that your whole life is built upon a lie."

"Carry on," said Mathieu. "I don't mind. Tell me what it is I'm trying to evade."

"You are trying," said Jacques, "to evade the fact that you're a bourgeois and ashamed of it. I myself reverted to bourgeoisie after many aberrations and contracted a marriage of convenience with the party, but you are a bourgeois by taste and temperament, and it's your temperament that's pushing you into marriage. For *you are married,* Mathieu," said he forcibly.

"First I heard of it," said Mathieu.

"Oh yes, you are, only you pretend you aren't because you are possessed by theories. You have fallen into a habit of life with this young woman: you go to see her quietly four days a week and you spend the night with her. That has been going on for seven years, and there's no adventure left in it; you respect her, you feel obligations towards her, you don't want to leave her. And I'm quite sure that your sole object isn't pleasure. I even imagine that, broadly speaking, however vivid the pleasure may have been, it has by now begun to fade. In fact, I expect you sit beside her in the evening and tell her long stories about the events of the day and ask her advice in difficulties."

"Of course," said Mathieu, shrugging his shoulders. He was furious with himself.

"Very well," said Jacques, "will you tell me how that differs from marriage—except for cohabitation?"

"Except for cohabitation?" said Mathieu ironically. "Excuse me, but that's a quibble."

"Oh," said Jacques, "being what you are, it probably doesn't cost you much to do without that."

"He has never said so much about my affairs," thought Mathieu, "he is taking his revenge." The thing to do was to go out and slam the door. But Mathieu was well aware that he would stay until the end: he was seized by an aggressive and malicious impulse to discover his brother's true opinion.

"But why do you say it probably doesn't cost me much, *being what I am?*"

"Because you get a comfortable life out of the situation, and an appearance of liberty: you have all the advantages of marriage and you exploit your principles to avoid its inconveniences. You refuse to regularize the position, which you find quite easy. If anyone suffers from all this, it isn't you."

"Marcelle shares my ideas on marriage," said Mathieu acidly; he heard himself pronounce each word and felt extremely ill at ease.

"Oh," said Jacques, "if she didn't share them she would no doubt be too proud to admit it to you. The fact is you're beyond my comprehension: you, so prompt with indignation when you hear of an injustice, you keep this woman for years in a humiliating position, for the sole pleasure of telling yourself that you're respecting your principles. It wouldn't be so bad if it were true, if you really did adapt your life to your ideas. But I must tell you once more, you are as good as married, you have a delightful apartment, you get a competent salary at fixed intervals, you have no anxiety for the future because the State guarantees you a pension . . . and you like that sort of life—placid, orderly, the typical life of an official."

"Listen," said Mathieu, "there's a misunderstanding here; I care little whether I'm a bourgeois or whether I'm not. All I want is"—and he uttered the final words through clenched teeth and with a sort of shame—"to retain my freedom."

"I should myself have thought," said Jacques, "that freedom consisted in frankly confronting situations into which one has deliberately entered, and accepting all one's responsibilities. But that, no doubt, is not your view: you condemn capitalist society, and yet you are an official in that society; you display an abstract sympathy with Communists, but you take care not to commit yourself, you have never voted. You despise the bourgeois class, and yet you are bourgeois, son and brother of a bourgeois, and you live like a bourgeois."

Mathieu waved a hand, but Jacques refused to be interrupted.

"You have, however, reached the age of reason, my poor Mathieu," said he, in a tone of pity and of warning. "But you try to dodge that fact too, you try to pretend you're younger than you are. Well—perhaps I'm doing you an injustice. Perhaps you haven't in fact reached the age of reason, it's really a moral age—perhaps I've got there sooner than you have."

• • •

She felt languid and clammy, still quite disheveled from sleep: the familiar steel helmet gripped her head, there was a taste of blotting-paper in her mouth, a lukewarm feeling down her sides, and beneath her arms, tipping the black hairs, beads of sweat. She felt sick, but restrained herself: her day had not yet begun, it was there, propped precariously against Marcelle, the least movement would bring it crashing down like an avalanche. She laughed sardonically and muttered: "Freedom!"

A human being who wakened in the morning with a queasy stomach, with fifteen hours to kill before next bedtime, had not much use for freedom. Freedom didn't help a person to live. . . .

❖ *from* St. Genet: Actor and Martyr ❖

A Dizzying Word

> *Our sentence is not severe. Whatever commandment the culprit has violated is simply written upon his skin by the harrow.*
>
> —Kafka,
> *In the Penal Colony*

The child was playing in the kitchen. Suddenly he became aware of his solitude and was seized with anxiety, as usual. So he "absented" himself. Once again, he plunged into a kind of ecstasy. There is now no one in the room. An abandoned consciousness is reflecting utensils. A drawer is opening; a little hand moves forward.

Caught in the act. Someone has entered and is watching him. Beneath this gaze the child comes to himself. He who was not yet anyone suddenly becomes Jean Genet. He feels that he is blinding, deafening; he is a beacon, an alarm that keeps ringing. *Who* is Jean Genet? In a moment the whole village will know. . . . The child alone is in ignorance. In a state of fear and shame he continues his signal of distress. Suddenly

> . . . a dizzying word
> From the depths of the world abolishes
> the beautiful order. . . .[1]

A voice declares publicly: "You're a thief." The child is ten years old.

That was how it happened, in that or some other way. In all probability, there were offenses and then punishment, solemn oaths and relapses. It does not matter. The important thing is that Genet lived and has not stopped reliving this period of his life as if it had lasted only an instant.

It is the moment of awakening. The sleepwalking child opens his eyes and realizes he is stealing. It is revealed to him that he *is* a thief and he pleads guilty, crushed by a fallacy which he is unable to refute; he stole, he is therefore a thief. Can anything be more evident? Genet, thunderstruck, considers his act, looks at it from every angle. No doubt about it, it is a theft. And theft is an offense, a crime. What he *wanted* was to steal; what he *did,* a theft; what he *was,* a thief. A timid voice is still protesting within him; he does not *recognize* his intentions. But soon the voice grows silent. The act is so luminous, so sharply defined, that there is no mistaking its nature. He tries to go back, to understand himself, but it is too late, he has lost his bearings. The dazzlingly evident present confers its meaning on the past; Genet now *recalls* that he cynically decided to steal. What happened? Actually, almost nothing: an action undertaken without reflection, conceived and carried out in the secret, silent inwardness in which he often takes refuge, has just *become objective.* Genet learns what he *is objectively.* It is this *transition* that is going to determine his entire life.

The metamorphosis occurs immediately. He is nothing more than what he was before, yet he is now unrecognizable. Driven from the lost paradise, exiled from childhood, from the immediate, condemned to see himself, suddenly provided with a monstrous and guilty "ego," isolated, separated, in short changed into a bug. An evil principle dwelt in him unperceived, and now it has been discovered. It is this principle which is the source of everything. It produces the slightest impulses of his soul. The child lived at peace with himself; his desires seemed to him limpid and simple. Their transparency now appears to have been deceptive. They had a double bottom. Little Genet's shame

---

[1] Genet, *Poèmes,* p. 56.

reveals eternity to him. He is a thief by birth, he will remain one until his death. Time is only a dream in which his evil nature is refracted into a thousand gleams, a thousand petty thefts, but does not belong to the temporal order. *Genet is a thief;* that is his truth, his eternal essence. And, if he *is* a thief, he must therefore always be one, everywhere, not only when he steals, but when he eats, when he sleeps, when he kisses his foster mother. Each of his gestures betrays him, reveals his vile nature in broad daylight. At any moment the teacher may interrupt the lesson, look Genet in the eyes and cry out: "There's a thief!" It would be vain for him to think he deserved leniency by admitting his errors, by mastering the perversity of his instincts. All the impulses of his heart are equally guilty because all alike express his essence.

• • •

A thief cannot have an intuition of himself *as thief.* The notion of "thief" is on principle incommensurate with the realities of the inner sense. It is of social origin and presupposes a prior definition of society, of the property system, a legal code, a judiciary apparatus and an ethical system of relationships among people. There can therefore be no question of a mind's *encountering* theft within itself, and with immediacy. On the other hand, the *Others,* all the Others, have this intuition at will; a thief is a palpable reality, like a tree, like a Gothic church. Here is a man being dragged along by two cops: "What has he done?" I ask. "He's a crook," answer the cops. The word strikes against its object like a crystal falling into a supersaturated solution. The solution immediately crystallizes, enclosing the word inside itself. In prose, the word dies so that the object may be born. "He's a crook!" I forget the word then and there, I see, I touch, I breathe a crook; with all my senses I feel that secret substance: crime. . . .

• • •

I Will Be the Thief

Pinned by a look, a butterfly fixed to a cork, he is naked, everyone can see him and spit on him. The gaze of the adults is a *constituent power* which has transformed him into a *constituted nature.* He now has to live. In the pillory, with his neck in an iron collar, he still has to live. We are not lumps of clay, and what is important is not what people make of us but what we ourselves make of what they have made of us. By virtue of the option which they have taken on his being, the decent folk have made it necessary for a child to decide about himself prematurely. We can surmise that this decision will be of capital importance. Yes, one *must* decide. To kill oneself is also to decide. He has chosen to live; he has said, in defiance of all, I will be the Thief. I deeply admire this child who grimly *willed* himself at an age when *we* were merely playing the servile buffoon. So fierce a will to survive, such pure courage, such mad confidence within despair will bear their fruit. Twenty years later, this absurd determination will produce the poet Jean Genet.

❖ Marxism and Existentialism ❖

Philosophy appears to some people as a homogeneous milieu: there thoughts are born and die, there systems are built, and there, in turn, they collapse. Others take Philosophy for a specific attitude which we can freely adopt at will. Still others see it as a determined segment of culture. In our view *Philosophy* does not exist. In whatever form we consider it, this shadow of science, this Gray Eminence of humanity, is only a hypostatized abstraction. Actually, there are *philosophies*. Or rather—for you would never at the same time find more than *one* living philosophy—under certain well-defined circumstances *a* philosophy is developed for the purpose of giving expression to the general movement of the society. So long as a philosophy is alive, it serves as a cultural milieu for its contemporaries. This disconcerting object presents itself *at the same time* under profoundly distinct aspects, the unification of which it is continually effecting.

A philosophy is first of all a particular way in which the "rising" class becomes conscious of itself.[1] This consciousness may be clear

[1] If I do not mention here the person who is objectified and revealed in his work, it is because the philosophy of a period extends far beyond the philosopher who first gave it shape—no matter how great he may be. But conversely we shall see that the

or confused, indirect or direct. At the time of the *noblesse de robe*[2] and of mercantile capitalism, a bourgeoisie of lawyers, merchants, and bankers gained a certain self-awareness through Cartesianism; a century and a half later, in the primitive stage of industrialization, a bourgeoisie of manufacturers, engineers, and scientists dimly discovered itself in the image of universal man which Kantianism offered to it.

• • •

If philosophy is to be simultaneously a totalization of knowledge, a method, a regulative Idea, an offensive weapon, and a community of language, if this "vision of the world" is also an instrument which ferments rotten societies, if this particular conception of a man or of a group of men becomes the culture and sometimes the nature of a whole class—then it is very clear that the periods of philosophical creation are rare. Between the seventeenth century and the twentieth, I see three such periods, which I would designate by the names of the men who dominated them: there is the "moment" of Descartes and Locke, that of Kant and Hegel, finally that of Marx. These three philosophies become, each in its turn, the humus of every particular thought and the horizon of all culture; there is no going beyond them so long as man has not gone beyond the historical moment which they express. I have often remarked on the fact that an "anti-Marxist" argument is only the apparent rejuvenation of a pre-Marxist idea. A so-called "going beyond" Marxism will be at worst only a return to pre-Marxism; at best, only the rediscovery of a thought already contained in the philosophy which one believes he has gone beyond. As for "revisionism," this is either a truism or an absurdity. There is no need to readapt a living philosophy to the course of the world; it adapts itself by means of thousands of new efforts, thousands of particular pursuits, for the philosophy is one with the movement of so-

study of particular doctrines is inseparable from a real investigation of philosophies. Cartesianism illuminates the period and situates Descartes within the totalitarian development of analytical reason; in these terms, Descartes, taken as a person and as a philosopher, clarifies the historical (hence the particular) meaning of the new rationality up to the middle of the eighteenth century.

[2] Noblesse de robe was originally the designation given in France to those members of the bourgeoisie who were awarded titles of nobility in recognition of outstanding achievement or service to the State. Later it was used loosely to refer to any "new" nobility. (Translator's note.)

ciety. Despite their good intentions, those very people who believe themselves to be the most faithful spokesmen for their predecessors transform the thoughts which they want simply to repeat; methods are modified because they are applied to new objects. If this movement on the part of the philosophy no longer exists, one of two things is true: either the philosophy is dead or it is going through a "crisis." In the first case there is no question of revising, but of razing a rotten building; in the second case the "philosophical crisis" is the particular expression of a social crisis, and its immobility is conditioned by the contradictions which split the society. A so-called "revision," performed by "experts," would be, therefore, only an idealist mystification without real significance. It is the very movement of History, the struggle of men on all planes and on all levels of human activity, which will set free captive thought and permit it to attain its full development.

Those intellectuals who come after the great flowering and who undertake to set the systems in order or to use the new methods to conquer territory not yet fully explored, those who provide practical applications for the theory and employ it as a tool to destroy and to construct—they should not be called philosophers. They cultivate the domain, they take an inventory, they erect certain structures there, they may even bring about certain internal changes; but they still get their nourishment from the living thought of the great dead. They are borne along by the crowd on the march, and it is the crowd which constitutes their cultural milieu and their future, which determines the field of their investigations, and even of their "creation." These *relative* men I propose to call "ideologists." And since I am to speak of existentialism, let it be understood that I take it to be an "ideology." It is a parasitical system living on the margin of Knowledge, which at first it opposed but into which today it seeks to be integrated.

●   ●   ●

[Conclusion to *Search for a Method*]

These considerations enable us to understand why we can at the same time declare that we are in profound agreement with Marxist philosophy and yet for the present maintain the autonomy of the existential ideology. There is no doubt, indeed, that Marxism appears today to be the only possible anthropology which can be at once historical and structural. It is the only one which at the same time takes man in his totality—that is, in terms of the materiality of his condition. Nobody can propose to it another point of departure, for this would be to offer to it *another man* as the object of its study. It is *inside* the movement of Marxist thought that we discover a flaw of such a sort that despite itself Marxism tends to eliminate the questioner from his investigation and to make of the questioned the object of an absolute Knowledge. The very notions which Marxist research employs to describe our historical society—exploitation, alienation, fetishizing, reification, etc.—are precisely those which most immediately refer to existential structures. The very notion of *praxis* and that of dialectic—inseparably bound together—are contradictory to the intellectualist idea of a knowledge. And to come to the most important point, *labor,* as man's reproduction of his life, can hold no meaning if its fundamental structure is not to pro-ject. In view of this default—which pertains to the historical development and not to the actual principles of the doctrine—existentialism, at the heart of Marxism and taking the same givens, the same Knowledge, as its point of departure, must attempt in its turn—at least as an experiment—the dialectical interpretation of History. It puts nothing in question except a mechanistic determinism which is not exactly Marxist and which has been introduced from the outside into this total philosophy. Existentialism, too, wants to situate man in his class and in the conflicts which oppose him to other classes, starting with the mode and the relations of production. But it can approach this "situation" in terms of *existence*—that is, of comprehension. It makes itself the questioned and the question as questioner; it does not, as Kierkegaard did apropos of Hegel, set the irrational singularity of the individual in opposition to universal Knowledge. But into this very Knowledge and into the universality of concepts, it wants to reintroduce the unsurpassable singularity of the human adventure.

Thus the comprehension of existence is presented as the human foundation of Marxist anthropology. Nevertheless, we must beware here of a confusion heavy with consequences. In fact, in the order of Knowledge, what we know concerning the principle or the foundations of a scientific structure, even when it has come—as is ordinarily the case—later than the empirical determinations, is set forth first; and one deduces from it the determinations of Knowledge in the same way that one constructs a building after having secured its foundations. But this is because the foundation is itself a knowing; and if one can deduce from it certain propositions already guaranteed by experience, this is because one has induced it in terms of them as the most general hypothesis. In contrast, the foundation of Marxism, as a historical, structural anthropology, is man himself inasmuch as human existence and the comprehension of the human are inseparable. Historically Marxist Knowledge produces its foundation at a certain moment of its development, and this foundation is presented in a disguised form. It does not appear as the practical foundations of the theory, but as that which, on principle, pushes forward all theoretical knowing. Thus the singularity of existence is presented in Kierkegaard as that which on principle is kept outside the Hegelian system (that is, outside total Knowledge), as that which can in no way be *thought* but only *lived* in the act of faith. The dialectical procedure to reintegrate existence (which is never *known*) as a foundation at the heart of Knowledge could not be attempted then, since neither of the current attitudes—an idealist Knowledge, a spiritual existence—could lay claim to concrete actualization. These two terms outlined abstractly the future contradiction. And the development of anthropological knowing could not lead then to the synthesis of these formal positions: the movement of ideas—as the movement of society—had first to produce Marxism as the only possible form of a really concrete Knowledge. And as we indicated at the beginning, Marx's own Marxism, while indicating the dialectical opposition between knowing and being, contained implicitly the demand for an existential foundation for the theory. Furthermore, in order for notions like reification and alienation to assume their full meaning, it would have been necessary for the questioner and the questioned to be made one. What must be the nature of human relations in order for these relations to be capable of appearing in certain definite societies as the relations of things to each other? If the reification of human relations is possible, it is because these relations, even if reified, are fundamentally distinct from the relations of things. What kind of practical organism is this which reproduces its life by its work so that its work and ultimately its very reality are alienated; that is, so that they, *as others,* turn back upon him and determine him? But before Marxism, itself a product of the social conflict, could turn to these problems, it had to assume fully its role as a practical philosophy—that is, as a theory clarifying social and political *praxis.* The result is a profound *lack* within contemporary Marxism; the use of the notions mentioned earlier—and many others—refers to a comprehension of human reality which is missing. And this lack is not—as some Marxists declare today—a localized void, a hole in the construction of Knowledge. It is inapprehensible and yet everywhere present; it is a general anemia.

• • •

It is precisely this expulsion of man, his exclusion from Marxist Knowledge, which resulted in the renascence of existentialist thought outside the historical totalization of Knowledge. Human science is frozen in the non-human, and human-reality seeks to understand itself outside of science. But this time the opposition comes from those who directly demand their synthetic transcendence. Marxism will degenerate into a non-human anthropology if it does not reintegrate man into itself as its foundation. But this comprehension, which is nothing other than existence itself, is disclosed at the same time by the historical movement of Marxism, by the concepts which indirectly clarify it (alienation, etc.), and by the new alienations which give birth to the contradictions of socialist society and which reveal to it its abandonment; that is, the incommensurability of existence and practical Knowledge. The movement can *think* itself only in Marxist terms and can *comprehend* itself only as an alienated existence, as a human-reality made into a thing. The moment which will surpass this opposition must reintegrate comprehension into Knowledge as its non-theoretical foundation.

In other words, the foundation of anthropology is man himself, not as the object of practical Knowledge, but as a practical organism producing Knowledge as a moment of its *praxis*. And the reintegration of man as a concrete existence into the core of anthropology, as its constant support, appears necessarily as a stage in the process of philosophy's "becoming-the-world." In this sense the foundation of anthropology cannot precede it (neither historically nor logically). If *existence*, in its free comprehension of itself, preceded the awareness of alienation or of exploitation, it would be necessary to suppose that the free development of the practical organism historically preceded its present fall and captivity. (And if this were established, the historical precedence would scarcely advance us in our comprehension, since the retrospective study of vanished societies is made today with the enlightenment furnished by techniques for reconstruction and by means of the alienations which enchain us.) Or, if one insisted on a logical priority, it would be necessary to suppose that the freedom of the project could be recovered in its full reality *underneath* the alienations of our society and that one could move dialectically from the concrete existence which understands its freedom to the various alterations which distort it in present society. This hypothesis is absurd. To be sure, man can be enslaved only if he is free. But for the historical man who *knows* himself and *comprehends* himself, this practical freedom is grasped only as the permanent, concrete condition of his servitude; that is, across that servitude and by means of it as that which makes it possible, as its foundation. Thus Marxist Knowledge bears on the alienated man; but if it doesn't want to make a fetish of its knowing and to dissolve man in the process of knowing his alienations, then it is not enough to describe the working of capital or the system of colonization. It is necessary that the questioner understand how the questioned—that is, himself—*exists his alienation,* how he surpasses it and is alienated in this very surpassing. It is necessary that his very thought should at every instant surpass the intimate contradiction which unites the comprehension of man-as-agent with the knowing of man-as-object and that it forge new concepts, new determinations of Knowledge which emerge from the existential comprehension and which regulate the movement of their contents by its dialectical procedure. Yet this comprehension—as a living movement of the practical organism—can take place only within a concrete situation, insofar as theoretical Knowledge illuminates and interprets this situation.

Thus the autonomy of existential studies results necessarily from the negative qualities of Marxists (and not from Marxism itself). So long as the doctrine does not recognize its anemia, so long as it founds its Knowledge upon a dogmatic metaphysics (a dialectic of Nature) instead of seeking its support in the comprehension of the living man, so long as it rejects as irrational those ideologies which wish, as Marx did, to separate being from Knowledge and, in anthropology, to found the knowing of man on human existence, existentialism will follow its own path of study. This means that it will attempt to clarify the givens of Marxist Knowledge by indirect knowing (that is, as we have seen, by words which regressively denote existential structures), and to engender within the framework of Marxism a veritable *comprehensive knowing* which will rediscover man in the social world and which will follow him in his *praxis*—or, if you prefer, in the project which throws him toward the social possibles in terms of a defined situation. Existentialism will appear therefore as a fragment of the system, which has fallen outside of Knowledge. From the day that Marxist thought will have taken on the human dimension (that is, the existential project) as the foundation of anthropological Knowledge, existentialism will no longer have any reason for being. Absorbed, surpassed and conserved by the totalizing movement of philosophy, it will cease to be a particular inquiry and will become the foundation of all inquiry. The comments which we have made in the course of the present essay are directed—to the modest limit of our capabilities—toward hastening the moment of that dissolution.

❖ Sartre on Angst ❖

BENNY LEVY: You said to me once, "I've talked about despair, but that's bunk. I talked about it because other people were talking about it, because it was fashionable. Everyone was reading Kierkegaard then."

JEAN-PAUL SARTRE: That's right. Personally, I have never despaired, nor for one moment have I thought of despair as something that could possibly be a characteristic of mine. Yet I had to consider that despair must exist for other people, since they were talking about it. But it was a passing moment. I see that in many philosophers: Early in their work they talk from hearsay about some idea, they give it importance. Then, little by little, they stop talking about it, because they realize that for them its content doesn't exist—they've merely picked it up from other people.

From a series of interviews with Jean-Paul Sartre, conducted by Benny Levy, his assistant, in the last years before Sartre's death in April 1980. The interviews originally appeared in the French magazine Le Nouvel Observateur *and are published in English translation in* Hope Now: The 1980 Interviews, *by the University of Chicago Press. Translated by Adrian van den Hoven.*

LEVY: Is that true of anguish, too?

SARTRE: I have never known anguish. That was a key philosophical notion from 1930 to 1940. It was one of the notions we made use of all the time, but to me it meant nothing. Of course, I knew grief or boredom or misery, but—

LEVY: Misery?

SARTRE: Well, I knew it through others. I saw it. But anguish and despair, no.

Maurice Merleau-Ponty

(1908-1961)
FRENCH

Merleau-Ponty has too often been viewed in the shadow of
Sartre, as the younger classmate, as the "other" founder of *Les
Temps Modernes,* as the "other" French existential phenomenol-
ogist and Marxist. In his phenomenological work, Merleau-
Ponty far surpasses Sartre in his knowledge and development of
Husserl's theory of perception. His early *Structure of Behavior* is
an important attempt to argue against the pervasive Cartesian
model of man as consciousness + machine-body. His important
Phenomenology of Perception is the most ambitious attempt to
correct certain persistent problems in Husserl's theory of perception. It begins with Husserl's basic techniques of phenomenology, provides an insightful account of the role of "sensation"
in phenomenology and psychology, then quickly moves to
Husserl's later works, adding a thorough appreciation of Heidegger's *Being and Time* and arguing that perception is primarily more than a relationship between consciousness and its acts
and certain objects or meanings. Against Descartes and Husserl,
and with Heidegger, Merleau-Ponty holds that essentially
human existence is not knowing and thinking, but living, valuing. Against both Husserl and Sartre, Merleau-Ponty argues that
it is not consciousness, but the human body that is intentional,
through "motility." Our bodies are not simply objects in the
world (to which each of us has privileged but yet contingent access). The body is our Being-in-the-world, the perspective from

which we perceive, judge, value. Accordingly, Merleau-Ponty adopts a notion of freedom which is also less Cartesian than Sartre's. Freedom is never, as Sartre insists, absolute or total freedom. It is "progressive," a reorientation of our demands on the basis of "pre-evaluated meanings" and motivation. True, one is always free, but to be always free is not to be totally free. One must act in accordance with his motives and interests as well as in obeyance with his situation and facticity (contingency). Politically, Merleau-Ponty was actively involved in the Left before Sartre. His *Humanism and Terror* had a deep effect on Sartre and marked an important break from the Communist party for both of them. Merleau-Ponty remained a moral individualist in his politics, which carried him increasingly further from the orthodox Left and ultimately caused the destruction of his lifelong friendship with Sartre.

❖ *from* "Merleau-Ponty" ❖
by Jean-Paul Sartre

One day in 1947, Merleau told me that he had never recovered from an incomparable childhood. He had known that private world of happiness from which only age drives us. Pascalian from adolescence, without even having read Pascal, he experienced his singular selfhood as the singularity of an adventure. To be someone, is something which happens and unhappens, but not without first tracing the ribs of a future, always new and always begun anew. What was he, if not this paradise lost, a wild and undeserved piece of luck, a gratuitous gift transformed, after the fall, into adversity, depopulating the world and disenchanting him in advance? This story is both extraordinary and commonplace. Our capacity for happiness is dependent upon a certain equilibrium between what we refuse and concede to our childhood. Completely deprived or completely en-

From Situations *by Jean-Paul Sartre, translated from the French by Benita Eisler. English translation copyright 1965 by George Braziller, Inc. Reprinted by permission of George Braziller, Inc.*

dowed, we are lost. Thus, there are an infinite number of lots we can draw. His was to have won too soon. He had to live, nonetheless. To the end, it remained for him to make himself as the event had made him. That way and other ways. Seeking the golden age, and with that as his point of departure he forged his myths and what he has since called his "style of life." It established his preferences—choosing, at the same time, the traditions which recalled the rituals of childhood, and the "spontaneity" which evoked childhood's superintended liberty. This naïveté, by starting from *what has happened,* also discovered the meaning of *what is happening,* and finally, it made a prophecy based on this inventory and its evaluation. This is what he felt as a young man, without as yet being able to express it. Through these detours, he finally arrived at philosophy. He wondered—nothing more. . . .

❖ Prospectus (A Report to the ❖ Collège de France)

We never cease living in the world of perception, but we go beyond it in critical thought—almost to the point of forgetting the contribution of perception to our idea of truth. For critical thought encounters only *bare propositions* which it discusses, accepts or rejects. Critical thought has broken with the naive evidence of *things,* and when it affirms, it is because it no longer finds any means of denial. However necessary this activity of verification may be, specifying criteria and demanding from our experience its credentials of validity, it is not aware of our contact with the perceived world which is simply there before us, beneath the level of the verified true and the false. Nor does critical thought even define the positive steps of thinking or its most valid accomplishments.

My first two works sought to restore the world of perception. My works in preparation aim to show how communication with others,

From The Primacy of Perception *by Maurice Merleau-Ponty, translated from the French by Arlene Dallery for Northwestern University Press, Inc. Reprinted by permission of Northwestern University Press. First published as an "Unpublished Text" in the Revue de métaphysique et de morale, no. 4, 1962.*

and thought, take up and go beyond the realm of perception which initiated us to the truth.

The perceiving mind is an incarnated mind. I have tried, first of all, to re-establish the roots of the mind in its body and in its world, going against doctrines which treat perception as a simple result of the action of external things on our body as well as against those which insist on the autonomy of consciousness. These philosophies commonly forget—in favor of a pure exteriority or of a pure interiority—the insertion of the mind in corporeality, the ambiguous relation which we entertain with our body and, correlatively, with perceived things. When one attempts, as I have in *The Structure of Behavior,* to trace out, on the basis of modern psychology and physiology, the relationships which obtain between the perceiving organism and its milieu one clearly finds that they are not those of an automatic machine which needs an outside agent to set off its preestablished mechanisms. And it is equally clear that one does not account for the facts by superimposing a pure, contemplative consciousness on a thinglike body. In the conditions of life—if not in the laboratory—the organism is less sensitive to certain isolated physical and chemical agents than to the constellation which they form and to the whole situation which they define. Behaviors reveal a sort of prospective activity in the organism, as if it were oriented toward the meaning of certain elementary situations, as if it entertained familiar relations with them, as if there were an "a priori of the organism," privileged conducts and laws of internal equilibrium which predisposed the organism to certain relations with its milieu. At this level there is no question yet of a real self-awareness or of intentional activity. Moreover, the organism's prospective capability is exercised only within defined limits and depends on precise, local conditions.

The functioning of the central nervous system presents us with similar paradoxes. In its modern forms, the theory of cerebral localizations has profoundly changed the relation of function to substrate. It no longer assigns, for instance, a preestablished mechanism to each perceptual behavior. "Coordinating centers" are no longer considered as storehouses of "cerebral traces," and their functioning is qualitatively different from one case to another, depending on the chromatic nuance to be evoked and the perceptual structure to be realized. Finally, this functioning reflects all the subtlety and all the variety of perceptual relationships.

The perceiving organism seems to show us a Cartesian mixture of the soul with the body. Higher-order behaviors give a new meaning to the life of the organism, but the mind here disposes of only a limited freedom; it needs simpler activities in order to stabilize itself in durable institutions and to realize itself truly as mind. Perceptual behavior emerges from these relations to a situation and to an environment which are not the workings of a pure, knowing subject.

In my work on the *Phenomenology of Perception* we are no longer present at the emergence of perceptual behaviors; rather we install ourselves in them in order to pursue the analysis of this exceptional relation between the subject and its body and its world. For contemporary psychology and psychopathology the body is no longer merely *an object in the world,* under the purview of a separated spirit. It is on the side of the subject; it is our *point of view on the world,* the place where the spirit takes on a certain physical and historical situation. As Descartes once said profoundly, the soul is not merely in the body like a pilot in his ship; it is wholly intermingled with the body. The body, in turn, is wholly animated, and all its functions contribute to the perception of objects—an activity long considered by philosophy to be pure knowledge.

We grasp external space through our bodily situation. A "corporeal or postural schema" gives us at every moment a global, practical, and implicit notion of the relation between our body and things, of our hold on them. A system of possible movements, or "motor projects," radiates from us to our environment. Our body is not in space like things; it inhabits or haunts space. It applies itself to space like a hand to an instrument, and when we wish to move about we do not move the body as we move an object. We transport it without instruments as if by magic, since it is ours and because through it we have direct access to space. For us the body is much more than an instrument or a means; it is our expression in the world, the visible form of our intentions. Even our most secret affective movements, those most deeply tied to the humoral infrastructure, help to shape our perception of things.

Now if perception is thus the common act of all our motor and affective functions, no less than the sensory, we must rediscover the structure of the perceived world through a process similar to that of an archaeologist. For the structure of the perceived world is buried under the sedimentations of later knowledge. Digging down to the perceived world, we see that sensory qualities are not opaque, indivisible "givens," which are simply exhibited to a remote consciousness—a favorite idea of classical philosophy. We see too that colors (each surrounded by an affective atmosphere which psychologists have been able to study and define) are themselves different modalities of our co-existence with the world. We also find that spatial forms or distances are not so much relations between different points in objective space as they are relations between these points and a central perspective—our body. In short, these relations are different ways for external stimuli to test, to solicit, and to vary our grasp on the world, our horizontal and vertical anchorage in a place and in a here-and-now. We find that perceived things, unlike geometrical objects, are not bounded entities whose laws of construction we possess a priori, but that they are open, inexhaustible systems which we recognize through a certain style of development, although we are never able, in principle, to explore them entirely, and even though they never give us more than profiles and perspectival views of themselves. Finally, we find that the perceived world, in its turn, is not a pure object of thought without fissures or lacunae; it is, rather, like a universal style shared in by all perceptual beings. While the world no doubt co-ordinates these perceptual beings, we can never presume that its work is finished. Our world, as Malebranche said, is an "unfinished task."

If we now wish to characterize a subject capable of this perceptual experience, it obviously will not be a self-transparent thought, absolutely present to itself without the interference of its body and its history. The perceiving subject is not this absolute thinker; rather, it functions according to a natal pact between our body and the world, between ourselves and our body. Given a perpetually new natural and historical situation to control, the perceiving subject undergoes a continued birth; at each instant it is something new. Every incarnate subject is like an open notebook in which we do not yet know what will be written. Or it is like a new language; we do not know what works it will accomplish but only that, once it has appeared, it cannot fail to say little or much, to have a history and a meaning. The very productivity or freedom of human life, far from denying our situation, utilizes it and turns it into a means of expression.

❖ Freedom ❖

Again, it is clear that no causal relationship is conceivable between the subject and his body, his world or his society. Only at the cost of losing the basis of all my certainties can I question what is conveyed to me by my presence to myself. Now the moment I turn to myself in order to describe myself, I have a glimpse of an anonymous flux,[1] a comprehensive project in which there are so far no "states of consciousness," nor, *a fortiori,* qualifications of any sort. For myself I am neither "jealous," nor "inquisitive," nor "hunchbacked," nor "a civil servant." It is often a matter of surprise that the cripple or the invalid can put up with himself. The reason is that such people are not for themselves deformed or at death's door. Until the final coma, the dying man is inhabited by a consciousness, he is all that he sees, and enjoys this much of an outlet. Consciousness can never objectify itself into invalid-consciousness or cripple-consciousness, and even if the old man complains of his age or the cripple of his deformity, they can do so only by comparing themselves with others, or seeing themselves through the eyes of others, that is, by taking a statistical and objective view of themselves, so that such complaints are never absolutely genuine: when he is back in the heart of his own consciousness, each one of us feels beyond his limitations and thereupon resigns himself to them. They are the price which we automatically pay for being in the world, a formality which we take for granted. Hence we may speak disparagingly of our looks and still not want to change our face for another. No idiosyncrasy can, seemingly, be attached to the insuperable generality of consciousness, nor can any limit be set to this immeasurable power of escape. In order to be determined (in the two senses of that word) by an external factor, it is necessary that I should be a thing. Neither my freedom nor my universality can admit of any eclipse. It is inconceivable that I should be free in certain of my actions and determined in others: how should we understand a dormant freedom that gave full scope to determinism? And if it is assumed that it is snuffed out when it is not in action, how could it be rekindled? If *per impossible* I had once succeeded in

From The Phenomenology of Perception *by Maurice Merleau-Ponty, translated from the French by Colin Smith for Routledge, Inc. Reprinted by permission of Routledge Inc.*

[1] In the sense in which, with Husserl, we have taken this word.

making myself into a thing, how should I subsequently reconvert myself to consciousness? Once I am free, I am not to be counted among things, and I must then be uninterruptedly free. Once my actions cease to be mine, I shall never recover them, and if I lose my hold on the world, it will never be restored to me. It is equally inconceivable that my liberty should be attenuated; one cannot be to some extent free, and if, as is often said, motives incline me in a certain direction, one of two things happens: either they are strong enough to force me to act, in which case there is no freedom, or else they are not strong enough, and then freedom is complete, and as great in the worst torments as in the peace of one's home. We ought, therefore, to reject not only the idea of causality, but also that of motivation.[2] The alleged motive does not burden my decision; on the contrary my decision lends the motive its force. Everything that I "am" in virtue of nature or history—hunchbacked, handsome or Jewish—I never am completely for myself, as we have just explained: and I may well be these things for other people, nevertheless I remain free to posit another person as a consciousness whose views strike through to my very being, or on the other hand merely as an object. It is also true that this option is itself a form of constraint: if I am ugly, I have the choice between being an object of disapproval or disapproving of others. I am left free to be a masochist or a sadist, but not free to ignore others. But this dilemma, which is given as part of the human lot, is not one for me as pure consciousness: it is still I who cause the other to be for me, and who cause us both to be as members of mankind. Moreover, even if existence as a human being were imposed upon me, the manner alone being left to my choice, and considering this choice itself and ignoring the small number of forms it might take, it would still be a free choice. If it is said that my temperament inclines me particularly to either sadism or masochism, it is still merely a manner of speaking, for my temperament exists only for the second order knowledge that I gain about myself when I see myself as others see me, and in so far as I recognize it, confer value upon it, and in that sense, choose it. What misleads us on this, is that we often look for freedom in the voluntary deliberation which examines one motive after another and seems to opt for the weightiest or most convincing. In reality the deliberation follows the decision, and it is my secret decision which brings the motives to light,

---

[2] See J. P. Sartre, *L'Être et le Néant,* pp. 508 and ff.

for it would be difficult to conceive what the force of a motive might be in the absence of a decision which it confirms or to which it runs counter. When I have abandoned a project, the motives which I thought held me to it suddenly lose their force and collapse. In order to resuscitate them, an effort is required on my part to reopen time and set me back to the moment preceding the making of the decision. Even while I am deliberating, already I find it an effort to suspend time's flow, and to keep open a situation which I feel is closed by a decision which is already there and which I am holding off. That is why it so often happens that after giving up a plan I experience a feeling of relief: "After all, I wasn't so very particular"; the debate was purely a matter of form, and the deliberation a mere parody, for I had decided against from the start.

We often see the weakness of the will brought forward as an argument against freedom. And indeed, although I can will myself to adopt a course of conduct and act the part of a warrior or a seducer, it is not within my power to be a warrior or seducer with ease and in a way that "comes naturally"; really to *be* one, that is. But neither should we seek freedom in the act of will, which is, in its very meaning, something short of an act. We have recourse to an act of will only in order to go against our true decision, and, as it were, for the purpose of proving our powerlessness. If we had really and truly made the conduct of the warrior or the seducer our own, then we should *be* one or the other. Even what are called obstacles to freedom are in reality deployed by it. An un-climbable rock face, a large or small, vertical or slanting rock, are things which have no meaning for anyone who is not intending to surmount them, for a subject whose projects do not carve out such determinate forms from the uniform mass of the *in itself* and cause an orientated world to arise—a significance in things. There is, then, ultimately nothing that can set limits to freedom, except those limits that freedom itself has set in the form of its various initiatives, so that the subject has simply the external world that he gives himself. Since it is the latter who, on coming into being, brings to light significance and value in things, and since no thing can impinge upon it except through acquiring, thanks to it, significance and value, there is no action of things on the subject, but merely a signification (in the active sense), a centrifugal *Sinngebung*. The choice would seem to lie between scientism's conception of causality, which is incompatible with the consciousness which we have of ourselves, and the assertion of an absolute freedom divorced from the outside. It is impossible to decide beyond which point things cease to be ἐφ ἡμιν. Either they all lie within our power, or none does.

The result, however, of this first reflection on freedom would appear to be to rule it out altogether. If indeed it is the case that our freedom is the same in all our actions, and even in our passions, if it is not to be measured in terms of our conduct, and if the slave displays freedom as much by living in fear as by breaking his chains, then it cannot be held that there is such a thing as *free action,* freedom being anterior to all actions. In any case it will not be possible to declare: "Here freedom makes its appearance," since free action, in order to be discernible, has to stand out against a background of life from which it is entirely, or almost entirely, absent. We may say in this case that it is everywhere, but equally nowhere. In the name of freedom we reject the idea of acquisition, since freedom has become a primordial acquisition and, as it were, our state of nature. Since we do not have to provide it, it is the gift granted to us of having no gift, it is the nature of consciousness which consists in having no nature, and in no case can it find external expression or a place in our life. The idea of action, therefore, disappears: nothing can pass from us to the world, since we are nothing that can be specified, and since the non-being which constitutes us could not possibly find its way into the world's plenum. There are merely intentions immediately followed by their effects, and we are very near to the Kantian idea of an intention which is tantamount to the act, which Scheler countered with the argument that the cripple who would like to be able to save a drowning man and the good swimmer who actually saves him do not have the same experience of autonomy. The very idea of choice vanishes, for to choose is to choose *something* in which freedom sees, at least for a moment, a symbol of itself. There is free choice only if freedom comes into play in its decision, and posits the situation chosen as a situation of freedom. A freedom which has no need to be exercised because it is already acquired could not commit itself in this way: it knows that the following instant will find it, come what may, just as free and just as indeterminate. The very notion of freedom demands that our decision should plunge into the future, that something should have been *done* by it, that the subsequent instant should benefit from its predecessor and, though not necessitated, should be at least required by it. If freedom is doing, it is necessary that what it does should not be immediately undone by a new freedom. Each instant, therefore, must not be a closed world; one instant must be able to commit its successors and, a decision once taken and action once begun, I must have something acquired at my disposal, I must benefit from my impetus, I must be inclined to carry on, and there must be a bent or propensity of the mind. It was Descartes who held that conservation demands a power as great as does creation; a view which implies a realistic notion of the instant. It is true that the instant is not a philosopher's fiction. It is the point at which one project is brought to fruition and another begun[3]—the point at which my gaze is transferred from one end to another, it is the *Augen-Blick*. But this break in time cannot occur unless each of the two spans is of a piece. Consciousness, it is said, is, though not atomized into instants, at least haunted by the spectre of the instant which it is obliged continually to exorcise by a free act. We shall soon see that we have indeed always the power to interrupt, but it implies in any case a power to *begin,* for there would be no severance unless freedom had taken up its abode somewhere and were preparing to move it. Unless there are cycles of behaviour, open situations requiring a certain completion and capable of constituting a background to either a confirmatory or transformatory decision, we never experience freedom. The choice of an intelligible character is excluded, not only because there is no time anterior to time, but because choice presupposes a prior commitment and because the idea of an initial choice involves a contradiction. If freedom is to have *room*[4] in which to move, if it is to be describable as freedom, there must be something to hold it away from its objectives, it must have a *field,* which means that there must be for it special possibilities, or realities which tend to cling to being. As. J. P. Sartre himself observes, dreaming is incompatible with freedom because, in the realm of imagination, we have no sooner taken a certain significance as our goal than we already believe that we have intuitively brought it into being, in short, because there is no obstacle and nothing *to do.*[5] It is established that freedom is not to be confused with those abstract decisions of will at grips with motives or passions, for the classical conception of deliberation is relevant only to a freedom "in bad faith" which secretly harbours antagonistic motives without

---

[3] J. P. Sartre, *L'Être et le Néant,* p. 544.

[4] "avoir du chamn"; in this sentence there is a play on the word "champ" = field (Translator's note).

[5] J. P. Sartre, *L'Être et le Néant,* p. 562.

being prepared to act on them, and so itself manufactures the alleged proofs of its impotence. We can see, beneath these noisy debates and these fruitless efforts to "construct" us, the tacit decisions whereby we have marked out round ourselves the field of possibility, and it is true that nothing is done as long as we cling to these fixed points, and everything is easy as soon as we have weighed anchor. This is why our freedom is not to be sought in spurious discussion on the conflict between a style of life which we have no wish to reappraise and circumstances suggestive of another: the real choice is that between our whole character and our manner of being in the world. But either this total choice is never mentioned, since it is the silent upsurge of our being in the world, in which case it is not clear in what sense it could be said to be ours, since this freedom glides over itself and is the equivalent of a fate—or else our choice of ourselves is a genuine choice, a conversion involving our whole existence. In this case, however, there is presupposed a previous acquisition which the choice sets out to modify and it founds a new tradition: this leads us to ask whether the perpetual severance in terms of which we initially defined freedom is not simply the negative aspect of our universal commitment to a world, and whether our indifference to each determinate thing does not express merely our involvement in all; whether the ready-made freedom from which we started is not reducible to a power of initiative which cannot be transformed into *doing* without taking up the world as posited in some shape or form, and whether, in short, concrete and actual freedom is not to be found in this exchange. It is true that nothing has *significance* and value for anyone but *me* and through anyone but me, but this proposition remains indeterminate and is still indistinguishable from the Kantian idea of a consciousness which "finds in things only what it has put into them," and from the idealist refutation of realism, as long as we fail to make clear how we understand significance and the self. By defining ourselves as a universal power of *Sinn-Gebung,* we have reverted to the method of the "thing without which" and to the analytical reflection of the traditional type, which seeks the conditions of possibility without concerning itself with the conditions of reality. We must therefore resume the analysis of the *Sinngebung,* and show how it can be both centrifugal and centripetal, since it has been established that there is no freedom without a field.

When I say that this rock is unclimbable, it is certain that this attribute, like that of being big or little, straight and oblique, and indeed like all attributes in general, can be conferred upon it only by the project of climbing it, and by a human presence. It is, therefore, freedom which brings into being the obstacles to freedom, so that the latter can be set over against it as its bounds. However, it is clear that, one and the same project being given, one rock will appear as an obstacle, and another, being more negotiable, as a means. My freedom, then, does not so contrive it that this way there is an obstacle, and that way a way through, it arranges for there to be obstacles and ways through in general; it does not draw the particular outline of this world, but merely lays down its general structures. It may be objected that there is no difference; if my freedom conditions the structure of the "there is," that of the "here" and the "there," it is present wherever these structures arise. We cannot distinguish the quality of "obstacle" from the obstacle itself, and relate one to freedom and the other to the world in itself which, without freedom, would be merely an amorphous and unnameable mass. It is not, therefore, outside myself that I am able to find a limit to my freedom. But should I not find it in myself? We must indeed distinguish between my express intentions, for example the plan I now make to climb those mountains, and general intentions which evaluate the potentialities of my environment. Whether or not I have decided to climb them, these mountains appear high to me, because they exceed my body's power to take them in its stride, and even if I have just read *Micromégas,* I cannot so contrive it that they are small for me. Underlying myself as a thinking subject, who am able to take my place at will on Sirius or on the earth's surface, there is, therefore, as it were a natural self which does not budge from its terrestrial situation and which constantly adumbrates absolute valuations. What is more, my projects as a thinking being are clearly modelled on the latter; if I elect to see things from the point of view of Sirius, it is still to my terrestrial experience that I must have recourse in order to do so; I may say, for example, that the Alps are *molehills.* In so far as I have hands, feet, a body, I sustain around me intentions which are not dependent upon my decisions and which affect my surroundings in a way which I do not choose. These intentions are general in a double sense: firstly in the sense that they constitute a system in which all possible objects are simultaneously included; if the mountain appears high and upright, the tree appears small and sloping; and furthermore in the sense that they are not of my own making, they originate from outside me, and I am not surprised to find them in all psycho-physical subjects organized as I am.

• • •

The rationalist's dilemma—either the free act is possible, or it is not, either the event originates in me or is imposed on me from outside, does not apply to our relations with the world and with our past. Our freedom does not destroy our situation, but gears itself to it: as long as we are alive, our situation is open, which implies both that it calls up specially favoured modes of resolution, and also that it is powerless to bring one into being by itself.

We shall arrive at the same result by considering our relations with history. Taking myself in my absolute concreteness, as I am presented to myself in reflection, I find that I am an anonymous and prehuman flux, as yet unqualified as, for instance, "a working man" or "middle class." If I subsequently think of myself as a man among men, a bourgeois among bourgeois, this can be, it would seem, no more than a second order view of myself; I am never in my heart of hearts a worker or a bourgeois, but a consciousness which freely evaluates itself as a middle class or proletarian consciousness. And indeed, it is never the case that my objective position in the production process is sufficient to awaken class consciousness. There was exploitation long before there were revolutionaries. Nor is it always in periods of economic difficulty that the working class movement makes headway. Revolt is, then, not the outcome of objective conditions, but it is rather the decision taken by the worker to will revolution that makes a proletarian of him. The evaluation of the present operates through one's free project for the future. From which we might conclude that history by itself has no significance, but only that conferred upon it by our will. Yet here again we are slipping into the method of "the indispensable condition failing which . . .": in opposition to objective thought, which includes the subject in its deterministic system; we are setting idealist reflection which makes determinism dependent upon the constituting activity of the subject. Now, we have already seen that objective thought and analytical reflection are two aspects of the same mistake, two ways of overlooking the phenomena. Objective thought derives class-consciousness from the objective condition of the proletariat. Idealist reflection reduces the proletarian condition to the awareness of it, which the proletarian arrives at. The former traces class-consciousness to the class defined in terms of objective characteristics, the latter on the other hand reduces "being a workman" to the consciousness of being one. In each case we are in the realm of abstraction, because we remain torn between the *in itself* and the *for itself*. If we approach the question afresh with the idea of discovering, not the causes of the act of becoming aware, for there is no cause which can act from outside upon a consciousness—nor the conditions of its possibility, for we need to know the conditions which actually produce it—but class-consciousness itself, if, in short, we apply a genuinely existential method, what do we find? I am not conscious of being working class or middle class simply because, as a matter of fact, I sell my labour or, equally as a matter of fact, because my interests are bound up with capitalism, nor do I become one or the other on the day on which I elect to view history in the light of the class struggle: what happens is that "I exist as working class" or "I exist as middle class" in the first place, and it is this mode of dealing with the world and society which provides both the motives for my revolutionary or conservative projects and my explicit judgements of the type: "I am working class" or "I am middle class," without its being possible to deduce the former from the latter, or vice versa. What makes me a proletarian is not the economic system or society considered as systems of impersonal forces, but these institutions as I carry them within me and experience them; nor is it an intellectual operation devoid of motive, but my way of being in the world within this institutional framework.

● ● ●

. . . class is a matter neither for observation nor decree; like the appointed order of the capitalistic system, like revolution, before being thought it is lived through as an obsessive presence, as possibility, enigma and myth. To make class-consciousness the outcome of a decision and a choice is to say that problems are solved on the day they are posed, that every question already contains the reply that it awaits; it is, in short, to revert to immanence and abandon the attempt to understand history. In reality, the intellectual project and the positing of ends are merely the bringing to completion of an existential project. It is I who give a direction, significance and future to my life, but that does not mean that these are concepts; they spring from my present and past and in particular from my mode of present and past co-existence. Even in the case of the intellectual who turns revolutionary, his decision does not arise *ex nihilo;* it may follow upon a prolonged period of solitude: the intellectual is in search of a doctrine which shall make great demands on him and cure him of his subjectivity; or he may yield to the clear light thrown by a Marxist interpretation of history, in which case he has given knowledge pride of place in his life, and that in itself is understandable only in virtue of his past and his childhood. Even the decision to become a revolutionary without motive, and by an act of pure freedom, would express a certain way of being in the natural and social world, which is typically that of the intellectual. He "throws in his lot with the working class" from the starting point of his situation as an intellectual and from nowhere else (and this is why even fideism, in his case, remains rightly suspect). Now with the worker it is *a fortiori* the case that his decision is elaborated in the course of his life. This time it is through no misunderstanding that the horizon of a particular life and revolutionary aims coincide: for the worker revolution is a more immediate possibility, and one closer to his own interests than for the intellectual, since he is at grips with the economic system in his very life. For this reason there are, statistically, more workers than middle class people in a revolutionary party. Motivation, of course, does not do away with freedom. Working class parties of the most unmistakable kind have had many intellectuals among their leaders, and it is likely that a man such as Lenin identified himself with revolution and eventually transcended the distinction between intellectual and worker. But these are the virtues proper to action and commitment; at the outset, I am not an individual beyond class, I am situated in a social environment, and my freedom, though it may have the power to commit me elsewhere, has not the power to transform me instantaneously into what I decide to be. Thus to be a bourgeois or a worker is not only to be aware of being one or the other, it is to identify oneself as worker or bourgeois through an implicit or existential project which merges into our way of patterning the world and coexisting with other people. My decision draws together a spontaneous meaning of my life which it may confirm or repudiate, but not annul. Both idealism and objective thinking fail to pin down the coming into being of class-consciousness, the former because it deduces actual existence from consciousness, the latter because it derives consciousness from de facto existence, and both because they overlook the relationship of motivation.

• • •

What then is freedom? To be born is both to be born of the world and to be born into the world. The world is already constituted, but also never completely constituted; in the first case we are acted upon, in the second we are open to an infinite number of possibilities. But this analysis is still abstract, for we exist in both ways *at once*. There is, therefore, never determinism and never absolute choice, I am never a thing and never bare consciousness. In fact, even our own pieces of initiative, even the situations which we have chosen, bear us on, once they have been entered upon by virtue of a state rather than an act. The generality of the "rôle" and of the situation comes to the aid of decision, and in this exchange between the situation and the person who takes it up, it is impossible to determine precisely the "share contributed by the situation" and the "share contributed by freedom." Let us suppose that a man is tortured to make him talk. If he refuses to give the names and addresses which it is desired to extract from him, this does not arise from a solitary and unsupported decision: the man still feels himself to be with his comrades, and, being still involved in the common struggle, he is as it were incapable of talking. Or else, for months or years, he has, in his mind, faced this test and staked his whole life upon it. Or finally, he wants to prove, by coming through it, what he has always thought and said about freedom. These motives do not cancel out freedom, but at least ensure that it does not go unbuttressed in being. What withstands pain is not, in short, a bare consciousness, but the prisoner with his comrades or with those he loves and under whose gaze he lives; or else the awareness of his proudly willed solitude, which again is a certain mode of the *Mit-Sein*. And probably the individual in his prison daily reawakens these phantoms, which give back to him the strength he gave to them. But conversely, in so far as he has committed himself to this action, formed a bond with his comrades or adopted this morality, it is because the historical situation, the comrades, the world around him seemed to him to expect that conduct from him. The analysis could be pursued endlessly in this way. We choose our world and the world chooses us. What is certain, in any case, is that we can at no time set aside within ourselves a redoubt to which being does not find its way through, without seeing this freedom, immediately and by the very fact of being a living experience, take on the appearance of being and become a motive and a buttress. Taken concretely, freedom is always a meeting of the inner and the outer—even the prehuman and prehistoric freedom with which we began—and it shrinks without ever disappearing altogether in direct proportion to the lessening of the *tolerance* allowed by the bodily and institutional data of our lives. There is, as

Husserl says, on the one hand a "field of freedom" and on the other a "conditioned freedom";[6] not that freedom is absolute within the limits of this field and non-existent outside it (like the perceptual field, this one has no traceable boundaries), but because I enjoy immediate and remote possibilities. Our commitments sustain our power and there is no freedom without some power. Our freedom, it is said, is either total or nonexistent. This dilemma belongs to objective thought and its stable-companion, analytical reflection. If indeed we place ourselves within being, it must necessarily be the case that our actions must have their origin outside us, and if we revert to constituting consciousness, they must originate within. But we have learnt precisely to recognize the order of phenomena. We are involved in the world and with others in an inextricable tangle. The idea of situation rules out absolute freedom at the source of our commitments, and equally, indeed, at their terminus. No commitment, not even commitment in the Hegelian State, can make me leave behind all differences and free me for anything. This universality itself, from the mere fact of its being experienced, would stand out as a particularity against the world's background, for existence both generalizes and particularizes everything at which it aims, and cannot ever be finally complete.

The synthesis of *in itself* and *for itself* which brings Hegelian freedom into being has, however, its truth. In a sense, it is the very definition of existence, since it is effected at every moment before our eyes in the phenomenon of presence, only to be quickly re-enacted, since it does not conjure away our finitude. By taking up a present, I draw together and transform my past, altering its significance, freeing and detaching myself from it. But I do so only by committing myself somewhere else. Psychoanalytical treatment does not bring about its cure by producing direct awareness of the past, but in the first place by binding the subject to his doctor through new existential relationships. It is not a matter of giving scientific assent to the psychoanalytical interpretation, and discovering a notional significance for the past; it is a matter of reliving this or that as significant, and this the patient succeeds in doing only by seeing his past in the perspective of his co-existence with the doctor. The complex is not dissolved by a non-instrumental freedom, but rather displaced by a new pulsation of time with its own supports and motives. The same applies in all cases of coming to awareness: they are real only if they

---

[6] Fink, *Vergegenwärtigung und Bild,* p. 285.

are sustained by a new commitment. Now this commitment too is entered into in the sphere of the implicit, and is therefore valid only for a certain temporal cycle. The choice which we make of our life is always based on a certain givenness. My freedom can draw life away from its spontaneous course, but only by a series of unobtrusive deflections which necessitate first of all following its course—not by any absolute creation. All explanations of my conduct in terms of my past, my temperament and my environment are therefore true, provided that they be regarded not as separable contributions, but as moments of my total being, the significance of which I am entitled to make explicit in various ways, without its ever being possible to say whether I confer their meaning upon them or receive it from them. I am a psychological and historical structure, and have received, with existence, a manner of existing, a style. All my actions and thoughts stand in a relationship to this structure, and even a philosopher's thought is merely a way of making explicit his hold on the world, and what he is. The fact remains that I am free, not in spite of, or on the hither side of, these motivations, but by means of them. For this significant life, this certain significance of nature and history which I am, does not limit my access to the world, but on the contrary is my means of entering into communication with it. It is by being unrestrictedly and unreservedly what I am at present that I have a chance of moving forward; it is by living my time that I am able to understand other times, by plunging into the present and the world, by taking on deliberately what I am fortuitously, by willing what I will and doing what I do, that I can go further. I can pass freedom by, only if I try to get over my natural and social situation by refusing, in the first place, to take it up, instead of using it as a way into the natural and human world. Nothing determines me from outside, not because nothing acts upon me, but, on the contrary, because I am from the start outside myself and open to the world. We are *true* through and through, and have with us, by the mere fact of belonging to the world, and not merely being in the world in the way that things are, all that we need to transcend ourselves. We need have no fear that our choices or actions restrict our liberty, since choice and action alone cut us loose from our anchorage. Just as reflection borrows its wish for absolute sufficiency from the perception which causes a thing to appear, and as in this way idealism tacitly uses that "primary opinion" which it would like to destroy as opinion, so freedom flounders in the contradictions of commitment, and fails to realize that, without the roots which it thrusts into the world, it would not be freedom at all. Shall I make this promise? Shall I risk my life for so little? Shall I give up my liberty in order to save liberty? There is no theoretical reply to these questions. But there are these *things* which stand, irrefutable, there is before you this person whom you love, there are these men whose existence around you is that of slaves, and *your* freedom cannot be willed without leaving behind its singular relevance, and without willing freedom *for all*. Whether it is a question of things or of historical situations, philosophy has no function other than to teach us once more to see them clearly, and it is true to say that it comes into being by destroying itself as separate philosophy. But what is here required is silence, for only the hero lives out his relation to men and the world. "Your son is caught in the fire; you are the one who will save him. . . . If there is an obstacle, you would be ready to give your shoulder provided only that you can charge down that obstacle. Your abode is your act itself. Your act is you. . . . You give yourself in exchange. . . . Your significance shows itself, effulgent. It is your duty, your hatred, your love, your steadfastness, your ingenuity. . . . Man is but a network of relationships, and these alone matter to him."[7]

---

[7] A. de Saint-Exupéry, *Pilote de Guerre,* pp. 171 and 174.

Simone de Beauvoir

(1908–1986)
FRENCH

De Beauvoir shares with Merleau-Ponty the disadvantage of frequently being viewed in the shadow of Sartre, in her case often
with doubly barbed comments that she was Sartre's "companion" or "disciple." In fact, there is ample evidence that they
worked out many of their ideas together, and that de Beauvoir
was an equal partner in the development of existentialist philosophy. De Beauvoir was one of France's foremost novelists
and, far from reiterating Sartre's views, she provided us with an
"existential ethics" that Sartre himself never gave us. In her
Ethics of Ambiguity freedom is again the central concept, but in
an explicitly ethical role. Freedom and morality are paired, as
they are not in Sartre ("To will freedom and to will to be moral
are one and the same"). A free action is also a universalizable
action, an action that essentially takes account of social values
and institutions as well as personal interests and consequences.

In *The Second Sex* de Beauvoir applied the concepts of freedom and universality to a concrete though universal ethical problem in what must count as one of the most insightful sociophilo-
sophical treatises of the century. The problem is woman; What is
a woman? What is it for a woman to be a woman as well as a
human being? What is it for a woman to be a woman as opposed
to a human being? In de Beauvoir's analysis the apparatus of existential philosophy is used to destroy both the views that a
woman is a woman (has an essence that defines her actions, feel-

ings, and roles) and the equally deceptive doctrine that a woman
is only a human being, without distinctive features that distinguish her from men. The following selections are from *The Ethics
of Ambiguity* and *The Second Sex,* respectively.

❖ *from* The Ethics of Ambiguity ❖

As for us, whatever the case may be, we believe in freedom. Is it true
that this belief must lead us to despair? Must we grant this curious
paradox: that from the moment a man recognizes himself as free, he
is prohibited from wishing for anything?

On the contrary, it appears to us that by turning toward this freedom we are going to discover a principle of action whose range will
be universal. The characteristic feature of all ethics is to consider
human life as a game that can be won or lost and to teach man the
means of winning. Now, we have seen that the original scheme of
man is ambiguous: he wants to be, and to the extent that he coincides with this wish, he fails. All the plans in which this will to be is
actualized are condemned; and the ends circumscribed by these
plans remain mirages. Human transcendence is vainly engulfed in
those miscarried attempts. But man also wills himself to be a disclosure of being, and if he coincides with this wish, he wins, for the fact
is that the world becomes present by his presence in it. But the disclosure implies a perceptual tension to keep being at a certain distance, to tear oneself from the world, and to assert oneself as a freedom. To wish for the disclosure of the world and to assert oneself as
freedom are one and the same movement. Freedom is the source
from which all significations and all values spring. It is the original
condition of all justification of existence. The man who seeks to justify his life must want freedom itself absolutely and above everything
else. At the same time that it requires the realization of concrete ends,
of particular projects, it requires itself universally. It is not a ready-
made value which offers itself from the outside to my abstract ad-

herence, but it appears (not on the plane of facility, but on the moral plane) as a cause of itself. It is necessarily summoned up by the values which it sets up and through which it sets itself up. It can not establish a denial of itself, for in denying itself, it would deny the possibility of any foundation. To will oneself moral and to will oneself free are one and the same decision.

• • •

Every man is originally free, in the sense that he spontaneously casts himself into the world. But if we consider this spontaneity in its facticity, it appears to us only as a pure contingency, an upsurging as stupid as the clinamen of the Epicurean atom which turned up at any moment whatsoever from any direction whatsoever. And it was quite necessary for the atom to arrive somewhere. But its movement was not justified by this result which had not been chosen. It remained absurd. Thus, human spontaneity always projects itself toward something. The psychoanalyst discovers a meaning even in abortive acts and attacks of hysteria. But in order for this meaning to justify the transcendence which discloses it, it must itself be founded, which it will never be if I do not choose to found it myself. Now, I can evade this choice. We have said that it would be contradictory deliberately to will oneself not free. But one can choose not to will himself free. In laziness, heedlessness, capriciousness, cowardice, impatience, one contests the meaning of the project at the very moment that one defines it. The spontaneity of the subject is then merely a vain living palpitation, its movement toward the object is a flight, and itself is an absence. To convert the absence into presence, to convert my flight into will, I must assume my project positively. It is not a matter of retiring into the completely inner and, moreover, abstract movement of a given spontaneity, but of adhering to the concrete and particular movement by which this spontaneity defines itself by thrusting itself toward an end. It is through this end that it sets up that my spontaneity confirms itself by reflecting upon itself. Then, by a single movement, my will, establishing the content of the act, is legitimized by it. I realize my escape toward the other as a freedom when, assuming the presence of the object, I thereby assume myself before it as a presence. But this justification requires a constant tension. My project is never founded; it founds itself. To avoid the anguish of this permanent choice, one may attempt to flee into the object itself, to

engulf one's own presence in it. In the servitude of the serious, the
original spontaneity strives to deny itself. It strives in vain, and meanwhile it then fails to fulfill itself as moral freedom.

• • •

However, man does not create the world. He succeeds in disclosing it only through the resistance which the world opposes to him.
The will is defined only by raising obstacles, and by the contingency
of facticity certain obstacles let themselves be conquered, and others
do not. This is what Descartes expressed when he said that the freedom of man is infinite, but his power is limited. How can the presence of these limits be reconciled with the idea of a freedom con-
firming itself as a unity and an indefinite movement?

In the face of an obstacle which it is impossible to overcome, stubbornness is stupid. If I persist in beating my fist against a stone wall,
my freedom exhausts itself in this useless gesture without succeeding in giving itself a content. It debases itself in a vain contingency.
Yet, there is hardly a sadder virtue than resignation. It transforms into
phantoms and contingent reveries projects which had at the beginning been set up as will and freedom. A young man has hoped for a
happy or useful or glorious life. If the man he has become looks
upon these miscarried attempts of his adolescence with disillusioned
indifference, there they are, forever frozen in the dead past. When an
effort fails, one declares bitterly that he has lost time and wasted his
powers. The failure condemns that whole part of ourselves which we
had engaged in the effort. It was to escape this dilemma that the Stoics preached indifference. We could indeed assert our freedom
against all constraint if we agreed to renounce the particularity of our
projects. If a door refuses to open, let us accept not opening it and
there we are free. But by doing that, one manages only to save an
abstract notion of freedom. It is emptied of all content and all truth.
The power of man ceases to be limited because it is annulled. It is
the particularity of the project which determines the limitation of the
power, but it is also what gives the project its content and permits it
to be set up. There are people who are filled with such horror at the
idea of a defeat that they keep themselves from ever doing anything.
But no one would dream of considering this gloomy passivity as the
triumph of freedom.

The truth is that in order for my freedom not to risk coming to
grief against the obstacle which its very engagement has raised, in

order that it might still pursue its movement in the face of the failure, it must, by giving itself a particular content, aim by means of it at an end which is nothing else but precisely the free movement of existence. Popular opinion is quite right in admiring a man who, having been ruined or having suffered an accident, knows how to gain the upper hand, that is, renew his engagement in the world, thereby strongly asserting the independence of freedom in relation to thing. Thus, when the sick Van Gogh calmly accepted the prospect of a future in which he would be unable to paint any more, there was no sterile resignation. For him painting was a personal way of life and of communication with others which in another form could be continued even in an asylum. The past will be integrated and freedom will be confirmed in a renunciation of this kind. It will be lived in both heartbreak and joy. In heartbreak, because the project is then robbed of its particularity—it sacrifices its flesh and blood. But in joy, since at the moment one releases his hold, he again finds his hands free and ready to stretch out toward a new future. But this act of passing beyond is conceivable only if what the content has in view is not to bar up the future, but, on the contrary, to plan new possibilities. This brings us back by another route to what we had already indicated. My freedom must not seek to trap being but to disclose it. The disclosure is the transition from being to existence. The goal which my freedom aims at is conquering existence across the always inadequate density of being.

• • •

. . . not only do we assert that the existentialist doctrine permits the elaboration of an ethics, but it even appears to us as the only philosophy in which an ethics has its place. For, in a metaphysics of transcendence, in the classical sense of the term, evil is reduced to error; and in humanistic philosophies it is impossible to account for it, man being defined as complete in a complete world. Existentialism alone gives—like religions—a real role to evil, and it is this, perhaps, which makes its judgments so gloomy. Men do not like to feel themselves in danger. Yet, it is because there are real dangers, real failures and real earthly damnation that words like victory, wisdom, or joy have meaning. Nothing is decided in advance, and it is because man has something to lose and because he can lose that he can also win.

❖ *from* The Second Sex ❖

For a long time I have hesitated to write a book on woman. The sub-ject is irritating, especially to women; and it is not new. Enough ink has been spilled in the quarreling over feminism, now practically over, and perhaps we should say no more about it. It is still talked about, however, for the voluminous nonsense uttered during the last century seems to have done little to illuminate the problem. After all, is there a problem? And if so, what is it? Are there women, really? Most assuredly the theory of the eternal feminine still has its adher-ents who will whisper in your ear: "Even in Russia women still are *women*"; and other erudite persons—sometimes the very same—say with a sigh: "Woman is losing her way, woman is lost." One wonders if women still exist, if they will always exist, whether or not it is de-sirable that they should, what place they occupy in this world, what their place should be. "What has become of women?" was asked re-cently in an ephemeral magazine.

But first we must ask: what is a woman? *"Tota mulier in utero,"* says one, "woman is a womb." But in speaking of certain women, connoisseurs declare that they are not women, although they are equipped with a uterus like the rest. All agree in recognizing the fact that females exist in the human species; today as always they make up about one half of humanity. And yet we are told that femininity is in danger; we are exhorted to be women, remain women, become women. It would appear, then, that every female human being is not necessarily a woman; to be so considered she must share in that mys-terious and threatened reality known as femininity. Is this attribute something secreted by the ovaries? Or is it a Platonic essence, a prod-uct of the philosophic imagination? Is a rustling petticoat enough to bring it down to earth? Although some women try zealously to in-carnate this essence, it is hardly patentable. It is frequently described in vague and dazzling terms that seem to have been borrowed from the vocabulary of the seers, and indeed in the times of St. Thomas it was considered an essence as certainly defined as the somniferous virtue of the poppy.

But conceptualism has lost ground. The biological and social sciences no longer admit the existence of unchangeably fixed entities that determine given characteristics, such as those ascribed to woman, the Jew, or the Negro. Science regards any characteristic as a reaction dependent in part upon a *situation*. If today femininity no longer exists, then it never existed. But does the word *woman,* then, have no specific content? This is stoutly affirmed by those who hold to the philosophy of the enlightenment, or rationalism, of nominalism; women, to them, are merely the human beings arbitrarily designated by the word *woman.* Many American women particularly are prepared to think that there is no longer any place for woman as such; if a backward individual still takes herself for a woman, her friends advise her to be psychoanalyzed and thus get rid of this obsession. In regard to a work, *Modern Woman: The Lost Sex,* which in other respects has its irritating features, Dorothy Parker has written: "I cannot be just to books which treat of woman as woman. . . . My idea is that all of us, men as well as women, should be regarded as human beings." But nominalism is a rather inadequate doctrine, and the antifemininists have had no trouble in showing that women simply *are not* men. Surely woman is, like man, a human being, but such a declaration is abstract. The fact is that every concrete human being is always a singular, separate individual. To decline to accept such notions as the eternal feminine, the black soul, the Jewish character, is not to deny that Jews, Negroes, women exist today—this denial does not represent a liberation for those concerned, but rather a flight from reality. Some years ago, a well-known woman writer refused to permit her portrait to appear in a series of photographs especially devoted to women writers; she wished to be counted among the men. But in order to gain this privilege she made use of her husband's influence! Women who assert that they are men lay claim none the less to masculine consideration and respect. I recall also a young Trotskyite standing on a platform at a boisterous meeting and getting ready to use her fists, in spite of her evident fragility. She was denying her feminine weakness; but it was for love of a militant male whose equal she wished to be. The attitude of defiance of many American women proves that they are haunted by a sense of their femininity. In truth, to go for a walk with one's eyes open is enough to demonstrate that humanity is divided into two classes of individuals whose clothes, faces, bodies, smiles, gaits, interests, and occupations are manifestly different. Perhaps these differences are superficial, perhaps they are destined to disappear. What is certain is that right now they do most obviously exist.

If her functioning as a female is not enough to define woman, if we decline also to explain her through "the eternal feminine," and if nevertheless we admit, provisionally, that women do exist, then we must face that question: what is a woman?

To state the question is, to me, to suggest, at once, a preliminary answer. The fact that I ask it is in itself significant. A man would never get the notion of writing a book on the peculiar situation of the human male. But if I wish to define myself, I must first of all say: "I am a woman"; on this truth must be based all further discussion. A man never begins by presenting himself as an individual of a certain sex; it goes without saying that he is a man. The terms *masculine* and *feminine* are used symmetrically only as a matter of form, as on legal papers. In actuality the relation of the two sexes is not quite like that of two electrical poles, for man represents both the positive and the neutral, as is indicated by the common use of *man* to designate human beings in general: whereas woman represents only the negative, defined by limiting criteria, without reciprocity. In the midst of an abstract discussion it is vexing to hear a man say: "You think thus and so because you are a woman"; but I know that my only defense is to reply: "I think thus and so because it is true," thereby removing my subjective self from the argument. It would be out of the question to reply: "And you think the contrary because you are a man," for it is understood that the fact of being a man is no peculiarity. A man is in the right in being a man; it is the woman who is in the wrong. It amounts to this: just as for the ancients there was an absolute vertical with reference to which the oblique was defined, so there is an absolute human type, the masculine. Women has ovaries, a uterus, these peculiarities imprison her in her subjectivity, circumscribe her within the limits of her own nature. It is often said that she thinks with her glands: Man superbly ignores the fact that his anatomy also includes glands, such as the testicles, and that they secrete hormones. He thinks of his body as a direct and normal connection with the world, which he believes he apprehends objectively, whereas he regards the body of woman as a hindrance, a prison, weighed down by everything peculiar to it. "The female is a female by virtue of a certain *lack* of qualities," said Aristotle: "we should regard the female nature as afflicted with a natural defectiveness." And St. Thomas for his part pronounced woman to be an "imperfect man," an "incidental" being. This is symbolized in Genesis where Eve is depicted as made from what Bossuet called "a supernumerary bone" of Adam.

Thus humanity is male and man defines woman not in herself but as relative to him; she is not regarded as an autonomous being. Michelet writes: "Woman, the relative being. . . ." And Benda is most positive in his *Rapport d'Uriel:* "The body of man makes sense in itself quite apart from that of woman, whereas the latter seems wanting in significance by itself. . . . Man can think of himself without woman. She cannot think of herself without man." And she is simply what man decrees; thus she is called "the sex," by which is meant that she appears essentially to the male as a sexual being. For him she is sex—absolute sex, no less. She is defined and differentiated with reference to man and not he with reference to her; she is the incidental, the inessential as opposed to the essential. He is the Subject, he is the Absolute—she is the Other.

The category of the *Other* is as primordial as consciousness itself. In the most primitive societies, in the most ancient mythologies, one finds the expression of a duality—that of the Self and the Other. This duality was not originally attached to the division of the sexes; it was not dependent upon any empirical facts. It is revealed in such works as that of Granet on Chinese thought and those of Dumézil on the East Indies and Rome. The feminine element was at first no more involved in such pairs as Varuna-Mitra, Uranus-Zeus, Sun-Moon, and Day-Night than it was in the contrasts between Good and Evil, lucky and unlucky auspices, right and left, God and Lucifer. Otherness is a fundamental category of human thought.

Thus it is that no group ever sets itself up as the One without at once setting up the Other over against itself. If three travelers chance to occupy the same compartment, that is enough to make vaguely hostile "others" out of all the rest of the passengers on the train. In small-town eyes all persons not belonging to the village are "strangers" and suspect; to the native of a country all who inhabit other countries are "foreigners"; Jews are "different" for the anti-Semite, Negroes are "inferior" for American racists, aborigines are "natives" for colonists, proletarians are the "lower class" for the privileged.

Lévi-Strauss, at the end of a profound work on the various forms of primitive societies, reaches the following conclusion: "Passage from the state of Nature to the state of Culture is marked by man's ability to view biological relations as a series of contrasts; duality, alternation, opposition, and symmetry, whether under definite or vague forms, constitute not so much phenomena to be explained as fundamental and immediately given data of social reality." These phenomena would be incomprehensible if in fact human society were simply a *Mitsein* or fellowship based on solidarity and friendliness. Things become clear, on the contrary, if, following Hegel, we find in consciousness itself a fundamental hostility toward every other consciousness; the subject can be posed only in being opposed—he sets himself up as the essential, as opposed to the other, the inessential, the object.

But the other consciousness, the other ego, sets up a reciprocal claim. The native traveling abroad is shocked to find himself in turn regarded as a "stranger" by the natives of neighboring countries. As a matter of fact, wars, festivals, trading, treaties, and contests among tribes, nations, and classes tend to deprive the concept *Other* of its absolute sense and to make manifest its relativity; willy-nilly, individuals and groups are forced to realize the reciprocity of their relations. How is it, then, that this reciprocity has not been recognized between the sexes, that one of the contrasting terms is set up as the sole essential, denying any relativity in regard to its correlative and defining the latter as pure otherness? Why is it that women do not dispute male sovereignty? No subject will readily volunteer to become the object, the inessential; it is not the Other, who, in defining himself as the Other, establishes the One. The Other is posed as such by the One in defining himself as the One. But if the Other is not to regain the status of being the One, he must be submissive enough to accept this alien point of view. Whence comes this submission in the case of woman?

There are, to be sure, other cases in which a certain category has been able to dominate another completely for a time. Very often this privilege depends upon inequality of numbers—the majority imposes its rule upon the minority or persecutes it. But women are not a minority, like the American Negroes or the Jews; there are as many women as men on earth. Again, the two groups concerned have often been originally independent; they may have been formerly unaware of each other's existence, or perhaps they recognized each other's autonomy. But a historical event has resulted in the subjugation of the weaker by the stronger. The scattering of the Jews, the introduction of slavery into America, the conquests of imperialism are examples in point. In these cases the oppressed retained at least the memory of former days; they possessed in common a past, a tradition, sometimes a religion or a culture.

The parallel drawn by Bebel between women and the proletariat is valid in that neither ever formed a minority or a separate collective unit of mankind. And instead of a single historical event it is in both cases a historical development that explains their status as a class and accounts for the membership of *particular individuals* in that class. But proletarians have not always existed, whereas there have always been women. They are women in virtue of their anatomy and physiology. Throughout history they have always been subordinated to men, and hence their dependency is not the result of a historical event or a social change—it was not something that *occurred*. The reason why otherness in this case seems to be an absolute is in part that it lacks the contingent or incidental nature of historical facts. A condition brought about at a certain time can be abolished at some other time, as the Negroes of Haiti and others have proved; but it might seem that a natural condition is beyond the possibility of change. In truth, however, the nature of things is no more immutably given, once for all, than is historical reality. If woman seems to be the inessential which never becomes the essential, it is because she herself fails to bring about this change. Proletarians say "We"; Negroes also. Regarding themselves as subjects, they transform the bourgeois, the whites, into "others." But women do not say "We," except at some congress of feminists or similar formal demonstration; men say "women," and women use the same word in referring to themselves. They do not authentically assume a subjective attitude. The proletarians have accomplished the revolution in Russia, the Negroes in Haiti, the Indo-Chinese are battling for it in Indo-China; but the women's effort has never been anything more than a symbolic agitation. They have gained only what men have been willing to grant; they have taken nothing, they have only received.

The reason for this is that women lack concrete means for organizing themselves into a unit which can stand face to face with the correlative unit. They have no past, no history, no religion of their own; and they have no such solidarity of work and interest as that of the proletariat. They are not even promiscuously herded together in the way that creates community feeling among the American Negroes, the ghetto Jews, the workers of Saint-Denis, or the factory hands of Renault. They live dispersed among the males, attached through residence, housework, economic condition, and social standing to certain men—fathers or husbands—more firmly than they are to other women. If they belong to the bourgeoisie, they feel solidarity with men of that class, not with proletarian women; if they are white, their allegiance is to white men, not to Negro women. The proletariat can propose to massacre the ruling class, and a sufficiently fanatical Jew or Negro might dream of getting sole possession of the atomic bomb and making humanity wholly Jewish or black; but woman cannot even dream of exterminating the males. The bond that unites her to her oppressors is not comparable to any other. The division of the sexes is a biological fact, not an event in human history. Male and female stand opposed within a primordial *Mitsein,* and woman has not broken it. The couple is a fundamental unity with its two halves riveted together, and the cleavage of society along the line of sex is impossible. Here is to be found the basic trait of woman: she is the Other in a totality of which the two components are necessary to one another.

• • •

. . . it is doubtless impossible to approach any human problem with a mind free from bias. The way in which questions are put, the points of view assumed, presuppose a relativity of interest, all characteristics imply values, and every objective description, so called, implies an ethical background. Rather than attempt to conceal principles more or less definitely implied, it is better to state them openly at the beginning. This will make it unnecessary to specify on every page in just what sense one uses such words as *superior, inferior, better, worse, progress, reaction,* and the like. If we survey some of the works on women, we note that one of the points of view most frequently adopted is that of the public good, the general interest; and one always means by this the benefit of society as one wishes it to be maintained or established. For our part, we hold that the only public good is that which assures the private good of the citizens; we shall pass judgment on institutions according to their effectiveness in giving concrete opportunities to individuals. But we do not confuse the idea of private interest with that of happiness, although that is another common point of view. Are not women of the harem more happy than women voters? Is not the housekeeper happier than the working-woman? It is not too clear just what the word *happy* really means and still less what true values it may mask. There is no possibility of measuring the happiness of others, and it is always easy to describe as happy the situation in which one wishes to place them.

In particular those who are condemned to stagnation are often pronounced happy on the pretext that happiness consists in being at rest. This notion we reject, for our perspective is that of existentialist ethics. Every subject plays his part as such specifically through exploits or projects that serve as a mode of transcendence, he achieves liberty only through a continual reaching out toward other liberties. There is no justification for present existence other than its expansion into an indefinitely open future. Every time transcendence falls back into immanence, stagnation, there is a degradation of existence into the "*en-soi*"—the brutish life of subjection to given conditions—and of liberty into constraint and contingence. This downfall represents a moral fault if the subject consents to it: if it is inflicted upon him, it spells frustration and oppression. In both cases it is an absolute evil. Every individual concerned to justify his existence feels that his existence involves an undefined need to transcend himself, to engage in freely chosen projects.

Now, what peculiarly signalizes the situation of woman is that she—a free and autonomous being like all human creatures—nevertheless finds herself living in a world where men compel her to assume the status of the Other. They propose to stabilize her as object and to doom her to immanence since her transcendence is to be overshadowed and forever transcended by another ego (*conscience*) which is essential and sovereign. The drama of woman lies in this conflict between the fundamental aspirations of every subject (ego)—who always regards the self as the essential—and the compulsions of a situation in which she is the inessential. How can a human being in woman's situation attain fulfillment? What roads are open to her? Which are blocked? How can independence be recovered in a state of dependency? What circumstances limit woman's liberty and how can they be overcome? These are the fundamental questions on which I would fain throw some light. This means that I am interested in the fortunes of the individual as defined not in terms of happiness but in terms of liberty.

• • •

A world where men and women would be equal is easy to visualize, for that precisely is what the Soviet Revolution *promised:* women raised and trained exactly like men were to work under the same conditions and for the same wages. Erotic liberty was to be recognized by custom, but the sexual act was not to be considered a "service" to be paid for; woman was to be *obliged* to provide herself with other ways of earning a living; marriage was to be based on a free agreement that the spouses could break at will; maternity was to be voluntary, which meant that contraception and abortion were to be authorized and that, on the other hand, all mothers and their children were to have exactly the same rights, in or out of marriage; pregnancy leaves were to be paid for by the State, which would assume charge of the children, signifying not that they would be *taken away* from their parents, but that they would not be *abandoned* to them.

But is it enough to change laws, institutions, customs, public opinion, and the whole social context, for men and women to become truly equal? "Women will always be women," say the skeptics. Other seers prophesy that in casting off their femininity they will not succeed in changing themselves into men and they will become monsters. This would be to admit that the woman of today is a creation of nature; it must be repeated once more that in human society nothing is natural and that woman, like much else, is a product elaborated by civilization. The intervention of others in her destiny is fundamental: if this action took a different direction, it would produce a quite different result. Woman is determined not by her hormones or by mysterious instincts, but by the manner in which her body and her relation to the world are modified through the action of others than herself. The abyss that separates the adolescent boy and girl has been deliberately opened out between them since earliest childhood; later on, woman could not be other than what she *was made,* and that past was bound to shadow her for life. If we appreciate its influence, we see clearly that her destiny is not predetermined for all eternity.

We must not believe, certainly, that a change in woman's economic condition alone is enough to transform her, though this factor has been and remains the basic factor in her evolution; but until it has brought about the moral, social, cultural, and other consequences that it promises and requires, the new woman cannot appear. At this moment they have been realized nowhere, in Russia no more than in France or the United States, and this explains why the woman of today is torn between the past and the future. She appears most often as a "true woman" disguised as a man, and she feels herself as ill at ease in her flesh as in her masculine garb. She must shed her old skin and cut her own new clothes. This she could do only through a social evolution. No single educator could fashion a *female human being* today who would be the exact homologue of the *male human being;* if she is raised like a boy, the young girl feels she is an oddity and thereby she is given a new kind of sex specification. Stendhal understood this when he said: "The forest must be planted all at once." But if we imagine, on the contrary, a society in which the equality of the sexes would be concretely realized, this equality would find new expression in each individual.

• • •

As a matter of fact, man, like woman, is flesh, therefore passive, the plaything of his hormones and of the species, the restless prey of his desires. And she, like him, in the midst of the carnal fever, is a consenting, a voluntary gift, an activity; they live out in their several fashions the strange ambiguity of existence made body. In those combats where they think they confront one another, it is really against the self that each one struggles, projecting into the partner that part of the self which is repudiated; instead of living out the ambiguities of their situation, each tries to make the other bear the abjection and tries to reserve the honor for the self. If, however, both should assume the ambiguity with a clear-sighted modesty, correlative of an authentic pride, they would see each other as equals and would live out their erotic drama in amity. The fact that we are human beings is infinitely more important than all the peculiarities that distinguish human beings from one another; it is never the given that confers superiorities: "virtue," as the ancients called it, is defined at the level of "that which depends on us." In both sexes is played out the same drama of the flesh and the spirit, of finitude and transcendence; both are gnawed away by time and laid in wait for by death, they have the same essential need for one another; and they can gain from their liberty the same glory. If they were to taste it, they would no longer be tempted to dispute fallacious privileges, and fraternity between them could then come into existence.

I shall be told that all this is utopian fancy, because woman cannot be "made over" unless society has first made her really the equal of man. Conservatives have never failed in such circumstances to refer to that vicious circle; history, however, does not revolve. If a caste is kept in a state of inferiority, no doubt it remains inferior; but liberty can break the circle. Let the Negroes vote and they become worthy of having the vote; let woman be given responsibilities and she is able to assume them. The fact is that oppressors cannot be expected to make a move of gratuitous generosity; but at one time the revolt of the oppressed, at another time even the very evolution of the privileged caste itself, creates new situations; thus men have been led, in their own interest, to give partial emancipation to women: it remains only for women to continue their ascent, and the successes they are obtaining are an encouragement for them to do so. It seems almost certain that sooner or later they will arrive at complete economic and social equality, which will bring about an inner metamorphosis.

• • •

To begin with, there will always be certain differences between man and woman; her eroticism, and therefore her sexual world, have a special form of their own and therefore cannot fail to engender a sensuality, a sensitivity, of a special nature. This means that her relations to her own body, to that of the male, to the child, will never be identical with those the male bears to his own body, to that of the female and to the child; those who make much of "equality in difference" could not with good grace refuse to grant me the possible existence of differences in equality. Then again, it is institutions that create uniformity. Young and pretty, the slaves of the harem are always the same in the sultan's embrace; Christianity gave eroticism its savor of sin and legend when it endowed the human female with a soul; if society restores her sovereign individuality to woman, it will not thereby destroy the power of love's embrace to move the heart.

It is nonsense to assert that revelry, vice, ecstasy, passion, would become impossible if man and woman were equal in concrete matters; the contradictions that put the flesh in opposition to the spirit, the instant to time, the swoon of immanence to the challenge of transcendence, the absolute of pleasure to the nothingness of forgetting, will never be resolved; in sexuality will always be materialized the tension, the anguish, the joy, the frustration, and the triumph of existence. To emancipate woman is to refuse to confine her to the relations she bears to man, not to deny them to her; let her have her independent existence and she will continue none the less to exist for him *also:* mutually recognizing each other as subject, each will yet remain for the other an *other.* The reciprocity of their relations will not do away with the miracles—desire, possession, love, dream, adventure—worked by the division of human beings into two separate categories; and the words that move us—giving, conquering, uniting—will not lose their meaning. On the contrary, when we abolish the slavery of half of humanity, together with the whole system of hypocrisy that it implies, then the "division" of humanity will reveal its genuine significance and the human couple will find its true form. "The direct, natural, necessary relation of human creatures is the *relation of man to woman*," Marx has said.[1] "The nature of this relation determines to what point man himself is to be considered as a *generic being*, as mankind; the relation of man to woman is the most natural relation of human being to human being. By it is shown, therefore, to what point the *natural* behavior of man has become *human* or to what point the *human* being has become his *natural* being, to what point his *human nature* has become his *nature*."

The case could not be better stated. It is for man to establish the reign of liberty in the midst of the world of the given. To gain the supreme victory, it is necessary, for one thing, that by and through their natural differentiation men and women unequivocally affirm their brotherhood.

---

[1] *Philosophical Works,* Vol. VI (Marx's italics).

Hazel E. Barnes

(B. 1915)
AMERICAN

Barnes is best known for her English translation of Sartre's *Being and Nothingness,* but she is also a Sartre scholar and an important existentialist in her own right. She received her Ph.D. from Yale University in 1941 and taught for many years at the University of Colorado. Her *An Existentialist Ethics* was published in 1967. Her autobiography, *The Story I Tell Myself: A Venture in Existentialist Autobiography,* was published in 1998. In this recent essay, Barnes reexamines Sartre's odd reputation as both a misogynist and an early defender of feminism.

❖ Sartre and Feminism ❖
Aside from *The Second Sex* and All That

While Sartre's *Critique of Dialectical Reason* could hardly be called a drama, the first volume has a distinct sense of rising and falling action. The dramatic climax comes in the cluster of passages describing the emergence of the group-in-fusion and the formation of the fused group. Rhetorical excitement abounds as Sartre puts us in the

From "Sartre and Feminism," by Hazel E. Barnes, in Julien S. Murphy, Feminist Interpretations of Sartre. *Published by Penn State Press, Inc. Reprinted with permission of Penn State Press, Inc.*

midst of the group at white heat, running on "its hundred pairs of legs," shouting with "its hundred mouths," each one of us the same in a body of "myselves" (*des moi-même*). Then, on the bright morning after the battle, when all vote to continue their existence as a pledged group, emotion mounts still higher. This act Sartre declares to be "the origin of humanity." Our committed freedoms unite us. We are brothers, but not like tinned peas in a can. Sartre grandly proclaims, "We are our common creation, we are our own sons." What a thud! Why couldn't Sartre have written, "We are our own children"? The French *enfants* is a nonsexual generic, *fils* is not.

Perhaps one might say that the logic of rhetoric requires the masculine. Sartre's description is loosely based on the taking of the Bastille, the revolutionary group comes into being on the field of battle, and so on. The further we go, the worse it gets. "The origin of humanity" is in a military camp; we pledge ourselves to invoke terror against traitors and defectors. "We?" Sartre may say "we," but I cannot. And where are the women? One may assume that they are cooking a meal for the men busy signing the new constitution. Whatever the women are doing, one can only imagine them. In the text itself there is no room for them. Women are nowhere. To label the formation of this male club the "origin of humanity" is a travesty.

I begin with this dismal illustration because I want to acknowledge at the outset that it is not without reason that some feminists have found Sartre's aggressive masculinity, shown in a passage such as this and in the sexist language of certain rhetorical images in *Being and Nothingness,* sufficient to render suspect, in their opinion, his overt approval of *The Second Sex* and women's liberation. I find this judgment overhasty but understandable. Sartre is not *my* ego ideal either. What I cannot accept is the often heard pronouncement that Sartre's entire philosophy is so irremediably male that it excludes women. Nor the view that it is based on the notion of a purely male consciousness, presented as an all but disembodied, hostile stare. Nor the charge that Sartre's concept of human freedom is so abstract as to be virtually unrelated to the real world. Nor even the conclusion that, while Beauvoir managed to bend Sartre's ontology to suit her own purpose, the only way to find Sartre's philosophy at all useful for feminism today is to concentrate on his later work and regard *Being and Nothingness* as preenlightened Sartre.

In a small, limited response to such attacks on Sartre, I will do two things here. First, I will ask whether Sartre's philosophical writings (I will exclude his literary works) do in fact put us into a wholly male world. He frequently employs examples in which women are present. What do these show us about Sartre's attitude? Second, I want to look once again at Sartre's early description of consciousness in relation to the body and the ego. Is the for itself in truth a bizarre creation that can exist only on the printed page?

• • •

First then, what are the implications of those examples in which Sartre selects women to clarify or to illustrate points in his philosophy? Without attempting to be exhaustive, I find that a surprisingly large number comes readily to mind. They are of various types:

Among those that refer to women to illustrate negative points, the one most strongly reflecting male bias is, of course, the woman in the café who demonstrates bad faith as she tries to deceive herself with regard to her companion's sexual overtures and her own responses to him. This woman's behavior is by no means unusual. I suspect that Sartre was expressing his frustration in having often encountered it. Yet he could, drawing on even more intimate personal experience, have analyzed the conduct of a self-deceiving male seducer. Perhaps more offensive, because more general, is a remark in *Notebooks for an Ethics*. In the context Sartre is discussing devices in bad faith by which people attempt to protect their unfounded beliefs from rational argument. One of these is the appeal to intuition, which Sartre finds frequent among women, especially "wives or girl friends of professionals (engineers, lawyers, doctors) who regularly beat them in discussion; they can protect their truths only by putting them beyond the control of discussions and discourse, of criticism." Sartre softens his charge by pointing out that resorting to intuition is an inoffensive weapon of the weak. And, of course, he is speaking of the untrained in the presence of experts. Still, the tacit assumption is that only rationality counts; the implication is that women's appeal to other than established forms of reason is a sign of inferiority.

Other examples of women illustrating self-deception are not necessarily reflections of male chauvinism. In *Saint-Genet* Sartre makes an extended comparison of Saint Theresa with two would-be saints, Jouhan-deau and Genet. Sartre is unkind to Saint Theresa, labeling her a "fake saint," who in her professed self-abasement risked far less than the other two and was more thoroughly steeped in self-deception. But, if Sartre is unfair to her, surely here the cause is his lack of sympathy for Christianity, not sexual bias. In *Truth and Existence,* Sartre chooses a woman to exemplify a willed ignorance that is almost indistinguishable from bad faith, a woman who will find reasons not to consult a doctor, who refuses even to try to interpret her own symptoms because she does not want to risk knowing that she has tuberculosis. Sartre could just as easily have imagined a man. But aside from the coincidental fact that he probably had in mind a real woman of his acquaintance, I find it hard to see his choice as expressive of contempt for women. In a couple of examples taken from psychoanalytical studies, Sartre introduces women. From *The Emotions* we recall the woman who fainted at the sight of the bay tree *in order to* (in Sartre's view) repress a painful recollection of an episode that once took place near such a tree. In *The Transcendence of the Ego* Sartre refers to Janet's account of the young bride, who found herself suddenly feeling, in a panic, that she *could,* that she was *free* to call down invitations to men in the street though nothing in her past suggested that she was capable of such behavior. This last example is of special interest. Rather than seeking an explanation of the woman's impulse in a repressed past, Sartre views her as experiencing what he believes is a frightening but potentially liberating revelation of the truth of our condition: no human consciousness is walled in or protected by the ego, it is gloriously and terrifyingly free to restructure its own ego. While hardly an example of authenticity, the young bride is, albeit neurotically, expressing our human reality.

Even with just these examples we would have to acknowledge that Sartre has at least peopled his world with women, introduced them into his discussion; the "men only" setting of the fused group appears to be more the exception than the rule.

What conclusions may we draw from this brief consideration of Sartre's use of women in examples? There are a few, remarkably few, traces of what I will call *unintended* male chauvinism. (For anyone but Sartre I would say "unconscious.") One assumption is all pervasive: that the human and the personal have existential priority over sex differentiation. We see this not only in the lack of mention of any determining "femininity" or "masculinity" but positively in the ease with which Sartre chooses, often as if at random, both males and females to illuminate the most basic principles in his phenomenological description of human consciousness in-the-world. There is a recognition of ways in which men have made it difficult for women freely to "make themselves" and a condemnation of the male bad faith that is responsible. We see some evidence that Sartre attempted to grasp the particular quality of the kind of situation that only women confronted. By implication, there seems to be room for women leaders in another sort of fused group. In the case of the Belgian women, there is a suggestion that women's unique experience might lead them to change social practice in a particular instance. There is no more general claim that women, in the name of feminine values, might effectively challenge the prevailing "subhumanity," which Sartre believes to be our present environment. In short, Sartre's *attitudes,* as shown here, are, for the most part, compatible with Beauvoir's in *The Second Sex.* They do not clearly point to a feminism more radical than she proposed there; nor, I add, do they preclude it.

If Beauvoir had not (at Sartre's suggestion, we should not forget) written *The Second Sex,* I doubt that Sartre would have attempted a work of his own on women's condition. (One cannot be sure, of course. This strictly heterosexual intellectual did not hesitate to describe the inner life of the homosexual, convicted felon, Saint Genet.) Sartre allowed his favorite character, Hoederer, to say that he was not interested in the cause of women's liberation. In Sartre's case, I think his making relatively few statements on the subject was not due to lack of interest but to the conviction that this was a specific area for the application of general principles and a sphere for social action rather than for philosophical investigation, just as he firmly believed that the education and the treatment of children within the family called for a revolution in our thinking and practice but never wrote an article devoted to child psychology. In taking over the task herself, Beauvoir built primarily on two major themes in Sartre—the subject-object conflict and his insistence that human beings are not born with a given nature but make themselves. All of this is so fully developed in *The Second Sex* that I will not touch on it here. If there is any point on which all feminists agree, surely it is the view that women historically have been the losers in the conflict and that self-definition must be the first step in any effort by women to develop their potentialities, whether as human beings or as women.

In his later work, Sartre went beyond not only *Being and Nothingness* but also *The Second Sex* in his emphasis on the interplay of freedom and conditioning. A summary statement of his position with regard to the relation between the sexes is found in *Critique* 2. "The sexual relationship . . . is perhaps the deepest incarnation of the relation of reciprocity between human beings, at once as free organisms and as products of the society in which they live." He goes on to say that it is not just the couple but the society that is set up for judgment in this "free incarnation." Embodiment as a free incarnation of organisms, the paradox of men and women declared to be free in a society that has produced them, a society on which a judgment can be brought to bear: this passage could not have come from *Being and Nothingness*. Nevertheless, its roots are there. There has been much misunderstanding of Sartre's view on the relation of a consciousness to its body and its ego. It has been particularly consequential in feminists' judgment of his philosophy. Let us look at his position again, beginning with what he says about the body.

I have noticed that translators (myself included) tend to choose the English work "incarnation" in translating the French cognate, rather than "embodiment," which is the more usual term in philosophical contexts. Why not use "embodiment"? My guess is that we translators have nonreflectively responded to our sense that it suggests more of a fixed enrooting than seems right for Sartre. In connotation at least, "incarnation" implies that something is one with its setting and yet more than it. Strictly speaking, a consciousness, for Sartre, is nether more nor other than its body. He states firmly, "The body is what this consciousness is; it is not even anything except body. The rest is nothingness and silence." The "nothingness," we know, makes all the difference. Consciousness both is and is not its body. As intentional activity, consciousness lives its relation with the body in three different ways. Or, as Sartre puts it, the human body has three ontological dimensions: (1) the body as being-for-itself; in nonreflective action my body's instrumentality is so fused with conscious intentions that the two are no more separable than a skier's leg is separable from his skiing; (2) the body-for-others, or my body as others perceive it; and (3) my body as I am aware that it is known by others.

Let us look specifically now at the first dimension—the body as being-for-itself. It is here that we can best understand Sartre's statement that consciousness both is and is not its body. Consciousness is not its body in that it nihilates (or transcends) its body as it does everything else, including its own past acts of consciousness. Properly and fully understood, this claim by Sartre has been rightly held to be the cornerstone of at least Beauvoir's feminism; I myself believe

it to be essential to any feminism that is not deterministic and re-
gressive. It is also a controversial issue to a few later feminists. If, in
some ultimate significant sense, consciousness is not its body, then
neither anatomy nor physiology makes us what we are as persons.
Judith Butler, in an excellent article, showed how Beauvoir, taking
Sartre at his non-Cartesian best (as Butler expresses it), used Sartre's
view that consciousness always goes beyond its body as support for
the position that—while we are our bodies as we are our situation,
our field of possibilities—still, our sex is not the same as our gender.
We are born female or male (though some extremists would argue
that things are not quite that simple); we become women or men.
Gender traits we develop ourselves, partly independently, partly as
we yield to social expectations and pressures. So-called feminine
qualities are on exactly the same level as cowardliness, generosity,
irascibility, and so on, all of which, according to Sartre and Beauvoir,
are qualities attributed to behavior but are not fixed structures of a
person's being.

I think that no feminist would want to reject the basic distinction
between sex and gender. Many, however, have argued that Sartre, in
denying the determinism of body over consciousness, has actually
postulated a disembodied consciousness, as an ideal if not as an existential reality. That he himself valued the feeling of being in control
as opposed to yielding and receiving, I do not deny. This is not the
same as believing that a consciousness is, should be, or could be, in
any significant sense, disembodied. Quite to the contrary, Sartre argued that consciousness is a revealing presence to the world and that
the living body is a consciousness present in the world. Consciousness *is* its body. One's way of being in the world inevitably reflects
one's bodily structure and physiological condition—just as one's particular position in space and time de-limits the objective possibilities
of one's life. Sartre always acknowledged that every freedom is situated. If the body is deformed or diseased, its relation to the world is
altered. Beauvoir did not have to bend Sartre's theory to show how
woman's usually slighter physique, her menstruation, and her potentiality for voluntary or involuntary pregnancy place her in a situation different from that of a man. The woman with tuberculosis cannot prevent the racking cough and fever from weakening her, but she
transcends it in her choice to deny or to acknowledge her condition,
to surrender to it, or to fight it; she lives with it or dies with it on her
own terms. Sartre said in *Critique* 1 that his philosophy gave full

weight to both materiality and consciousness. Even in his late work, and despite his heavy emphasis on the alienating power of the practico-inert, he insisted that some measure of subjectivity always contributes to how we live the situation that has been imposed on us. Similarly, a consciousness, while not being something other than the body, is not its body, is not its body in exactly the same way that in every intentional act, consciousness is aware of not being its object—or, more precisely, aware that the awareness of the object is not the object. We are aware of the many ways by which consciousness at once transcends its body and makes itself one with its body in conduct which, as Sartre sees it, is intentional but not deliberate. Psychosomatic reactions testify to a consciousness's capability of expressing its intentions by means of bodily symptoms. In *The Family Idiot* Sartre examined this mode of passive activity in his study of Flaubert's recourse to hysteria (in the form of a pseudo-epileptic attack) as a way for Flaubert to rebel against his father.

Sartre's description of the second dimension of the body has been largely neglected by commentators although I believe that it is here that he most effectively shows the inextricability of body and consciousness and the possibilities for positive relations between individuals. Obviously, like Sartre, I must speak of the body-for-others in terms of the other's body for me, for this is what I know directly. Sartre begins by establishing that whatever my attitude toward a particular other, the other's body is always meaningful; it is a pathway from or to the other's intentional consciousness. The other's body appears graceful insofar as its movements seem to flow harmoniously from that consciousness, obscene if its flesh seems extraneous to consciousness's intentions. Already in *Being and Nothingness,* Sartre, while denying that one consciousness might ever merge with another, spoke of a "reciprocal incarnation" of consciousnesses in the union of lovers when each one, insofar as possible, sought to reach toward the other's consciousness through the body. Sartre appeared hardly to realize the full implications of what he said here, probably because his controlling purpose at this point was to show that neither love nor sex could satisfy the mistaken passion to be God. In *Notebooks for an Ethics* he explicitly designates the body-for-others as the seat of authentic love (love either erotic or nonerotic as in intimate friendship or emotional devotion to the leader of a cause one believes in).

Three things characterize what Sartre takes to be authentic love. First, I empathically read the other's actions and bodily expressions as manifestations of a free consciousness and grasp them in terms of the other's network of ends and means. I interpret the other's activities within a situation and sometimes more clearly than the other, I grasp the external possibilities and obstacles to the other's projects. I regard with love the very limitations of the other's body—for example, "the gauntness, the nervousness of this politician or that doctor, who properly brushes aside and overcomes the thin, nervous body and *forgets* it." This bodily vulnerability which I sense, Sartre says, is the body-for-others. He concludes, "To reveal the other in his being-in-the-midst-of-the-world is to love him in his body." Second, beyond empathic comprehension of the other's attempt to pursue his or her project, I shelter the other's freedom, making the other's goal a part of my own project but in such a way as to offer it support without substituting my own in place of the other's projected goal and chosen means. Finally, in authentic love, we do not have an abstract encounter of two impersonal consciousnesses following through on an existential principle. Sartre writes explicitly, "Freedom as such is not lovable, for it is nothing but negation and productivity. Pure being, in its total exteriority of indifference is not *lovable* either. But the other's body is lovable inasmuch as it is freedom in the dimension of being."

Sartre sums up his expanded view of the body-for-others in words that wholly refute the charge that the negative structures described in *Being and Nothingness* are the sole pattern for human relations. "Here is an original structure of authentic love . . . to reveal the other's being-in-the-midst-of-the-world, to take upon myself this revealing, hence this being—absolutely; to take delight in it without seeking to appropriate it, and to give it shelter in my freedom, and to go beyond it only in the direction of the other's ends."

This discussion of authentic love as a natural (though not necessary) way of living the second dimension, the body-for-others, is utterly radical in its full implications—for feminism as well as generally. To set up the goal of empathically comprehending the other's project and striving to enable its free self-realization is to demand a total transformation of the traditional relationship between a man and a woman and—if extended to the social sphere—the overall pattern of male-female relationships. To comprehend and give shelter to the others' ends and means is to open the door to recognition of what have been called feminine values, whatever their origin.

The third dimension of experience of the body, my body as I am aware that it is known by others, is obviously a necessary mediation between the first two dimensions. My awareness that my body and its acts in the world are perceived and interpreted by others is essential to all communication, and it is my practical defense against solipsism. It is also, when I myself look upon my body as an object (thereby assuming the point of view of the other), the tangible proof of my ongoing existence in space and time. It is as well, of course, the treacherous instrument that shows that the world has stolen my action from me, as we saw in the case of Sartre's ill-dressed woman. The significance of this dimension has already been fruitfully exploited by feminists, with and without specific reference to Sartre.

We learn from Sartre that we exist not only as bodies but as witnesses to our own bodily being, from Beauvoir that this 'doubling' is felt acutely by adolescent girls who learn to appraise themselves as they are shortly to be appraised. "Objectification becomes self-objectification." A woman suffering from this sort of self-estrangement, Bartky claims, lives in "a state of inner conflict wherein one is closeted with an enemy who is at the same time oneself. Estrangement from self can be likened to a 'colonization' of consciousness when inner conflict facilitates control from without and where such control is maintained by and in turn maintains a hierarchy of gender."

So, far from postulating a disembodied consciousness, Sartre seems to me to have examined the ontological complexity of our existence as conscious bodies more thoroughly than any other philosopher, with the possible exception of Merleau-Ponty, whose work is hardly thinkable without Sartre as his point of departure.

Martin Buber

(1878–1965)
AUSTRIAN (ISRAELI)

The central focus of Buber's philosophy is on "dialogue," between man and man, between man and God. He draws a sharp
cleavage between our relationships with things as objects of experience, contemplation, and use, and our relationships with
others. The first relation, I-It, is essentially "detached." The second relation, I-Thou, essentially "involves the whole person." In
the first relation, one sees the It in its context in the world, as
something that is interesting or useful. In the second relation,
one "addresses" a Thou and is "addressed" in return. In relating
to a Thou, one sees the world in the context of the Thou. One
experiences an It in a causal, deterministic context: one addresses a Thou "beyond causality." Of course, to be another person is not yet to be a Thou. One typically treats others as Its, as
interesting or useful. In an "age of sickness," such treatment is
the rule. Against such reduction of Thou to It, of I-Thou to I-It,
Buber insists that it is only through I-Thou that one is a man. On
the political side, Buber saw the emerging state of Israel as a living community of I-Thou relationships and developed a concept
of socialism—later realized in Israeli *kibbutzim*—which he opposed to the deterministic socialism of Marxism. Buber's I-Thou
relations have an ultimate theological aspect, of course. Every
I-Thou, he tells us, leads us to the Ultimate Thou, the one Thou
that cannot become an It for us. In his later works Buber moves

further from traditional political Zionism and more toward the Jewish mysticism of Hasidism.

The selection here is edited from Buber's best-known work, *I and Thou*.

❖ *from* I and Thou ❖

The world is twofold for human beings, corresponding to their twofold positioning.

The positioning of humans is twofold, corresponding to the double-sidedness of the founding words [the statements that ground all others] that the human can utter.

These founding words are not single words, but word pairs.

One founding word is the word pair I-Thou.

The other founding word is the word pair I-It; in this founding word, one of the words "he" or "she" can occupy the position of "it" without altering it.

Thus the *I* of humans is also twofold.

For the *I* of the founding word I-Thou is different from that of the founding word I-It.

Founding words do not signify things, but rather relations.

Founding words do not assert anything that would exist beyond them, but spoken, they ground an inventory of states of affairs [*Bestand*].

Founding words are uttered by the essence.

When the *Thou* is uttered, the *I* of the word pair I-Thou is uttered at the same time.

When the *It* is uttered, the *I* of the word pair I-It is uttered at the same time.

The founding word I-Thou can only be uttered with the entire essence.

From I and Thou *by Martin Buber, translated from the original German text of 1923 (Insel-verlag of Leipzig) by Markus Weidler and Katherine Arens (2004), and reprinted with the permission of Markus Weidler.*

The founding word I-It can never be uttered with the entire essence.

There is no *I* in itself, but only the *I* of the founding word I-Thou, and the *I* of the founding word I-It.

When a human being says *I,* he means one of the two. The *I* that he means is there, [at the moment] when he utters *I.* Likewise, when he utters the *Thou* or *It,* the *I* of one founding word or the other is present.

Being *I* and uttering the *I* are one. Uttering *I* and uttering one of the founding words are the same thing.

Whoever utters a founding word enters into that word and stands within it.

The life of the human essence does not exist solely within the purview of vector verbs [*zielende Zeitwörter*]. It does not consist solely of practices that have something as their object.

I become aware of something. I sense something. I represent something. I want something. I feel something. I think something. The life of the human essence is not constituted solely in all these, or in their equivalents.

All these, together with their equivalents, ground the realm of the *It.*

But the realm of the *Thou* has a different foundation.

Whoever utters the *Thou* is not taking any *thing* as the topic [of the utterance]. For where there is some*thing,* there is another something, each *It* borders on other *Its, It* comes to be only by bordering on others. Where, however, the *Thou* is uttered, there is no something. *Thou* does not border on.

Whoever says *Thou* has no some*thing,* has *nothing.* But he stands in [the process] of relating.

• • •

The world as experience belongs to the founding word I-It.
The founding word I-Thou grounds the world of relating.

Three are the spheres in which the world of relating establishes itself.

The first: living with nature. Here the relating is swinging in the dark and beneath language. Creations come to life before us but they are unable to approach us, and our saying *Thou* to them is stuck at the threshold of language.

The second: living with human beings. Here the relating is revealed and takes the form of language. We can give the *Thou* and receive it.

The third: living with spiritual essentialities. Here the relating is shrouded in clouds, yet revealing itself, without language, yet language-engendering. We perceive no *Thou* and still feel called upon, we answer—forming, thinking, acting: with our essence we utter the founding word, unable to say *Thou* with our mouths.

But how may we integrate what lies beyond language into the world of the founding word?

In each sphere, through everything that become present to us, we glance toward the rim of the eternal *Thou,* from out of each we perceive a breath of wind from that [eternal *Thou*], in every *Thou* we address the eternal *Thou,* in each sphere in its own way.

• • •

—What, then, does one experience of the *Thou?*
—Exactly nothing. For one does not experience it.
—What, then, does one know of the *Thou?*
—Only everything. For one no longer knows anything else about it in particular.

The *Thou* encounters me by grace—it cannot be found by searching. But that I utter the founding word to it is a deed of my essence, my essence's deed.

The *Thou* encounters me. But I enter into an unmediated relating to it. Thus the relating is being chosen and choosing, passive suffering and active initiative [*Passion und Aktion*] in one. Just as an active initiative of the whole essence will have to resemble passive suffering, insofar as it is taken as the suspension of all partial deeds and thus of all sensations of acting grounded solely in their liminality.

The founding word I-Thou can only be uttered with one's whole essence. Gathering and fusing them into a whole essence can never happen through me, can never happen without me. Meeting the *Thou,* I become. In the process of becoming the *I,* I utter *Thou.*

All real life is encounter.

• • •

The fundamental difference between the two founding words comes to light in the intellectual history of the primitive, so that the difference is already uttered in the original event of relating, in a natural but at the same time preformational way—thus before he has recognized himself as an *I*. By contrast, the founding word I-It becomes possible only by dint of this recognition, by dint of the detachment of the *I*.

The former [founding word in its primitive uttering] may split itself into *I* and *Thou,* but it did not originate in their composition, it has the character of preceding the *I;* the latter springs from the composition of *I* and *It,* it has the character of succeeding the *I*.

In the primitive event of relating, the *I* is encompassed: through the former's exclusivity. Insofar as [this event], according to its essence, comprises in itself only the two partners, the human being and his counterpart, in their full actuality—and insofar as the world becomes [in this event] a dual system, the human being already senses that cosmic pathos [*Pathetik*] of the *I,* yet without himself becoming aware of it.

By contrast, the *I* is not yet encompassed in the nature-like fact that will turn into the founding word I-It, into experiencing related to the *I*. This fact constitutes the distinctness of the human body as the bearer of its sensations, from its environment. In this particularity, the body learns to know and distinguish itself, but the distinction remains on the level of a pure juxtaposition and thus cannot adopt the character of an implicit *I-ness*.

But once the *I* of relating has distinguished itself and become existent in its particularity, it also reaches into the nature-like fact of the body's distinctness from its environment, diluting and functionalizing itself strangely, and awakens *I-ness* within it. Only now can the conscious I-act come into being, the first form of the founding word I-It, a way of experience related to the *I:* the now-distinct *I* decrees itself the carrier of sensations, the environment as their object. To be sure, this happens in a "primitive" manner, not in an "epistemological" one; yet once the sentence "I see the tree" is uttered so that it no longer narrates a relating of human-I and tree-Thou, but posits the perception of a tree-object by human-consciousness, it has already put up the barrier between subject and object; the founding word I-It, the word of separation, has been uttered.

• • •

The human being becomes *I* at the boundary of the *Thou*. The fact of juxtaposition comes and vanishes, events of relating coalesce and evanesce, and the consciousness of the partner who remains consistent, the I-consciousness comes to clarity, growing in each encounter. To be sure, it still only appears within the fabric of relating, in the relation to the *Thou,* as a becoming-recognizable of that which reaches for the *Thou* without being it; but it bursts forth ever more strongly, until finally the connectedness is shattered and the *I* confronts itself, its detached self, for a moment; as if it were a *Thou,* in order to soon take possession of itself and henceforth to enter into [instances of] relating at the level of consciousness.

Only now can the other founding word assemble itself. For while the *Thou* likely kept fading time and again, it never became the *It* of an *I,* never the object of an [instance of] perceiving and experiencing, as it will henceforth be; instead it became at the same instant an It for itself, something that initially went unnoticed, waiting for its assumption into a new event of relating. And the embodiment on its way to becoming a body, as bearer of its sensations and executive of its motives, likely set itself off from its environment, but only in the succession of instances of taking one's bearings, not in an absolute separation of *I* and object. Now, however, the detached *I* approaches in everything the "It in itself," transformed, shrunken from a substantial fullness into the set of functional points of an experiencing and utilizing subject; [the detached *I*] takes control of it and sets it together with itself in [the relating of] the other founding word. The human being who has become an *I-ness,* who utters I-It, takes a position over and against things, not as their counterpart in the current of reciprocity. Bent over the particulars with the objectifying loupe in his close-up view or ordering them into a [piece of] scenery with the objectifying field-glasses of his distant projection, isolating them in his regard without any feeling of exclusivity, or connecting them in his regard without any feeling of world-ness—he can only find the former in [instances of] relating, the latter only through that instance itself. Only now does he experience things as sums of properties: these properties have likely been left [behind] in his memory by each experience of relating, as belonging to the recollection of the *Thou,* but only now do things constitute themselves for him out of their properties; only out of the memory of [the instance of] relating, as dream or as image or as thought, each according to the kind of man he is, does he supplement the core that had revealed itself power-fully in the *Thou,* encompassing all properties, the substance. Only now does he set things into a scheme of spatio-temporal-causal con-stellation; only now does each [thing] acquire its place, its orderly course, its measurability, its state of being conditioned. To be sure, the *Thou* does appear in space, but only in the [instance of being an] exclusive counterpart, in which everything else can only be the back-ground, not the boundary or the measure, against which [the *Thou*] emerges; [the *Thou*] appears in time, but in the time of a process ful-filled in itself, which is lived not as a fragment of a constant and solidly articulated sequence, but in a "span of time" whose purely in-tensive dimension can be determined only by that *Thou;* at the same time, [the *Thou*] appears both as exerting and receiving effects, though not as set into a chain of causalities, but rather in its reci-procity with the *I,* beginning and end of what happens. This is part of the fundamental truth about the human world: Only *It* can be or-dered. Only if things turn from being our *Thou* to being our *It* can they be mapped onto coordinates. The *Thou* knows of no coordinate system.

· · ·

The naked present cannot be lived, it would consume one, if it had not been prearranged that it is quickly and thoroughly over-come. But the bare past can be lived, *only* in it can a life be set up. All one has to do is fill each moment with experiencing and utilizing, and it will burn no longer.

And in all of truth's seriousness, [let me tell] you: Without It the human being cannot live. But whoever lives with It alone, is not human.

· · ·

In the It-world, causality reigns without restriction. Every process that is sensually perceivable as "physical," like every "psychic" process discovered or found in introspection is necessarily consid-ered to be caused and causal. From among these, those processes are not exempted to which may be ascribed [the character of] purpo-siveness, as components of the It-world continuum: this [continuum] may tolerate some teleology, but only as a reversal fit into a certain aspect of causality, which does not impair [that causality's] cohesive completeness.

The unlimited purview of causality in the It-world, of fundamental importance for the scientific ordering of nature, as such, does not impose upon the human, who is not confined to the It-world but who rather can always enter into the world of relating again. Here, *I* and *Thou* stand across each other freely, in a reciprocity that is not implicated in any kind of causality, nor tainted by it; here is guaranteed to humans the freedom of their own essence and of essence itself. Only those who know about relating and about the present of the *Thou* are able to decide for themselves. Whoever makes a decision is free because he has stepped before the face of the Lord.

The fiery matter of all my willing power hugely surging, everything possible to me spinning primordially, intertwined and seemingly inseparable, the enticing glances of potentialities flickering from all sides, the universe as temptation, and I myself, having come forth in an instant, both hands [thrust] into the fire, deep into it, to where the single [matter] that intends me conceals itself, my deed, seized: Now! And already the threat of the abyss is banned; the coreless multitude no longer plays in the shimmering homogeneity of its claim—instead there are only Two next to each other, the Other and the One, madness and mission. Only now does realization begin within me. For that would not yet amount to having decided, if the One were done and the Other would remain a sediment [of] extinguished mass, congealing my soul, layer upon layer. Instead, only whoever channels the entire force of the Other into the doing of the One, who lets the undiminished passion of the unchosen into the becoming-real of the chosen, only who "serves God with the evil drive" makes a decision, decides what happens. If one has understood this, then one also knows that precisely this ought to be called what is just, that which has been adjudicated, for which one judges and decides; and if there a devil, it would not be the one who delivered a verdict against God but who remained undecided in eternity.

Causality does not subjugate the human being to whom freedom is guaranteed. He knows that his mortal life is, by its essence, an oscillation between *Thou* and *It,* and he has an inkling of its sense. He is content with the permission, to set foot repeatedly on the threshold of the sanctuary, in whose interior he could not remain; in fact, that he always has to leave again is integral to the meaning and the determination of his life. There, at the threshold, the answer, the spirit, kindles itself ever anew within him; here, in the unholy and needy land the spark has to prove itself. Whatever here is called necessity cannot terrify him; because there he has recognized true necessity: fate.

Fate and freedom are promised to each other. Only he who realizes freedom encounters fate. That I discover the deed which intends me, in that, in the movement of my freedom, the secret reveals itself to me; yet also [in the fact] that I cannot accomplish [freedom] as I intended to, the secret also reveals itself to me in resistance. Whoever forgets all states of being caused and makes his decision from out of the depths, whoever dispenses with personal goods and garments and comes naked before the face of the Lord: fate looks to the free as the reflection of his freedom. It is not his limit but his complement; freedom and fate embrace each other to yield sense; and within that sense, fate, as those ever so strict eyes full of light, sees itself as grace. No, causal necessity does not oppress the human who returns to the It-world carrying the spark. And in the eras of healthy lives, confidence emanates out from humans of spirit and to all people; encounter, presence, to be sure, has happened to all, even the most obtuse, like nature, like a compulsion, like a darkening, all have sensed the *Thou* somewhere or other; now the spirit construes this guarantee for them.

But in sick ages, it [can] happen that the It-world is no longer infused with and made fertile by the influx of the Thou-world, as if by living streams: cut off and stagnant, a gigantic swamp phantom, it overpowers humans. As they settle themselves within a world of objects that no longer become presences to them, they succumb to it. Then, familiar causality increases to the oppressive, suffocating level of ordained fate [*Verhängnis*].

Every great culture encompassing multitudes rests on an original event of encounter, on a response that has reached its emanation point, given to the *Thou;* [it rests on] an essential act of the spirit. This act, reinforced by the force of the following generations, aligned in the same direction, creates an unusual version of the cosmos in the spirit—only through this [act] does cosmos become possible again and again, as comprehended world, homelike, houselike world, the world-dwelling [*Weltbehausung*] of humans; only now can humans ever and again build houses of god and humankind, out of a solaced soul, in a peculiar grasp of space, can [they] fill swinging time with new hymns and songs and bring the human community itself into a form. But only just as long as the human possesses that act of essence in his own life, actively and passively, as long as he himself disappears into the relating; for that length of time he is free and thus creative. If a culture is no longer centered in the living, inexorably renewed process of relating, only then does it petrify into the It-world, which the glowing deeds of isolated spirits only eruptively and sporadically break through. Henceforth, the familiar causality increases to the oppressive and suffocating [level of] ordained fate, which until this point had never been able to disturb the cosmos, up to now was not able to disturb the spiritual composure of the cosmos. The wise and masterful fate, which, attuned to the cosmos' wealth of meaning, presided over all causality, has collapsed into that causality, transformed into an absurd demonic state. The same karma that struck the ancestors as a beneficial providence—for what we do in life raises us into higher sphere for a future life—now allows itself to be recognizes as tyranny: because the [*karma*] of a previous life, to which we are oblivious, has locked us into a dungeon, from which we cannot escape in this life. Where previously a heaven's law of meaning arched over us, where the spindle of necessity hung upon its bright arch, there the meaningless and subjugating power of the planets holds sway; they said that it was only necessary to give one's self over to *Dike,* the heavenly "path" that was meant to be ours, too, in order to dwell in the total dimension [*Allmass*] of destiny, with a free heart—now the *heimarmene,* alien to our spirit, coerces us, whatever it is we do, and forces onto every back the entire burden of the dead world-mass. The surging desire for redemption remains unsatisfied to the last, despite many trials, until someone quenches it, someone who teaches how to escape from the wheel of rebirth, or someone who saves the souls who have fallen prey to mighty powers, [delivering them] into the freedom of God's children. Such a work results from a new event of relating become substance, from a new fate-determining response of a human being to his *Thou.* As the effect of this central act of essence, one culture can be relieved by another, dedicated to the vector of this act, yet that one culture can also be renewed within itself.

The sickness of our age does not resemble that of any other, for it belongs among those of all of them. The history of cultures is not an arena of the eons, where one runner after another would have to pace off the same death circle, cheerfully and without a clue. A nameless path leads through their ascensions and declines. Not a path of progress and development; a descent through the spirals of the spiritual underworld, probably also to become known as an ascent to the innermost, finest, most convoluted vortex, where there is no way onward and even less one back, only the unheard-of turning back [*Umkehr*] the breakthrough. Will we have to walk this path to its [very] end, [up] to the test of the final darkness? Yet, where there is danger, that which saves also grows.

The biologistic and historiosophic thoughts of our age, regardless of how differently they conceived of themselves, have cooperated to produce a faith in ordained fate, more resilient and more anxious than any such faith before. It is no longer the power of karma or the power of the stars that inexorably rule the human lot; various forces lay claim to this rulership but, eventually, most contemporaries believe in an amalgam of these forces, just as the late Romans believed in a mixture of gods. That [believing] is made easier by the [specific] rendering of such claims. Whether it is the "law of life" in the ultimate struggle, in which everyone must join or forfeit life; or the "spiritual law" of a complete construction of the psychic person out of inborn conventional drives; or the "social law" of an inexorable social process that the will and consciousness may only accompany; or the "cultural law" of an unalterably even rising and passing of historical formations; and whatsoever other forms there are: it always means that humans are yoked into an inescapable occurrence against which they cannot defend themselves or only through madness. Initiation into the mysteries freed [humans] from the coercion of the stars, the Brahmanic sacrifice bringing enlightenment, delivered from the coercion of karma, and both prepared the way for salvation; the bastard idol does not tolerate any faith in deliverance. It is considered foolish to imagine a freedom for oneself; one would only have the choice between a resolute and a hopelessly rebellious slavery. No matter how much is spoken in the laws about teleological development and organic becoming, all of them are based on an obsession with ordered process; that is, with an unrestricted causality. The dogma of a gradual ordered process is the abdication of humanity in the face of a burgeoning It-world. The name of destiny is abused by [this dogma]; destiny is no glass dome tipped over on top of the human world; no one encounters it except he who goes out into freedom. The dogma of ordered process, however, leaves no room for freedom, no room for its most real revelation, whose serene power changes the face of the earth: turning back. The dogma knows nothing of the human being who overcomes total struggle by turning back [from it]; who shreds the fabrication of common drives by turning back from it; who, by turning his back, upsets, rejuvenates, and transforms secure historical formations. The dogma of ordered process leaves you only one choice on its game board: to observe the rules or drop out; but he who turns his back knocks over the chess pieces. The dogma will nonetheless allow you to execute its conditionality with your life and "to remain free" in your soul; but he who turns back scorns this freedom as the most disgraceful bondage.

The only thing that can become a human's ordained fate is the belief in ordained fate: [for] it arrests the movement of turning back.

The belief in ordained fate is from its [very] inception a delusion. Considering anything as ordered process is only an ordering of that which is nothing more than a having-become of isolated world-events, of the physically present as history; the presence of the *Thou,* the becoming that grows out of being bound is inaccessible to this perspective. [This perspective] does not know the reality of the spirit, and its scheme is not valid for the spirit. Divination based on the physically present is only valid for those who do not know the temporally present. Anyone overpowered by the It-world must see in the dogma of unalterable ordered process a truth that creates a clearing in the proliferating tangle; in truth, this dogma renders him all the more subservient to the It-world. But the world of the *Thou* is not closed off. Whoever sets out for it, with his essence gathered together, with his resurrected capacity to relate, will become aware of freedom. And to become free from the belief in unfreedom is to become free.

• • •

The prolonged lines of relatings intersect in the eternal *Thou.*

Each individuated *Thou* is a vision through to it. Through each individuated *Thou,* the founding word addresses the eternal *Thou.* From this mediatorship of the *Thou* of all essences springs the fulfillment of their relatings, and the lack of fulfillment. The innate *Thou* realizes itself in every [relating] but never completes itself in any one. It completes itself only in unmediated relating to the *Thou* that, according to its essence, cannot become an *It.*

Paul Tillich

(1886–1965)
GERMAN (AMERICAN)

Tillich was one of the most influential religious philosophers of the twentieth century. However, his "religion" must be carefully qualified. He does not believe in a supreme personal deity, and thus he moves away from Kierkegaard and Buber, for whom a personal God is the essential mark of the religious. Yet Tillich's "Ultimate Concern" is neither a return to pantheism nor a reversion to mysticism before an impersonal transcendent force. His "faith" is first of all a living answer to the anxieties of life, the (ontic) anxiety of death and fate, the (spiritual) anxiety of meaninglessness and emptiness, and the (moral) anxiety of guilt and condemnation. Like Kierkegaard, Tillich stresses the *how*, that is, the *dynamics*, of faith and deemphasizes the *what*, or objects, of faith. His Christianity is neither a set of doctrines nor a focal point for an existential "leap" so much as it is the foremost symbol of Ultimate Concern and existential courage.

The following discussion of anxiety and courage is excerpted from Tillich's *The Courage to Be*.

❖ *from* The Courage to Be ❖

The Interdependence of Fear and Anxiety

Anxiety and fear have the same ontological root but they are not the same in actuality. This is common knowledge, but it has been emphasized and overemphasized to such a degree that a reaction against it may occur and wipe out not only the exaggerations but also the truth of the distinction. Fear, as opposed to anxiety, has a definite object (as most authors agree), which can be faced, analyzed, attacked, endured. One can act upon it, and in acting upon it participate in it—even if in the form of struggle. In this way one can take it into one's self-affirmation. Courage can meet every object of fear, because it is an object and makes participation possible. Courage can take the fear produced by a definite object into itself, because this object, however frightful it may be, has a side with which it participates in us and we in it. One could say that as long as there is an *object* of fear love in the sense of participation can conquer fear.

But this is not so with anxiety, because anxiety has no object, or rather, in a paradoxical phrase, its object is the negation of every object. Therefore participation, struggle, and love with respect to it are impossible. He who is in anxiety is, insofar as it is mere anxiety, delivered to it without help. Helplessness in the state of anxiety can be observed in animals and humans alike. It expresses itself in loss of direction, inadequate reactions, lack of "intentionality" (the being related to meaningful contents of knowledge or will). The reason for this sometimes striking behavior is the lack of an object on which the subject (in the state of anxiety) can concentrate. The only object is the threat itself, but not the source of the threat, because the source of the threat is "nothingness."

One might ask whether this threatening "nothing" is not the unknown, the indefinite possibility of an actual threat? Does not anxiety cease in the moment in which a known object of fear appears? Anxiety then would be fear of the unknown. But this is an insufficient explanation of anxiety. For there are innumerable realms of the unknown, different for each subject, and faced without any anxiety. It is the unknown of a special type which is met with anxiety. It is the unknown which by its very nature cannot be known, because it is nonbeing.

Fear and anxiety are distinguished but not separated. They are immanent within each other: The sting of fear is anxiety, and anxiety strives toward fear. Fear is being afraid of something, a pain, the rejection by a person or a group, the loss of something or somebody, the moment of dying. But in the anticipation of the threat originating in these things, it is not the negativity itself which they will bring upon the subject that is frightening but the anxiety about the possible implications of this negativity. The outstanding example—and more than an example—is the fear of dying. Insofar as it is *fear* its object is the anticipated event of being killed by sickness or an accident and thereby suffering agony and the loss of everything. Insofar as it is *anxiety* its object is the absolutely unknown "after death," the nonbeing which remains nonbeing even if it is filled with images of our present experience. The dreams in Hamlet's soliloquy, "to be or not to be," which we may have after death and which make cowards of us all are frightful not because of their manifest content but because of their power to symbolize the threat of nothingness, in religious terms of "eternal death." The symbols of hell created by Dante produce anxiety not because of their objective imagery but because they express the "nothingness" whose power is experienced in the anxiety of guilt. Each of the situations described in the *Inferno* could be met by courage on the basis of participation and love. But of course the meaning is that this is impossible; in other words they are not real situations but symbols of the objectless, of nonbeing.

The fear of death determines the element of anxiety in every fear. Anxiety, if not modified by the fear of an object, anxiety in its nakedness, is always the anxiety of ultimate nonbeing. Immediately seen, anxiety is the painful feeling of not being able to deal with the threat of a special situation. But a more exact analysis shows that in the anxiety about any special situation anxiety about the human situation as such is implied. It is the anxiety of not being able to preserve one's own being which underlies every fear and is the frightening element in it. In the moment, therefore, in which "naked anxiety" lays hold of the mind, the previous objects of fear cease to be definite objects. They appear as what they always were in part, symptoms of man's basic anxiety. As such they are beyond the reach of even the most courageous attack upon them.

This situation drives the anxious subject to establish objects of fear. Anxiety strives to become fear, because fear can be met by courage. It is impossible for a finite being to stand naked anxiety for more than a flash of time. People who have experienced these moments, as for instance some mystics in their visions of the "night of the soul," or Luther under the despair of the demonic assaults, or Nietzsche-Zarathustra in the experience of the "great disgust," have told of the unimaginable horror of it. This horror is ordinarily avoided by the transformation of anxiety into fear of something, no matter what. The human mind is not only, as Calvin has said, a permanent factory of idols, it is also a permanent factory of fears—the first in order to escape God, the second in order to escape anxiety; and there is a relation between the two. For facing the God who is really God means facing also the absolute threat of nonbeing. The "naked absolute" (to use a phrase of Luther's) produces "naked anxiety"; for it is the extinction of every finite self-affirmation, and not a possible object of fear and courage. . . . But ultimately the attempts to transform anxiety into fear are vain. The basic anxiety, the anxiety of a finite being about the threat of nonbeing, cannot be eliminated. It belongs to existence itself.

• • •

Sartre draws consequences from the earlier Heidegger which the later Heidegger did not accept. But it remains doubtful whether Sartre was historically right in drawing these consequences. It was easier for Sartre to draw them than for Heidegger, for in the background of Heidegger's ontology lies the mystical concept of being which is without significance for Sartre. Sartre carried through the consequences of Heidegger's Existentialist analyses without mystical restrictions. This is the reason he has become the symbol of present-day Existentialism, a position which is deserved not so much by the originality of his basic concepts as by the radicalism, consistency, and psychological adequacy with which he has carried them through. I refer above all to his proposition that "the essence of man is his existence." This sentence is like a flash of light which illuminates the whole Existentialist scene. One could call it the most despairing and the most courageous sentence in all Existentialist literature. What it says is that there is no essential nature of man, except in the one point that he can make of himself what he wants. Man creates what he is. Nothing is given to him to determine his creativity. The essence of his being—the "should-be," "the ought-to-be,"—is not something which he finds; he makes it. Man is what he makes of himself. And the courage to be as oneself is the courage to make of oneself what one wants to be.

There are Existentialists of a less radical point of view. Karl Jaspers recommends a new conformity in terms of an all-embracing "philosophical faith" while Gabriel Marcel moves from an Existentialist radicalism to a position based on the semicollectivism of medieval thought. Existentialism in philosophy is represented more by Heidegger and Sartre than by anybody else.

The Courage of Despair in the Noncreative Existentialist Attitude

I have dealt in the last sections with people whose creative courage enables them to express existential despair. Not many people are creative. But there is a noncreative Existentialist attitude called cynicism. A cynic today is not the same person the Greeks meant by the term. For the Greeks the cynic was a critic of contemporary culture on the basis of reason and natural law; he was a revolutionary rationalist, a follower of Socrates. Modern cynics are not ready to follow anybody. They have no belief in reason, no criterion of truth, no set of values, no answer to the question of meaning. They try to undermine every norm put before them. Their courage is expressed not creatively but in their form of life. They courageously reject any solution which would deprive them of their freedom of rejecting whatever they want to reject. The cynics are lonely although they need company in order to show their loneliness. They are empty of both preliminary meanings and an ultimate meaning, and therefore easy victims of neurotic anxiety. Much compulsive self-affirmation and much fanatical self-surrender are expressions of the noncreative courage to be as oneself.

The Limits of the Courage to Be as Oneself

This leads to the question of the limits of the courage to be as oneself in its creative as well as its uncreative forms. Courage is self-affirmation "in spite of," and the courage to be as oneself is self-affirmation of the self as itself. But one must ask: What is this self that affirms itself? Radical Existentialism answers: What it makes of itself. This is all it can say, because anything more would restrict the absolute freedom of the self. The self, cut off from participation in its world, is an empty shell, a mere possibility. It must act because it lives, but it must redo every action because acting involves him who acts in that upon which he acts. It gives content and for this reason it restricts his freedom to make of himself what he wants. In classical theology, both Catholic and Protestant, only God has this prerogative: He is *ā sē* (from himself) or absolute freedom. Nothing is in him which is not by him. Existentialism, on the basis of the message that God is dead, gives man the divine "a-se-ity." Nothing shall be in man which is not by man. But man is finite, he is given to himself as what he is. He has received his being and with it the structure of his being, including the structure of finite freedom. And finite freedom is not aseity. Man can affirm himself only if he affirms not an empty shell, a mere possibility, but the structure of being in which he finds himself before action and nonaction. Finite freedom has a definite structure, and if the self tries to trespass on this structure it ends in the loss of itself. The nonparticipating hero in Sartre's *The Age of Reason* is caught in a net of contingencies, coming partly from the subconscious levels of his own self, partly from the environment from which he cannot withdraw. The assuredly empty self is filled with contents which enslave it just because it does not know or accept them as contents. This is true too of the cynic, as was said before. He cannot escape the forces of his self which may drive him into complete loss of the freedom that he wants to preserve.

This dialectical self-destruction of the radical forms of the courage to be as oneself has happened on a world-wide scale in the totalitarian reaction of the twentieth century against the revolutionary Existentialism of the nineteenth century. The Existentialist protest against dehumanization and objectivation, together with its courage to be as oneself, have turned into the most elaborate and oppressive forms of collectivism that have appeared in history. It is the great tragedy of our time that Marxism, which had been conceived as a movement for the liberation of everyone, has been transformed into a system of enslavement of everyone, even of those who enslave the others. It is hard to imagine the immensity of this tragedy in terms of psychological destruction, especially within the intelligentsia. The courage to be was undermined in innumerable people because it was the courage to be in the sense of the revolutionary movements of the nineteenth century. When it broke down, these people turned either to the neocollectivist system, in a fanatic-neurotic reaction against the cause of their tragic disappointment, or to a cynical-neurotic indifference to all systems and every content.

It is obvious that similar observations can be made on the transformation of the Nietzschean type of the courage to be as oneself into the fascist-Nazi forms of neocollectivism. The totalitarian machines which these movements produced embodied almost everything against which the courage to be as oneself stands. They used all possible means in order to make such courage impossible. Although, in distinction to communism, this system fell down, its aftermath is confusion, indifference, cynicism. And this is the soil on which the longing for authority and for a new collectivism grows.

• • •

The Courage to Accept Acceptance

Courage is the self-affirmation of being in spite of the fact of nonbeing. It is the act of the individual self in taking the anxiety of nonbeing upon itself by affirming itself either as part of an embracing whole or in its individual selfhood. Courage always includes a risk, it is always threatened by nonbeing, whether the risk of losing oneself and becoming a thing within the whole of things or of losing one's world in an empty self-relatedness. Courage needs the power of being, a power transcending the nonbeing which is experienced in the anxiety of fate and death, which is present in the anxiety of emptiness and meaninglessness, which is effective in the anxiety of guilt and condemnation. The courage which takes this threefold anxiety into itself must be rooted in a power of being that is greater than the power of oneself and the power of one's world. Neither self-affirmation as a part nor self-affirmation as oneself is beyond the manifold threat of nonbeing. Those who are mentioned as representatives of these forms of courage try to transcend themselves and the world in which they participate in order to find the power of being-itself and a courage to be which is beyond the threat of nonbeing. There are no exceptions to this rule; and this means that every courage to be has an open or hidden religious root. For religion is the state of being grasped by the power of being-itself. In some cases the religious root is carefully covered, in others it is passionately denied; in some it is deeply hidden and in others superficially. But it is never completely absent. For everything that is participates in being-itself, and everybody has some awareness of this participation, especially in the moments in which he experiences the threat of nonbeing. . . .

Keiji Nishitani

(1900–1990)
JAPANESE

Nishitani was educated in both Japan and Germany, and his writings combine the insights of Zen Buddhism with Existentialism, particularly on the topic of religion. Like the existentialists, he is centrally concerned with the question of self-identity and the question of passionate commitment. But like the Japanese Buddhists, Nishitani finds serious fault with the Western tendency to perceive the world as separate from the self. It is much more important to feel and be at one with the world, and this is the aim of all religion. Nevertheless, to even ask the question, so common in Western thinking, "What is the purpose of religion?" is to employ just that analytic attitude that Nishitani criticizes, and as such it distracts us from the important question, "What is the purpose of life?"

❖ *from* "What Is Religion?" ❖

"What is religion?" we ask ourselves, or, looking at it the other way around, "What is the purpose of religion for us? Why do we need it?" Though the question about the need for religion may be a familiar

From "What Is Religion?" from Religion and Nothingness *by Keiji Nishitani, translated by Jan Van Bragt. Published by University of California Press, Inc. Reprinted with permission of University of California Press, Inc.*

one, it already contains a problem. In one sense, for the person who poses the question, religion does not seem to be something he needs. The fact that he asks the question at all amounts to an admission that religion has not yet become a necessity for him. In another sense, however, it is surely in the nature of religion to be necessary for just such a person. Wherever questioning individuals like this are to be found, the need for religion is there as well. In short, the relationship we have to religion is a contradictory one: those for whom religion is *not* a necessity are, for that reason, the very ones for whom religion *is* a necessity. There is no other thing of which the same can be said.

When asked, "Why do we need learning and the arts?" we might try to explain in reply that such things are necessary for the advancement of mankind, for human happiness, for the cultivation of the individual, and so forth. Yet even if we can say why we need such things, this does not imply that we cannot get along without them. Somehow life would still go on. Learning and the arts may be indispensable to living well, but they are not indispensable to living. In that sense, they can be considered a kind of luxury.

Food, on the other hand, is essential to life. Nobody would turn to somebody else and ask him why he eats. Well, maybe an angel or some other celestial being who has no need to eat might ask such questions, but men do not. Religion, to judge from current conditions in which many people are in fact getting along without it, is clearly not the kind of necessity that food is. Yet this does not mean that it is merely something we need to live *well*. Religion has to do with life itself. Whether the life we are living will end up in extinction or in the attainment of eternal life is a matter of the utmost importance for life itself. In no sense is religion to be called a luxury. Indeed, this is why religion is an indispensable necessity for those very people who fail to see the need for it. Herein lies the distinctive feature of religion that sets it apart from the mere life of "nature" and from culture. Therefore, to say that we need religion for example, for the sake of social order, or human welfare, or public morals is a mistake, or at least a confusion of priorities. Religion must not be considered from the viewpoint of its *utility,* any more than life should. A religion concerned primarily with its own utility bears witness to its own degeneration. One can ask about the utility of things like eating for the natural life, or of things like learning and the arts for culture. In fact, in such matters the question of utility should be of constant concern.

Our ordinary mode of being is restricted to these levels of natural or cultural life. But it is in breaking through that ordinary mode of being and overturning it from the ground up, in pressing us back to the elemental source of life where life itself is seen as useless, that religion becomes something we need—a *must* for human life.

Two points should be noted from what has just been said. First, religion is at all times the individual affair of each individual. This sets it apart from things like culture, which, while related to the individual, do not need to concern each individual. Accordingly, we cannot understand what religion is from the outside. The religious quest alone is the key to understanding it; there is no other way. This is the most important point to be made regarding the essence of religion.

Second, from the standpoint of the essence of religion, it is a mistake to ask "What is the purpose of religion for us?" and one that clearly betrays an attitude of trying to understand religion apart from the religious quest. It is a question that must be broken through by another question coming from within the person who asks it. There is no other road that can lead to an understanding of what religion is and what purpose it serves. The counterquestion that achieves this breakthrough is one that asks, "For what purpose do I myself exist?" Of everything else we can ask its purpose for us, but not of religion. With regard to everything else we can make a *telos* of ourselves as individuals, as man, or as mankind, and evaluate those things in relation to our life and existence. We put ourselves as individuals/man/mankind at the center and weigh the significance of everything as the *contents* of our lives as individuals/man/mankind. But religion upsets the posture from which we think of ourselves as *telos* and center for all things. Instead, religion poses as a starting point the question: "For what purpose do I exist?"

We become aware of religion as a need, as a must for life, only at the level of life at which everything else loses its necessity and its utility. Why do we exist at all? Is not our very existence and human life ultimately meaningless? Or, if there is a meaning or significance to it all, where do we find it? When we come to doubt the meaning of our existence in this way, when we have become a question to ourselves, the religious quest awakens within us. These questions and the quest they give rise to show up when the mode of looking at and thinking about everything in terms of how it relates to us is broken through, where the mode of living that puts us at the center of everything is overturned. This is why the question of religion in the form, "Why do we need religion?" obscures the way to its own answer from the very start. It blocks our becoming a question to ourselves.

The point at which the ordinarily necessary things of life, including learning and the arts, all lose their necessity and utility is found at those times when death, nihility, or sin—or any of those situations that entail a fundamental negation of our life, existence, and ideals, that undermine the roothold of our existence and bring the meaning of life into question—become pressing personal problems for us. This can occur through an illness that brings one face-to-face with death, or through some turn of events that robs one of what had made life worth living. . . .

Nihility refers to that which renders meaningless the meaning of life. When we become a question to ourselves and when the problem of why we exist arises, this means that nihility has emerged from the ground of our existence and that our very existence has turned into a question mark. The appearance of this nihility signals nothing less than that one's awareness of self-existence has penetrated to an extraordinary depth.

Normally we proceed through life, on and on, with our eye fixed on something or other, always caught up with something within or without ourselves. It is these engagements that prevent the deepening of awareness. They block off the way to an opening up of that horizon on which nihility appears and self-being becomes a question. This is even the case with learning and the arts and the whole range of other cultural engagements. But when this horizon does open up at the bottom of those engagements that keep life moving continually on and on, something seems to halt and linger before us. This something is the meaninglessness that lies in wait at the bottom of those very engagements that bring meaning to life. This is the point at which that sense of nihility, that sense that "everything is the same" we find in Nietzsche and Dostoevski, brings the restless, forward-advancing pace of life to a halt and makes it take a step back. In the Zen phrase, it "turns the light to what is directly underfoot."

In the forward progress of everyday life, the ground beneath our feet always falls behind as we move steadily ahead; we overlook it. Taking a step back to shed light on what is underfoot of the self—"stepping back to come to the self," as another ancient Zen phrase has it—marks a conversion in life itself. This fundamental conversion in life is occasioned by the opening up of the horizon of nihility at the ground of life. It is nothing less than a conversion from the self-centered (or man-centered) mode of being, which always asks what *use* things have for us (or for man), to an attitude that asks for what *purpose* we ourselves (or man) exist. Only when we stand at this turning point does the question "What is religion?" really become our own.

Colin Wilson

(B. 1931)
ENGLISH

Wilson made a huge splash at the young age of twenty-five with his novel *The Outsider,* which was inspired by and got its title from Camus's *The Stranger.* Accordingly, comparison and competition with Camus and Sartre marked much of Wilson's career. After considering suicide as a teenager, Wilson spent much of his life trying to express how life is worthwhile even if it is pointless. Wilson confronted what he saw as the defeatism of existentialism and, in the spirit of Nietzsche, he pursued existentialism as a life-affirming philosophy. Wilson employed both phenomenology and linguistic philosophy, but he remained very much an "outsider" with regard to academia. His mission was to show how one could use self-discipline to avoid the despair that seemed to underlie the classic existentialists. Accordingly, the targets of much of his thinking were Sartre and Camus. The following is taken from Wilson's insightful but harsh essay, *Anti-Sartre.*

❖ *from* Anti-Sartre ❖

[In February 1936] Sartre had been engaged on a kind of novel which began life as a pamphlet about "contingency." This was an idea he seems to have developed early—Simone de Beauvoir mentions that he was already speaking of it at the age of twenty-three (in 1928). Sartre defined "Contingency" as the recognition that "existence is not necessary." What Sartre means is that things have a causal, unimportant quality, as if it didn't matter whether they exist or not. When we read about something in a book, or see it in a painting, it seems to have a dimension of "importance" that it does not possess in real life. A volume of philosophy may give the impression that the universe is significant and necessary, but when you encounter the universe, actuality seems oddly unnecessary. . . .

In the novel, the idea of contingency was expressed by a character called Roquentin, a historian; the novel was to express the contrast between the "reality" and "necessity" that he gives to events when he puts them on paper, and the contingency of his own existence.

A mescalin experience [in early 1936] seems to have given the novel a new direction, a new depth. What Roquentin now experiences in sudden flashes is a sense of horrified meaninglessness. We can see the development of one of its major themes from an early letter to Simone de Beauvoir. It begins: "I have been to look at a tree. . . . It was extremely beautiful, and I have no hesitation about setting down here two vital pieces of information for my future biography; it was in Burgos that I first understood the meaning of a cathedral, and it was in Le Havre that I first understood the meaning of a tree. . . . [Simone de Beauvoir, *The Prime of Life*, p. 8].

In the famous passage of the published novel, *La Nausee* (which appeared in 1938), the tree has become—like his mescalin visions—rather horrifying—a "black, knotty lump, entirely raw, frightening me." And as he stares at the tree, Roquentin is overcome by an insight. We see things, but we do not really *believe they exist;* we treat them as if they were a painting or stage scenery—mere sense impressions. And now, he says, he is suddenly overwhelmed with the realization that things exist in their own right, and their sheer reality seems to mock our attempt to categorize them, to keep them "in their proper place." Reality, says Sartre, is "naked with a frightful and obscene nakedness." "Turning a tree into something other than itself" with literary comparisons is now no longer seen as a harmless and pleasant amusement; it has become an instance of the way in which we all deceive ourselves.

Sartre calls this revelation of contingency (or meaninglessness) "nausea." And it becomes, in a sense, the cornerstone of his philosophy. Human beings are so wrapped up in themselves that they treat reality as if it was there for their convenience. (We can also sense here the basic attitude that turned Sartre into a Marxist, for this is also the way that the spoilt rich treat their servants.) They take things for granted with a kind of silly conceit. They are not interested in the real complexity of things; only in what happens to suit their self-absorbed little purposes. If they are suddenly forced to recognize that things exist in their own right, they experience a kind of distress, like a child confronted with a page of mathematical equations. This is "nausea"—revulsion. It keeps happening to Roquentin as he tries to write his book about the diplomat Rollebon, producing the feeling that this attempt to endow Rollebon's life with meaning is a charade.

Inevitably, the sense of the "contingency" of things gives him a feeling that his own life is meaningless. He recalls how, when he was asked to join an archaeological mission to Bengal, he had a sudden sense of waking up. "What was I doing there? Why was I talking to these people? Why was I dressed so oddly?" He feels that he is an actor in a play—an actor who has suddenly forgotten what it is all supposed to be about. Here Sartre is echoing a theme that Tolstoy had explored in a story called, "Memoirs of a Madman," in which a landowner who is traveling to a distant place to buy more land suddenly wakes up in the middle of the night with the feeling: "What am I doing here? Who am I?" The desire for more land suddenly strikes him as an absurdity. But in the Tolstoy story, this is the prelude to a kind of religious conversion—as it was in Tolstoy's own life.

We should note that Sartre did his best to live up to his own standards. Simone de Beauvoir notes: "Torpor, somnolence, escapism, intellectual dodges and truces, prudence and respect were all unknown to him. He was interested in everything and never took anything for granted. Confronted with an object, he would look it straight in the face instead of trying to explain it away with a myth, a word, an impression or a preconceived idea: he wouldn't let it go until he had grasped all its ins and outs and all its multiple significations" [Simone de Beauvoir: *Memoirs of a Dutiful Daughter,* p. 342]. That is to say, Sartre did not try to ignore the complexity of things. He referred to the kind of people who ignore it as "salauds"—shits. The act of ignoring complexity he calls "mauvais-fois"—bad faith or self-deception.

On this foundation, Sartre constructs both his existential metaphysic and his political philosophy. It is an impressive structure—made more so by his use of "phenomenological" procedures derived from Husserl and Heidegger. Kierkegaard objected to philosophy on the ground that it is too vague and abstract to apply to real life—like trying to find your way around Copenhagen with a map on which Denmark is the size of a postage stamp. No one could throw this accusation in Sartre's face. He insists on bringing philosophy down to minute particulars—like how a man can be an idealist when his mistress needs the money for an abortion. His immense works on Genet and Flaubert show the same obsessive need to bring real life within the bounds of philosophy. No one can deny that he has shown an almost heroic determination to keep one foot in the world of reason and the other in the realm of practical necessity.

Anyone who has never read Sartre might be excused for assuming that this tremendous effort has resulted in a philosophy of great subtlety and complexity. It comes as something of a shock to turn to the end product and discover a crude pessimism combined with political extremism. Somehow, it seems incongruous to hear an aging philosopher proclaim himself an atheist, and state his belief that true progress now lies in the attempt of the colored races to liberate themselves through violence. This is the kind of thing we associate with the young—which is to say that it is the kind of thing that most reasonable people dismiss as hot-headed nonsense. But in Sartre's case, it is clearly not unthought-out nonsense.

Let us begin by considering Sartre's account of perception and consciousness in *La Nausee*. The substance of Roquentin's "vision" is that we treat the external world *as though it were unreal.* "I was like the others . . . I said, like them; 'The sea *is* green; that white speck up there *is* a seagull,' but I didn't feel that it existed or that the seagull was an 'existing seagull'. . . ." Now that existence has "unveiled itself," Roquentin feels negated, superfluous. "We were a heap of existences, embarrassed at ourselves, we hadn't the slightest reason to be there . . . In vain I tried to count the chestnut trees, to locate them by their relationship . . . each of them eluded the relations in which I tried to enclose it, isolated itself and overflowed. I felt the arbitrariness of these relations (which I obstinately maintained in order to delay the collapse of the human world of measurements, quantities, directions). *Superfluous . . .*"

But is this an accurate analysis of the way our senses deal with the "world?" Babies are born into a confusing world of sights and sounds and smells. Little by little, their senses discern order in the chaos: the mother's face, the brightly colored toy, the smell of food. Their senses have to learn to ignore "irrelevancies" and to concentrate on the comfortable, the familiar. This "filtering"—ignoring the irrelevant—is not due to "bad faith," or even laziness; it is not an attempt to pretend that the world is something that it isn't. It is an attempt to bring order into chaos; the alternative would be to be overwhelmed by it.

As the child grows up, he is forced to extend his command of the chaos—a new school can be a traumatic experience for the first few days—but he cannot run away from it. If he is basically confident and determined, he gradually learns to order his "reality" with some degree of skill; his attitude to "chaos" is like that of a Sergeant Major with a squad of raw recruits. But it would hardly be fair to call the Sergeant an authoritarian "salaud," for if he declines to accept authority, the result will be nervous breakdown.

There are, of course, occasions when human beings attempt to ignore things that worry or frighten them; but this is relatively rare, compared to the number of times we grapple with new complexities and try to absorb them. We know instinctively that running away is dangerous.

So how *do* we fall into states of "nausea?" The most familiar pattern involves becoming "overwhelmed"—that is, problems increase until they become uncontrollable. In effect, we become "shell-shocked." The same kind of thing happens if we are forced to cope with problems that strike us as basically futile or boring; in this case, our vitality seems to leak away. Finally, we may simply find life *too* unchallenging—unproblematic but dull. Here again, the problem is due to a diminution in vitality. The Sergeant Major can see no point in drilling the recruits; in fact, he wonders why he ever bothered.

Clearly, it is the third case that fits Roquentin—and Sartre. Sartre was bored with his *locum* job as a professor in Le Havre; Roquentin is bored with his academic research in a town obviously based on Le Havre. But we must also take into account the mescalin experience on which Roquentin's "attacks" seem to be based. Psychedelic drugs have an "uninhibiting" effect; they remove some of the "filters" that protect us from being overwhelmed by the complexity of experience. They also make us more vulnerable to our unconscious attitudes. "Reality" is suddenly magnified. The effect could be compared to waking up suddenly on a train and finding a stranger with his face within an inch of your own. Most people would find the experience unpleasant because our attitude towards strangers is basically mistrustful. A baby would probably smile with delight, because he is used to seeing his mother's face at close quarters; his attitude is basically trustful. Sartre's own mescalin experiences contrast sharply—for example—with those of Aldous Huxley, as described in *The Doors of Perception*. His unconscious attitudes towards the world are plainly a great deal more mistrustful than Huxley's.

So Roquentin is devitalized by boredom, and he suffers the equivalent of a "bad trip" because his attitude to the world is mistrustful and defensive. Yet Sartre ignores—or is unaware—of these factors, and tries to convince us that Roquentin is seeing things "as they really are." We might illustrate Roquentin's view of perception by the example of a wealthy man who has always regarded servants as machines, and who is shocked and embarrassed to realize that they are human beings like himself. In short, Roquentin believes that we habitually ignore the *complexity* of the world, and try to impose our own false categories on it. We have seen that this view is untrue. We do not "ignore" the complexity, in the sense of pretending it does not exist. We are fully aware that it exists; we mostly do our best to absorb and control it. We "filter" it for the sake of survival. The filtering is not an act of self-deception, but a necessity of survival, like breathing. So Roquentin's perception, far from being a vision of things "as they really are," is a kind of chaos.

The point might become clearer if we compare this world of experience with an orchestra tuning-up. If a stranger walks into the concert hall, he hears only a confusion of sound. But the conductor can distinguish various instruments, and even observe that the second violin is out of tune. Who has the "truer" perception of the reality of the orchestra—the conductor or the inexperienced stranger? Clearly, the conductor. Roquentin's unconscious "conductor" (or Sergeant Major) has abdicated, and he only hears a chaos of sound.

I apologize for spending so long on what may seem to be a rather technical matter. In fact, it goes to the heart of Sartre's philosophy. We might say that he is attempting to convict the mind on a "trumped up" charge. Moreover, he assumes the charge to be proven, and makes this the basis of a philosophy of pessimism. In fact, he is simply failing to grasp the mechanics of perception. "Nausea" is a form of bewilderment in the face of complexity. But how can complexity be meaningless—surely it is a contradiction in terms? The image of the schoolboy dismayed by a page of algebraic equations provides the answer. He is perfectly aware that they are not meaningless; he is really appalled by the effort he is being asked to make to grasp their meaning. It is true that they are meaningless *for him,* at this particular moment; but that is a purely subjective matter. Roquentin tells us about his sense of meaninglessness, and insists that it is an objective fact. We can only tell him that he is blaming "reality" when he should be blaming himself.

What is happening is that Sartre is allowing his inborn tendency to pessimism to sneak into his philosophy as if it were some kind of logical premise. . . .

. . . Nietzsche felt the same at the same epoch in his life—at the time he discovered Schopenhauer. But Nietzsche later rejected this early pessimism as Byronic *weltschmerz,* based on self-pity. Whether or not we can accept the philosophy of the later Nietzsche, there can be no doubt that statements like "we are free but helpless—everything is too weak" are expressions of a mood rather than the kind of objective statements philosophy attempts to make.

The same objection applies to Sartre's analysis of "contingency." To be contingent, says Sartre, is to be unnecessary or superfluous. Elsewhere in *Nausea* he prefers (like Camus) to use the word "absurd" rather than contingent. "A circle is not absurd . . . But neither does a circle exist. This root, in contrast, existed in such a way that I could not explain it. Knotty, inert, nameless, it fascinated me, filled my eyes, brought me back unceasingly to its own existence." A circle is an idea; it belongs to the realm of the "necessary," the meaningful. The same applies to art; we think of Beethoven's Ninth Symphony as "necessary," meaningful. We are making a kind of innate distinction between the meaningful and the futile or trivial. When a man sets out to write a novel, he is attempting to raise the triviality of everyday life to a level of more general meaning—rather as Euclid attempted to state general propositions of geometry. We are all familiar with the experience of going out into the street from a cinema or theatre, and finding "real life" confused and bewildering in contrast to the world of art. (It is worth mentioning, in parenthesis, that Sartre and de Beauvoir seem to have spent an enormous amount of time in cinemas.) Does this "prove" that real life is chaotic and meaningless? Obviously not, for we have moods in which we can walk down a crowded street, or sit outside a boulevard cafe, and find the complexity satisfying and exciting. But are "moods" relevant to a philosophical discussion? In this case, yes, for we are again discussing which is "truer"—the perception of the conductor or of the unmusical stranger. For this same stranger, Beethoven's Ninth Symphony may seem confused and bewildering; but we would have no hesitation in agreeing that he is failing to hear the meaning that is so plain to the rest of us. This is not a matter of relativity—of two equivalent judgments. If the stranger learned to understand Beethoven, and *still* felt the Ninth Symphony was meaningless, we would be in altogether deeper waters in trying to contradict him. But where he simply fails to grasp what is being said, there is no question of respecting his "judgment."

We might turn aside briefly to mention a similar fallacy in the work of Camus—who, in *The Myth of Sisyphus,* uses the word "absurdity" to express what Sartre means by contingency. Camus's clarity makes him rather easier to lay by the heel than Sartre. He begins by speaking frankly of boredom: "Rising, streetcar, four hours in the office or the factory, meal, streetcar, four hours of work, meal, sleep, and Monday, Tuesday, Wednesday, Thursday, Friday and Saturday according to the same rhythm. . . . But one day the 'why' arises and everything begins in that weariness tinged with amazement." That is to say, the feeling of "absurdity" begins in a sense of futility, with the question "Why-on earth am I wasting my life like this?" He goes on: "A step lower and strangeness creeps in; perceiving that the world is 'dense,' sensing to what degree a stone is foreign and irreducible to us, and what intensity of nature or a landscape can negate us." Here, very clearly, we are speaking of Roquentin's nausea—the "denseness" of reality, the "foreignness" of a stone. He goes on: "Men, too, secrete the inhuman. At certain moments of lucidity, the mechanical aspects of their gestures, their meaningless pantomime, make silly everything that surrounds them. A man is talking on the telephone behind a glass partition; you cannot hear him, but you see his incomprehensible dumb show; you wonder why he is alive. This discomfort in the face of man's own inhumanity, this incalculable tumble before the image of what we are, this 'nausea' as a writer of today calls it, is also the absurd. Likewise the stranger who at certain seconds comes to meet us in a mirror, the familiar and yet alarming brother we encounter in our own photographs is also the absurd."

These examples really reveal the flaw in the argument. If you turn down the sound of the television set at a moment of high drama, the faces of the characters look "absurd," with their mouths opening and closing, their expressions tense or horrified. But this is because you have deliberately *robbed* them of a dimension of reality—a dimension necessary to grasp fully what is going on. Similarly, if you walked into a play halfway through, it would mean less to you than to someone who had watched it from the beginning. But you would not argue that your lack of understanding was somehow "truer" than the view of the other person. The same argument applies to the man gesticulating in a telephone booth. He has been stripped of certain essential "clues" that would enable you to complete the picture. But it is hardly fair to allege that your incomprehension somehow proves his "inhumanity." The image of the photograph shows the fallacy most clearly of all. Photographs are notoriously deceptive. You might see a thousand snapshots of a man, and yet still know less of him than would be revealed in ten seconds of actually talking to him, or seeing him on the screen in a cinema. The same applies to places. You may have studied a thousand views of the pyramids; the moment you actually see them, it is quite different; they then stay in your mind with their own peculiar "smell" of reality, which could not be supplied by an infinite number of photographs. A photograph can seem "absurd" because it lacks this dimension of reality.

The mirror image is an even more interesting case. Simone de Beauvoir has also used this (in *Pyrrhus et Cineas*) to demonstrate "contingency." "I look at myself in vain in a mirror, tell myself my own story, I can never grasp myself as an entire object, I experience in myself the emptiness that is myself, I feel that I am not." What is happening is that the mirror image is being misinterpreted by your "alienated" senses *as another person,* while you realize consciously that it is you; it is the clash between these two contradictory views that produces the sense of the absurd. But again, it is because the Sergeant Major has gone on strike, so that what you are seeing is *less* true than your normal view.

In short, the "absurd" is due basically to a *falsification* of the data. *Private Eye* prints photographs of a politician making some expansive gesture, with an absurd caption coming out of his mouth; but it is, so to speak, a deliberate frame-up; he is being *made* to look absurd. No one would claim that the picture "tells the truth." Similarly, you could take a Sunday school picture of Jesus extending his arms and saying "Come unto me all ye that are heavily laden," and substitute the caption "You should have seen the one that got away." It might be regarded by some people as funny, but only a fool would pretend it was a valid criticism of Christianity.

But the really important observation is one we have already made: that the "nausea" reaction is basically like that of a schoolboy confronting a page of equations. It is not meaninglessness, but the sense of too much meaning, that produces the nausea. Nausea is the mind's sense of its own inadequacy. What really produces the unease, in certain moments of intuitive perception, is that our minds are quite inadequate to grasp the meaning that surrounds us. Mystics have always asserted that their "moments of vision" reveal that human perceptions filter and cramp and distort the meaning of the reality that surrounds us—and this view *is* perfectly consistent with what we know about the operation of the senses.

To summarize this section of the argument: we must strive to make a distinction between the subjective and objective elements in perception. If a child watches television for too long, he becomes dull and bored, and finally, everything he watches strikes him as dull and boring. His sense of reality is blunted; he finds it hard to remember whether something actually happened, or whether he saw it on TV. If he persisted in watching, for lack of anything better to do, he would end by experiencing "nausea"—the feeling "What am I doing here, watching these meaningless events?" His nausea would tell us something about the state of his perceptions, but not about the quality of the television programs. Similarly, if we knew a man was suffering from indigestion through overeating, we would not take his word for it if he said "This food is awful." We would recognize that a healthy appetite is an essential prerequisite for judging a meal. In failing to make this distinction, Sartre and Camus are guilty of a misunderstanding that amounts to a schoolboy howler. . . .

Viktor E. Frankl

(1905–1997)
AUSTRIAN

Frankl was the founder of "Logotherapy," a successor to Freud's
psychoanalysis. Logotherapy was a therapeutic theory and technique aimed at the future and finding meaning in life, as opposed to Freud's emphasis on the burdens of the past. It was a
theory born of Frankl's great personal suffering. He spent several years in Auschwitz and Dachau, where daily existence and
meaning were always under enormous pressure. Before World
War II Frankl had received both medical degrees and a Ph.D.
from the University of Vienna, and after the war he visited several North and South American universities and served as president of the Austrian Medical Society of Psychotherapy.

❖ Man's Search for Meaning ❖

Life in a concentration camp tore open the human soul and exposed
its depths. Is it surprising that in those depths we again found only
human qualities which in their very nature were a mixture of good
and evil? The rift dividing good from evil, which goes through all
human beings, reaches into the lowest depths and becomes appar-

ent even on the bottom of the abyss which is laid open by the concentration camp.

And now to the last chapter in the psychology of a concentration camp—the psychology of the prisoner who has been released. In describing the experiences of liberation, which naturally must be personal, we shall pick up the threads of that part of our narrative which told of the morning when the white flag was hoisted above the camp gates after days of high tension. This state of inner suspense was followed by total relaxation. But it would be quite wrong to think that we went mad with joy. What, then, did happen?

With tired steps we prisoners dragged ourselves to the camp gates. Timidly we looked around and glanced at each other questioningly. Then we ventured a few steps out of camp. This time no orders were shouted at us, nor was there any need to duck quickly to avoid a blow or kick. Oh no! This time the guards offered us cigarettes! We hardly recognized them at first; they had hurriedly changed into civilian clothes. We walked slowly along the road leading from the camp. Soon our legs hurt and threatened to buckle. But we limped on; we wanted to see the camp's surroundings for the first time with the eyes of free men. "Freedom"—we repeated to ourselves, and yet we could not grasp it. We had said this word so often during all the years we dreamed about it, that it had lost its meaning. Its reality did not penetrate into our consciousness; we could not grasp the fact that freedom was ours.

We came to meadows full of flowers. We saw and realized that they were there, but we had no feelings about them. The first spark of joy came when we saw a rooster with a tail of multicolored feathers. But it remained only a spark; we did not yet belong to this world.

• • •

But for every one of the liberated prisoners, the day comes when, looking back on his camp experiences, he can no longer understand how he endured it all. As the day of his liberation eventually came, when everything seemed to him like a beautiful dream, so also the day comes when all his camp experiences seem to him nothing but a nightmare.

The crowning experience of all, for the homecoming man, is the wonderful feeling that, after all he has suffered, there is nothing he need fear any more—except his God.

❖ *Logotherapy* ❖

The Will to Meaning

Man's search for meaning is the primary motivation in his life and not a "secondary rationalization" of instinctual drives. This meaning is unique and specific in that it must and can be fulfilled by him alone; only then does it achieve a significance which will satisfy his own *will* to meaning. There are some authors who contend that meanings and values are "nothing but defense mechanisms, reaction formations and sublimations." But as for myself, I would not be willing to live merely for the sake of my "defense mechanisms," nor would I be ready to die merely for the sake of my "reaction formations." Man, however, is able to live and even to die for the sake of his ideals and values!

Existential Frustration

Man's will to meaning can also be frustrated, in which case logotherapy speaks of "existential frustration." The term "existential" may be used in three ways: to refer to (1) *existence* itself, i.e., the specifically human mode of being; (2) the *meaning* of existence; and (3) the striving to find a concrete meaning in personal existence, that is to say, the *will* to meaning.

Existential frustration can also result in neuroses. For this type of neuroses, logotherapy has coined the term "noögenic neuroses" in contrast to neuroses in the traditional sense of the word, i.e., psychogenic neuroses. Noögenic neuroses have their origin not in the psychological but rather in the "noölogical" (from the Greek *noös* meaning mind) dimension of human existence. This is another logotherapeutic term which denotes anything pertaining to the specifically human dimension.

Noögenic neuroses do not emerge from conflicts between drives and instincts but rather from existential problems. Among such problems, the frustration of the will to meaning plays a large role.

. . . Not every conflict is necessarily neurotic; some amount of conflict is normal and healthy. In a similar sense suffering is not always a pathological phenomenon; rather than being a symptom of neurosis, suffering may well be a human achievement, especially if the suffering grows out of existential frustration. I would strictly deny that one's search for a meaning to his existence, or even his doubt of it, in every case is derived from, or results in, any disease. Existential frustration is in itself neither pathological nor pathogenic. A man's concern, even his despair, over the worthwhileness of life is an *existential distress* but by no means a *mental disease*. It may well be that interpreting the first in terms of the latter motivates a doctor to bury his patient's existential despair under a heap of tranquilizing drugs. It is his task, rather, to pilot the patient through his existential crisis of growth and development.

Logotherapy regards its assignment as that of assisting the patient to find meaning in his life. Inasmuch as logotherapy makes him aware of the hidden *logos* of his existence, it is an analytical process. To this extent, logotherapy resembles psychoanalysis. However, in logotherapy's attempt to make something conscious again it does not restrict its activity to *instinctual* facts within the individual's unconscious but also cares for *existential* realities, such as the potential meaning of his existence to be fulfilled as well as his *will* to meaning. Any analysis, however, even when it refrains from including the noölogical dimension in its therapeutic process, tries to make the patient aware of what he actually longs for in the depth of his being. Logotherapy deviates from psychoanalysis insofar as it considers man a being whose main concern consists in fulfilling a meaning, rather than in the mere gratification and satisfaction of drives and instincts, or in merely reconciling the conflicting claims of id, ego and superego, or in the mere adaptation and adjustment to society and environment.

The Existential Vacuum

The existential vacuum is a widespread phenomenon of the twentieth century. This is understandable; it may be due to a twofold loss which man has had to undergo since he became a truly human being. At the beginning of human history, man lost some of the basic animal instincts in which an animal's behavior is imbedded and by which it is secured. Such security, like Paradise, is closed to man forever; man has to make choices. In addition to this, however, man has suffered another loss in his more recent development inasmuch as the traditions which buttressed his behavior are now rapidly diminishing. No instinct tells him what he has to do, and no tradition tells him what he ought to do; sometimes he does not even know what he wishes to do. Instead, he either wishes to do what other people do (conformism) or he does what other people wish him to do (totalitarianism).

The existential vacuum manifests itself mainly in a state of boredom. Now we can understand Schopenhauer when he said that mankind was apparently doomed to vacillate eternally between the two extremes of distress and boredom. In actual fact, boredom is now causing, and certainly bringing to psychiatrists, more problems to solve than distress. And these problems are growing increasingly crucial, for progressive automation will probably lead to an enormous increase in the leisure hours available to the average worker. The pity of it is that many of these will not know what to do with all their newly acquired free time.

❖ Tragic Optimism ❖

Let us first ask ourselves what should be understood by "a tragic optimism." In brief it means that one is, and remains, optimistic in spite of the "tragic triad," as it is called in logotherapy, a triad which consists of those aspects of human existence which may be circumscribed by: (1) pain; (2) guilt; and (3) death. How is it possible to say yes to life in spite of all that? How, to pose the question differently, can life retain its potential meaning in spite of its tragic aspects? After all, "saying yes to life in spite of everything" presupposes that life is potentially meaningful under any conditions, even those which are most miserable. And this in turn presupposes the human capacity to creatively turn life's negative aspects into something positive or constructive. In other words, what matters is to make the best of any given situation. "The best," however, is that which in Latin is called *optimum*—hence the reason I speak of a tragic optimism, that is, an optimism in the face of tragedy and in view of the human potential which at its best always allows for: (1) turning suffering into a human achievement and accomplishment; (2) deriving from guilt the opportunity to change oneself for the better; and (3) deriving from life's transitoriness an incentive to take responsible action.

It must be kept in mind, however, that optimism is not anything to be commanded or ordered. One cannot even force oneself to be optimistic indiscriminately, against all odds, against all hope. And what is true for hope is also true for the other two components of the triad inasmuch as faith and love cannot be commanded or ordered either.

Gabriel Garcia Márquez

(B. 1928)
COLOMBIAN

Marquez was a newspaperman in Bogotá and a foreign corre-
spondent when he became an international celebrity with his
"magical realist" novel *One Hundred Years of Solitude,* a book
that "lays bare the miraculous in everyday life." He was awarded
the Nobel Prize for Literature in 1982. "Magical realism" was a
term popularized by Cuban novelist Alejo Carpentier to describe
the uniquely Latin style of combining the everyday and the fab-
ulous nature of Latin American folklore. Marquez's *Love in the
Time of Cholera* is a love story, of sorts. Fermina Daza loses her
husband of many years and is a grieving widow in her seventies
when a childhood would-be suitor arrives to declare his undy-
ing love for her. Fermina—and the reader—are at first put off,
then perplexed, and finally moved, suggesting both the absurdity and the persistence of love.

❖ *from* Love in the Time of Cholera ❖

From her first moment as a widow, it was obvious that Fermina Daza
was not as helpless as her husband had feared. She was adamant in

her determination not to allow the body to be used for any cause, and she remained so even after the honorific telegram from the President of the Republic ordering it to lie in state for public viewing in the Assembly Chamber of the Provincial Government. With the same serenity she opposed a vigil in the Cathedral, which the Archbishop himself had requested, and she agreed to the body's lying there only during the funeral Mass. Even after the mediation of her son, who was dumbfounded by so many different requests, Fermina Daza was firm in her rustic notion that the dead belong only to the family, and that the vigil would be kept at home, with mountain coffee and fritters and everyone free to weep for him in any way they chose. There would be no traditional nine-night wake: the doors were closed after the funeral and did not open again except for visits from intimate friends.

The house was under the rule of death. Every object of value had been locked away with care for safekeeping, and on the bare walls there were only the outlines of the pictures that had been taken down. Chairs from the house, and those lent by the neighbors, were lined up against the walls from the drawing room to the bedrooms, and the empty spaces seemed immense and the voices had a ghostly resonance because the large pieces of furniture had been moved to one side, except for the concert piano which stood in its corner under a white sheet. In the middle of the library, on his father's desk, what had once been Juvenal Urbino de la Calle was laid out with no coffin, with his final terror petrified on his face, and with the black cape and military sword of the Knights of the Holy Sepulcher. At his side, in complete mourning, tremulous, hardly moving, but very much in control of herself, Fermina Daza received condolences with no great display of feeling until eleven the following morning, when she bade farewell to her husband from the portico, waving goodbye with a handkerchief.

It had not been easy for her to regain her self-control after she heard Digna Pardo's shriek in the patio and found the old man of her life dying in the mud. Her first reaction was one of hope, because his eyes were open and shining with a radiant light she had never seen there before. She prayed to God to give him at least a moment so that he would not go without knowing how much she had loved him despite all their doubts, and she felt an irresistible longing to begin life with him over again so that they could say what they had left unsaid and do everything right that they had done badly in the past. But she had to give in to the intransigence of death. Her grief exploded into a blind rage against the world, even against herself, and that is what filled her with the control and the courage to face her solitude alone. From that time on she had no peace, but she was careful about any gesture that might seem to betray her grief. The only moment of pathos, although it was involuntary, occurred at eleven o'clock Sunday night when they brought in the episcopal coffin, still smelling of ship's wax, with its copper handles and tufted silk lining. Dr. Urbino Daza ordered it closed without delay since the air in the house was already rarefied with the heady fragrance of so many flowers in the sweltering heat, and he thought he had seen the first purplish shadows on his father's neck. An absent-minded voice was heard in the silence: "At that age you're half decayed while you're still alive." Before they closed the coffin Fermina Daza took off her wedding ring and put it on her dead husband's finger, and then she covered his hand with hers, as she always did when she caught him digressing in public.

"We will see each other very soon," she said to him.

Florentino Ariza, unseen in the crowd of notable personages, felt a piercing pain in his side. Fermina Daza had not recognized him in the confusion of the first condolences, although no one would be more ready to serve or more useful during the night's urgent business. It was he who imposed order in the crowded kitchens so that there would be enough coffee. He found additional chairs when the neighbors' proved insufficient, and he ordered the extra wreaths to be put in the patio when there was no more room in the house. He made certain there was enough brandy for Dr. Lácides Olivella's guests, who had heard the bad news at the height of the silver anniversary celebration and had rushed in to continue the party, sitting in a circle under the mango tree. He was the only one who knew how to react when the fugitive parrot [who had caused Dr. Urbino's death] appeared in the dining room at midnight with his head high and his wings spread, which caused a stupefied shudder to run through the house, for it seemed a sign of repentance. Florentino Ariza seized him by the neck before he had time to shout any of his witless stock phrases, and he carried him to the stable in a covered cage. He did everything this way, with so much discretion and such efficiency that it did not even occur to anyone that it might be an intrusion in other people's affairs; on the contrary, it seemed a priceless service when evil times had fallen on the house.

He was what he seemed: a useful and serious old man. His body was bony and erect, his skin dark and clean-shaven, his eyes avid behind round spectacles in silver frames, and he wore a romantic old-fashioned mustache with waxed tips. He combed the last tufts of hair at his temples upward and plastered them with brilliantine to the middle of his shining skull as a solution to total baldness. His natural gallantry and languid manner were immediately charming, but they were also considered suspect virtues in a confirmed bachelor. He had spent a great deal of money, ingenuity, and willpower to disguise the seventy-six years he had completed in March, and he was convinced in the solitude of his soul that he had loved in silence for a much longer time than anyone else in this world ever had.

The night of Dr. Urbino's death, he was dressed just as he had been when he first heard the news, which was how he always dressed, even in the infernal heat of June: a dark suit with a vest, a silk bow tie and a celluloid collar, a felt hat, and a shiny black umbrella that he also used a walking stick. But when it began to grow light he left the vigil for two hours and returned as fresh as the rising sun, carefully shaven and fragrant with lotions from his dressing table.

• • •

Florentino Ariza was one of the few who stayed until the funeral was over. He was soaked to the skin and returned home terrified that he would catch pneumonia after so many years of meticulous care and excessive precautions. He prepared hot lemonade with a shot of brandy, drank it in bed with two aspirin tablets, and, wrapped in a wool blanket, sweated by the bucketful until the proper equilibrium had been reestablished in his body. When he returned to the wake he felt his vitality completely restored. Fermina Daza had once again assumed command of the house, which was cleaned and ready to receive visitors, and on the altar in the library she had placed a portrait in pastels of her dead husband, with a black border around the frame. By eight o'clock there were as many people and as intense a heat as the night before, but after the rosary someone circulated the request that everyone leave early so that the widow could rest for the first time since Sunday afternoon.

Fermina Daza said goodbye to most of them at the altar, but she accompanied the last group of intimate friends to the street door so that she could lock it herself, as she had always done, as she was prepared to do with her final breath, when she saw Florentino Ariza, dressed in mourning and standing in the middle of the deserted drawing room. She was pleased, because for many years she had erased him from her life, and this was the first time she saw him clearly, purified by forgetfulness. But before she could thank him for the visit, he placed his hat over his heart, tremulous and dignified, and the abscess that had sustained his life finally burst.

"Fermina," he said, "I have waited for this opportunity for more than half a century, to repeat to you once again my vow of eternal fidelity and everlasting love."

Fermina Daza would have thought she was facing a madman if she had not had reason to believe that at that moment Florentino Ariza was inspired by the grace of the Holy Spirit. Her first impulse was to curse him for profaning the house when the body of her husband was still warm in the grave. But the dignity of her fury held her back. "Get out of here," she said. "And don't show your face again for the years of life that are left to you." She opened the street door, which she had begun to close, and concluded:

"And I hope there are very few of them."

When she heard his steps fade away in the deserted street she closed the door very slowly with the crossbar and the locks, and faced her destiny alone. Until that moment she had never been fully conscious of the weight and size of the drama that she had provoked when she was not yet eighteen, and that would pursue her until her death. She wept for the first time since the afternoon of the disaster, without witnesses, which was the only way she wept. She wept for the death of her husband, for her solitude and rage, and when she went into the empty bedroom she wept for herself because she had rarely slept alone in that bed since the loss of her virginity. Everything that belonged to her husband made her weep again: his tasseled slippers, his pajamas under the pillow, the space of his absence in the dressing table mirror, his own odor on her skin. A vague thought made her shudder: "The people one loves should take all their things with them when they die." She did not want anyone's help to get ready for bed, she did not want to eat anything before she went to sleep. Crushed by grief, she prayed to God to send her death that night while she slept, and with that hope she lay down, barefoot but fully dressed, and fell asleep on the spot. She slept without realizing it, but she knew in her sleep that she was still alive, and that she had half a bed to spare, that she was lying on her left side on the left-hand side of the bed as she always did, but that she missed the weight of the other body on the other side. Thinking as she slept, she thought that she would never again be able to sleep this way, and she began to sob in her sleep, and she slept, sobbing, without changing position on her side of the bed, until long after the roosters crowed and she was awakened by the despised sun of the morning without him. Only then did she realize that she had slept a long time without dying, sobbing in her sleep, and that while she slept, sobbing, she had thought more about Florentino Ariza than about her dead husband.

Samuel Beckett

(1906–1989)
IRISH

From our perspective, Beckett's theater is a paradigm of existentialist literature. Two of his best-known plays, *Waiting for Godot* and *Endgame*, capture the nameless despair and unavoidable religious hope of vulgar man as well as any plays by Camus or Sartre. Because it is the overall effect of such plays rather than any particular dialogue or action within them that makes them so effective, no selections from them could do them justice. What follows is a short but complete one-act play without words that illustrates Beckett's existentialism.

❖ Act Without Words ❖

Desert. Dazzling light.

The man is flung backwards on stage from right wing. He falls, gets up immediately, dusts himself, turns aside, reflects.

Whistle from right wing.

He reflects, goes out right.

Act Without Words *by Samuel Beckett. Published by Grove Press, Inc. Reprinted by permission of Grove Press, Inc.*

Immediately flung back on stage he falls, gets up immediately, dusts himself, turns aside, reflects.

Whistle from left wing.

He reflects, goes out left.

Immediately flung back on stage he falls, gets up immediately, dusts himself, turns aside, reflects.

Whistle from left wing.

He reflects, goes towards left wing, hesitates, thinks better of it, halts, turns aside, reflects.

A little tree descends from flies, lands. It has a single bough some three yards from ground and at its summit a meager tuft of palms casting at its foot a circle of shadow.

He continues to reflect.

Whistle from above.

He turns, sees tree, reflects, goes to it, sits down in its shadow, looks at his hands.

A pair of tailor's scissors descends from flies, comes to rest before tree, a yard from ground.

He continues to look at his hands.

Whistle from above.

He looks up, sees scissors, takes them and starts to trim his nails.

The palms close like a parasol, the shadow disappears.

He drops scissors, reflects.

A tiny carafe, to which is attached a huge label inscribed WATER, descends from flies, comes to rest some three yards from ground.

He continues to reflect.

Whistle from above.

He looks up, sees carafe, reflects, gets up, goes and stands under it, tries in vain to reach it, renounces, turns aside, reflects.

A big cube descends from flies, lands.

He continues to reflect.

Whistle from above.

He turns, sees cube, looks at it, at carafe, reflects, goes to cube, takes it up, carries it over and sets it down under carafe, tests its stability, gets up on it, tries in vain to reach carafe, renounces, gets down, carries cube back to its place, turns aside, reflects.

A second smaller cube descends from flies, lands.

He continues to reflect.

Whistle from above.

He turns, sees second cube, looks at it, at carafe, goes to second cube, takes it up, carries it over and sets it down under carafe, tests its stability, gets up on it, tries in vain to reach carafe, renounces, gets down, takes up second cube to carry it back to its place, hesitates, thinks better of it, sets it down, goes to big cube, takes it up, carries it over and puts it on small one, tests their stability, gets up on them, the cubes collapse, he falls, gets up immediately, brushes himself, reflects.

He takes up small cube, puts it on big one, tests their stability, gets up on them and is about to reach carafe when it is pulled up a little way and comes to rest beyond his reach.

He gets down, reflects, carries cubes back to their place, one by one, turns aside, reflects.

A third still smaller cube descends from flies, lands.

He continues to reflect.

Whistle from above.

He turns, sees third cube, looks at it, reflects, turns aside, reflects.

The third cube is pulled up and disappears in flies.

Beside carafe a rope descends from flies, with knots to facilitate ascent.

He continues to reflect.

Whistle from above.

He turns, sees rope, reflects, goes to it, climbs up it and is about to reach carafe when rope is let out and deposits him back on ground.

He reflects, looks around for scissors, sees them, goes and picks them up, returns to rope and starts to cut it with scissors.

The rope is pulled up, lifts him off ground, he hangs on, succeeds in cutting rope, falls back on ground, drops scissors, falls, gets up again immediately, brushes himself, reflects.

The rope is pulled up quickly and disappears in flies.

With length of rope in his possession he makes a lasso with which he tries to lasso carafe.

The carafe is pulled up quickly and disappears in flies.

He turns aside, reflects.

He goes with lasso in his hand to tree, looks at bough, turns and looks at cubes, looks again at bough, drops lasso, goes to cubes, takes up small one, carries it over and sets it down under bough, goes back for big one, takes it up and carries it over under bough, makes to put it on small one, hesitates, thinks better of it, sets it down, takes up small one and puts it on big one, tests their stability, turns aside and stoops to pick up lasso.

The bough folds down against trunk.

He straightens up with lasso in his hand, turns and sees what has happened.

He drops lasso, turns aside, reflects.

He carries back cubes to their place, one by one, goes back for lasso, carries it over to cubes and lays it in a neat coil on small one.

He turns aside, reflects.

Whistle from right wing.

He reflects, goes out right.

Immediately flung back on stage he falls, gets up immediately, brushes himself, turns aside, reflects.

Whistle from left wing.

He does not move.

He looks at his hands, looks around for scissors, sees them, goes and picks them up, starts to trim his nails, stops, reflects, runs his finger along blade of scissors, goes and lays them on small cube, turns aside, opens his collar, frees his neck and fingers it.

The small cube is pulled up and disappears in flies, carrying away rope and scissors.

He turns to take scissors, sees what has happened.

He turns aside, reflects.

He goes and sits down on big cube.

The big cube is pulled from under him. He falls. The big cube is pulled up and disappears in flies.

He remains lying on his side, his face towards auditorium, staring before him.

The carafe descends from flies and comes to rest a few feet from his body.

He does not move.

Whistle from above.

He does not move.

The carafe descends further, dangles and plays about his face.

He does not move.

The carafe is pulled up and disappears in flies.

The bough returns to horizontal, the palms open, the shadow returns.

Whistle from above.

He does not move.

The tree is pulled up and disappears in flies.

He looks at his hands.

Curtain

Luis Borges

(1899-1986)
ARGENTINIAN

Borges began his literary career as a rebellious poet, one of the founders of the "ultraist movement" that declared war on conventional poetry and defended, in his words, "metaphor above all." Later, Borges started to write the brilliant short stories and essays that continue to confuse and even bamboozle readers, essays that are in fact brilliant fictions; for example, his fantastic character Ireneo Funes, who remembered utterly everything, or his seemingly scholarly report on Pierre Menard, a man in the twentieth century who writes Don Quijote. Borges was master of an elegant and beautiful Spanish, but most important for us is his incredible sense of the absurd and of the remotest possibilities of human experience. But Borges was a writer who eschewed politics, which earned him the wrath of such "committed" writers as Jean-Paul Sartre. In "Borges and I" he tackles head-on the paradox of self-identity, the ultimate existentialist quandary.

❖ Borges and I ❖

Things happen to him, the other one, to Borges. I stroll about Buenos Aires and stop, almost mechanically now perhaps, to look at the arch of an entranceway and the ironwork gate; news of Borges reaches me in the mail and I see his name on an academic ballot or in a biographical dictionary. I like hourglasses, maps, eighteenth-century typography, etymologies, the taste of coffee, and Robert Louis Stevenson's prose; he shares these preferences, but with a vanity that turns them into the attributes of an actor. It would be an exaggeration to say that our relationship is a hostile one; I live, I go on living, so that Borges may contrive his literature; and that literature justifies me. I do not find it hard to admit that he has achieved some valid pages, but these pages can not save me, perhaps because what is good no longer belongs to anyone, not even to him, the other one, but to the language or to tradition. In any case, I am destined to perish, definitively, and only some instant of me may live on in him. Little by little, I yield him ground, the whole terrain, though I am quite aware of his perverse habit of magnifying and falsifying. Spinoza realized that all things strive to persist in their own nature: the stone eternally wishes to be stone and the tiger a tiger. I shall subsist in Borges, not in myself (assuming I am someone), and yet I recognize myself less in his books than in many another, or than in the intricate flourishes played on a guitar. Years ago I tried to free myself from him, and I went from the mythologies of the city suburbs to games with time and infinity, but now those games belong to Borges, and I will have to think up something else. Thus is my life a flight, and I lose everything, and everything belongs to oblivion, or to him.

I don't know which one of the two of us is writing this page.

Harold Pinter

(B. 1930)
ENGLISH

Pinter is England's foremost playwright and an advocate of that peculiar British brand of existentialism that says—or rather shows—that we really have nothing to say to each other. The following extract is from *The Dwarfs*.

❖ *from* The Dwarfs ❖

LEN: Do you believe in God?
MARK: What?
LEN: Do you believe in God?
MARK: Who?
LEN: God.
MARK: God?
LEN: Do you believe in God?
MARK: Do I believe in God?
LEN: Yes.
MARK: Would you say that again?

From The Dwarfs *by Harold Pinter. Published by Grove Press, Inc. Reprinted by permission of Grove Press, Inc.*

Joseph Heller

(B. 1923)
AMERICAN (NEW JERSEY)

Joseph Heller was born in 1923 in Brooklyn, New York. He became immediately famous with his great anti-war, anti-bureaucracy novel, *Catch-22*. This was followed by *Something Happened* (1974) and *God Knows* (1984). The following very brief selection from *Catch-22* succinctly captures the biting philosophical satire that has now made that novel such an existential classic.

❖ *from* Catch-22 ❖

"From now on I'm thinking only of me."

Major Danby replied indulgently with a superior smile, "But Yossarian, suppose everyone felt that way?"

"Then I'd certainly be a—fool to feel any other way, wouldn't I?"

Philip Roth

(B. 1933)
AMERICAN (NEW JERSEY)

Roth was born in 1933 in Newark, New Jersey. His fiction frequently drew on Jewish culture and family life in New Jersey.
He first drew attention in 1959 with a collection called *Goodbye,
Columbus.* In 1969 Roth shocked and amused the world with
Portnoy's Complaint. In the 1980s, he wrote the Zuckerman tril-
ogy, and in 2000 *The Human Stain.* In all Roth's books, an obsession with personal identity serves as a philosophical leitmo-
tif. He is the subject of a recent bio-flick by esteemed Berlin
documentary film maker Christa Maerker.

❖ *from* The Human Stain ❖

"You think—if you ever want to know—is there a God? You want to
know why am I in this world? What is it about? It's about this. It's
about. You're here, and I'll do it for you. It's about not thinking
you're someone else somewhere else. You're a woman and you're in
bed with your husband, and you're not fucking for fucking, you're
not fucking to come, you're fucking because you're in bed with your
husband and it's the right thing to do. You're a man and you're with
your wife and you're fucking her, but you're thinking you want to be

fucking the post office janitor. Okay—you know what? You're with the janitor."

He says softly, with a laugh, "And that proves the existence of God."

"If that doesn't, nothing does."

"Keep dancing," he says.

"When you're dead," she asks, "what does it matter if you didn't marry the right person?"

"It doesn't matter. It doesn't even matter when you're alive. Keep dancing."

"What is it, Coleman? What does matter?"

"This," he said.

"That's my boy," she replies. "Now you're learning."

"Is that what this is—you teaching me?"

"It's about time somebody did. Yes, I'm teaching you. But don't look at me now like I'm good for something other than this. Something more than this. Don't do that. Stay here with me. Don't go. Hold on to this. Don't think about anything else. Stay here with me. I'll do whatever you want. How many times have you had a woman really tell you that and mean it? I will do anything you want. Don't lose it. Don't take it somewhere else, Coleman. This is all we're here to do. Don't think it's about tomorrow. Close all the doors, before and after. All the social ways of thinking, shut 'em down. Everything the wonderful society is asking? The way we're set up socially? 'I should, I should, I should'? Fuck all that. What you're supposed to be, what you're supposed to do, all that, it just kills everything. I can keep dancing, if that's the deal. The secret little moment—if that's the whole deal. That slice you get. That slice out of time. It's no more than that, and I hope you know it."

"Keep dancing."

Arthur Miller

(B. 1915)
AMERICAN

Death of a Salesman is Miller's classic American tragedy. Its protagonist, Willy Loman, is destroyed in the abyss between the American promise of success and the realities of failure. He is a firm believer in individual initiative, a broad smile, and polished shoes. But Loman has grown old and ineffective, and, like his two sons, reared on the same ethic of success, he is a failure. When he is fired from his job and deserted by his sons, Loman is forced to confront himself, and he makes a final heroic gesture. He kills himself in the family car to provide the insurance money for his wife. *Requiem* is the epilogue of the play, with Willy's wife and sons and his sole friend Charley standing before the simple grave. If existentialism is to force us "to know who we are," *Requiem* is a fitting epilogue to our collection as well.

❖ *from* Death of a Salesman ❖

Requiem

> CHARLEY: It's getting dark, Linda.
> *Linda doesn't react. She stares at the grave.*

BIFF: How about it, Mom? Better get some rest, heh? They'll be closing the gate soon.

Linda makes no move. Pause.

HAPPY (*deeply angered*): He had no right to do that. There was no necessity for it. We would've helped him.

CHARLEY (*grunting*): Hmmm.

BIFF: Come along, Mom.

LINDA: Why didn't anybody come?

CHARLEY: It was a very nice funeral.

LINDA: But where are all the people he knew? Maybe they blame him.

CHARLEY: Naa. It's a rough world, Linda. They wouldn't blame him.

LINDA: I can't understand it. At this time especially. First time in thirty-five years we were just about free and clear. He only needed a little salary. He was even finished with the dentist.

CHARLEY: No man only needs a little salary.

LINDA: I can't understand it.

BIFF: There were a lot of nice days. When he'd come home from a trip; or on Sundays, making the stoop; finishing the cellar; putting on the new porch; when he built the extra bathroom; and put up the garage. You know something, Charley, there's more of him in that front stoop than in all the sales he ever made.

CHARLEY: Yeah. He was a happy man with a batch of cement.

LINDA: He was so wonderful with his hands.

BIFF: He had the wrong dreams. All, all, wrong.

HAPPY (*almost ready to fight Biff*): Don't say that!

BIFF: He never knew who he was.

CHARLEY (*stopping Happy's movement and reply. To Biff*): Nobody dast blame this man. You don't understand: Willy was a salesman.

And for a salesman, there is no rock bottom to the life. He don't put a bolt to a nut, he don't tell you the law or give you medicine. He's a man way out there in the blue, riding on a smile and a shoeshine. And when they start not smiling back—that's an earthquake. And then you get yourself a couple of spots on your hat, and you're finished. Nobody dast blame this man. A salesman is got to dream, boy. It comes with the territory.

BIFF: Charley, the man didn't know who he was.

HAPPY (*infuriated*): Don't say that!

BIFF: Why don't you come with me, Happy?

HAPPY: I'm not licked that easily. I'm staying right in this city, and I'm gonna beat this racket (*He looks at Biff, his chin set.*) The Loman Brothers!

BIFF: I know who I am, kid.

HAPPY: All right, boy. I'm gonna show you and everybody else that Willy Loman did not die in vain. He had a good dream. It's the only dream you can have—to come out number-one man. He fought it out here, and this is where I'm gonna win it for him.

BIFF (*with a hopeless glance at Happy, bends toward his mother*): Let's go, Mom.

LINDA: I'll be with you in a minute. Go on, Charley. (*He hesitates.*) I want to, just for a minute. I never had a chance to say good-by.

Charley moves away, followed by Happy. Biff remains a slight distance up and left of Linda. She sits there, summoning herself. The flute begins, not far away, playing behind her speech.

LINDA: Forgive me, dear. I can't cry. I don't know what it is, but I can't cry. I don't understand it. Why did you ever do that? Help me, Willy, I can't cry. It seems to me that you're just on another trip. I keep expecting you. Willy, dear, I can't cry. Why did you do it? I search and search and I search, and I can't understand it, Willy. I made the last payment on the house today. Today, dear. And there'll be nobody home. (*A sob rises in her throat.*) We're free and clear. (*Sobbing more fully, released.*) We're free. (*Biff comes slowly toward her.*) We're free . . . We're free . . .

Biff lifts her to her feet and moves out up right with her in his arms. Linda sobs quietly. Bernard and Charley come together and follow them, followed by Happy. Only the music of the flute is left on the darkening stage as over the house the hard towers of the apartment buildings rise into sharp focus, and

The Curtain Falls